Intimate Selving in Arab Families

Gender, Culture, and Politics in the Middle East
Leila Ahmed, Miriam Cooke, and Simona Sharoni, *Series Editors*

Intimate Selving in Arab Families

Gender, Self, and Identity

Edited by

Suad Joseph

Syracuse University Press

First edition 1999

05 06 07 08 09 10   7 6 5 4 3 2

The paper used in this publication meets the minimum requirements of American National Standard for Information Sciences—Permanence of Paper for Printed Library Materials, ANSI Z39.48–1984. ∞™

Library of Congress Cataloging-in-Publication Data

Intimate selving in Arab families : gender, self, and identity / edited by Suad Joseph. — 1st ed.
    p. cm. — (Gender, culture, and politics in the Middle East)
    Includes bibliographical references (p. -) and index.
    ISBN 0-8156-2808-0 (cloth : alk. paper)
    ISBN 0-8156-2817-X (paper : alk. paper)
    1. Family—Arab countries—Psychological aspects.   2. Sex role—Arab countries—Psychological aspects.   3. Self.   I. Joseph, Suad.   II. Series.
    HQ1784 .I58 1999
    306.85'0917'4927—dc21   99-16643

Manufactured in the United States of America

To our families

Contents

Preface

The subject of selving has a long intellectual history in Western scholarship and popular literature that has represented itself as speaking on behalf of or for humanity. That universalizing intellectual legacy had, for some time, left me disconcerted. Struggling (and coming up short) in my efforts to become its descendent, I tried to understand: Were the shortcomings mine? Were they my family's? Were they my class's? Were they my gender's? Were they my "culture's"? Answers for these questions did not rest easily in my mind in the 1970s and 1980s when I began taking notes on systematic differences I observed in relational dynamics among Arab and American associates. At first the differences appeared to be specific to the persons in the relationships. As the number of relationships I observed increased, patterns emerged that clearly were not person specific.

Trained to look at structure and material conditions, I found it initially difficult to recognize the issue as about the "self" and the process of becoming a self in intimate relationships—a process I have come to call "intimate selving." The difficulty was compounded by the fact that the 1970s and 1980s were a low point for cross-cultural studies in psychological anthropology. Additionally, although much research in psychological anthropology or cross-cultural psychology had been carried out in other parts of the world, Middle East scholarship had produced little empirical or theoretical scholarship on psychodynamics.[1] Works like Daniel Lerner's, moreover, with little concern for on-the-ground complexities and differences, painted the whole Middle East with one psychological brush stroke and colored it largely as "traditional" and backward.[2] Such modernization theorists were coloring much of the Third World in similar shades of dysfunctionality. By the mid-1980s, however, the surge of scholarship (especially by feminists and women of color) reassessing *individualism, selfhood, relationality,* and their gendering (and racing and classing) offered new vocubularies for those of us attempting to theorize, in nonpathologizing terminologies, notions of selfhood that did not conform to the hegemonic Western bounded, autonomous, separative, individualist self.

Seeking venues for clarifying the differences with vocabularies that did not pathologize whole cultural patterns, I organized a series of workshops on families in the Arab world. One workshop met sporadically and lasted for several years, in the 1970s, in New York City. In 1987 I organized a panel, "Reassessing Arab Family Studies," at the Middle East Studies Association. Most directly, the book is an outgrowth of a panel I organized, "Culture and Psychodynamics in Arab Families: Interdisciplinary Approaches," at the Middle East Studies Association meetings in 1991. The focus of the project crystallized as contributors were added. For some, this undertaking represented a new look at their research questions; for others, it was an opportunity to refine or further develop their current work. We exchanged some of each other's work and engaged, at times, in lengthy discussions on the meanings of our experiences of self and other both in our own lives and in our research. The encounter has been rich.

We offer here notions of self and selving in intimate contexts that describe ways of being "othered" by Western constructs, but which are considered legitimate in their cultures. The book is not written in praise of such alternative notions. Rather, it is a critical and close investigation of the conflicting ideas, the struggles to selfhood, and the intersections of selving within family systems that embue the self with gendered and aged dynamics of domination. Some of these dynamics may be culturally and historically specific. Others may have relevance beyond the families and societies described. Some may appear to be relevant to a number of Arab societies; others may not. These close-up depictions offer crucial insights into the complexities of selving in intimate relationships in families across a number of Arab countries. In the process, they dispel both essentializing notions of culture and essentializing notions of humanity.

Suad Joseph
Davis, California

Acknowledgments

As with any edited work, there are more people to thank than can be credited here. I thank, first of all, the contributors who patiently reworked revisions and waited for each other and for me to see the book through. The many people whose stories appear in these chapters generously and graciously invited us into their lives and shared with us their intimate experiences of selving. My family gave me my first experiences and insights into the dynamics and struggles of intimate selving in Arab families (and no doubt the families of the contributors to this volume gave them theirs). To no person, however, do I owe more than to my mother. Mama Rose's profound wisdom concerning the complexities of relationships was my early schooling in relationality. I am still learning from the lessons she taught me.

I also thank Lin Nutile, a University of California, Davis, Women's Studies major, who worked tirelessly to format the final manuscript. Her meticulous attention to details and her calm control in the face of the final frenzy helped enormously in completion of this project. Royce McClellan's (Anthropology Department, University of California, Davis) unwavering cheerfulness in the first phase of formatting alleviated some of the editor's burden, and Faith Boucher took on the second phase of formatting. The editors at Syracuse University Press, Mary Selden Evans and Cynthia Maude Gembler were most helpful in manuscript preparation.

I engaged many colleagues in discussions on the theorization for my chapters: Paul Aikin, Rachelle Taqqu, Ylana Miller, Smadar Lavie, Etel Adnan, Simone Fattal, May Rihani, Mary Farha, Patricia Joseph, Rosemary Sayigh, Julie Peteet, Carol A. Smith, G. William Skinner, Carol Stack, Judith Stacey, Judith Newton, Barbara Metcalf, Carole Joffe, Lata Mani, Angie Chabram-Dernersesian, Ruth Frankenberg, Jacob Olapuna,

Valerie Matsumoto, Christine DiStefano, Dorinne Kondo, Rosa Linda Fregoso, Lyn Roller, Stephanie Shields, Kari Lokke, Anna Kuhn, Cynthia Brantley, Patricia Turner, Yvette Flores-Ortiz, Juliana Schiesari, Deborah Luepnitz, and Catherine Lutz. The errors or limitations are, of course, my own.

Most especially, I thank my daughter, Sara Rose Joseph, for her patience and tolerance as Mama spent what must have seemed endless hours at the computer, competing with playtime, snacks, and bedtime stories. Sara Rose has taught me new meanings of Khalil Gibran's verses on children (her song of liberation).

Contributors

Magda M. Al-Nowaihi is currently associate professor of Arabic literature, Columbia University. She has also been a lecturer at Princeton University, 1989–94, and a research fellow at Annenberg Research Institute, 1990–91. She received her Ph.D. from Harvard University, 1988, and her bachelor's at American University in Cairo, 1978. Her publications include: *The Poetry of Ibn Khafajah: A Literary Analysis* (Leiden; New York: E. J. Brill, 1993); "Memory and Imagination in Edwar al-Kharrat's Turabuha Za'faran," in *Journal of Arabic Literature*, 1993; "Resisting Silence in Arab Women's Autobiographies," in *Rewriting the Orient* ed. by H. Dabashi and T. Riccardi (forthcoming); "The Mountain Poem," in S. Jayyusi's *The Legacy of Muslim Spain* (New York: E. J. Brill, 1992); and "Arabic Literature and the Post colonial Predicament," ed. by Sangeeta Ray and Henry Schwartz (Blackwell, in press).

Soraya Altorki is a professor of anthropology at the American University in Cairo. She is author of *Women in Saudi Arabia: Ideology and Behavior among the Elite* (New York: Columbia Univ. Press, 1986), and coeditor of *Arab Women in the Field* (Syracuse, N.Y.: Syracuse Univ. Press, 1988). She is coauthor of *Arabian Oasis City: The Transformation of Unayzah* (Austin: Univ. of Texas Press, 1989), and of *Bedouin, Settlers, and Holiday-Makers* (Cairo: American Univ. in Cairo Press, 1998).

Najla Hamadeh received her Ph.D. in philosophy from Georgetown University. She has been an assistant professor, then lecturer, in the Civilization Sequence Program at the American University of Beirut from 1988 to 1999. She has published works in Arabic and English on the philosophy of psychoanalysis and feminist issues. Her latest publications in English are "Lacan's Technique: Looking for Consistency in Freud's Theory of the Death Instinct," *Clinical Studies: International Journal of Psychoanalysis*, no. 1 (1998); "The Values and Self-Identity of Bedouin and Urban Women: A Comparative Analysis" (field study, Bekaa valley,

Lebanon), Economic and Social Commission for Western Asia, Studies on Arab Women and Development, no. 26, (N.Y.: United Nations, 1997); "Islamic Family Legislation: The Authoritarian Discourse of Silence," in *Feminism and Islam,* ed. May Yamain (Beirut: Ithaca Press, 1996). She is co-editing a forthcoming book entitled "Gender and Citizenship in Lebanon."

Mervat F. Hatem is an associate professor of political science at Howard University. Her chapter on 'A'isha Taymur is part of a larger work on the critique of modernity and its representation in nineteenth- and twentieth-century Egypt. Her latest publication is "'A'isha Taymur's Tears and the Critique of the Modernist and Feminist Discourses on Nineteenth-Century Egypt," in *Remaking Women: Feminism and Modernity in the Middle East,* ed. Lila Abu-Lughod (Princeton, N.J.: Princeton Univ. Press, 1998).

Suad Joseph is professor of anthropology and women's studies at the University of California, Davis. She has carried out urban and rural fieldwork in her native Lebanon for thirty years on issues ranging from the politicization of religion, state and community organization, education, youth, family systems, women's networks, and transformations in notions of rights and citizenship. She is currently carrying out a longitudinal study on how children in Lebanon learn gendered notions of rights, nationality, and citizenship. She has coedited with Barbara L. K. Pillsbury, *Muslim Christian Conflicts: Economic, Political and Social Origins* (Boulder, Colo.: Westview Press, 1978). She authored "Gender and Relationality among Arab Families in Lebanon," *Feminist Studies* 19, no. 3 (fall 1993): 465–86, and "Problematizing Gender and Relational Rights: Experiences from Lebanon," *Social Politics* 1, no. 3 (fall 1994): 271–85. She is editing two books, "Gender and Citizenship in the Middle East and Women and Human Rights in Muslim Communities," and coediting three books: "Citizenship in Lebanon," "Gender and Citizenship in Lebanon," "Gender, Culture, and Politics in the Middle East."

Jean Said Makdisi is an independent writer, living in Beirut, Lebanon. She holds a master's degree from George Washington University (Washington, D.C.), and taught English and humanities for many years at the Beirut University College. She is the author of *Beirut Fragments: A War Memoir* (New York: Persea Books, 1990) as well as articles on women's issues, including "The Mythology of Modernity: Women and Democracy in Lebanon," in *Feminism and Islam: Legal and Literary Perspectives,* ed. by Mai Yamani (London: Ithaca Press, 1996). She is editing a book of memoirs by Serene Husseini Shahid titled *Windows on the Past: Memories of Palestine,* and is coediting two books, *Gender and Citizenship in Lebanon* and the fifth annual volume of *Bahithat.*

Maysoon Melek is an Iraqi economist, development expert, and mother of two girls. Most of her professional life has been in the fields of human resource development, poverty, and gender issues in the Arab region. She received her primary and secondary education in Baghdad, Iraq, then traveled to England and Lebanon where she received a degree in economics from the University of York, England, and a master's degree in development planning from the American University of Beirut. She has worked on development issues in Iraq, Egypt, Tunisia, Jordan, Saudi Arabia, and Yemen. She lives at the moment between Egypt and Jordan. She also has written a number of short stories in Arabic and is presently preparing her first collection of short stories for publication.

Scheherazade is an anonymous writer.

Intimate Selving in Arab Families

Introduction

Theories and Dynamics of Gender, Self,
and Identity in Arab Families

SUAD JOSEPH

Intimate Selving

Western psychological theory has focused on the analysis of and conditions for the emergence of a bounded, autonomous, and separate self. Such an individuated self has been assumed to be the hallmark of maturity in most Western psychodynamic theorizing. The central site for the construction of the mature individualized self has been iconized as a nuclear family that includes one father, one mother, and their joint children. That other models of selfhood and other sites of construction of self exist in the West and other areas of the world has long been recognized, most especially by anthropologists. To a large extent, however, Western psychodynamic theory has dysfunctionalized, even pathologized, notions of selving that do not conform to the individualized self.

Many feminist and critical theorists, particularly scholars of color, during the 1980s and 1990s have contested this homogenizing strategy of Western psychology. Working on questions of self, identity, gender, ethnicity, and race, many scholars have argued that these accounts of self negate or devalue the realities of cultural difference, hybridity, and the heterogeneity found globally and even in Western societies. They have suggested a need for greater complexity and specificity in the analysis of self and identity.[1]

Relationality has emerged as a central trope for scholars with reservations about a hegemonic individualized construct of selfhood. For some scholars the notion of relationality simply means that selves are shaped in relationship to others. Selving is a lifelong process, imbued with contradictions, impinged upon by social and cultural processes, actively engaged by multiple actors in diverse relationships in the microdynamics of their day-to-day lives. That no one makes her/him self in isolation is self-evident and not questioned, even by the most ardent proponents of normalizing the "individual." To say that every person's notion of self is shaped by relationships is also to assert the obvious. That notion of relationality is not the subject of this book.

This book is about historically and culturally specific constructs of relationality in the context of intimate relationships in families in the Arab world. It is about intimate relationality as a foundational framework, underwriting notions of self that do not conform to the individualist, separative, bounded, autonomous constructs subscribed to in much of Western psychodynamic theory. It is about selves woven through intimate relationships that are lifelong, which transform over the course of personal and social history and which shape and are shaped by shifts and changes of the self. It is about notions of maturity that valorize rather than pathologize the embeddedness of self and other. It is about selves in which embeddedness still encompasses agency. It is about notions of self and relationality that are gendered because of culturally specific (not universal) notions of gendered child "development" and because of locally specific and changing dynamics of power. It is about notions of relational selfhood that exist side by side with individualist and other notions of self in the same society and even within the same person.

In the chapters in this book we focus on intimate relationships in familial contexts: mother-son, mother-daughter-granddaughter, father-son-grandson, father-daughter, husband-wife, co-wives, sisters, cousins. The scholars investigate the ways in which relationality can become conjoined with structures of domination. Most commonly, these structures are gendered and aged forms of domination moralized by kinship rules, moralities, and idioms. Most commonly, then, the relational notions of self described in this book are co-constructed with forms of patriarchy. But patriarchy, as understood by scholars in this collection, is not a fixed, stable social structure. Patriarchy is seen as historically changing, contextual, and subject to the power of specific personas.

Quite critically, all contributions to this volume document multiple and changing notions of agency. Relational selfhood and patriarchy are not seen to be inimical to the coexistence of agency of the self. All the authors document women and men, children and adults as actively engaged in their own self-making besides the self-making of others. The agency of the self emerges experientially and existentially although it may not be the agency of the bounded, separative "individual," nor may it necessarily be the same notion of agency throughout the lifetimes of the persons described or the societies discussed.

In the book we enjoin the biographical and autobiographical (part 1) with the ethnographic and historical (part 2) and the literary (part 3). The chapters are testimony to the recognition that we learn as much from self-representation as from representation by others, from "reporting" as from "interpreting," from "scientific" accounts as from "fictional." Ultimately, our categories of viewing and writing the self are fluid and culturally specific, and the constructed boundaries between them are continually changing.

This book, then, is about the constructedness of self and selving. It rejects both universalizing and culturally specific accounts that essentialize and naturalize the self. Such accounts are strategic knowledge productions to be viewed as social contestations rather than as "objective" accounts of the nature of selving. Ideas are always struggled for, and hegemonic ideas, even in the realm of science, expose more about the nature of society and its social relations than about the "essence" of the subject of study. Every society produces multiple and competing notions of self. That one may be dominant, more institutionally supported, may reveal more about class, race, ethnicity, religion, and gender in that society than about the human possibilities of selving.

Selving is the most complex of human phenomena. The "truth" of what is seen/imagined/reported about the process of selving must be partial, situated, and imbued with the meanings of the moment and the localities of both the investigator and the investigated. These limitations make the competing accounts of greater, not less, interest and value because they make them more human, more a souvenir of the most human of human endeavors—the struggle to understand oneself. The book is a series of stories of struggle for self and understanding. In these narratives the self is always situated, contextualized, and embedded in relationalities.

Relationality in Psychological Theory

Relational selfhood, when it has been theorized in psychology, has been often dysfunctionalized. Western psychology has tended to assume that autonomy and relationality are oppositional. The valorization of autonomy for maturity in Western culture has led many theorists to regard relationality as an obstacle to maturity. Western psychodynamic theory has tended to presume that autonomy of the self entails the *individuation* of the self (the self separated from the other by clear and firm boundaries). Such theorization has also presumed that individuation is necessary for agency.[2] There has been a tendency to naturalize the individuated self as the only possible repository of an agential self. Relationality, in these frameworks, is not only an obstacle to maturity but destructive of agency.

Salvador Minuchin, among the most interesting theorists of relationality, described relational selves in terms of enmeshment.[3] The concept of enmeshment describes a process by which selves are crafted with diffuse boundaries. The enmeshed self privileges relationships and context rather than inner psyches and identifies persons as active agents rather than passive victims. A family system theorist, Minuchin identified each person in the family system as an active participant whose behavior is both caused and causative.

The concept of enmeshment, although useful descriptively, is embedded in Western-centric notions of the family and person situated in functionalist theoretical paradigms committed to individualism as universally normative for maturity and agency. Minuchin presumed a nuclear family model with the mother as the primary caretaker and with the parents enacting "executive roles," not delegated to or preempted by children. He, therefore, pathologized families in which older children might take on primary caretaking responsibilities for younger siblings and families in which mothers and fathers were not the administrative heads of households. His account of normativity would discount the psychodynamic health of many extended family systems in which authority might be more diffuse or shared. By neglecting culturally diverse family and social histories, he undermined the usefulness of the notion of enmeshment as an analytical tool for examining the functionality of different systems of selving.

Minuchin also did not take account of patriarchy. Feminist psychotherapist Deborah Anna Luepnitz[4] observed that Minuchin, in therapeutic situations, was more likely to challenge the mother than the father. Not seeing the connection between enmeshment and patriarchy, he often reinscribed patriarchy in his efforts to reintegrate fathers into family systems.[5] Presuming that individuation, autonomy, and separateness are psychodynamic necessities, Minuchin concluded that enmeshment is dysfunctional. Enmeshment may be problematical for the construction of productive selves in market-based societies. Such societies, organized around contractual relations, may require individuation, autonomy, and separateness to produce mobile, detachable persons. In many societies, however, despite the presence of markets, other factors pressure for and support functional relationality.

Cross-cultural psychologists, at times, have offered interesting data and insights for conceptualizing relational selves. Alan Roland,[6] arguing that "the prevailing psychological maps and norms assumed to be universal are in fact Western-centric," has criticized Western individualist assumptions, noting that focusing on intrapsychic phenomena ignores the ways in which historical, social, and cultural patterns shape the inner world. Judgments of psychopathology should be based on what is normal in a particular culture, he contended. Studying India and Japan, he found three organizations of the self: the familial self, the individualized self, and the spiritual self. The familial self is highly relational, with permeable outer boundaries. The familial self, according to Roland, experiences a "we-self," which derives self esteem from constant affective exchange (where high levels of empathy and receptivity are nurtured) and from strong identification with the honor of hierarchal family, community groups, and idealized elders. The familial self is sustained by mirroring throughout life, by observation of traditional responsibilities, and by modes of cognition that are highly contextual. The individualized self is an autonomous, individuated, separated self with relatively self-contained outer ego boundaries adapted to societies organized around contractual and egalitarian relationships and valuing rational, self-reflective, and efficient modes of cognition. Defining the spiritual self as an "inner spiritual reality" within everyone, Roland concluded that Indians and Japanese have traditionally integrated a familial and spiritual self, with little of the individualized self; whereas American psychological makeup is predominately based on the individualized self, with little of the familial self.

Roland's acute appreciation of cultural difference leads him to offer culturally sensitive notions of selving. The familial self is a particular recognition of the centrality of family in these cultures. It incorporates many of the characteristics summarized by the notion of enmeshment but decouples them from a judgment of dysfunctionality. Unlike Minuchin, Roland acknowledged the operation of systems of gender and age hierarchy. His analysis, although allowing for the functionality of the familial relational self in India and Japan, nevertheless is problematical. Roland's cultural topologies of the self suffer from the assumptions that have often blinded well-intended cultural relativists. Like most cultural relativists, he presumed the existence of bounded cultural wholes; he even assumed systematic cultural differences between East and West. In so doing, he essentialized East and West as "intrinsically antithetical to each other."[7] His view of Indians and Japanese as "collective man" and Westerners as a "collection of individuals who as the ultimate unit of society are equal to each other and are essentially similar in nature" glossed over differences based on race, ethnicity, class, gender, and age in the West.[8] Arguing that the individualized self[9] does not characterize most American ethnic and racial subcultures and is less present in women than in men, he left himself in a position of conflating the Western individual with white middle- and upper-class males. That he did not decouple relationality from family-based systems of hierarchy also complicates efforts to analyze systematically the relationship between constructs of self and other systems of domination.

Kenneth Gergen,[10] suggesting one should move away from the Western notion of self-contained individualism premised on the problematic assumption of dualism, argued for a relational concept of knowledge, social understanding, emotions, and selves. Like Minuchin, Gergen contended relationships among persons, rather than the single person, are the center of biological, social and psychological life.[11] "When any two of us come together, it is essentially the meeting point for the multiple systems of relatedness in which each of us is embedded."[12]

Minuchin offered a concept of context-embedded selves with diffuse boundaries, a profound (but pathologized) insight into a nonindividualist construct of self. Roland offered a culturally sensitized (but essentialized) concept of a functional self embedded in family and community. Gergen offered a notion of relationality that is nonculturally specific and redirects attention to the basic social character of humanity. In different ways each contributed to the study of relationality. Our project is still to find analytical tools to study relational notions of self that are not pathologized, which take account of culturally specific differences based on gender, race, class, religion, ethnicity, and power.

Relationality in Feminist Theory

Much feminist theory since the 1980s has transformed from hypothesis to axiom the claim that women are more relationally oriented than men. Assertions that women have more complex psychic structures with more fluid ego boundaries than do men emerged from feminist revisions of psychoanalytically based object relations theory in the important work of Nancy Chodorow.[13] Chodorow, assuming a predominate pattern of exclusive female parenting, argued that because mothers are likely to see daughters and not sons as extensions of themselves, then girls, who fashion their femininity by sustaining primary attachment to the mother, are likely to cultivate selves with an affinity to sameness and relatedness. Boys, constructing their masculinity by distancing from mothers and identifying abstractly with largely absent fathers, experience their selves in terms of difference and separateness. As a result, Chodorow[14] reasoned, feminine personality comes to be defined relationally (less individuated, with more fluid boundaries) and masculine personality as denial of relation (more individuated, with more autonomy and separate, firm boundaries).[15]

Building on this feminist reconstruction of object relations theory, feminist have derived explanations of gender differences in areas ranging from moral behavior[16] to methods of research and theorizing science,[17] to metaphysical and political thought,[18] to the rationality and modes of erotic, scientific, and technical domination in advanced capitalism,[19] to capacities for gendered domination,[20] and to subjective accounts of familial power relations.[21] Earlier assertions of the universality of gendered relational capacity[22] inspired generalizations across social and cultural boundaries and influenced theoretical[23] and popular[24] guides to therapeutic intervention.

Some feminists have challenged these theories as circular, as methodologically flawed, as reifying a decontextualized dualism, as neglecting historical and cultural specificity, as essentialist and reductionist in their glossing of economic, political, and social structures and the experiences of class, race, and ethnicity, as privileging ideational forms, and as reinforcing culturally institutionalized mother blaming.[25] Elizabeth Spelman,[26] in a cogently argued critique of Chodorow's work, observed that white middle-class American men may deny relationality, but that denial is not equivalent to absence of connection. The public, "masculine," sphere of work, which Chodorow described as nonrelational, is filled with relation and affect among men, according to Spelman.

The problem is not that feminists have not taken Chodorow's work seriously, Spelman observed,[27] but that they have not taken it seriously enough. Chodorow called for an analysis of the reproduction of gendering situated in its social context, including a call[28] for deessentializing gender theory by locating gender in relation to other identities and situated aspects of social and cultural organization. But, according to Spelman, by deriving an explanation of masculine and feminine identities that does not consider the impact and inseparability of racial, class, and ethnic identities on gender identity, Chodorow glossed some of her own insights.

The emphasis in feminist object relations theory on sexual difference also has deflected analysis of gender as a social relation.[29] As Barrie Thorne[30] noted, when the topic is gender, there may be no escaping discussions of difference and the hold dualisms have on one's way of thinking about gender. But focusing on social relations and context situates gendering in multiple determinations in which cultural, ethnic, racial, regional, religious, and class variables are "always already" embedded in notions of masculinity and femininity[31] and helps unravel the plural/shifting basis of identity.

Psychoanalytical theory is based on Western philosophical axioms, particularly the split between self and object, and self-representation and object-representation that flows from Cartesian dualistic assumptions.[32] This dualism has been a foundational assumption in the formation of Western epistemology—how one knows what one knows and how the knowing subject is presumed to have agency.[33] Feminist object relations theory incorporated the Western-centric binaries on which the ideological commitments to individuation, separation, and autonomy were built. Dualisms, as Yanagisako and Collier observed,[34] impede the recognition that one views the world only through the lens of one's own culture and that such binaries are not universal. Despite the seemingly endless scholarly debates on difference, dualisms, and gender and their anchoring in individualist notions of self,[35] as yet there has been relatively little ethnographic and cross-cultural research on gender differences in selving, agency, and relationality.

Few of the proponents or critics of feminist object relations theory have examined these issues using ethnographically based cross-cultural research.[36] Fewer yet have systematically investigated the impact of patriarchy on relationality. These scholars have mainly sought to integrate the analytical, sociological, and experiential categories present in American society, but glossed or excluded from American white feminist middle-class discourse, or used them to displace psychoanalytical constructs.[37] Local, national, and international political realities, though, also deeply influence the local possibilities for gender construction,[38] a problem little explored by feminists, even though feminists have argued for consideration of race, class, and ethnicity.

Recent cross-cultural studies, however, contribute to de-essentializing the self, destabilizing the hegemony of Western psychological constructs, and challenging Western binaries between thought/feeling, self/society, experiential/theoretical, which have been incorporated into some Western feminist thought. Such research thereby offers insights into the varieties of selfhood among men and women cross-culturally.[39]

Relationality

Relational selving may not be dysfunctional in societies (including Western societies) in which persons are expected to remain in close proximity to their families and to be responsible for and to each other much of their lives. In societies in which the family or community is as or more valued than the person, in which persons achieve meaning in the context of family or community and in which survival depends upon integration into family or community, such relationality may support the production of what is locally recognized as healthy, responsible and mature persons. Relationality, then, becomes, not an explanation of dysfunctionality but rather a description of a process by which persons are socialized into social systems that value linkage, bonding, and sociability. Relationality is a process by which socially oriented selves are produced under different regimes of political economy. There may be multiple kinds of relationality (and individualism) in various cultures and historical periods. Relationality and individualism, although seemingly contradictory constructs, can and do exist side by side in specific societies. In the Arab world, where various forms of relationality are highly valued and institutionally supported, forms of individualism also thrive and receive support. In the chapters in this volume the focus is on relationality. We however, also lend insight to the dynamics of individualism and the interplay of diverse forms of relationality and individualism.

Intimate Selving in the Arab World

Little work on the Arab world has focused on theorizing selving. In both scholarly research and popular culture, the centrality of family in the Arab world has been so axiomatic that there has been relatively little problematizing of the psychodynamics of family life.[40] This hypervalorization of the family has placed the family in a sacrosanct space, which may be seen as inviolate except on peril of accusations of betrayal. That the most profound insights into the interior dynamics of family life often come from literary, "fictional," accounts is further testimony to the sanctity of the family. Because the Arab family is the center of controversy in the literature and popular culture of the Middle East, new efforts have been made to study Arab families.[41] Most scholars concerned with Arab families, however, focus on social structural and cultural dimensions. Those who have considered psychodynamics have applied Western rather than culturally situated theories.[42]

John Gulick noted,[43] a generation ago, that scholars tend to describe the Arab world as either extremely group oriented or extremely individualistic. He observed a "peril-refuge" polarity in which danger is experienced in every security zone.[44] Although security requires investing in collectivities, the danger in every zone applies to the collective as well. This makes corporate action difficult, according to Gulick, thus presenting opportunities for individualist action. I suggest, however, that neither the individualist nor corporatist view of Arab society offers the analytical tools necessary for more nuanced understandings of intimate selving.

The individualist view of Arab culture has a following.[45] George Hakim, for example, has argued: "Lebanese society is individualistic and petty bourgeois. . . . Social and economic relations are mainly between individuals. Group formations and group relations are not strong."[46] The corporatist view of the Arab world, however, has a larger following. Scholars differ, though, on the functionality of corporatism. Whereas many scholars argue that interests of collectivities may override those of individual persons in Arab societies,[47] some have suggested corporatism is problematical.[48] Halim Barakat asserted that the deep integration of selves into the family leads to a neglect of the person and society.[49] Hisham Sharabi contended that socialization by an authoritarian father and a smothering mother leads to a reflexive deference to authority and an inability to separate from the mother.[50] Juliette Minces claimed that Arab women are not able to stay by themselves "even for a few days."[51]

Andrea Rugh, arguing for the validity, rationality (and, in some ways, even, at times, the superiority) of corporateness, contended that Egyptians see social groups as indivisible and superordinate to their members.[52] Rugh later argued that Syrians teach their children to put obligation to others before the self, discouraged their children from thinking independently, encouraged the children to fit themselves into the family hierarchy, and inculcated the notion that their long-term interests were best served by commitment to their families.[53] Cynthia Nelson and Virginia Olesen have suggested Muslim gender and family organization is premised on complementarity, based on corporatist assumptions, rather than equality, based on individualist assumptions.[54] For Samir Khalaf the political and economic deployment of corporatists' primordial ties can be a productive mechanism of modernization.[55]

The debate between individualist and corporatist orientations in Arab societies has been charged by the tendency to judge the goodness or badness of these psychodynamic processes. The individualist and some corporatist views share a common prognosis about Arab society, but for different reasons. Individualists tend to regard Arab society as fragmented by individuals and incapable of collective societal action because of individualism. Corporatists tend to view Arab society as fragmented by tribal, ethnic, or religious groups, rendering it incapable of collective societal action—but because of corporatism. Both sets of scholars consider these patterns dysfunctional.

I suggest a construct that is neither individualist nor corporatist, but relational. It is productive to view persons in Arab societies as embedded in relational matrices that shape their sense of self but do not deny them their distinctive initiative and agency. The relational matrixes should not be read as equivalent to or coterminus with the "collective." Relational matrixes, although primarily embedded in kinship and relationships of proximity, are shifting and situational. Arab sociocultural systems often have supported the primacy of the family over the person, the family of origin over the family of procreation. Children have been socialized to feel lifelong responsibility for their parents and siblings. Older children, often, have been given parental responsibility for younger ones. Men have been encouraged to control and be responsible for their female kin. Women have been called upon to serve and to regard male kin as their protectors. Non-kin relationships have been absorbed into the family or appropriated family idioms and morality to legitimate patriarchal connectivity outside kin groups.[56] Yet despite these apparent "corporatist" family norms, persons in these Arab families have often resisted, constructed alternatives, or created networks that crossed the boundaries of family, neighborhood, class, religion, ethnicity, and nation, emerging with notions of self that, while privileging relationality, are quite hybrid.

To capture some of these dynamics, I suggest a construct of connective selfhood that, when coupled with patriarchy, produces patriarchal connectivity. Patriarchal connectivity is one of a number of culturally subsidized dynamics of selving. It does not exclusively or inclusively conceptualize all that the self is or that selving entails in Arab societies. As demonstrated in the chapters in this volume, there are multiple, competing and compatible notions of self coexisting in each Arab society and in many families and persons. The construct of patriarchal connectivity, however, describes processes that are culturally specific and, although they may have relevance beyond the Arab world, are widely supported in many Arab societies.

Patriarchal Connectivity

By connectivity I mean relationships in which a person's boundaries are relatively fluid so that persons feel a part of significant others. Persons do not experience themselves as bounded, separate, or autonomous. They may try to read each other's minds, answer for each other, anticipate each other's needs, expect their needs to be anticipated by significant others, and often shape their likes and dislikes in accordance with the likes and dislikes of others. Maturity is signaled in part by the successful enactment of a myriad of connective relationships. In a culture in which the family is valued over and above the person, identity is defined in familial terms, and kin idioms and relationships pervade public and private spheres, connective relationships are not only functional but necessary for successful social existence. I, like Catherine Keller, use *connectivity* to imply an "activity or an intention,"[57] rather than a state of being. Whereas Keller builds her idea of connective selfhood on Jungian theory to envision a liberatory construct of a self that is both autonomous and relational, I use the term here to connote a relationality that can take various forms under different political economy regimes.

Connectivity necessitates neither inequality in general (hierarchy) nor the subordination of women and juniors in particular (patriarchy). Among Arab families, however, connectivity is often intertwined with local patriarchy to produce what I call *patriarchal connectivity*. I use patriarchy here to mean the privileging of males and seniors and the mobilization of kinship structures, morality, and idioms to legitimate and institutionalize gendered and aged domination.

I use patriarchal connectivity to mean the production of selves with fluid boundaries organized for gendered and aged domination in a culture valorizing kin structures, morality, and idioms. By kin structures, I refer to the institutional arrangements that provide the rules of relationships by which kinship is governed. By morality, I mean the values shaping the beliefs and guiding the behavior of members of the society. Kinship idioms are the various terms that are used for relatives ("sister," "son of my father's brother") that are evoked to bring to bear the rules and morality of kinship.

Patriarchy entails cultural constructs and structural relations that privilege the initiative of males and elders in directing the lives of others. Connectivity entails cultural constructs and structural relations in which persons invite, require, and initiate involvement with others in shaping the self. In patriarchal societies, then, connectivity can support patriarchal power by crafting selves responding to, requiring, and socialized to initiate involvement with others in shaping the self, and patriarchy can help reproduce connectivity by crafting males and seniors prepared to direct the lives of females and juniors and females and juniors prepared to respond to the direction of males and seniors.

Connectivity can be critical to the reproduction of patriarchy in societies and subcultures in which family and/or community are valued more highly than the person. The production of persons with diffuse boundaries, responding to and requiring the involvement of others, may facilitate the exercise of patriarchal power by crafting selves potentially subject to control. Thus, in patriarchal societies connectivity can become a psychodynamic instrument of domination, and patriarchy can become a structural means of reproducing fluid selves. Out of this intersection patriarchal connectivity emerges.

Connectivity has reinforced family solidarity where solidarity was necessary for social, economic, and political survival. Connectivity has helped produce patterns that *locally* signaled healthy, responsible, and mature individuals (even though that measure of maturity, like any measure, may be contested). The fluidity of boundaries, the affiliative proclivity, the sense of responsibility for and to others, the experience of one's self as an extension of others and others as an extension of one's self that has been entailed in connectivity has not been gender or age specific. It has not necessitated hierarchy. The gendered and aged domination legitimated by kin structures, morality, and idioms that has been entailed in patriarchy subsidized and has subsidized psychodynamic processes that helped craft heirarchical oriented selves. Intertwined, connectivity and patriarchy have helped produce selves trained in the psychodynamics of domination, knowing how to control and be controlled.

Men in patriarchal connective systems usually are also raised with diffuse boundaries, responding to and requiring the involvement of others. In patriarchal systems, though, men and elders have the right of initiation. Males and elders are privileged to enter the boundary of the self of others, shape its contours, and direct its relationships. The connective patriarch may view his wife (wives), sisters, junior siblings, and children as extensions of himself. He may speak for them, make decisions for them, read and expect to be read by them.

Patriarchy has operated effectively in part because both men and women were socialized to view themselves relationally. Connectivity has held family together in part because men and women, adults and children internalized the psychological demands of compliance with gendered and aged hierarchies. Intertwined, patriarchy and connectivity have under-written the crafting of relationally oriented selves, socialized to negotiate gendered and aged hierarchies and *locally* recognized as healthy, mature, and responsible.

Connectivity and patriarchy intertwine in variable ways. I caution, however, against seeing men or fathers as prime movers or causes of these complex relationships. Each person, including women and juniors, is an active participant, both caused and causative of the relations of inequality in patriarchal systems. The actions of persons are always embedded in re-lational matrices. Viewing relationships in their complexity, plurality, and multiple agency may enjoin persons from solving the problem of "mother-blaming" by replacing it with "father-blaming."

Neither am I arguing that connectivity is the cause of patriarchy or that patriarchy is the cause of connectivity. Connectivity exists independently of patriarchy and probably occurs in most cultures (or subcultures) in which individuation, autonomy, and separation are not valued or sup-ported. Patriarchal societies, although not causing connectivity, may sup-port some form of connectivity among a significant proportion of their members.

Relationality in Arab families has not been feminized but has been gen-der and age marked. Recognizing men and seniors' connectivity chal-lenges the Western-centric gendering of relationality. The gender and age marking of relationality has been the result not of the primacy of female parenting but of the centrality of patriarchy and the pervasiveness of id-iomatic kinship modeled on patriarchal connectivity. It has been patri-archy, privileging male and senior initiative, that differentiated the experiences and expressions of connectivity and shaped connectivity into a crucible of domination. And it is the intersections of patriarchy and rela-tionality that have gone largely unproblematized in feminist object rela-tions theory.

In the context of states organized around familial ties reinforced by class, religious, ethnic, regional, and ideological alliances, leaders and fol-lowers often offer and obtain access to information, services, and protec-tions by mobilizing networks grounded in relations of proximity, the most central of which is kinship.[58] In such political arenas relationality can be a motorizing force. What family one comes from, who one knows, and what face-to-face networks one can mobilize may be critical in achieving political ends in societies in which there are fluid boundaries between state and family, public and private, the personal and the political, and kin and non-kin.

By decoupling relationality and patriarchy and then analyzing their linkages, one can recognize that it may not be relationality in and of itself that limits autonomy, but relationality coupled with patriarchy. By decoupling relationality and patriarchy, one may reevaluate Western constructs of the self that relegate relationality to dysfunctionality. By decoupling connectivity and patriarchy, one can challenge the dysfunctionalization of relationality. The limits to autonomy may then turn out to have emerged from the conjunction of relationality with patriarchy. By recognizing the multiplicity of culturally legitimate paths to mature selfhood across cultures and within any one culture, one avoids the hazards of ethnocentricism and the essentializing assumptions of cultural relativism as well. Through such culturally contextualized constructs of relationality, one can develop more productive and recuperative constructs of self.

Contributions of This Volume

In this volume we ground relationality in specificities of culture, history, and the intimate context of particular intimate familial relationships. A number of forms of relationality (besides other forms of selving) are depicted in the various chapters although dynamics of connectivity and patriarchy seem to underpin most of the descriptions. Throughout the discussions of relationality, the authors never lose sight of agency of the self. The self is represented as an active agent, not as a passive object of kin structures, moralities, or idioms. Such agency, however, rarely conforms to the hegemonic Western homogenized individual—bounded, self-contained, autonomous, separative. The agency of the self is situated, contextual, and relational. The actors are discussed as embedded in webs of relationships that coshape their desires, interests, ambitions, and behavior. Both shaped and shaping, the self, in these depictions, is neither individualist or collectivist, but absorbing and actively defining self and other, each of which shifts as each actor acts.

For example, Flaur, in my chapter on brother-sister relationships, seems, on the one hand, dominated by her brother Hanna, who appears to be supported by his mother and the patriarchal kinship system in asserting authority over his younger sister. Yet Flaur actively both rejects and invites, resists and submits to Hanna's interventions in her life. In the process of actively engaging Hanna, drawing him into her life, Flaur not only shapes her role of "sister" and her "femininity" but also what it means for Hanna to be "brother" and "masculine." Hanna similarly is both active and reactive to Flaur's actions. He takes initiative, but his initiative is also shaped by her responses. His willingness to be proactive in her life not only shapes Flaur's life and her role as sister (and, thus, her femininity) but also shapes his role as brother (and his masculinity). Their relationship shifts, transforms as each absorbs the action of the other and takes action. Flaur "becomes" a sister, defined by a certain femininity in relationship to Hanna. Hanna "becomes" a brother, defined by a certain masculinity in relationship to Flaur. The process of "becoming" a sister or a brother is shaped, but not preordained, by the kinship structures, moralities, and idioms. The analysis of the love and power that mutually shape what Flaur and Hanna become as sister (and feminine) and brother (and masculine) focuses on one time period in that relationship, a period of almost two and one-half years. But the process of becoming sister and brother continues throughout their lives, changing as their situations and context change. As the process changes, so do their notions of self and siblingship, and as their notions of self and siblingship change, so does the process of becoming "sister" and "brother."

The book is divided into three parts. Part 1 engages the practice of selving represented in biographical and autobiographical accounts. Part 2 offers ethnographic and historical narratives of selving. Authors in part 3 evoke the literary imagination and interpret representations of selving in a number of novels by highly respected Arab writers.

In part 1, Jean Said Makdisi records an intimate portrayal of three generations of women in her family (her grandmother, mother, and herself) living in Lebanon during the transformative changes of the twentieth century. In chapter 2, I recollect the struggle of a daughter, caught between Western and Arab worlds, to understand a father embedded in the relational matrices of Lebanon. Maysoon Melek portrays the profound influence of extended family by painting a portrait of growing up in Iraq under the tutelage of her relationship with her famous cousin, Nazik al-Malaika. The centrality of sisters to intimate selving is the subject of Scheherazade's reflections.

In part 2, we expand the stories into ethnographic and historical accounts. I center stage the brother-sister relationship in Lebanon in the intimate selving of both, a relationship often neglected in Western psychology. Najla Hamadeh compares co-wives in urban and rural settings, focusing attention on an understudied and little-understood relationship in Muslim families in Lebanon. The mother-son relationship, although much discussed, is rarely studied in ethnographic detail. In chapter 7, I suggest alternative views of the functionality of mother-son relationality in Lebanon. Mother-daughter, father-daughter, and husband-wife relationalities are rarely investigated historically. In chapter 8, Mervat F. Hatem offers a provocative insight into a little-researched important Egyptian historical figure 'A'isha Taymur in relationship to her daughter.

In part 3, we engage the literary notions of intimate selving in the Arab world, which are also semiautobiographical. Soraya Altorki offers critical insights into father-son relationships in Naguib Mahfrouz's prize-winning Cairo trilogy. She suggests important connections between Naguib's literary imaginings of intimate selving and the literary critique of colonialism. Magda M. Al-Nowaihi finds the novel a site for the construction of masculinity in Egyptian novels by 'Abd al-Hakim Qasim and Mahmud Diyab.

This volume is concerned with the culturally specific constructs of selving in which intimate relationality is foundational, functional, and valorized. What is being contested are the culturally imbued assumptions of what constitutes a self, a person, a woman, a man. Western psychology and liberal feminism largely have accepted individualist tenets of Western psychology built in part on the untheorized gender binary. Central to these tenets has been a naturalization of individualism through the Western psychotherapeutic assumption that individuation is necessary for maturation and agency. This has been the hegemonic view in Western psychodynamic theory despite the critiques by some feminists of the limitations of masculinized autonomy. Other standards of maturity are valued by many people, including feminists, of other cultures, and by many people of the West. This volume is not a judgment of the relative merits of individualism or relationality, nor do we propose yet another binary. Individualism and relationality are variegated and the relationships between them not oppositional, but fluid. They often co-reside in the same societies, families, and persons.

In this volume we call neither for abandonment of models that work for persons in their settings nor for uncritical valorizing of other cultural modes of being. Yet I hope for theoretical works that recognize that one's vision is always already filtered through the fine lens of culture through which one views the world. Scholars cannot hope to even begin to hear what women and men in other cultures want until they develop descriptive languages that neutralize the ethnocentrism of Western formations of the self.

PART ONE

Intimate Selving as a Practice of Biography
and Autobiography in Arab Families

The Context

The chapters in part 1 are all biographical or autobiographical. Focusing on grandmother-mother-daughter relationships (Jean Said Makdisi), father-daughter relationships (Suad Joseph), cousin relationships (Maysoon Melek), and sister-sister relationships (Scheherazade), they explore the dance of intimate selving within the immediate family circle. Each chapter is written by one of the actors in the relationship described. One chapter is set primarily in Iraq (Melek), two in Lebanon (Makdisi and Scheherazade), and one between Lebanon and the United States (Joseph). All four authors, however, describe relationships that move across national boundaries. Makdisi's narrative moves across Syria, Palestine, Egypt, the United States, and Lebanon; Joseph's moves between Lebanon and the United States several times; Melek transverses Iraq, England, and Italy; and Scheherazade travels between Syria, Lebanon, France, and the United States. Families begin in village settings for some (Makdisi, Joseph) and urban settings for others (Melek, Scheherazade) although all seem destined for urban life, either in small cities (Joseph) or large (Makdisi, Melek, Scheherazade). The actors come from peasant (Joseph) to middle-class (Melek, Makdisi) to relatively wealthy (Scheherazade) backgrounds. The families are Christian (Makdisi, Joseph) and Muslim (Melek, Scheherazade). Educational levels vary from elementary school to doctoral degrees. This span of the social spectrum from the eastern Arab countries might provoke easy generalizations. But generalizations might suggest a premature calculus. Both similarities and differences are intriguing and must be given their due.

Makdisi weaves a three-generational tapestry of grandmother-mother-daughter relationships spanning one century. History, understood politically and culturally, is woven within the narrative. Often foregrounded, at times backgrounded, political and cultural history always is a central thread that ties the actors to their society for Makdisi and helps explain the transformations in selves and relationalities. History is also personal as Makdisi discovers she did not know her grandmother or mother as well as she had assumed and must excavate family memoirs and letters and carry out interviews to learn even some of the basic facts of their lives. The grandmother who appeared submissive and frail to her granddaughter emerges, upon examination of family history, as a "vital, tough, and bustling matriarch, dominating the life of her family" earlier in her life. Makdisi's mother changes as well, coming to dominate her own mother who had earlier dominated her. Makdisi investigates how these changes came about and how different notions of selfhood are contested for or against. The story is one of intimate relationships cast in the throes of political and social upheaval, holding onto themselves and each other, yet changing each other and their selves as cultural transformations sweep through the many lands the three generations of women call home. Makdisi delicately interlaces the macro- and microhistorical narratives of dynamically changing selves and relationalities bound to each other in silence and in word, knowing and not knowing self and other and yet in the knowing and not knowing, both shaped and shaping self and intimate other.

For myself, in some ways like Makdisi, the death of a parent provoked a journey into the soul of the relationship. I knew, at some level, that my theories of selfhood and relationality were informed and enriched by my family history and relationships. But I had always thought of those notions of selfhood as being most influenced by my mother, the dominant figure in my family and life. I had long assumed I would write my mother's story someday. I was surprised to find myself writing about my father first. Perhaps it was my father's death, like the death of Makdisi's mother, coming after my mother's and sealing the end of that generation, that consolidated my will to write. But perhaps it was the timing of his departure. His death came in the midst of my efforts to conceptualize a theoretical construct of selfhood encompassed neither by "individualist" nor "collectivist" notions; a notion of selfhood that recognized the power of structure yet insisted on the agency of the self; a notion of selfhood that respected the functionality and rationality of forms of selving that had been either dysfunctionalized or not theorized by Western psychodynamic scholarship; a notion of selfhood informed by feminists' insistence that the political is personal and the personal is political and my conviction, hard-learned through years of teaching, that the personal is theoretical and the theoretical is personal. The personal journey to Lebanon, to deal with my father's estate, was a pathway toward theory. And theory opened a door back to the personal. The journey unravels the wide web of relatives (whom my father always seemed to fight but never wanted to lose) entangled in my father's estate; his complicated multigenerational patrilineal co-ownership of land; his messy citizenship records, whose story was told as mysterious interventions by vengeful relatives; his seemingly unfathomable name changes, which the Lebanese state accepted but could not reconcile. The journey chronicles Baba's self-making in the context of patriarchal connective family-making and state-making. His was a self reticulated within a structure that seemed to engulf him, yet within which he held himself to be a supreme actor.

Maysoon Melek offers a story of self-making in the context of a family in which the boundaries between nuclear and extended are fluid and in which, contrary to generic scholarship on Arab families, the maternal line is forefronted. Here, the literary is personal and the personal is literary. Melek's relationship with her maternal first cousin, the distinguished Iraqi poet Nazik al-Malaika, is formative. Al-Malaika is a second mother to Melek. She is a revolutionary figure in Arabic literature, a formidable agent for literary and social change. As a woman poet, writing groundbreaking romatic poetry, she frees poetry from classical forms. But for Melek, she does more. She frees herself from classical structure while being deeply immersed in classical Arabic language and poetry "of which she had been an extremely serious student." For Melek, al-Malaika was a "true daughter of her culture," yet a free agent within that culture. It is this nuanced reading of the connection between literary and personal revolution, between structure and innovation, between culture and the self, and between intimate first cousins in a close family system that makes Melek's contribution here a powerful insight into the dynamics of self-making within Arab family and culture.

Scheherazade's biographical/autobiographical account of her relationship with her sister, Isabelle, probes one of the least-theorized relationships in Arab family systems. She painstakingly demystifies a relationship that is as romanticized as it is untheorized. Told from the voice of the younger sister, the narrative discloses the complexities of love and power in sister relationships, much as Joseph does for brother-sister relationships. The details of jealousies, the willingness to do damage, the consequent fear and uncertainty belie the descriptions of sister relationships, often found in anthropological texts, as generically loving and nurturing. Age, birth order, gender, all factor into the relationship between the sisters. The sisters have different relationships with their father and their mother and that, it seems, all the difference makes. The profound impact of the older sibling on the younger challenges the hyper-privileging of the parent-child relationship in much of Western psychodynamic theory. And the tensions in the same-sex sibling relationships call for further investigation of this little-recognized, but obviously highly important, relationship for intimate selving.

The authors in this section offer important insights for understanding intimate familial relationships crucial to the shaping of self in these Arab families. They unhinge some standing theories privileging parent-child relationships. They shed light on relationships little described or theorized. They closely chronicle the impact of macro- and microhistorical changes on changing notions of selfhood. They link the political, social, cultural, theoretical, literary, and the personal. Their power is not only in the insights they offer, but in the call for dymystification of family relationships, for closer scrutiny of intimate dynamics, and for examining the similarities and differences in family experiences across age, gender, class, religion, nationality, time, and place.

1

Teta, Mother, and I

JEAN SAID MAKDISI

My maternal grandmother, Munira Badr, or "Teta" (the Arabic equivalent of "Gramma"), was the only grandparent I ever knew. She was always there, hauntingly, in the background of my childhood, her aging face and figure delicate and vulnerable. Her silence and general air of submission spoke of an intense past pain, one that I felt rather than knew about. Although stooped with age, she never lost her dignity, and even when we were young, her grandchildren recognized her goodness and her stoicism.

She died in Beirut in 1973 at the age of ninety-three after several months in the fog of an agonizing senility. During that time I felt her vulnerability more than ever. I resolved that one day I would write about Teta, about her only daughter, my mother, about myself and my sisters, that I would trace our lives and watch to see what, if anything, had changed in our respective lifetimes. When my mother died in 1990 in the United States, to which she had fled from the war in Lebanon, my resolve was hastened.[1] I thought mine would be an easy task, a biographical act of love. No sooner had I started to work, however, than I encountered several huge surprises. The first was when I realized that I would have to do historical research: I had never thought of my grandmother, my mother, or myself as having anything in particular to do with history, as though it were something utterly irrelevant to us and we to it. As I worked, however, I found that their lives, and mine, were intricately bound up with history of which I found myself astonishingly ignorant.

Second, I found that I did not know all that much about Mother and Teta, whom I thought I knew so intimately and thoroughly. About Teta I

25

knew next to nothing. I had spent surely thousands of hours with her; when she died I was in my thirties. Yet even for the simplest questions— Where had she gone to school? What language had she spoken with her parents? What clothes had she worn in her youth? Where had she met my grandfather? What were the conditions of her early married life?—I had no answers.

I wrote to my mother's oldest surviving brother, and he sent me a memoir with answers to some of my questions. Later Mother's youngest brother wrote down his memories as well.

During the long and terrible war in Lebanon, I had prodded Mother to write her memories of her childhood, her early schooling, her early married life. She wrote very reluctantly at first, but with growing interest and, I fear, with growing pain so that she did not continue the task for very long. I did not read her memoir through until after her death, and then it was too late for questions.

It is from these sources, as well as family letters and many conversations with uncles, aunts, cousins, and older members of the community, that I came to know some of the particulars of my grandmother's and mother's lives. Histories of the area, in addition to the published memoirs and personal correspondence of contemporaries, filled in the background.

The Teta who emerged from the memories of others was radically different from the Teta I had known. Instead of the silent, submissive, frail woman I knew, there emerged from an earlier time, especially from the accounts of her children, a vital, tough, and bustling matriarch, dominating the life of her family.

To my astonishment I found that my grandmother had once been a professional woman, one who had helped create new social forms. How, I kept asking myself, had she changed so thoroughly? My question evolved: To what extent had the particular vagaries of her individual life and character been influenced by the world from which she had seemed so separate and alien but which, I found out as I worked, had molded her, and she it?

Mother, too, changed. Although the force of her character was clearly there from her earliest days, she became gradually a truly dominant figure over an increasingly small territory. Furthermore, a great transformation had taken place in their relationships with each other as time passed: where Teta had dominated Mother, Mother came to dominate Teta, and this was, I believe, at least partly a direct result of social and political history.

When Teta was born in the Syrian town of Hums in 1880, the countries that today are Syria, Lebanon, Palestine, Israel, and Jordan did not exist as separate political entities. Israel did not exist at all, although Palestine and Lebanon were known as distinct entities from ancient times. The whole area was known as Syria, or, in Arabic, *bilad al-Sham*. Syria was, in those days, a province of the vast Ottoman Empire.

Mother was born in Nazareth in Palestine in March 1914, on the eve of World War I. "I opened my eyes to war," she used to say. The Great War brought unimaginable suffering to the area. Famine, epidemics, and plagues of locusts, not to mention invading armies, occupations, mass exiles, and hangings, engulfed Syria, especially in the last two years of the war. In addition, the war was to bring overwhelming political and cultural change to Syria. When the Ottoman army was defeated, the British and French divided up the spoils between themselves, carved up Syria, and created the new countries, each with either Britain or France as the mandatory power.

The British and French did not just impose fixed political boundaries where none had existed before: they imposed their language, a different culture, an altogether new and alien political organization, the so-called "modern" nation-state, and with it a new economic organization.

Though they lived through this period, neither Mother nor Teta ever said much about it, nor did it ever give rise to tales about them told around the dining table and in the nursery. My father, by contrasts often talked of his experiences during the war. The family narrative received from that time was exclusively my father's, as the public one has been that of other men.

This lack of narration no longer surprises me. Women in the family did not talk much about public issues or about themselves. Even privately, their principal focus was on others, especially their husbands. The women took on the stories of their men, even as they took their names, and let them speak while they stood looking on, listening. The narrative of public history was not perceived, by them or anyone else, as belonging to the women. And just as they were silent about the outside world, so it was silent about them. The history books to which I turned scarcely mention the women or their concerns, scarcely nod at the rich tapestry of everyday life that they wove and that in the end constitutes a major aspect of the social world.

As I worked, I began to see that I did, after all, know many things about my grandmother and mother, but that these had nothing to do, at least not obviously, with history or politics. When I asked myself, for instance, what my mother and grandmother actively, explicitly, *taught* me, I immediately thought of recipes and stitches, ways of bathing and swaddling a baby; how to sew on a button or darn a stocking; how to make the coffee and tea; how to wait until you could count to ten with your finger in the boiled and cooling milk before adding the culture for the yogurt; how to add cinnamon sticks to the syrup to give it that extra touch of flavor—domestic secrets that I first dismissed, disappointed, as insignificant and then understood to be enormously important.

It gradually came to me that the world of women, the world of the interior, the domestic life, with all its mysteries and rituals, could not be separated from the outer life, the world of politics and armies and treaties; that the one world is the complement to the other, in no way inferior, in no way less important or significant; and that neither world can be understood without the other.

The domestic life Teta and Mother lived, with its clutter of kitchens and nurseries, was at the heart of a vastly changing world. More than anywhere else, one could trace in it, as in the patterns of one of those crocheted doilies that Teta regularly made, the patterns of those changes. Social change was as significant as political. The facades of towns and cities were being altered. My grandmother's parents, of rural origin, belonged to a middle class just then emerging; by the time my mother was mature, it had become well established.

It was the women, with their enormous domestic power, with the clothes they wore and dressed their children in, with the table manners, songs, and games they taught their children, with the way they organized their households, who concretized and gave form to the changes. And in their relationships with their husbands and sons, and with their mothers and daughters, new definitions, new boundaries were created, as alien and revolutionary as the political ones on the map.

As I tried to trace our relationships, which, against the calmest background imaginable would naturally have been complex and deeply entangled with entirely personal and particular complications, I found the strands repeatedly leading me to historical knots. I found not only that, in order to understand Teta and Mother, and myself, I had first to know history: I found that history was a very difficult thing to know.

Just as my apparently thorough knowledge of Teta and Mother turned out to be not nearly as thorough as I had thought it, so history, deceptively clear and discernible in its progress, was full of puzzles and conundrums. I found that into our personal history, as into our social and political history, an intrusive outside presence had insinuated itself, distorting our perceptions of ourselves, of each other, of our surroundings, and of our past. I have tried to disentangle the knotted strands, to clear up the puzzles, and to fill in the empty spaces.

Teta's earliest schooling was at the American Presbyterian mission school in Hums where she was born in 1880. Her father, the Reverend Youssef Badr, native of a preponderantly Greek Catholic village in Mount Lebanon and son of a weaver, had studied theology with the American missionaries and was ordained in 1872. In the same year he had married my great-grandmother, who was also from a village in Mount Lebanon, and they had moved to Hums where the mission had sent him to be the first "native" pastor of the newly founded Protestant community there.

The most important monument of the American missionaries, who began their work here in the 1830s, is today the American University of Beirut, founded in 1866 as the Syrian Protestant College. The Americans were by no means the only foreign missionaries in the largely Muslim Ottoman Empire. European missions, including Catholics, Orthodox, and other Protestants, had preceded them. Later a European Jewish mission became active as well. Whether they were aware of it or not, the missionaries spearheaded the European imperial penetration that was to come to full flower early in the twentieth century.

During the nineteenth century, the missions, protected by powerful European consulates, became an increasingly important cultural presence in the declining empire. This was particularly true in Syria, where large concentrations of Christians and Jews lived, on whose behalf the European powers justified their frequent and aggressive interventions in Ottoman affairs.[2]

The "natives" involved in the missionary venture, although they were crucial to its success, enjoyed none of the power or privileges of the foreigners. But by the time the war ended, hundreds of students and teachers had been through the mission schools and were in place, able to make the uneasy transition, speaking the languages and knowing the ways of the British and the French—and later the Americans—in the post-Ottoman era. Ironically, from the ranks of these students emerged nationalist thinkers and leaders who, influenced by the political ideas of the West, turned against the imperialist camp and worked toward political and cultural independence.

In 1890 the Badrs moved to Beirut where my great-grandfather became the first Arab pastor of the Beirut Protestant church and where Teta and her sisters entered the Training College of the British Syrian mission. The school had been founded in the 1860s by an English gentlewoman, Elizabeth Bowen-Thompson.[3] The curriculum at this important and influential school included such subjects as physiology, botany, history, and geography, besides English, Arabic, and mathematics. The greatest stress was laid on the Bible, which was not only studied itself but used as a text for the study of language. In music the girls most probably learned to sing hymns.

The all-important field of comportment, manners, and personal conduct was a continuous and regular part of the curriculum and led to a new domestic reality. Girls were given marks for "housework," "needlework," "cutting out," and "Scripture," and they were marked also on "conduct" and "order." Prizes awarded for good work and good behavior included workbaskets, hymnals, prayer books, and Bibles.

Not surprisingly, the world taught by the missionaries reflected their own reality as can be seen clearly in the nature of the prizes. In the early years of the twentieth century, several years after Teta had left the school, the feminist movement emerged in England, and the prizes began to include books on historic heroines, ancient goddesses, and the lives of influential women. Such titles as *Noble Deeds of the World's Heroines, Heroines of History and Travel, Florence Nightingale, Four Noble Women,* and *Women Who Have Worked and Won* never replaced the hymnals, prayer books and workbaskets, but their presence among them is nonetheless striking.[4]

On graduating, Teta and her sisters taught in this and other mission schools, becoming the embodiments of that most interesting and important figure in nineteenth-century Syrian cultural history, the Christian female schoolteacher. Trained by foreign missions and spreading their ways, they quietly helped to transform the world in which they lived. Later, two of Teta's sisters emigrated to the United States. A third went to Cairo where she made important contributions to the feminist movement and to female education. After completing their education at the Syrian Protestant College, their two brothers went to the Sudan, where they joined the British civil administration. In many ways this was an adventurous group, fearlessly ready to travel and to taste the world outside the narrow limits of their own background, bringing back with them new ideas and opening up new paths.

In 1905, at what was then considered the ripe old age of twenty-five, Teta married my grandfather, Shukri Musa. He was a Greek Catholic native of Safad, a town in Galilee in northern Palestine, and had been working as a postal clerk in Jerusalem. When he decided to seek a bride, he was taken by a friend of his to Marjeyoun, now in Israeli-occupied southern

Lebanon, to which the Reverend Youssef had been transferred by the mission in 1893, and there was introduced to the Badrs.

After their marriage, my grandparents settled in his native Safad, where he made a living in commerce. After the birth of their first son, he took the bold step in 1908 of going to America where he somehow made his way to Texas. He became intrigued with the Baptist faith, converted, and, after a short period of intense study in Waco, was ordained. He returned to Palestine a couple of years later as a member of the Southern Baptist Convention Near East Mission. He opened his church in Nazareth, where Christianity had begun, and at this point his family, including his widowed mother and his brother, moved with him from Safad to this provincial town. His wife, mother, and brother were his first converts.

The First Baptist Church of Nazareth was, predictably, not well received by the local population, which was mostly Greek Orthodox. By the time my grandfather died, however, the church, along with its pastor and his family, had, if not an important congregation of vast proportions, a respected place in the community.

My grandparents had six children, only five of whom, my mother and four brothers, survived: a daughter born to Teta while her husband was in America died of cholera during his absence, causing Teta a sorrow from which I think she never fully recovered. The story of the birth and death of this beloved infant is the only one from her early life that Teta ever told me—or the only one I remember her telling me.

My mother, Hilda Musa, the fourth child of the family, was born in March 1914. The Ottoman Empire entered the war on the side of Germany in November. Religious figures were normally exempted from conscription; my grandfather, however, had not achieved official recognition from the Ottomans for his sect. He was, therefore, not granted the privilege of exemption but was drafted into the army early in 1916. Luckily, he was spared the ravages of the battlefield, remaining until the end of the war in a town in the Beqaa valley as an assistant pharmacist to the Turkish army.

In the meantime, as an employee of an institution from an enemy state—by this time the United States had entered the war—his salary was stopped, and Teta had a difficult time of it. She was now in charge of four children—her next-to-youngest son was born during this time—and her husband's sister and mother, who were living with her. When the war ended and my grandfather returned, his salary was restored, and the arrears paid. The next few years were the family's happiest time. The church grew and prospered although the political situation was extremely unsettled.

Not only had the Ottomans been replaced by the British and French but the Balfour Declaration of 1917 had promised "a national home" for the Jewish people in Palestine. Under British occupation large numbers of Jews began to pour in from Europe, and the Arab population of Palestine, feeling threatened and engulfed, soon began a series of strikes and revolts. The culmination of the struggle was the defeat of 1948 and the creation of the Jewish state of Israel and of the Palestinian Arab diaspora, to which both my mother's and father's family belonged.

In the shade of these events, although apparently sheltered from them, Mother attended first the public school of Nazareth and then in 1925 the Scots College in her father's native Safad. She had a great love for Safad and had pleaded with her parents to send her to this mission school.

In August 1928, after catching a chill, her father died of pneumonia. This was the single most traumatic event of Mother's early life, perhaps of her entire life; she was fourteen years old. For Teta, who was only forty-eight, it was the end of the world. For the family as a whole, it was a catastrophe.

Teta was devastated; she suffered a major depression, lost more than twenty kilograms in a few weeks, and had to be hospitalized for some time. Eventually she recovered enough to be able to come home, to work, and to take care of her children, but she was never the same. For a brief period she went on with her work in the mission and was paid a small salary. Eventually, however, as a result of the Great Depression then devastating the United States, her salary was stopped, and Teta now became thoroughly redundant.

For some time after her retirement, Teta supported herself and the family from the sale of olives and olive oil from their olive trees and the sale of some goats that her husband had bought just before he died. She was able to keep her home for a while, and her place in it. In 1936, however, the great revolt against the British occupation and the growing Zionist presence occurred in Palestine, including a six-month-long strike during which all economic activity stopped. Teta lost whatever income she had and whatever independence. She had to close her house, and from this time to the end of her long life, she lived with one or another of her children, with whom she later shared the exile from Palestine.

In the meantime, at the end of the traumatic summer of 1928 and after a deeply emotional farewell with her mother, Mother was sent to the

American School for Girls (ASG) in Beirut, the principal American mission school for girls, where her cousins were already studying. From the ASG she went on to another important mission institution in Beirut, the American Junior College. She was a brilliant student and until the day she died looked back to these years of accomplishment and promise as among the happiest of her life.

Preparation for her schooling in Beirut had been made before her father's death. In one of his last letters he mentions his hope that, upon completion of her education, Hilda would ultimately come back to Nazareth and open a school attached to the Baptist mission. He had wished her to follow in her mother's footsteps and become a school-teacher, but this was not to be her destiny.

After only one year at the junior college, at the age of eighteen, Mother became engaged to my father, who was from Jerusalem. The reduced circumstances of her family after the death of her father was a major factor in her decision to marry. My father was a good deal older than she and had earlier emigrated to the United States. He had returned to Palestine in the 1920s. His beloved only sister was married to their cousin; he went into business with him in Jerusalem. Eventually, they opened a branch of the business, for which he took charge, in Cairo, where he resided most of the year.

Soon, a prosperous but lonely man, he started to look for a bride. He was introduced to my mother by his sister and the wife of the pastor of the Jerusalem Anglican church to which he belonged. They had, of course, already inspected Mother and inquired into her background. Impressed with her beauty, intelligence, scholarship, virtue, and impeccable family background—daughter of an accomplished mother and an upright father of modest, but respectable, means—they had pronounced her an excellent prospect and arranged a meeting. He fell madly and utterly in love with her.

My parents were married in Nazareth on Christmas Eve, 1932. They had a prolonged honeymoon in Europe, including tours of the great cities of Italy, France, and England, where the adoring groom bought the diffident bride the latest fashions. Finally, they returned to Egypt and to his bachelor apartment in Cairo. Every holiday and special occasion took them home to Jerusalem.

Their six children—two boys, of whom the first was stillborn, and four girls—were born either in Cairo or Jerusalem. I was born in Jerusalem in 1940, the middle child of the family. The British, who had occupied

Egypt since 1882, were on the defensive as the German army under General Rommel advanced in the desert. The British victory at Alamein entrenched them more than ever in Egypt.

In Cairo my parents moved in the elite business circles of cosmopolitan prerevolutionary Cairo, and especially in the circle of that interesting group of people known in Egypt as the *shawwam,* those originating from bilad al-Sham. A prosperous and sophisticated community, including writers, teachers, journalists, professionals, and businessmen, the shawwam made many important contributions to social and domestic history.

In Jerusalem my siblings and I attended mission schools. In Cairo, however, after a period in which my parents seemed to have tried various schools for us, we were sent to English lay schools. Principally intended for the children of the British residents of British-controlled Egypt, the schools admitted as well the children of the local elite and members of the diplomatic service. Not intended for the "improvement" (or conversion) of the "natives," as the mission schools had been, they thus provided the same education as would have been had in England for the same social class of English children. Later, we would attend colleges and universities in the United States. In this important way was my education, and that of my siblings, different from my mother's and grandmother's.

After the war, the situation in Palestine became explosive. In 1948 the Palestine war and the creation of the state of Israel became the central political event in the life of our family, and of the region, as it has remained to this day. The loss not just of property but of a rooted home base and of historic continuity; the scattering of the family; the sense of being blown about by political winds—all this dominated the family, both as individuals and as a group. All my parents' friends and relatives, including Teta and her sons, my father's sister and her family, became refugees, and many of them came to Cairo. Thus I grew up in a world that had been blown asunder, a world of fragments and falling debris, of displaced people and of alienation.

Partly as a result of the Palestine war, the Egyptian Revolution led by Gamal Abdel Nasser took place in 1952, and the region entered a new phase of change.

In 1956 the Suez crisis that began in the summer with the nationalization of the Suez Canal culminated in the tripartite invasion of Egypt and was certainly the formative political experience of my life. The following year I went to Vassar College.

When I married after my graduation, my parents were in the process of moving from Cairo to Beirut as private businesses and homes were being nationalized and sequestered by the socialist revolution. My Lebanese husband had just completed his doctorate in the United States, having done his lower studies at the American University of Beirut (AUB) to which he had now returned as assistant professor. His father had for decades been a professor of Arabic at the AUB.

Immediately after our wedding, my husband and I left for the United States where he had been appointed to a post in the International Monetary Fund. We lived in the Washington, D.C., area for the next ten years. It was during this time that our three sons were born, that I did my graduate work and experienced the doldrums of American suburban life against the intensely passionate background of the American revolution of the 1960s.

It was also during this time that the catastrophic 1967 war took place, and what was left of my native Jerusalem along with all the towns on the west bank of the Jordan were taken by the Israelis.

In 1972 my husband again accepted a post at the American University of Beirut, and, with our young children in tow, we moved back to Beirut where my father had died in 1970. I started to teach at the Beirut College for Women, (now the Lebanese American University), successor of the American Junior College where Mother had spent a blissfully happy year. Perhaps because I identify the college with her, I have clung to it as to a vague strand in my elusive past.

In 1973, three months after Teta died, the October war took place. In April 1975 the first shots of the war in Lebanon were fired, and the next sixteen years of our lives were lived in its terrible shade. In 1990 Mother died of cancer in Washington, D.C., where she had gone to live with my sister, both having left behind the devastation of Beirut. I am the last of my family to live in Beirut.

Thus have our lives been tied up in some of the principal historical and social events in this area over the last hundred years.

Teta often lived with us, as she did with her other children's families. This used to be a common arrangement, part of the natural order of things. It was as entirely unexceptional for a widow to live with her adult children, especially her sons, as it was for sons to bring their brides into the family home. Teta's mother-in-law lived with her. So did her mother when she was widowed because her sons, with the eldest of whom she would have been expected to live, were in the Sudan. The natural course of a woman's life was to start out with her mother-in-law and to end up with her daughter-in-law.

This was in the age of communal relationships, the age of a relatively stable social life, when families stayed together. In the provincial towns and in the villages, the family used to eat from a common dish, sitting around the low, round table called a *tabliyye,* dipping their bread and spoons into the food, fingers touching fingers, elbows touching elbows. But then some of them learned other ways, manners based on a Western style brought in at least in part by the missionaries. The puritanical Victorian missionaries of England and America, often of the upper classes, brought with them the domestic ethics, the social and economic attitudes of an entirely alien culture, as did the Catholic priests and nuns who came mostly from France. The dining table gradually replaced the tabliyye, the individual plate replaced the common dish, individual ambition and identity replaced family, and the individual purse replaced family possessions.

Teta was one of those who learned, and then one of those who taught, the imported domestic ways and manners as she taught history and Arabic. When Mother was a girl in Nazareth, she remembered decades later, theirs was the only family of her acquaintance to sit on chairs at a Western-style dining table, eating out of individual plates, using forks and knives. Theirs was the only family of her acquaintance in which every member had his or her own bed: The normal sleeping arrangement was to lay out cotton mattresses at night and in the morning to stack them neatly in a closet or *youk* for the day. In Teta's household these mattresses were only brought out when the large family had guests because there was no room for more bedsteads even in the pastor's spacious house. "We were different," Mother wrote in her notebook, outsiders, not only because they were not natives of the town, not only because of their Baptist faith, but because of the way they lived.

In her notebook Mother remembers her father scoffing occasionally at the domestic manners Teta took so seriously. For a provincial Palestinian the fuss over manners learned from Victorian missionaries and taken utterly to heart by his wife must have seemed the height of absurdity, but he humored her because he loved and admired her.

All accounts of this period of Teta's life that I have culled, and which create that utterly different portrait of her from the one I knew, agree that Teta's contribution was enormous, invaluable to the success of her husband's mission. His engaging personality, his talent as a public speaker, his sincerity and goodness were complemented and completed by her accomplishments.

She was famous not only as pastor's wife and helpmate in his pastoral and civic duties, organist of the church, account-keeper, hostess, Sunday School teacher, conductor of women's Bible study classes, and so on, but also as model matriarch of a large family. She became well known and admired among both the members of the congregation and the town at large, visiting the sick, comforting mourners, congratulating or commiserating with members of the community, exchanging visits and hospitality. She was particularly admired for her learning and for her refinement and "ladylike" behavior.

Compared to the provincial women of Nazareth she must indeed have shone. Certainly, she was far better educated than most of the women in her circle. She had also traveled far more than most of them; she had rubbed shoulders with foreigners, especially with Europeans and Americans; she knew American and English hymns and those translated into Arabic as well. She had lived in Beirut, then in the midst of its transformation into the sophisticated metropolis it was to become in my time. She had been to Hums and to the important cities of Damascus and Aleppo.

She played the piano and the organ. She knew enough arithmetic to keep the accounts of the church and those of their home: this was almost unheard of at the time, not only because of the knowledge involved but because of the implied power of such account-keeping. Unlike most other women of Nazareth she did not cover herself with a *millaya* or a *habara* when she went out, nor did she ever cover her face as many of them continued to do well into the 1930s. (Few people are aware that there were traditionally few distinctions between the dress of Syrian Muslims and that of Christians although there were between classes and between rural people and townspeople. This similarity is, I believe, still true.) When they went out together, she never walked behind her husband, as was the custom. This is one of the few things about her past I remember her telling me, proudly. My uncle remembers his father saying that, on the contrary, if anything, she should walk *in front* of him, in such high esteem did he hold her.

They had a happy home. Although my grandfather was unbendingly severe in his religious beliefs, they played games and sang songs and hymns. A favorite game, remembered fondly decades later, was played during meals. One person, usually my grandfather, who particularly loved this pastime, would recite a line of poetry. The next player had to find a line whose first word was the same as the last of his, and so on around the table, over and over. Thus was the love of the Arabic language, which Mother never lost, instilled into her and her brothers.

They had a loving extended family. Often, Teta's sisters and brothers and their children came to Nazareth to visit. Mother's female cousins, girls of her age, came from Cairo and Beirut wearing the latest European fashions. My mother was a provincial girl then with a strictly religious father who allowed her to shorten her hemlines and sleeves, and "bob" her hair in the Western fashion of the time only after family intervention.

As a child Mother always preferred Safad, her father's hometown, and Rameh, her paternal grandmother's home town, to Nazareth because she felt more at home there, accepted, unexceptional. They had many relatives in both these towns, and she used to delight in accompanying her father on his frequent visits to them. She hated the feeling of being an outsider, which status was a natural result of their situation in Nazareth.

Through her father, and through his family in Safad and Rameh, Mother kept a connection with the earth, with the common people, with the mainstream of cultural life. In her notebook she writes lovingly of walks in the country with her father, picking flowers and herbs whose names he taught her. She attended village weddings, was familiar with the *henna* evenings that preceded the wedding, and all the other ancient customs of the village; she knew the folk music, the *oud* and *dirbakki,* the songs and dances, the food and the clothes of tradition.

I was astonished when I discovered, after her death, Mother's true knowledge of tradition and of the earth. I never knew that Mother had been to village weddings; I never heard her talk about them during her lifetime. It was only from her notebook that I learned of these important connections, this important loss.

I grew up familiar with the flora and fauna referred to in the English poetry I was taught in school. I knew the names of those flowers, mostly imported, that Mother taught me to arrange in porcelain bowls. I knew the animals I saw in the zoos. But I knew little of the particulars of the natural world around me. My sisters and I never went to a village wedding, and if we ever should go, it would be as tourists, as curious onlookers, as outsiders. We learned English better than Arabic; we knew Western better than Arabic music; we learned the piano instead of the oud and danced ballet instead of the *dabke.*

Teta had been a daughter of the people. Although perhaps to a lesser extent, so had Mother. The process of being extracted from the mainstream and set on a path of differentiation that began with Teta's schooling was completed by ours. Another of the comments on the past that Teta made to me, repeatedly, and which I never understood until I discovered in Mother's notebook the memory of the village weddings, was this: "On my wedding day," she used to say, "I only washed my face." For Teta, daughter also of the mission, there was to be no henna, no dabke, no playing of the oud. It must have been a struggle to defy tradition as she did, wresting out of the past a future over which she was eventually to lose control.

I have been astonished by so much that I have learned about my mother and grandmother since their deaths. Most of all, I have been astonished at the incredible cultural spaces over which they leapt.

Like her mother before her, mine also had great power over her husband. With her beauty, intelligence, and background she had been an excellent catch as a bride. My father was also a great catch. Her youth, however, weakened his position. He knew she had other, younger suitors, and so keenly did he feel vulnerable about the difference in their ages that he did not tell her exactly how old he was until after they were married.

Their courtship was marked most of all by his intense love for her and her shy but growing fascination with him. It was also dominated by a quarrel between their respective families: Should the wedding be celebrated in his town and church, as patriarchal tradition dictated, or in hers? He was an Anglican from Jerusalem, she a Baptist from Nazareth. Arab tradition demands that when bride and groom come from different sects and backgrounds, the bride invariably "follows" her husband's. The conflict between the families was fought at some length, and the combatants were the women on either side. My father's sister, Auntie Nabiha, and the Anglican pastor's wife, apparently with all the power on their side, were pitted against Teta and Mother, impoverished widow and fatherless girl.[5]

The patriarch himself, my father, was at first entirely indifferent and then cared far less than any one of the warring factions. Indeed the issue, which had quite simply not occurred to him, had to be brought to his attention by his sister and the pastor's wife, both of whom were furious with him for agreeing without hesitation on one of his visits to marry in the Baptist Church in Nazareth. They stormed and cried when they heard; they threatened to boycott the wedding.

Mother and her mother, were adamant. The wedding would be held in their church in Nazareth or not at all. Teta's power came from her daughter's love for her and the daughter's fear of wounding the mother's feelings. Mother's power came entirely from her fiance's love for her and his fear of losing her and from her own powerful personality, which was then in its first flowering and which allowed her to handle the situation with astonishing coolness.

Mother and Teta's insistence on having the wedding in Nazareth was designed to protect the memory of their dead husband and father: This was to be the first wedding in the family, and if it were not held in the church he had worked so hard to establish, would it not be said that he had worked in vain? Although not as obviously, the patriarchy was at stake here as well.

Many questions were raised in the furor: Where would the bride stay if she went to Jerusalem? It was unthinkable for her to stay in a hotel, but equally unthinkable that she should stay in her prospective bridegroom's house before the wedding. Where would the reception be held? How many guests would be invited? Who would they be? Who would be bridesmaid? Best man? What about the choir and the music? Most of these questions had to do with a consciousness and a sense of propriety totally unrelated to the old traditions.

Thus what had been simply a custom, a way of life, was transformed into a major issue of decorum and principle. The battle for an ideologized patriarchy was fought by the women, and Mother and Teta won, hands down. Those protecting the system, my aunt and the Anglican pastor's wife, fought long and hard. They had money, position, power, but they lost the battle because the patriarch went over to the enemy. He had pleaded and cajoled, argued gingerly, appealed desperately to the better feelings on both sides, and then at last had given up in exasperation. In a letter to my mother he wrote his unequivocal surrender: he would go to the Mosque of Omar or to the Wailing Wall if that was that it would take to marry her!

At last, the wedding took place in the Baptist Church in Nazareth. His family, who had earlier threatened to boycott, were in full attendance.

Although ultimately the quarrel was forgotten, and the two families settled into the normal friendly relationship of *nussaytb* (those related by marriage) the pivotal position around which the quarrel had evolved had been Teta's. Her heroic stand was to protect the vestiges of her dead husband's work and also, thus, to preserve her own status, but her triumph was short-lived and ultimately meaningless. Her growing dependence on her children, the loss of her own home, the social and political changes that had been taking place terminally undermined her position.

Mother's stand vis-à-vis Teta began to change later. Although still emotionally dependent on her—when her first child was born dead, she writes in her notebook, all she wanted was to see her mother, to have her there by her side—she began to be embarrassed by Teta's dependence, which she sometimes attributed to her mother's "weakness." She often exhorted her daughters to "be strong."

It was as she wrote in her notebook, long after her mother's death, that she fully recaptured her earlier sympathy for her. Writing in the shadow of her own deeply felt widowhood, made relatively easy by comfortable means, and almost sixty years after the fact, she recalled Teta's traumatic early widowhood, and she felt her mother's tragedy. A new admiration for her mother grew in her and a new acknowledgment that, far from having exhibited "weakness," Teta had shown strength, gallantry, and courage in the face of impossible circumstances. Mother discovered her mother as she wrote about her, exactly as I discovered my mother and grandmother as I wrote about them.

Mother and her siblings and cousins remembered their grandmothers as weighty presences, matriarchs who claimed their rightful places in the household. Mother remembered her blind paternal grandmother, who had once been famous for her horsemanship, calling out peremptorily to Teta from her bed, "What's for lunch today?"

History and change robbed Teta of that high status that should have been granted her as a widowed matriarch. Although, as Teta aged, her children loved and protected her, although she lived with first one and then another of them, they did not—they could not—grant her the status she would have enjoyed in an earlier time.

When her husband died, she was powerless to protect her children or herself from the consequences of his death. His connection with America, made in that daring adventure of 1908, had defined their lives, but it snapped at the moment of his death and there was simply nothing she could do about that. Because of the new world that she had helped create, she had separated herself and her children from the mainstream of society and its view of life. This new world of hers, although it may have been a stepping stone to a rather more solid one, was in itself a mirage, and she was powerless to prevent its dissolution.

The new nuclear family, one that included property as a major pillar of its existence, had robbed her of traditional status. The arrival of the British and French had imposed a new form of society with its own requirements—birth certificates, fixed nuclear family names—all the "modern" bureaucracy surrounding identity, which forged a new definition of family and which twisted the old relationships, like wrought iron, to make a social shape that had no place for those without personal property. Capitalism and the modern nation-state were not good for Teta, I am sure.

The Palestine situation further diminished her status. When the Palestine war was lost and Israel created, her sons scattered to Beirut, Amman, Cairo; they had their own families, children to look after and educate in alien surroundings; they had their own problems with identity papers and lost jobs.

She *was*, however strenuously they might have denied this, an added burden, and she must have known it. She had to be looked after. Papers had to be got for her too. It was impossible for her to be treated as she might otherwise have been.[6]

She was without status in all ways. She had no husband, no money, no country, no papers, no property, and the old forms of society that would have required none of these things of her no longer existed. Poor Teta.

Yet she had an enormous influence on her grandchildren. As I look back on it, I feel sure that Teta somehow came to mean to all of us Goodness personified. We have all felt, I am sure, that we knew Goodness in a real, substantial, true, human form, and if one has once known that, it is difficult to forget.

Her silence was weighty, ponderous, although infinitely sweet. When she spoke, it seems to me it was mostly to tell Bible stories, to teach us our prayers, or to admonish us toward virtuous behavior. As all the world around us swirled and turned, as we lived through the turbulent events of our childhood, she was like a staying point, a leftover piece of another time, a silent reminder of our own long history.

Indeed, on this score, she was not always silent. Teta was famous as a chronicler. Even in her old age, with her memory failing, she was referred to as the ultimate authority on who of the community was born when and where, who was related to whom, and how. Family relationships were defined by her and set down in her memory as was the chronicle of the exodus from Palestine. Who left when? Who went where? I remember people coming to ask her to recall their own stories, lost from their own memories. No one that I talked to about her failed to mention this quality of hers. She was the unofficial historian, the unofficial record-keeper of the community. Although in some ways an outsider, she was the ultimate insider.

In her last months, utterly given up to the senility that did not permit her to recognize anyone and that put her in constant danger of repeated falls in the night as she wandered aimlessly about on an unhealed broken hip, Teta had been confined to the care of nuns in an old people's home. She required constant watching, and Mother, desperately restless in her own new widowhood, could not handle the task. I do not think the decision caused her as much guilt as the awareness later on as she wrote her notes of how much her mother had suffered earlier.

My father died in 1970, leaving my mother depressed and disoriented. Theirs had been a happy marriage. I was living in the United States when my father died: my youngest son was three months old. When I received a call informing me that he had slipped into a coma, I rushed to Beirut, leaving the children in the care of my husband and friends. By the time I arrived in Beirut, he had already died. For the next few days, I took my place near my mother, my sisters, and my brother, all of us receiving condolences before and after the funeral.

One of the most moving scenes in my memory between Mother and Teta occurred at this time. When the latter arrived that first evening, just a few minutes after I had entered, she stood for a few seconds at the door, trying to search for Mother among all the forms in black who filled the living room. Finally, she saw her, and moved in her direction, her arms held out, in preparation for the maternal embrace. Mother at the same time had seen Teta arrive and had risen. Walking toward her, she preempted the tears that would have come. "Remember, you promised," she said, almost desperately. "You promised. No crying." Teta valiantly nodded her obedience and silently, frailer than ever, took her place among the mourners. She did not cry, at least not then and there, not in front of Mother.

Although neither of them mentioned it, the memory of their earlier trauma must have haunted them that evening, but they were determined, both of them, not to allow devastation into their lives again. Teta, in any case, was by then almost ninety, and she had only three years more to live.

I have often wondered when that promise not to cry was made and what kind of scene prompted it. Was it made as my father lay dying, or was it earlier, much earlier, that they had resolved together never to cry again as they once had in that terrible, but unifying, summer of 1928?

The clearest lesson passed wordlessly from Teta to Mother and from Mother to me was that my principal function in life was to be Wife, Mother, and Keeper of the House and Hospitality. Doing my domestic duty has been as binding and necessary to me as oxygen to my heart: to this day, and struggle though I may, I could no more walk away from it than I could suspend my own breathing.

If I remember one thing Mother was always saying as my sisters and I were growing up, either directly to us or in overheard gossip sessions with her friends, it was that "marriages are made by women. If a marriage succeeds, it is because of her; if it fails, it is because of her." She and her friends said repeatedly: "Women always have to sacrifice; that is how they win," and "*She* has to know how to handle *him*. Men are like boys: you can make them do anything you want; you just have to know how to do it." Other than her tips on cooking and sewing, this simultaneously manipulative and self-sacrificing attitude was, it seems to me, her most fully articulated lesson to me and one that I have found impossible either to accept and absorb or to slough off completely.

It was only in the mid-1960s that I challenged her on it. I had been married for a few years and had faced the usual problems of adjusting. The American woman's movement was just beginning, and the unfairness of Mother's lesson rankled deep with me. I soon learned, however, that if I pursued the argument I would be in danger of quarreling with her, and so I dropped the issue and never spoke to her about it again.

My silence was a form of deference, an acknowledgment of the ancient tradition of respect for one's elders. It was also, perhaps, an instinctive recognition of the fact that her self-esteem depended on the vindication of the ideology that she had imbibed from her mother, and by whose unbending standards she had lived her life. Many decades later, Mother was to become infected by what she tried contemptuously to dismiss as "women's lib": then she denied herself the pride she had earlier felt in her role. She became depressed and anxious, feeling that the world had denied her her rightful place.

Although the function of women inside marriage was so carefully theorized and articulated, I do not remember ever hearing either Mother or Teta complain about domestic chores although both of them had large families. No doubt this was partly because they both had servants to spare them the worst forms of drudgery. Or perhaps they enjoyed helping each other, reenacting that time when housework was a community affair shared by all the women living under the same roof.

In any case, I did not grow up with the idea that domestic chores were soul-destroying or demeaning. On the contrary, the giving, nurturing function of women in the house was a form of power, perhaps the most relentless form of power. Through the apparently self-sacrificing love of women, men were appropriated together with all their functions. I remember my father often saying, only, I think, half-jokingly, "The man is the head of the family; but the woman is the neck that turns the head about as it pleases."

The domestic world was not only one of power but of pleasure. Domesticity was sometimes worldlessly, sometimes openly, glorified by both Teta and Mother. Housekeeping and child-rearing were given sensual, total, absolute meaning and importance, to be felt and tasted, delectable, enviable. Accomplishment in these tasks was the summit of pleasure and power and in no way a lower form of achievement than a man's.

For both my mother and grandmother the domestic empire they governed was an integral aspect of the social status of the family. For them it was the husband who, through his occupation, provided one's place in society, but it was the wife who defined the nature of that place and who gave it organization and meaning; who could, depending on the degree of her skill and her dedication, either fulfill or destroy its potential.

As I grew up, it was clear to me that if Mother held a position of invincible power in our household, the world outside it, the world of finance, lawyers, government, business, belonged to men and was a dangerous place for women. My father often used to refer jokingly to Mother as "the minister of the interior" while he was the "minister of finance" and sometimes the "minister of foreign affairs."

If the outside men's world was one of danger for women, then the world of women was as puzzling and threatening to men. A man was expected to feel as confused and alienated in the kitchen and nursery as his wife would feel in the bank or courts of law. Never did Mother have to renew a passport, go to the bank, or talk to a lawyer. It is not that she was forbidden to do these things; it is that if she had she would have been trespassing on my father's territory as much as he would have been trespassing on hers if he had tried to cook a *mouloukhiyye* or arrange lilies and roses in a porcelain bowl.

The connection between the two worlds was established inside the home within the marriage. My father was very much a part of our lives, never a remote, threatening figure of power. The ministers of interior, finance, and foreign affairs catered to each other, supported each other. Most important of all was the ministry of defense, for all the other functions of the father and the husband were secondary to that principal one of protection.

My mother's lifelong and deep anxiety over my father's health, based no doubt on the early death of her father, emphasized the danger that eternally lurked in family life. Over the patriarchal nuclear family, far more than over the extended family, hangs a Damoclean sword, the potential death of the patriarch, which would leave the family vulnerable to all threats, unprotected from the world.

As I think back to my childhood, I see that my earliest perception of myself was as a being lovingly protected by the household. In a thousand incidents that come to mind I recognize now that I was regarded not only as a being looked at as though from a distance but also as one forbidden, inviolate, protected. I was always aware that someone—my mother, my father, my brother, an aunt, an uncle, the family driver—was watching over me, protecting me from a mysterious, sinister, unspoken danger.

The threat was never real as a physical danger; I do not believe anyone ever really thought for a minute that the slightest danger of rape or murder or any other kind of bodily harm existed. The worst that one could expect was a rough touch on the street, a bit of harmless ogling, a remark of innuendo, a bottom pinched on the crowded bus. There was nothing immediately practical or useful about the protectiveness. The threat existed only as a potential violation of a protected area for which a clear demarcation line was drawn around me.

I believe now that the unsettling historical and social changes that my family lived through, especially after the Palestine war robbed them of a grounding home base, led them to cling to personal relationships to an unusual degree. This was especially true of my mother and grandmother, who, as I have shown, had gradually become separated from the outside world. Children, and especially daughters, were thus naturally held in a protective embrace. The strong women who surrounded us in childhood, I believe, used their domestic power above all to protect their children, putting up inner and outer barricades between them and that threatening outside world.

This protection created, invented, a new space, a domestic area that surrounded me, like an aura, even when I was outside the physical space of the house. Wherever I went, I sensed the impervious presence of those protective walls and grew up sheltered by them to a degree that separated me utterly from the real world outside them. The nature of the society in which we lived, deeply divided along class lines, my schooling,[7] only shored up those walls.

Groomed by Mother and Teta, I learned, very early on, how to behave. Inside the house I learned to obey, to smile, to please, to love and be loved. Outside, I learned how to walk down the street with my eyes fixed ahead, pretending I did not hear the remarks I heard. I learned to recognize the impudent look of a passing ogler and immediately to lower my eyes modestly, sending a clear message of rejection.

The awareness of modesty and inviolability was as intense in me, a teenager from a prosperous, urbane, sophisticated, cosmopolitan Christian family, wearing the latest European fashions and going to the best English schools, as it was in the most secluded and closely veiled Muslim girl of my age. More, perhaps. In her case, her clothes covered her, and perhaps her inner self was freer, more rebellious. I was taught to cover *myself* inwardly and to develop habits of self-restraint and sexual modesty far more demanding than hers.

Sexuality was an entirely secret function in my growing-up years. Ac-

companying this secrecy was a whole school of teachings about womanhood and propriety. "Little girls do not talk like that"—"that" being anything touching even the distant borders of the sexual—was a phrase as
familiar to me as I grew up as it was to Mother in her childhood. I also
became familiar with a little ditty often recited at home and surely picked
up from an American missionary teacher: "Little boys are made of toads
and snails and puppy dog tails; little girls are made of sugar and spice and
everything nice."

Sexual Puritanism of the kind I grew up with was, I believe, imported
by the missionaries. It was inherent in their culture, through whose eyes
they naturally viewed the world. In their writing, their attitude toward
local customs having to do with women is always disapproving in a tut-
tut, Victorian sort of way; sometimes it is scathing. They saw themselves
as having brought to the women here not only enlightenment but virtue
and modesty as well. Always, they ignore the appalling condition of working-class and rural women in England or America at this time, and rarely,
as they write about women here, do they distinguish one class from
another.

Mrs. Bowen-Thompson's sister writes in her autobiographical sketch
that on first going to Syria, Elizabeth's "full heart yearned over the dark-
ness and degradation of the women."[8] H. H. Jessup describes Muslim
women as "[s]ecluded at home, veiled when abroad, without training,
veracity, virtue or self-respect."[9]

The idea that women here desperately required salvation from the "degrading" customs of their own culture is everywhere seen in the missionary texts. It provided validation of the missionary educational endeavor,
much of which was directed at girls, in the same way that it provided im-
perialists such as Lord Cromer in Egypt with arguments for intervention
in national society.[10]

Mrs. Bowen-Thompson does seem aware of class differences and in
general is more sensitive to the nuances in the condition of women here
than her male colleagues. Still, in her eyes even Western clothes become a
symbol of moral advancement and sexual purity.

In an article published in England in the *Missing Link* magazine, Sep-
tember 1865, Mrs. Bowen-Thompson takes note of the class of the people she is describing, but is no less disapproving of them for that:

> While at Zachleh, we paid a visit to the ladies of the family of an
> Effendi. They were all reclining on the divan, smoking or idling, except
> one, a fine young woman, who was seated on the ground with a quantity

of white calico beside her, and several paper patterns, fitting and cutting out some garments. She looked up with a sweet smile, exclaiming, 'Ah dear lady, I learnt to work when I was in your schools, and now I am come from Damascus for a few days, and am helping my friends to make some apparel.' I assure you I watched her pretty little fingers adjusting the patterns, and then cutting out so neatly, with perfect admiration and respect. Her little nieces are now in our schools. A respectable young woman, in a plain lilac dress, fastened up to the throat, sat down on the divan beside the ladies. She, too, had been in the school at Beirut.[11]

The difference between, on the one hand, the ladies reclining on their divans, smoking *narguilehs* and in general luxuriating in what she perceived to be sinful idleness, and, on the other hand, the usefully employed girls "respectably" dressed, their long-sleeved dresses buttoned up to their throats, is stark statement, in Mrs. Bowen-Thompson's eyes, of the difference between "degrading" local culture and the superior values taught in her schools.

I cannot help but see in the reclining ladies, a certain kind of freedom, confidence, and assertiveness and in the mission girls, with their patterns and sewing and highnecked dresses, a contraction, a diminishment, above all, an estrangement.

As she reminisced about her childhood in her notebook Mother remembered that for her mother the most important thing in the world was how people regarded them: *shu biquoulou al-nas?* (What will people say?) was her most frequent admonition. The excruciating awareness of being scrutinized and judged by the community is surely one of the marks of the intruder into history and of the pioneer. Surely, this was a function of her having been to such a large degree a product of the missions. I believe they marginalized the girls they taught by removing them, not physically but mentally and ideologically, from their immediate environment and from the real political and social context in which they lived.

In all the years that I knew Teta, in that matriarchal enclave at home, I do not remember once hearing a political comment pass her lips. The Bible played a far more important role in her life than the modern political world: I cannot but believe that it was a much more real place to her, much more familiar, than the geographical, historical, political world in which she lived.

No doubt some of this had to do with her personality and her particular experience. Teta was, after all, daughter and wife of pastors and was schooled utterly in the missionary context. She was by nature sweeter, more pliant, than her fiery, ferociously independent older sister, Emelia, who played a role in female education and the feminist movement in Egypt. But it was clearly Aunt Emelia who was the exception, not Teta: she never married, and, however notable and respected, she was generally considered an exception.

I do not remember anyone discussing with me the earthshaking events in whose shade I grew up. Never once was it even hinted to me that the world in which I lived was a world to which I belonged and which belonged to me; that I should act in it as it acted on me; that I had a say in how things should turn out.

It has been my growing conviction that the "Westernization" brought by the Western mission schools, and to this day often claimed as the deliverer of women, and as the emblem of a "modern" way of life, helped to marginalize my mother and grandmother and to make them politically silent. Female education in the eyes of the Victorian missionaries was not only a function of arithmetic and reading and writing; heavy emphasis was laid, as noted, on such specifically "womanly" duties as needlework, housework, and modesty. Rather than freeing women, the missionaries added, it seems clear to me, a layer of repression and separation to their status; they closed new doors on them rather than opening whatever ones already existed. The aim was never to "liberate" the girls but to domesticate them, to tame them into becoming "better" wives and mothers in the Victorian manner. The society set up in England to support Mrs. Bowen-Thompson's missionary work called itself "The Ladies' Association for the Moral and Religious Improvement of Syrian Females." [12] Mrs. Bowen-Thompson writes in 1865, in the same article quoted above:

> The long neglected and despised Syrian woman is beginning to rise from her abject ignorance and degradation and is manifesting in her life and conversation that she is what God made our first mother, a help-meet for man. [13]

These Victorian attitudes were passed down from Teta to Mother and from Mother to me. But Mother and Teta also inherited, and bequeathed, along with this narrowing tendency the generosity and openness of the ancient Arab tradition of hospitality. There was nothing acquisitive about them; they were utterly innocent of the graspingness and pure materiality inherent in the capitalist background of the Victorian domestic model. They had open hearts as they prided themselves on having open homes—*beit maftouh*—open to guests and family alike. They created spaces of comfort and warmth that were of immense benefit to those who enjoyed them.

The form of nurture and hospitality that they offered is, I fear, disappearing; I do not know many people of the urban middle class that they helped create who are quite as innocently, as ungraspingly, as sincerely generous as they were. Teta and Mother—and, no doubt, the other mission-educated girls like them—thought they had merely refined the old hospitality; they were quite unaware of having helped transform it. This form of openness and attachment to the real world from which they had been separated was for me to discover: What they *taught* me, were the rules of domestic life. But the world imposes itself on all, and the grasp of the marginalizing influence on me was gradually loosened by an insistent and often violent reality.

Although I have clear memories of World War II, and of the Palestine War, I was far too young to grasp the issues. By the time of the Egyptian Revolution, however, I was beginning my awakening, and was deeply impressed by the person and politics of Gamal Abdel Nasser. Yet at first Abdel Nasser was all power and I was all listening.

But Suez! Suez! That was different. Political understanding became inevitable, and marginalization inevitably receded. All of Cairo was alive with the excitement of the nationalization of the canal and of the righteous indignation that met the tripartite invasion and of the triumph that followed its ignominious end. Rousing marches and nationalist anthems, many sung by Um Kulthoum and Abdel Halim Hafez, were played in the cinemas and blared through loudspeakers on the streets. I remember particularly the marching song "Allahu Akbar," whose urgent rhythms and stirring melody, sung by a vigorous male chorus, were heard again in another important political period of my life, the 1982 Israeli invasion of Lebanon.

This time, instead of being an excited teenager, I was a grown woman with children of my own. As a young matron I had followed in the footsteps of my mother. The doors that Suez had swung open had gradually been drawn shut again. To those invisible domestic walls I had inherited I had added layers of my own. The social imperatives of the American professional class among whom I lived in the United States were no less demanding than the domestic skills and hospitality my mother taught me. I kept an impeccable house, cooked gourmet food, and became an avid consumer of all the latest domestic machines. I took my children to the doctor and to the park and to their Montessori school. I read the *Wash-*

ington Post, the *New York Times,* and the *New Yorker,* and I joined several book clubs.

Soon after my marriage I had begun to work on a master's degree. It never occurred to me then that I should aim for a doctorate. The master's degree, at the time, made me something of a pioneer: I was married, pregnant, and studying. At the time, this was not common even in America; when I came to Beirut on home leave, many of my mother's friends congratulated me. Others laughed at me. Several of them said: "Why do you want an MA? You will soon be peeling potatoes on it." Or: "You will hang your diploma in the kitchen."

Mother herself was, I think, amazed. That my older sister, at the time unmarried, was working on a doctorate put these reactions into a very clear context: professional life was an alternative to marriage, and an inferior one at that. If one tried to do both, one was clearly an anomaly. Those were still, after all, the days when remarks such as "Men do not like clever girls" were very common.

When the American woman's movement began in the middle sixties, I was deeply influenced by it as I was by all the aspects of the revolutionary spirit of the 1960s. Yet I had continued to live the domestic life for which I felt I had been fated. Increasingly, I resented its narrowness and closeness made more terrible in the context of the culturally and emotionally arid life of the suburbs.

I started to teach and, for the first time in my life, to earn money soon after I settled in Lebanon in 1972. I had been freed from the drudgery of domestic life, although not from its framework, because of the nature of the society in which I now found myself. I had reluctantly surrendered to social pressure by employing a housekeeper. Thus, my entrance into professional life could scarcely be called a liberation although it often is. Nothing had changed in the social demands made of me. What changed was the execution of the housework for which I was still responsible although I no longer did much of it myself. Having help at home was made possible by the class divisions with which I felt deeply uncomfortable although I continued to live with them as with something over which I had absolutely no control.

The war in Lebanon forced me to take stands for which nothing in our lives had prepared me or anyone else. We were treading new ground, and convention, although often life preserving, was as often irrelevant in the face of the continuously unexpected and life-threatening situations in which we found ourselves. Once more, we were all, women and men, creating the world as we went along.

As the war progressed, I began to lose the overwhelming sense of my own powerlessness. The more trials and tests the war offered, the closer I felt to the real world from which I had earlier been so isolated. As I lived them and dealt with them, I appropriated the horrific events and found in myself an unexpected strength with which to cope.

Then I took a step beyond mere coping. I wrote about the war. Like my grandmother and, like my mother, I became a chronicler, but whereas their chronicles were entirely private, mine was public. My first book, a memoir of the war, was published in 1990.[14]

I am trying to become used to speaking up, to stop leaving the public positions to my husband, my brother, my sons. It is not easy to break out of the modest silence imposed on me by the marginalizing tradition. It has been very difficult, so very difficult, to wrench myself out of the narrow—although in its own way fruitful and unregretted—path created for me by my mother and grandmother.

My grandmother had been a daughter of the people, and so, although to a lesser extent, had my mother. I have spent many years of my life trying to find the point where Teta began to be extricated from her surroundings, and to make it mine. I have tried to recapture some of the old connections. I have tried to learn the names of the flowers and herbs that my mother knew so well. I have concentrated my efforts on trying to master the Arabic language and Arabic music although I know I shall never be quite as much at home in either of these as I am in English and in Western music.

In doing all this, I do not propose to move backward, into a lost past, but forward to a new time, a new state. I am in a race to catch up with my past and with my future and to reconcile them with each other. I need to find a way to reconcile my desire to embrace the memory of my mother and grandmother, to salute them and their lives, their weaknesses and failures, and their strength and courage. I wish to pay homage to their legacy even while breaking loose from it.

I do not know if this can be done.

2

Searching for Baba

SUAD JOSEPH

Friday, February 5, 1993, 2:15 P.M.

The phone rings: "Sis, this is Violet. Have you heard about Dad? Dad died this morning. Su, he died alone."

My sister's story registers as abstractions. I ask: How? When? The circumstances? I realize I am reacting rationally. Violet's voice comes back, "Su, we're orphans now."

What does she mean? How can we be orphans? We are both adults, parents, nearing or in our fifties.

I am still at my computer. I had been working on a paper for a volume by Arab-American feminists. The paper reflects my experiences as a working-class female immigrant from Lebanon, growing up in a large Lebanese Maronite Catholic family in a small upstate New York town in the 1950s. I try to position myself in relation to feminist, nationalist, ethnic, and class-based identity movements. In the paper I search for peace-making among multiple, conflicting, and powerful loyalties and identities, filtered through my relationship to my family(ies) and my culture(s).

But now I must make arrangements to return to Lebanon with my brother. We must face the complexities of dealing with the Lebanese state to settle Baba's estate. In the best of times, dealing with the Lebanese state required the ability to call up and maneuver brokerage networks, the financial capacity to pay bribes, the patience to deal with delays and inefficiencies. After seventeen years of civil war, the worst features of the state system have been exaggerated. In addition, processing inheritance matters is inordinately complex in Lebanon. The complexity is increased when families, such as Baba's, have not subdivided properties.

53

As I prepare for the journey to Lebanon, I realize there is also an inner journey. The inner journey is a search for my parentage, my heritage, a sense of identity. It feels primordial. Violet's words come back to me, "We're orphans." Without parents. But leaving Lebanon at the age of six, I left my larger parentage, the extended family, the lineage, the history that gave me roots three hundred years deep in our ancestral village.

Searching for Baba, my father, in our Lebanese patrilineal, patriarchal culture—it is a culture that channels personages through masculinized genealogies overpowering the specificities of their personas. It is a culture that embeds persons in familial relationships. Personhood is understood in terms of relationships woven into one's sense of self, identity, and place in the world. One is never without family, without relationships, outside the social body.

The self is not sealed within boundaries separating self from others. To be whole is to be part of, related, connected. To be pervious to others, to invite the engagement of others, to embrace the self in the other and the other in the self—these are the signs of maturity in Baba's culture. Relationships may change, break, mend. The boundaries and sense of self change, break, and mend. One's self is always "in relationship to."

Violet's voice comes back to me, "Su, he died alone." In Lebanon, my family keeps asking, "Is it true, he died alone?"

It is this self that I have come to call the relational or connective self, supported by patriarchy, that I grew up with, in, part of. It is this connective self that I observed in Baba. It was Baba's connective self that kept slipping through my hands until I began to develop a vocabulary to understand it.[1] It was Baba's connective self that my brothers struggled with when they were trying to wrench Baba away from the influence of his brothers and nephews. It was Baba's connective self that left a legal nightmare for his children to wake up to in Lebanon. It was Baba's connective self that the modern Lebanese state could not stabilize.

Searching for Baba means searching through the maze of his relationality. His family, his property, his travels left a webbed trail that keeps rerouting me onto itself but somehow always through different routes. The search winds through village Lebanon where, like my father and three hundred years of male ancestors, I was born. It winds through Baba's patriline's joint property interlaced with a legacy of swindles. It winds through the Lebanese legal system where Baba left a trail of conflicting documents, mismatching names, dates, and histories. It deadends, maybe, in the Lebanese state that adjudicates names, identity, and property and is now claiming some of our land inherited from Baba for its own roads.

It was the property that took my brother and I back to Lebanon. Baba left us land in our ancestral village and in our coastal hometown. Of the four pieces in our ancestral village, three had never been subdivided with his brothers. So now we were co-owners with my father's brothers' children, and their grandchildren. Now we were co-owners with the cousins my brothers had fought to wrench Baba away from. Like them or not, we inherited Baba's relations and relationality. They came with the joint property my brothers wanted to liquidate.

Mama had tried for twenty years to persuade Baba to subdivide the property or to sell it. She had died three and one-half years before Baba, not having made peace with his refusal/inability to resolve the property in Lebanon. A visionary woman living Lebanese cultural rules to perfection, Mama somehow molded matrifocal familial dynamics within our patriarchal culture. Mama's story is woven into Baba's. She struggled in and against his web of relationality to create opportunities of upward mobility for her children. The epitome of her culture, she succeeded, paradoxically, to transcend it in crucial ways to build her family in Lebanon and America. Yet she could not extract Baba from his familial relationality to deal with the property.

Uncle Fred, a first cousin I always called uncle, came to pay his respects to Baba at his death. Firmly stout at eighty-three, with a handshake of which his boxer brother would have been proud, he eagerly told the story of coming with Baba to the United States in 1919. "Sam was between sixteen and nineteen years old. I was ten when we came," Uncle Fred started. Baba had recounted to me in January, when I had last seen him, that his nephews had been like brothers to him and he had wanted to come with them to the States. His mother and sister had also come but had been turned back in Marseilles because they had glaucoma. Together, they had spent a couple of months in Marseilles until money arrived from Baba's brothers in America for their mother's and sister's return tickets to Lebanon.

"We spent two months on Ellis Island waiting clearances," Uncle Fred explained. "Then we went to Cortland, New York.[2] We lived together, with brothers, sisters, uncles, aunts, or cousins until we could afford to have our own places," Uncle Fred continued. "We all worked. We helped each other."

Eight to twelve of the Lebanese, including Baba, my uncles, aunts, and cousins worked in Wickwire Brothers, a wire and nail factory. Like many young Lebanese, Baba worked long hours for little pay, saved his money, and sent as much as he could back to his mother in Lebanon. She wrote to tell him to return to Lebanon to marry the woman she had found for him. An obedient son, he did. Three days after they met in 1928, Mama, at eighteen, and Baba, between twenty-five and twenty-eight (he was not sure of his age),[3] married. Baba's mother had arranged the marriage with Mama's brothers because Mama's parents had died when she was seven to eight years old.[4]

Mama had told me that her brothers made Baba promise to stay in Lebanon. Having raised her, their only sister, they were attached to her. Baba broke his promise, returning to Cortland in 1929 with Mama and their firstborn, Linda. Putting Linda in childcare, Mama began working in the Crescent Corset Company, a sweatshop garment factory. Baba returned to Wickwire's.

The Great Depression drove Baba, Mama, their first- and secondborn to Lebanon in 1932. Mama told me she argued against going to Lebanon and tried to persuade Baba to return to the States. After living here, she saw more hope for her children in the States, she explained. After the war, Mama, surmounting the opposition of some of Baba's relatives, won. In 1948 Baba returned to Cortland with two of his sons to prepare a home for the rest of us. The remaining five children, my mother, and my sister's husband joined them in 1949.

Baba was back working at the Wickwire's and Mama and Linda at the Crescent. Our tiny two bedroom flat, across from the railroad station, housed ten of us for a year until Baba bought a house down the street. Everyone who could worked, even below work age, to support the family.

The journey through the educational system began. Two brothers were high school class presidents, two were student council presidents, my sister was student council secretary, and I was editor of the school newspaper. The family journal of newspaper clippings of school achievements grew. The *Schenectady Gazette* did a one-page article on my three brothers in the same engineering school. "Prove Education Can Be Earned," the article headlined.

"Education was my father's friend and foe," my oldest brother said in his eulogy for Baba. Education brought advancement. Six college graduates, two Ph.D.s, master's degrees, three engineers, a physicist, a teacher, a university professor. Baba never earned more than six thousand dollars in one year. Mama always made less and never did learn to read or write.

Baba jokingly called himself an engineer because he sometimes tended the fire at the factory's engine.

But education took us away from our home. We returned only for visits and reunions. Education took us away from the nest of familial relationships. Education took us away from Lebanon. Education took us away from our culture. "The more education you get, the stupider you become," Mama would half-tease me. I thought she meant to assert her greater wisdom in life. She must have sensed that the more education we had, the more we left the shared cultural heritage that authorized her knowledge and Baba's.

Baba loved to tell the story of his Italian buddy who jokingly asked him, "Eh, Sam, how come stupid man like you has smart children?" Baba would put on his sly grin and repeat his answer, "How many smart men you know have stupid children?"

"Work hard, study, don't do hanky-panky. Your education make your life," Baba told the students in my introductory Cultural Anthropology course at University of California, Davis, when he visited me in January 1990 after Mama had died. He had come to see me teach and had fallen asleep. I introduced him at the end of the lecture, telling the students that even my father was bored. They applauded. That woke him up. When he realized they had been clapping for him and not me, he asked to return to address them. For fifteen minutes, this eighty-seven to ninety-year-old man with an elementary school education lectured three hundred University of California students about the importance of education and family.

"Look at me," he said. "I have nothing. But I have my children. They do everything for me. Oh, students," he ended, "study hard. Do your work. Take care of your parents." Many students wrote in their evaluations that Baba's was the best lecture in the course.

Now, as I prepare for my departure, I remember my first trip to Lebanon in 1968. I was the first of the children to go back home. The dizzying impact of being met at the airport by fifty relatives, none of whom I remembered, swirls through my head. Uncles, aunts, cousins. They took me in. They claimed me. They said I belonged to them. For a euphoric summer I reveled in relationships.

A few years later, in 1972, during my doctoral fieldwork, I hosted Baba's and Mama's return visit to Lebanon (after their twenty-three and twenty-four year absences, respectively). For six weeks, I saw my parents reimmersed in the relationships that had shaped their earlier lives. The invigorating impact that familial enmeshment had on their health and well-being brought home the relative poverty of relationships in their American home. It also sharpened my recognition that it was embedment in relationships that gave meaning and vibrancy to both of their lives. Their relationship with each other also livened as they spent hours talking together about what so-and-so had said and meant and what changes had happened to this and that person. Remembering this, aware of my heightened vitality in the familial embrace of relationality, I wondered what I would find in Lebanon after the death of both parents.

Now I am going back to Lebanon, the first time since 1980. I make arrangements with my friends, Jane and Mark, to take care of my daughter Sara Rose (named after her Lebanese grandmother and great-grandmother) and fly her to Southern California to my brother's. I try to explain to Sara Rose what Mama will be doing in Lebanon. Mama has never been away from her for so long and so far away.

I wonder, what does Lebanon mean to your six-and-one-half-year-old mind? Mama's stories about childhood; Sito[5] and Gido's[6] stories; pictures of your great-grandparents in Ottoman attire; Arabic songs, Lebanese food, a *dirbakki;*[7] hundreds of cousins you've never seen; others who mysteriously appear at funerals and special occasions and who Mama introduces as "your cousins"? You respond *" 'a albik"* (to your heart) when I say *"sahtin"* (good health) and consider yourself fluent in Arabic. My blond, blue-eyed daughter, adopted at birth. What will Mama's Lebanon become for you?

On the way to the airport bus, Jane and I speak of the relationship between her son and Sara, who have been buddies since they were one and one-half years old. When we contemplate the study in contrast as we look in the mirror, Sara and I are fond of reminding each other that blond-haired Eric's father has curly black hair. Daily, these friendships jolt me out of lapses into cultural essentialism. I find myself closer to Jane's Swedish-American morality than that of many Arab Americans. I find myself closer to Jane's Swedish-American familial relationality than that of my brothers and sisters at times. The boundaries of cultures leak into each other. Other and self absorb each other.

As Sara waves goodbye from Jane's van, I feel the world I created speeding away down Route 80 back to Davis. I wave until after I can no longer see them; my hand stirring through the air, reaching for a slipping sense of self.

From My Journal

March 12, 1993. 4:00 P.M. San Francisco Airport

My journey to Lebanon begins. I carry a suitcase filled with presents from my dead Baba and Mama and letters from Baba to his nephews in Lebanon. Baba had given the presents to me in January, explaining that Mama had bought them before she died to take to Lebanon on her next trip and that he had planned to deliver them himself. He knew he could no longer travel. He asked me to deliver them.

I feel like a pilgrim. I dress in black. I have taken only black and navy-blue clothes with me. A Lebanese American friend tells me, "No one would expect you to wear black because you've lived in America." But in my return, I feel I must honor the part of my parents that remained at home in Lebanon. The black at once veils the specificity of my journey and publicly signals my inner state of being, my loss. It is a feminized state, for men are not expected to signal their losses publicly. My second-oldest brother, who will meet me in Heathrow Airport, will not, I expect, wear anything signaling Baba's death. In Lebanon my cousin asks me why I wear navy blue and not all black.

The fragments of the puzzle that is me are mirrored through pieced together memories of Baba and Mama, Sara Rose, my ex-husband, my siblings and their families, and the many places I have been. Baba and my brothers opposed my marriage to a man from India. Mama and my sister did, too. The women somehow always knew they had to heal the wounds afterward. For a while, India became a part of me. Baba and Mama did not want me to go away to graduate school. Baba offered to buy me a car if I would accept the fellowship from nearby Cornell. I left home, and for awhile Pittsburgh and New York City became a part of me. Baba and Mama were both thrilled when I returned to Lebanon and even more thrilled to see how much Lebanon became a part of me. Baba and Mama opposed my moving to California and the part of California that became me. Each relationship, each place found its way into the puzzle. Baba and Mama could only support those that drew me back to them. The more educated I became, the more I traveled, the more pieces there were, the more fragmented I seemed to become. "You were not meant to be a congealed, unified persona," a friend said. "You were meant to be all the pieces. They are you, and you make them into a whole." His gift to me was to affirm the multiplicity.

5:00 P.M. I call Sara Rose at Jane's home. "Mama, where are you?" Sara asks. The question strikes me as primordial. "At the San Francisco airport." "Mama, I couldn't find the combination to my suitcase," she complains. "It's on the envelope with Mama's travel schedule and family phone numbers." "I couldn't find it." "It's there, Honey." "You are not lost, the forest knows where you are. . . . Wherever you are is called here," a poet wrote. "You are not lost, Sara," I want to tell her, "Mama knows where you are." But Mama is not sure where Mama is. "I better hang up now, Mama, but I don't want to let you go." "Mama is always with you, Bunny-cat. Just cuddle the little bunny I got you, Sweetie. Mama loves you." Is it a coincidence, I wonder, that after two and one-half years of searching for a bunny like the one Sito had given Sara and Sara had lost, I found one last week?

The British Airline hostess makes her announcement in English, Spanish, French, German, and Italian. "Where is your final destination?" "Bei——," I almost slip. The American government still restricts travel to Lebanon. My Middle East Airlines ticket says Damascus. "Damascus." "Do you have a visa to Syria?" "No, I'll get one in London." "How long are you staying?" "A week." "Okay."

The pilgrimage must be done in secret. I cannot say I am going to Lebanon, to this home. But my brother has told his U.S. senator we are going. Lebanon, my country of origin, has become a description. "Lebanonization," "to Lebanonize" has come to mean to tear apart from within. It has come to mean terrorism, fanaticism, militias, snipers, kidnappings, the klashinkov generation. This Lebanon that was the intellectual center of the Arab world, the art and music capital, the banking, finance, and transportation hub, the vacation and resort land. This cosmopolitan, international Lebanon with its multiple languages, religions, cultures. This Lebanon that seemed to embrace differences, change, the future.

I think of Baba and Mama with daughters and sons-in-law with roots in England, Italy, France, Germany, Lebanon, India. My cousin in Lebanon used to say she was related to my husband because her married name was Hinnūd.[8] A Lebanese poet friend published an essay in his memoirs entitled "Suad and the Hindi." I think of their loving embrace of me and my husband. And I think of the tragedy that has become Lebanon where the multiplicity that had found its home lost its bearing.

<hr/>

March 13, 12:45 P.M. London.

Angie picks me up at Heathrow Airport. I will spend a night in England to catch my Middle East Airlines flight to Beirut the next day. For more than two years, I saw Angie daily as Sara's preschool teacher. She became a close friend, a confidante. We shared personal journeys, each day checking in. Now Angie has returned home. She talks of being finished with America. She's back home, her family, her community reembraced. No longer in need of a place to run away to. She gathers the many pieces of herself. Her American husband, her son, and her soulful journey to America made her into something else. Yet she has a home to come to. England belongs to her. I talk to her about feeling no place belongs to me, of having no home to return to, of Lebanon being a symbolic home.

It is only with parenting that I began to feel that I had a claim to American institutions. I had to claim my rights for Sara's sake. Her first year of public education taught me that regardless of my sense of belonging, I had to stake out claims in the institutional structure of educational America to make sure my daughter's needs would be met. That meant involvement, volunteerism, and creating relationships of accountability. Enacting rights on the local level, I found, was facilitated by creating relationships—a resonance with what I had learned in Lebanon.

Blond, green-eyed Angie is home with her dark-haired, dark-eyed, Italian-Spanish American husband, and dark-haired, blue-eyed, dual-citizen son. I had forgotten that Angie has Italian-English roots. Angie says that England is behind the States in understanding the new psychologies of the self, so her journey toward selfhood will be slower. But she chose to return to have her community. "Perhaps," I wonder out loud to Angie, "we can't have both continuity of communities and freedom of the self, at this point."

I begin to think about the connective self that I have been writing about in my work on Camp Trad, Lebanon, where I have done fieldwork since 1971. Connective selfhood brings with it rights persons have in each other. Connectivity gives persons claims in others. Moving, traveling destabilizes relationships, entitlements. Each time I leave, a part of me remains with those critical others. Each time I move, I lose some sense of rights. Unifying the self becomes a fleeting accomplishment. Reestablishing rights requires rebuilding relationalities for connective selves. I wondered what rights Baba lost and reclaimed in his many moves between Lebanon and the United States. I knew he always tried to hold onto familial relationships, no matter what the cost.

The poet Gary Snyder is reputed to have said that in the 1990s it is a radical act to stay put. Radical, to go to the roots. To keep my roots in place. New roots are still roots.

The reciprocal claims of connective selves can become mechanisms of control, however, particularly when combined with patriarchy. Baba and Mama reproduced, in their family, the privileging of men and elders of patriarchal connectivity. Patriarchal connectivity also entailed reciprocal rights, however. The paradox of connectivity is its particular blend of autonomy and control. I come to see Baba's struggle to be a patriarch as mandated by this culture of patriarchy but constrained by the claims of his siblings and their children on him. Belonging, to him, meant relationships. Having rights required having claims on others and claims from others. Being a patriarch meant more claiming than being claimed. Baba was always an uneasy patriarch.

Individualist culture rejects the claims of others in the self and the claims of the self in others. It locates rights in the self. One has property in one's self, but not in others. Individualism is the discourse for mobility, for autonomy, for uprooting, for the contractual self, for the freedom of the self from the constraints of others, including the state. For Baba, it was a difficult transition, one I think he never made. This, I suspect, may have been a source of tension between him and his sons.

~

March 14, 8:15 A.M. Heathrow Airport

Angie drops me off and runs to the party her family is giving to welcome her home. At Middle East Airlines. I barely believe I am seeing the familiar insignia again. Hearing the familiar Lebanese dialect. I find myself repeatedly asking if I am in the right terminal despite all the evidence. I enter a series of still picture frames, moving from one to another in a dream state. The MEA clerk says my name is not in the computer, but lets me check in anyway. No, she says, my brother has not checked in yet, but his name, or at least the family name (she assumes it must be his and not mine) is in the computer.

I am at the gate before I realize I am not supposed to be there. The long, empty corridor seems like a frame from "The Twilight Zone." Returning to the departure lounge, I start to sit when I recognize the familiar figure, standing with his back to me, searching. "Ray, Ray," I shout, almost running back to the present. My eyes wet from my condensed reentry. I feel grounded in my brother, but nothing else around me.

Raymond talks of the storm that just hit the East coast. I give him the watch he had given Baba that I had found while closing down our Cortland home. He cannot hear well out of his left ear, but his right ear tells him the watch is working. I feel tender toward the signs of his aging, our aging. This brother that I loved so much as a child, but scarcely know anymore. The pulls of time, careers, family pressures have created distances between us. After Mama died, Baba took on Mama's role of reminding us to call each other. "Have you called your brother?" he'd ask me. Who will remind us now, I wonder.

Ray tells me stories of our childhood, of Mama, Baba, Lebanon. He corrects my memory of family stories; we review the familiar dispute about when Baba was born, when I was born, when others were born. Baba was an American citizen when we were born but did not register us at the American Embassy until he was ready to return to the States. His sense of dates and names was situational, embedded in memories of specific relationships.

Raymond and I have told many stories, have talked our way to Lebanon. Through the clouds the mountains appear. The familiar, beautiful Jabal Lubnan (Mount Lebanon). I hold the frame in my mind's eye. *"Wa irka' taht ahla sama wa usalli"* (And I kneel under the most beautiful sky and pray), Fairuz[9] sings. I pray.

In the bus to the terminal I drink in the mountains. Inside the terminal half-a-dozen porters compete to get our luggage, and before we are out of the airport we pay fifteen dollars to six to eight men, each of whom claims *hilwiyat* (tips) by touching our luggage. I am surprised to remember how many blue-eyed Lebanese there are. I find myself spontaneously lowering my eyes at the inspectorial gaze of men. I notice the shy glance up, from the lowered eyes. Where did that come from? How can I still have that in me, I wonder? The always gendered, sexualized, hierarchalized dynamics of selfhood reemerge in their Lebanonized form. The airport brings me to the present. Pictures of Syrian president Hafez al-Asad abound. My brother notices one of Lebanese President Elias Hrawi, but I miss it.

Outside, my friend Mary and cousin Rose wait for us. Not wanting to bother people, I had told only Mary our arrival time. Rose had found out from Mary and had driven two hours from my mother's ancestral village to meet us. Mama's half-sister's only living child, Rose had gone to Mali with her mother and father and had stayed there for twenty years. She learned to speak Arabic at home, but cannot read or write it. She reads and writes French. Now Rose's mother and husband are gone. Rose is alone. Her son left Lebanon for the States during the war, her daughters are married. Rose was named after Mama. She has a granddaughter named Rosalie, after her. I wonder who Mama was named for.

Home. Lebanon. Mali. Middle East. Africa. America. Arabic. French. English.

Mary has been my friend since my first trip in 1968. Whenever I have returned to Lebanon, I have always stayed at her house first. A sister to me, she has helped me in almost everything I have done in Lebanon over the past twenty-five years: finding a field site, finding apartments, creating networks, finding work, emotional support. Her family has become my family. My family has become her family. She took me in. She gave me a home. She made me belong. Mary's family, although Lebanese, lost almost all their property in Palestine with the creation of Israel. She had to stop her schooling and go to work to help support her family. She never stopped working. Not even during the war. Not even under gunfire. The Lebanese government recognized her service with a national medal in 1992.

Mary wears black for her mother, who died a month before Baba. We look at each other in disbelief. We cry for more things than we can say. Muhammid, her neighbor who used to be a driver for her at the YWCA, still helping her drive, seems unchanged after twenty-five years of taking me to and bringing me from the airport. Mary has brought her housekeeper, Samra, a Sri Lankan, with her to give her a ride on this balmy Beirut Sunday.

I take in the multiplicity. Mary, a Christian. Muhammid, her Muslim neighbor, sometime employee. The neighbors took care of each other during the war, Mary tells me. Samra is one of sixty thousand, according to some estimates, Sri Lankans now working in Lebanon. Mary had brought her in to help with her mother before her death. Often, she appears like a member of the family.

March 15, 2:00 A.M. Monday morning in Honey Hotel, Beirut

I hear the beating of the drums, the call to break fast. I remember we are in the middle of Ramadan. Observing Muslims will be fasting all day. They must wake early in the morning to eat before the sun rises. Growing up in my enclosed Lebanese Christian community in Cortland, I didn't realize that most Arabs were Muslim until I went to school. Religion has come to have new meanings in Lebanon. Religion brought me to Lebanon for my doctoral research in the 1960s and 1970s. I argued that political leaders were using religious identities to build political bases. Mary reminded me of the argument we had when she visited me in California in 1976 after the war had begun. "You were right," she said. I had begun making my argument about the politicization of religious identity in Lebanon in the late 1960s and had predicted the collapse of the system in the early 1970s before the war broke out. But it was the brash confidence of a graduate student. I have much less confidence in predictions now.

"It's a historical necessity that this dissertation be published," Alexander Ehrlich had said during my doctoral defense. But I had not. I was too shocked by what happened, overtaken by the speed of developments, torn by the ripping apart of this country I loved. Lebanon was born fragmented. Seventeen religious sects formally recognized and represented in government. A political miracle, some called Lebanon in the 1960s. A disaster waiting to happen, others prophesied.

Lebanon, a puzzle with so many pieces groping to hold onto each other, themselves, something. Too many states had stakes in the pieces. I was born Maronite Catholic, a cultural minority in the Arab world (although the political elite in Lebanon). Critical of the politics of many Maronite leaders, I was a minority in the minority. I think how much easier identity politics must be when one can embrace the majority politics of an identity group. Maybe that is why I have been troubled by identity politics—often authoritarian, creating orthodoxies of being, essentializing, fixing, mandating what one must be to belong, to be a member, to have a home.

Baba never had fully formed views of politics. The war broke his heart, took away his home. I remember relatively little politics as I was growing up. It must have been there.

Mary abruptly shifts between laughter and tears to tell me stories about the war. "You can't know what it was like," she says. One night, her mother, Um Nazmi, saved their lives by refusing to go to the shelter during the bombing. Mary and her sister stayed with Um Nazmi. Minutes later, a rocket hit the shelter. As I listen, I know there will be many stories in the coming days. I listen, wanting to know, share, understand, take a part of it for myself. Mary and her sister wear black for Um Nazmi. Rose no longer wears black for her husband and mother, who died a few years earlier. But we all mourn. Our parents, our loved ones, our parentage, our heritage, our culture, our selves.

I stand on Mary's balcony. When I first stood here in 1968, there was an unobstructed view of Beirut and the Mediterranean. I remember our early morning coffees, sitting in our nightgowns, drinking in the moist ocean air, telling stories, sharing our histories. Mary's brother and sister stayed with me when they visited the States. I feel the familial bond with these friends of twenty-five years. The friendships did not stop at the boundary of the ego but took in the whole family. Mary took me along on all her family functions. I was expected to be there. They took me in, claimed me, made claims on me, entitled me to make claims on them.

It is this belonging that I have longed for and have fought against. I have wanted the familial home. But home making meant belonging to a tribe. Tribes fission and fuse. Family tribes, familylike tribes, Maronite tribes, Christian tribes, Lebanese tribes, Arab tribes. There are new world order tribes, too, I come to realize, as voluntary groups play out similar dynamics of loyalty and betrayal: gendered tribes, class tribes, religious, racial, ethnic, political tribes.

"La tunkirri al asil, aslik" (don't repudiate your origin, your origin is), we sang as children, filling in at times "Haddadiyya," Mama's maiden name, at times, "Awwadiyya," Baba's family name, at times "Lubnaniyya," at times "Arabiyya." There was never a single origin, a single identity to forsake. The identity was plural, fractured, contradictory in its roots. The struggle was misplaced in trying to unify, make the multiple whole into one.

"Ya nayyim, uum, bi rahmin allah" (Oh, you who are asleep, awake in the blessing of God), the muezzin calls as he drums. I wake up the pieces of me that have slept for thirteen years. I am in Lebanon again. I cannot sleep to the drumming. The drum thumping, my heart throbbing become one.

My brother sleeps in the room next door. I was surprised to see he is not as tall as I always had thought he was. Authority inflates bodies. As we age, we congeal. Someone said, as we age we become more like ourselves. Which self was I to become more like? My brother has been speaking to me in Arabic since we boarded the plane in London. I follow his lead although as adults we have rarely spoken to each other in our mother tongue. I find myself often finishing his sentences for him, supplying him with words when he gropes, translating to others for him, yet he remembers the music and poetry better than I. I feel disoriented connecting with my brother through Arabic. I remeet my brother through our common tongue of origin.

Coming from the airport, I noticed that Lebanon looks like a Third World country. It had never seemed so before the war. Until the early 1980s, the Lebanese lira (LL) had remained relatively constant, $1:3.25LL. Now it was $1:1,750LL. At points during the war, it had reached $1:3,000LL. "We pay for everything in dollars but get paid in liras," Mary quipped. The American dollar has become the daily currency.

Mary stayed in Lebanon during the war. Her family had lost almost everything in Palestine. She refused to lose Lebanon. She had made her home. She stayed, worked for it, risking her life, daily crossing the Green line between Muslim-controlled West Beirut and Christian-controlled East Beirut to go between home and work. Daily crossings, boundaries that are not metaphors. Barricades creating safety and danger; border zones risking life and death. Angie and Rose returned home. Mary refused to leave. I wonder if I have one.

The muezzin continues his drumming. The rumbling inside my head and outside have become one. Metaphors and reality merge. Fragmented souls and fragmented country. The fractures within mirrored without. I no longer wonder whether the fractures are inside or outside.

Mary said that Najla, a colleague, left a message for me. Atif, who had been a student at U.C. Davis called. Hanna, my brotherlike next-door neighbor in Camp Trad, where I did my research, called. Pieces of the past and present come together. *"Lubnan rah tikhlak 'an jadid,"* (Lebanon will be born again), Fairuz sings.

~

March 16, 1993, Tuesday, 11:30 P.M.

Raymond and I spend Monday, the first day in Beirut, talking to our Shi'i lawyer and his foreign ministry consul brother about Baba's property. Mary takes us to meet other lawyers and experts to help out. As if I had never left, Mary embraces me and my brother, calling us daily, insisting we eat at her house, making contacts for us, going with us to work on the estate. We become a part of her family.

Talking with the lawyers, working with government officials, I am struck again by the necessity of relationships in the Lebanese political arena. Without *wasta* (contacts, brokers, relationships) one gets nowhere. Without wasta there is little access. Without wasta there are few rights in practice. Without wasta there is little belonging. Claims in the political arena are generated from sets of relationships. I guarantee my rights in the Lebanese state by investing in family and friendships. My belonging, my home, my entitlements flow from neither birthright nor citizenship, but from my relationships, my relationships with my family, my friends, and their relationships with others.

We learn that settling the estate is even more complex than we feared it would be. The lawyer tells us that it would be easier if we were Lebanese citizens. The Lebanese state, like the United States, now honors dual citizenship. One does not lose citizenship by migration unless one actively chooses to do so, we are told. I had learned earlier, however, that Baba's name had been scratched from the citizen rolls for reasons that were unclear. We are alternately told that it will be easy and that it will be complicated to restore Baba's citizenship. It will happen, our lawyer and his brother claim. It is only a matter of finding the thread in the bureaucratic web that will lead to the solution. I read that to mean wasta.

Children receive citizenship only through their fathers in this patriarchal society. Mama had retained her Lebanese citizenship, never having become an American citizen. We learn that the Lebanese parliament is considering allowing children to gain citizenship through their mothers, which should then make our case straightforward. Whether or when such a law would be enacted, however, remains unclear.

I contemplate what it has meant to me to not have citizenship in the country in which I was born, in which my parents were born, in which our extended family remains, in which all of Baba and Mama's landed property exists. A white American friend of mine has Lebanese citizenship because she married a Lebanese man. Lebanese law automatically offers foreign wives of Lebanese men citizenship. Yet reclaiming ours is fraught with problems. The paradoxes of patriarchy.

What would it mean to gain citizenship through Mama? We gained American citizenship through Baba's citizenship. We lost Lebanese citizenship through Baba's loss. In patriarchal societies paternal heritage weighs heavily in descendant lines. Baba's gains and losses live on in the lives of his children.

Like many of his generation of Lebanese, Baba never subdivided the land he and his brothers inherited from his father. The land in our ancestral village is almost all registered in the names of a number of persons, making it impossible to sell to anyone but those family members who collectively own it with us. Whether we like it or not, whether we like them or not, we must communicate, negotiate, compromise with our families. Relationality is a structural, economic, political condition of social life in Lebanon.

Relationality, like so many aspects of Baba's life, was situational, shifting. His family was embedded in his property, his possibilities, and his personhood. The family ebbed and flowed in his life. Who his family was to him and what meaning he gave to them seemed both an eminent and contested issue. But modern states like to fix families, fix properties, fix personhoods. Baba resisted permanent positioning.

He left a legacy of eluding the state's fixity. He used different names, different ages in different government registries, and not only for himself but for his children. In some he called himself by his father's term of address. In Arab culture men and women are addressed as the father or mother of their eldest son. My grandfather's eldest son was named Mrad, and so Gido was called "Abu Mrad" (father of Mrad) and Sito was called "Um Mrad" (mother of Mrad). In some places Baba registered property as Salim (his first name) Yusif (his father's first name) Abu Mrad (his father's term of address). In other places Baba shortened the Abu to Bu (the colloquial for father). In other registers he dropped Abu altogether. In one registry he identified himself by his mother's maiden family name. Only in the American Embassy was he registered as Samuel (English for Salim) Joseph (English for Yusif, his father's first name), the name he used in the States. And rarely did he register himself by the family name of Awwad. To bring Mama with him to the States, he registered her in her Lebanese passport as Rose Abou Mrad while in his American passport he registered himself as Samuel Joseph. I wonder whether Baba ever felt a need to be one name, one identity, a congealed self? Did the multiplicity give more options, maneuverability, elasticity? I wonder, who was he for himself? Could he have passed a unified self on to us even if it had occurred to him?

I find in the records two different birth certificates for myself, one showing me born in our ancestral mountain village, the other showing me born in our coastal home. Mama always told me I was born in the mountain village. Mama and Baba disagreed about the year I was born, too. Even now, my oldest brothers argue that Baba registered me as having been born one year earlier than my birth date. Each of the children have contested birthdays and birth years. One of the forms explains that Baba did not register me in the American Embassy when I was born because he did not realize he was an American citizen. Other government records explain that he did not realize that he was not a Lebanese citizen. Some records indicate that he was living in Lebanon at the same time that other records indicate that he was in the States. I am tempted to think of this as a problem of Third World peasant classes until a friend tells me that her upper-class father, a leading member of parliament, did not register her birth until she was in high school. My father's brother's sons recently registered themselves under three different family names, even though they are brothers.

The legacy becomes a legal nightmare in the modern state that formally considers each person to have only one name, one identity. True to his culture, Baba defined himself in terms of the relationships and events that mattered at the moment. As relationships shifted, so did terms of address, identity, positionality, possibilities. The culture of Baba's Lebanon allowed for situationality, supported it, even encouraged it. But it was the culture of a premodern state. In some ways Baba made only a superficial journey to the modern state.

Mama was also ambivalent about the consequences of living in a modern state. But she understood the consequences more deeply, perhaps, than Baba. She urged him for years to straighten out the property problems, the citizenship problems, the name problems. He could not. He would not. He did not. Which was it? I think of the consequences for his children. It will take us years to straighten it out. To straighten—to rectify, align, make level, unbent, true—as if what was there before was false, crooked. Relationality must seem false, crooked, to the modern bureaucratic state that needs to fix properties, identities, personhoods. Baba's property is embedded in familial relationality. Baba's identity is embedded in familial relationality. The modern state must straighten, unwrap, unravel the self from its relationality to construct the modern fixed, essentialized, individualized, autonomous citizen. The Lebanese state must be ambivalent, however, about the individualized citizen. It insists on fixed names, but makes the subdivision of property, so essential for the autonomy of the individualized self, very difficult.

Searching for Baba. In this patriarchal culture that traces genealogies through male lines. But the lines are not straight. Baba crossed many boundaries. He zigzagged, veered, curved, circled, squared off, rotated, reeled, rose, pivoted, reversed, reverted, twisted, fell, coiled, detoured, advanced. The one thing he did not do was to straighten out, to fix, to become one.

"Don't romanticize relationality," Najla cautions, "*Mughtaribin*[10] romanticize Lebanon as a home," she adds. "You might be romanticizing individualism," I point out. We remind each other of the dangers of each side of the false polarity. She holds out that only the one who is able to stand apart, be alone, can accomplish something. I counter that one can be relational and agential. She offers a qualified agreement. We discuss the problems in relationality and autonomy, role and personhood, obligation and freedom, family and self, society and self.

"Relationality can kill," Najla's words reverberate in my head as I tug at the patriarchal structures embedded within familial relationality in Lebanon. I realize I can do little about Baba's estate without my brothers' agreement. Violet and I have always known that, even if we came up with the ideas, we had to get our brothers to accept them for anything major to be accomplished in the family. Our successes came when one of the brothers embraced an idea as his own and moved with it.

"Americans are deadened," Najla also said. Relationality can kill. Individualism can deaden.

I go to the government telephone central to call home. I talk to Sara Rose. "Mama, this is hard for me. I miss you. Can you come home?"

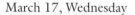

March 17, Wednesday

Raymond and I hired the Honey House driver to take us to Intilias, our coastal home. Raymond had been there in October 1992 but is not sure he can find our house. He asks me if I can. I say yes. I have not been this way in thirteen years. We take a turn too early off the autostrat but are still heading in the right direction. "Where are we?" Raymond keeps asking. We drive. I find the store my cousin's husband used to own in the adjacent village. It is closed down. We approach Intilias. I look for cousin Asad's gas station. "This is it!" I recognize Asad's station even though it has changed from Esso to Distral. His worker tells us the *mukhtar* (Asad is a mayor) is not there. I direct Raymond to Uncle Joe's house, my first cousin, who is the oldest living member of our family. Uncle Joe's aging wife answers. She recognizes Raymond before me, having seen him in October.

I had always been afraid of Uncle Joe as a child. He traveled back and forth from Lebanon to the States. We never knew when he would appear. Although he was Baba's nephew, he was one year older and claimed considerable authority for himself. He had the largest house in the family and more political connections than anyone else. Dressed in his pajamas and bathrobe, walking so slowly that Raymond jumps up to help him, seeing only with difficulty, even with the help of glasses, he now sits before us. He says he had not known that Baba died. "I loved him," he says. "He was brother to me." I give him the envelope with the gift from Baba. His eyes tear. I try to take in as much as I can of this man. He is one of the few links left to a passing epoch.

March 23, Tuesday, 8:00 P.M., House

Raymond wanted to go to the palace of Beit Eddine. Cousin Rose took us yesterday. Her son's friend, Roger, drove. Roger has become like a son to her, dropping by every Sunday to see if she needs anything, calling her, taking her places.

Syrian and Lebanese soldiers man barricades on all the roads. Roger says, "*'atikun al-'afi*" (God give you health, strength) to the Lebanese soldiers. He does not acknowledge the Syrian soldiers. Occupiers, he calls them.

Occupiers in Beirut, in the mountains. Israel occupies the South. Lebanon is fragmented. No one now, however, is talking of *taksim* (division) of Lebanon into different ethnic/religious states. I sense some hope that Lebanon will be reunified. Roger says everybody wants a piece of Lebanon—the Syrians, the Israelis, the Americans, the French. The Lebanese is born into conflicting claims. On the way back from Beit Eddine, we stop at Rose's daughter's house. Rose's teenage granddaughter sings Whitney Houston songs for us and dances hip-hop. She is fluent in Arabic, French, and English. The Lebanese is globalized. But the multiple pieces are held together by the glue of the family. Her father and mother and grandmother adoringly watch as she sings.

March 26, Friday

Tomorrow I will go to Amman, Jordan, for a job interview with UNICEF. I carry with me a letter from a friend of Mary's to her relatives in Amman.

March 28, Sunday

On the plane from Beirut to Amman I meet a Palestinian doctor who lives in Amman. His parents live in San Jose, California, and he had spent some time in Davis. In the Amman airport a Sri Lankan woman stands, looking lost, crying, as some Jordanian officials try to help her. The floors and benches of one airport room are filled with sleeping men and women from India or Sri Lanka. I deliver the letter from Mary's friend to her family. I learn that the person to whom I delivered it is married to a cousin of a dear friend of mine in Sacramento and that she is working with a friend of mine in Amman to organize a conference. She has been trying to reach me in Beirut to invite me to attend the conference in Amman.

In the evening I turn on the TV to watch CNN. A news item is broadcast from Davis, California. Davis's ban on smoking in public places has made international news. My friend Elaine is shown saying, "I'm pleased as punch. It's the first time I can breathe relaxed in years." From this hotel room the world seems small. I call Sara Rose, now with my oldest brother. He wants to know what we have accomplished. Sara says, "I love you, Mommie. I miss you. When are you coming home?"

On the plane back to Beirut I sit next to a woman from Sri Lanka in an orange sari. I smile. She smiles back. Mary's Sri Lankan housekeeper had worked in Kuwait before coming to Beirut. She cries when she talks of her children back home. "Do you speak English?" I ask my Sri Lankan neighbor. She stares back in confusion. *"Tihki Arabi"* (Do you speak Arabic)? "English, no; Arabi, no," she answers. As the plane descends into Beirut, she hands me her passport and her landing card without a word. I notice the eight to ten other Sri Lankan women on board are giving their cards and passports to people next to them to complete. Given name, "Deru." Occupation, "housemaid." Date of birth, October 8, 1972. I fill out her card.

Mary and Muhammid will meet me at the airport. I wonder who will meet Deru. As we walk through passport control, a man from outside the control station calls out to "Abu Emad." Abu Emad has connections and gets right through passport control ahead of all of us. When Mary's brother used to work at the airport, he would meet me or help send me off. In Lebanon one never is just a single person. One always is already a set of relationships, multiple intersections of connectivity. It is the relationships that position a person for access, rights, privileges, resources. It is the relationships that shape selfhood, identity.

⌒

April 2, 1993, Friday, 7:00 A.M.

It is our last day in Beirut. Yesterday, we visited Umti Marion, Baba's last surviving sibling. She looks so much like Baba, I just stare at her. Never tall, she has shrunk to my shoulder. Her large nose stands out even more against her sunken eyes. With her rich, full head of thick white hair, her eyes twinkle with delight at everything around her; she slaps her right hand into the palm of her left hand every few minutes to dramatize her response to information. Ummi Jibran, her husband, recovering from a fall, is bundled in a wool cap and sweaters in his heatless mountain home, close to the house in which I was born. I take in the simplicity and sweetness of the man and woman who have lived in our coastal home since we left Lebanon in 1949. We go see the *khuri* (priest), the son of Baba's oldest sister. He and Raymond recite poetry to each other and reminisce about things they did together as children.

Cousins Rose and Nakhli have come with us on this round of visits. I tell Nakhli that he's gotten to look more and more like his father, *khali* (my mother's brother). *"Ka'innu ibnu"* (Its as if I'm his son), he quips. He shows me his picture before his last heart attack. He looks shockingly like Mama.

I see Baba and Mama in Bsalim, our mountain village. I see them in Intilias, our coastal village. I see them in our cousins, our aunt and uncle. I know there is a part of them that remained in Lebanon. There is a part of them they left with their families. They planted a part of me here. It remains.

Earlier Nakhli had introduced us to a neighbor of his who sits on the government commission that determines values of properties that the government has claimed for public uses. He tells us that a decision has been made to put a road through our property in Intilias. The road will take the entire property. Nothing will be left. The government will compensate us. He will do the best he can for us, he says.

This is what we had feared. Nothing is official. It is not public information. Baba's property, our legacy from him and Mama, will be taken by the State. It will become public property. It will be fixed as a road, a straight road. The State controls citizenship. The State controls property. Property, like relationships, is central to selfhood in village Lebanon. Property, citizenship, relationships, selfhood, seem to route us into the State.

〜

April 4, Saturday, 2:40 P.M., Heathrow Airport

Lebanon has quickly become a series of snapshots in my mind, frozen in time. Quickly, Western time, Western sounds, Western views take over the moving scenes. Quickly, I normalize the West as I quickly normalized Beirut. Traveling with my brother has provided a luxurious constancy that has been absent in most of my travels.

〜

April 4, Saturday, Los Angeles

Sara Rose and D'Arcy meet me at the airport. I see them before they see me. Sara will not let me put her down. I carry her all the way to the car. "Mommie, when I saw you every day in Davis, I didn't realize how much I loved you. I love you Mama-di." "I love you Sara-di."

〜

April 8, Thursday, 5:30 A.M., Davis

I have been up since 2:30 A.M. My body does not know I am back. I call Mary in Beirut. Her image unfreezes from a series of still pictures to moving frames. She is following up on the citizenship and estate issues.

~~~

June 6, Sunday, 7:00 P.M., Cortland

I have come home for my last pilgrimage to Baba and Mama's last home. We have sold the house to my cousin. I want to be in it one more time before they move in. I intend to spend only one night, but my flight is canceled because of Chicago weather. I think Mama must have sent the weather. One night was not enough.

Cherry meets me at home. We have known each other since one year after my family arrived in the States and bought the house next to hers. One year younger than I, we have shared family and school joys and pains. She is the first person I want to see. She knew Mama, Baba, the family so well. We called her maternal Russian grandfather "Dida" and her Russian grandmother "Baba." Part Russian, part Native American, Cherry married her high-school sweetheart and stayed in Cortland. I treasure the continuities she brings into our friendship.

"I've made up a bed for you in case you change your mind about staying alone here," Cherry advises me as soon as she walks in. I tell her I feel I really need to be in the house alone that night to make my peace. "You always did the tough thing," she reminds me. Mama called me "stubborrrrrrrnnnnnn," when she was angry. Baba thought he was complimenting me when he said I was strong as a bull.

Maybe Cherry was right. I was always afraid and trying hard to be bigger than my fear. There were so many frightening things. Gypsies might kidnap me, Mama said. Violet was going to steal my growth while I was asleep, Alfred warned. I would get pregnant if I sat too close to the boys who chased me, Violet cautioned. Violet and I walked back to back up the stairs after watching late-night movies. Raymond said it would be my fault if anything happened to Mama because I married a man of color. I locked my car inside the locked garage when I first moved to Davis.

But Baba said to me in January, "Su, be a man! Don't be afraid of nobody. Be a man!"

I visit the cemetery each day, two to three times. I visit my brother-in-law, my cousins, my old professors, talk to my fifth grade teacher on the phone. I learn that one of the older Lebanese women has just passed away and talk to her son, my boss in my high-school part-time job. I meet a childhood friend who now works for the local college, SUNY Cortland. As I enter her office, I feel a bit dizzy. I realize that her desk is exactly in the same spot, the same room, that I sat in for three years as a work-study student working my way through college. Her boss, the chair of the department, comes. He has only two college yearbooks on his shelf. One is 1966, the year I graduated from Cortland. We leaf through the pages, reminiscing about people we know in common. I reclaim something from Cortland. I feel a coming home.

3

The Poet Who Helped Shape My Childhood

MAYSOON MELEK

Time and Place

I was born to a middle-class family in Baghdad in the mid-forties of the twentieth century. During the forties and the fifties, Baghdad was pregnant with dreams of a new history. The old generation dreamed of independence, the new of independence and a great deal more. The middle-class town dwellers took it upon themselves to lead the country not only to freedom from British rule but also to create a modern Iraq. To change the political status quo was of paramount importance, but equally important was to acquire the keys to modernity, which was diagnosed as knowledge and science.

Most middle-class families in Baghdad after the Second World War considered the education of their children the most important investment they could undertake. Education was attained not only through schooling but also through reading and discourse with the learned and the elderly. Knowledge and know-how were also acquired through exposure to the West, which was conceptualized then as both our occupier and our model of modernity. In my family, however, our ancient Iraqi and Arab heritage had always been revered and often discussed. We aspired to understand, assimilate, and apply modernization, but that was to be achieved without changing our skins or souls. This was one of the very first lessons I learned in my family.

The house where I was born belonged to my father and was situated not very far from my maternal grandfather's house. I do not have strong memories from early childhood of my father's family because they lived in Al-Amarah (a town in the south of Iraq) where their land and most of their business were. This meant that my father was away for extended periods, which caused a great deal of worry to my grandfather, uncles, and aunts (on my mother's side). When my brother was born one year after I was, my grandfather managed to convince my father that to make everybody happy our small family should move to my grandfather's house.

My grandfather's house was situated near the river Tigris. Six people lived there: my grandfather who was in his late seventies, my mother, an unmarried aunt, an unmarried uncle, my brother, and myself. My father was away most of the time, but we scarcely felt his absence because there were so many other sources of both authority and care within our household.

The house next to us belonged to Sadik al-Malaika, my uncle on my mother's side, where he lived with his wife, also his first cousin, and seven children. The two families maintained separate budgets, separate kitchens and separate sleeping quarters, but they shared the garden and much of life. There were no rules about where to eat, play, or spend the day. The two houses were "home" to all members of the clan.

During my childhood and teens, I had the luxury of having two homes where I was equally loved and cherished, two mothers (my mother and my cousin, Nazik al-Malaika, daughter of Sadik al-Malaika), and a family composed of thirteen members of all ages. The two houses were surrounded by a common garden where we played and spent summer evenings. The garden was surrounded by orange and narinj[1] trees; it had a palm tree, a cedar, a huge vine that climbed over the garage and reached the roof and a variety of shrubs and eastern flowers as well. In spring the youth of the family picked orange and lemon blossoms and made them into necklaces to give to their favorites. In Summer we waited for the palm climber to pick the matured dates so that we could taste the first pick of the season, or we would collect the morning jasmines and distribute them in between the two houses.

My earliest memories of my life in Baghdad were of people close and caring, of music and poetry, of trees and summer smells and shadows, of summer evenings on the terrace where the young and the elderly discussed politics, literature, society, arts, cinema, family affairs, and any future plans the younger members of the family had in mind. I learned my first lessons about the merits and the shortcomings of democracy during those summer evenings on the family terrace in Baghdad during the fifties of the twentieth century.

My brother and I were the youngest members of the clan. The elderly members of the family gave us love, security, protection, and sometimes the presents of which we dreamt. The younger ones looked after us, helped us with our lessons and took care of our daily needs. As for outings, we had to exercise thinking and choice and at a very early age because we often had more than one attractive offer to consider.

The Poet Who Helped Shape
My Childhood within the Family

Nazik al-Malaika[2] was my favorite in the family. She was the eldest of the my uncle's girls and in her twenties. To me, she was not only a second mother but an idol and an important source of learning. In the late forties she had already published her first collection of poems in her book "Asihkat al-Leil." This collection was so well received by Iraqi and Arab critics that articles appeared in the Iraqi press insinuating that such "mature poetry could not be written by a woman and a woman so young at that." Some critics said that the book of poems was written for her by her father, who was a well-established professor of Arabic and a poet. My uncle repudiated the accusation through the press, and he prophesized a great literary future for his gifted and hard-working daughter. He and the rest of the family had great admiration for that very exceptional woman: sensitive, revolutionary, creative, modest but highly obstinate where her literary standards are concerned.

I still have clear memories of the incident of accusing my uncle of writing poems which appeared in Nazik's name. Years later, when Nazik became an important figure in modern Arabic literature, I read about it in books and articles dealing with her life and poetry. I wish to highlight here the way the male members of the family responded to the incident. Both my grandfather, (who often practiced the reciting and writing of poetry), and her father found it their responsibility not only to defend Nazik but also to support her for any future literary endeavor she was planning. They believed in her, and they expressed this belief publicly.

"A woman publishing love poems in the well-respected Malaika family—what a disgrace!" cried some distant relatives and friends. But Nazik would not be hindered. She believed passionately in the poetry that was in her. She also believed that women had a right to express themselves in the new Iraq, and she had to participate in the making of this new Iraq.

Two years later she published "Shathaya Wa Ramad" her second collection, and she was true to her dream of being an effective agent of change in the new society. The book embraced the first Arabic poem, which did not fully adhere to the rules of the classical Arabic "Qafia."[3] She explained in the introduction of the collection her reasons for breaking with the old forms. Modern Arabic poetry has to free itself from classical forms established more than two thousand years ago, and it is the duty of young poets to create new structures that make use of the old forms but refuse to be their lifelong prisoner. The book became one of the most controversial publications in modern Arabic literature. For centuries no man or woman had dared to challenge the basic foundation on which all Arab poetry rested. Now this young, unheard of, fragile-looking, passionate Iraqi woman enters the scene and dares not only to shake the foundations but also to provide the criteria for the creation of a modern foundation.

Needless to say, Nazik, like all revolutionaries, became the target of attack by all who represented the establishment in literary circles. But Nazik remained strong and resilient. She was aware of the value of her contribution, and she knew that time and the young were on her side and that the new forms she established would open up new horizons for the younger generations of poets all over the Arab world.

Here I wish to stress an important point. One of Nazik's literary achievements was her deep knowledge of classical Arabic language and poetry of which she had been an extremely serious student. She was a true daughter of her culture, and her roots were firmly established in her heritage. But she was convinced that the world was changing rapidly and that Arabic poetry must prove that it could transcend the past and extend itself into the future.

My Relationship with Nazik

I think of the multiple facets of Nazik's personality I was impacted most by the creative and nonconformist part of her personality. She was a woman who could never be satisfied with the ordinary and always created ways and means to develop the exceptional and exciting. When Nazik was present at any family gathering or party, there was always something different to hear or to do. We "acted" songs, "drew" poetry, and "recited" political developments!

Nazik had always been very close to her aunt (on her father's side) 'A'isha al-Malaika, who was later to become my mother. They both enjoyed poetry, lute playing, music, and cinema going. In many ways the relationship between them was a very close friendship.

When I was born, Nazik began to spend more time with my mother. She was so attached to her aunt ʿAʾisha's baby girl that when her first collection appeared she wrote on my mother's copy "to my dear Aunt ʿAʾisha; in gratitude for the gift she gave us: our angel Maysoon." When I grew up a little, she used to make a point of spending an hour or so every day, playing her lute to me and teaching me Iraqi, Egyptian, and Lebanese songs or telling me stories from all over the world.

I still remember clearly an early childhood in which Nazik played a very central role. I thought of her as the most wonderful person in my world and followed her like a tiny shadow whenever she was around.

When I was five years old, I was registered in an English nursery and was extremely unhappy because all my cousins and friends went to Arabic schools. I think I "took the decision" not to learn the English alphabet, in the hope that my parents would change their minds and send me to the same school my cousins attended.

My mother was worried at my "inability" to learn. Knowing how much I loved Nazik, she resorted to her to give me my first English lessons. Nazik, being true to her creative self, decided to teach me the alphabet like no other child was taught.

She took me for a walk on the riverside for my first lesson. Decades later I can still see the scene; smell the river and the Baghdadi autumn, and hear her loving voice. We sat on a bench looking at the scene before us. She spoke to me of the wonder of the Tigris, the palm trees, and the Baghdad skies, so rich with depth and stars. I was bewitched. Then, suddenly she pointed to the sky and said to me: "Can you see the letter *S?*" . . . and there on the sky, she and I studied the shapes stars made of the letter *S, N, E,* and *Z.*

When I went home that evening, I was so enchanted with my lesson that I tried to teach my younger brother what I had learned. When I taught him, I drew the newly learned letters with tiny stars. The next day, Nazik spent the afternoon reading to me in English and translating Hans Anderson's story "The Prince and the Nightingale." When she finished, my eyes were full of tears, and it was then that she explained to me that had the translator not been bilingual, she and I would not have been able to know about the prince and the nightingale.

That was my second lesson; I was being taught to appreciate that tolerance of other cultures could expose one not only to learning but also to deep beauty and new horizons.

After my first two lessons, letters and words became my new hobby, and I still remember how I marveled at the way they took shape. In no time, I started formulating small sentences, and it was always to Nazik I would resort to "edit' them for me. After I mastered the English alphabet, I became frustrated. I wanted to read things other than what was in my school books. Nazik took care of that. Together we went book shopping to an ancient library that sold children stories in Al-Rasheed Street in the heart of Baghdad, and I would always come back with a treat. Two years later I learned the Arabic alphabet. By then I had already been convinced of the magic of words. Once I learned Arabic, a whole new world became wide open to me. I faced no difficulty in obtaining books. There was some sort of library in almost every room in our two houses.

Looking back at the child I was, I know now that my enthusiasm for reading was partly to attain Nazik's approval, but it was also because I found intrinsic pleasure in the act itself.

Since that first lesson when Baghdad skies became my blackboard, I have not stopped following letters and words, which have become an essential part of my life. Whenever I sense I am learning something new through the media of language, a strange excitement, almost physical, takes hold of me. This feeling, I think, has its roots in that first lesson when my new knowledge was being absorbed while I was fully aware of the colors, the smells, and the feeling of someone I loved.

I believe that if I have any intellectual content in me now, it is primarily the result of the care and teaching that Nazik invested in me as a child. She was determined to pass to her chosen daughter and little friend the knowledge that of all human experiences, learning was the most exciting.

Nazik's Second Fundamental Lesson: Helping Me to Be Critical of Myself

My primary school record was excellent. In my final year at primary school I achieved the highest aggregate among all primary school children in Iraq and was honored with a gift from the then king of Iraq, Faisal the Second. I was also the first student in my school to receive that honor. For some time after the event, I became the favorite topic of conversation within the family and among our friends. At school, the teachers showered me with praise and showed pride in my performance. This went to my head, and I became much too aware of my importance.

Nazik noticed the change in me and began to send me indirect messages reflecting her disapproval of my new image of myself. I think now that perhaps I did, at the time, comprehend her messages but decided to ignore them because I did not want to give up my newly acquired role of "star" in the family and at school.

One day, she told me that she wanted to have a serious talk with me. "Where has my beautiful Maysoon gone? I have been trying to locate her for some time, but I cannot find her."

As I am writing this now, I can still feel the fear that dawned on me as she uttered those words. I loved Nazik more than anyone, and I would have done anything to remain "beautiful" to her. And although I did not know where exactly she was leading, I was so full of fear I dared not ask her, so I started to cry.

For a while she remained silent and showed no response, then she took me into her arms and started to explain why she was upset with me. She quoted to me an old Arabic saying to the effect: "God has mercy with those who know their real self-worth." She continued: "To have pride in one's self because one is intelligent and hardworking is a beautiful thing, but to become vain is ugly. The young woman whom I always loved has become ugly because her lovely pride has turned into ugly vanity."

Was Nazik, who treated me as if I were her own daughter, expecting too much of the twelve-year-old girl I was then? Was the differentiation between pride and vanity an easy task for someone my age? Was she trying to model me according to an image in her mind that was too ideal, too difficult to attain?

Those are questions I am facing for the first time as I dwell on the past to write this chapter. I need to reflect upon those questions to find answers to them. I can think now of one thing that could partially explain Nazik's attitude toward me that day. We both belonged (she on her father's side and I on my mother's side) to a family well known in Baghdadi society not only for its intellectual but also for its high moral standing. The original name of the family was Al-Shalaby, but Malaika (which means angels in Arabic) was the name people bestowed on my great-grandfather's family because they "behaved not like humans but like angels." This story is recorded in a number of history books dealing with Baghdadi families and is also referred to in books and articles on Nazik's life and literature. Language, in our family was treated not as a mere tool of communication but foremost as the sacred container of values, culture, and heritage.

At twelve, as a member of that family, I was expected to know not only the difference between the words *pride* and *vanity* but more basically the difference between the values they reflected.

That incident left an imprint on me for a long time. For the first time in my life I was subjected to seeing my "self" through the perception of another whom I so loved and respected. I was shocked at the way Nazik depicted my new image, and it hurt me to realize that what she depicted was truly ugly. For sometime afterward I kept trying to understand fully the border between vanity and pride to see if Nazik was fair in her judgment of me.

I have carried that lesson with me all my life. Nazik's love for me was threatened because my newly acquired vanity made me "ugly" to her. I have never stopped, like the wicked queen who looked into her mirror to make sure that she was still the most beautiful women in her kingdom, asking myself every once in a while, "Am I still beautiful?" The voice from the mirror has always been Nazik's. In a recent get-together between my two daughters and Nazik, I told her that she has done much to shape what they are now because of her investment in what I was to become. I also told her that whenever any of my daughters commits an act of vanity or cruelty I look at her and use almost the same language she used with me: "But why do you look 'ugly' to me today?"

My First Encounter with Womanhood

Eleven is the average age for menstruation for girls in my country. When I reached that age, my mother talked with me about what I should expect physically. The talk focused on hygiene during menstruation. I was also told to ask permission from school to go home if my first period arrived during school hours. A few weeks later, Nazik talked with me about the same subject. Her approach was quite different from my mother's. We had a book that showed the anatomy of the female body, and my cousin explained to me in detail what takes place during menstruation. "After your first period, your uterus starts changing and developing in a wonderful manner. It prepares for the miracle of motherhood. It becomes a potential container of new life." Then she asked me to inform her when I had my first period. When at school I discussed all of this with my friends, I found that all of them, except for one whose mother was a doctor, had no idea what I was talking about. Menstruation was almost taboo, and mothers dealt with it only when it happened to their daughters. My newly acquired knowledge gave me a great sense of maturity at the time, and I felt that I was quite different from the rest of my girlfriends. When I had my first period, Nazik was true to her word. The event was celebrated, and I had a lovely present from her.

Three decades later, when my eldest daughter reached eleven, I repeated the same scenario with her from the explanations with the aid of a drawing of the female body to the celebration of her first menstruation with a card and a gift.

I think the way I was helped to be acquainted with my womanhood affected greatly the way I responded to my first pregnancy. It was customary for a woman in my country to keep her pregnancy unannounced until it became physically obvious.

I became pregnant for the first time in Rome where my husband was working. An overwhelming euphoria took hold of me when the doctor told me that I was with child, and the first thing I did when I went home was to write a heap of letters to all close members of my family and to my friends. It was an occasion to celebrate, and celebrations have to be shared with close ones.

"It is so typical of you to respond to the event as if it were a miracle!" one of my closest friends wrote to me jokingly. And I still remember the sadness I felt, as I reflected upon her words, at how women have become conditioned to bury the joy that they have within them whose sources lie deep in their bodies.

When my eldest daughter was born, my husband was away. I sent him a letter saying: "Tolstoy wrote in *War and Peace* that pure joy is not possible, and I used to believe this. But today I knew what pure joy was all about when the nurse handed me the life that is our daughter. As I was tasting the feeling of her, so warm and soft and alive, so much you and I, yet not really you and I, I knew from the depth of my soul that this is what pure joy is all about. Later on, as I was attempting to feed her, I reflected upon Tolstoy's statement and I think that now I know why he made it. For no man, since our father Adam, has known or will ever know the pure joy of giving birth for the first time. God has endowed only women with that gift."

The Wish for Weaning

At sixteen I started thinking about my university education. Nazik was not available to give me direct advice because she was away in the United States where she was working for her master's degree in comparative literature. She was very occupied with her new life, and it was difficult for her to give me the kind of advice I so needed at that stage. But she wrote to me beautiful and detailed letters, telling me about her new experiences and her work. Her discourse with me during this period was different from her previous discourse. She wrote to me as if I were really an equal, a friend with whom she could discuss almost everything.

It was during that period that I started playing with the idea of doing my university education abroad. At that time I did not realize that I was being highly influenced by the positive images that were emanating from Nazik's letters to me about her education in the United States. I truly believed that this new dream was totally my own. I started introducing the idea to my parents, who did not take me seriously at the beginning. Interestingly enough, I remember now that whenever I brought up the topic, I treated the matter as if they had already agreed to the principle, and all we needed to discuss were the details. Gradually, and with a great deal of intent and persistence on my part, they began to accept the idea.

Traveling abroad for higher university education was not uncommon for women in Iraq during the fifties. We had one university that offered first degrees, and women who wanted to continue their education could travel either to Egypt, Lebanon, Europe, or the United States.

It was not common, however, for young girls to travel abroad for a first degree. Some families sent their daughters to Beirut College for Women (BCW) to get their first degree because the BCW was a "safe" university for women of "good" families. It was a women's college, geographically near, and well known at the time for its "strict rules and regulations." As the first part of my campaign ended, and the idea of my traveling abroad was accepted, I realized that I had yet to undergo a much tougher campaign. My parents were willing to send me abroad, but it was to the BCW that I could go. That was not what I wanted. A number of young women among friends and relatives who had graduated from the BCW ended up as nonworking socialites.

A number of my male cousins were already applying to universities in England and the States, and my academic record was much better than theirs. Why, I kept thinking, should I not have at least the same opportunity they have?

My parents exercised a high degree of patience with me and tried to convince me to go to Beirut, but I would not listen. I remember the bitterness and sometimes the strong jealousy I felt in family gatherings when I heard of the preparations by some of my male cousins to find places in English or American universities. After one such gathering, I went home and wrote a letter asking for application forms. I copied the letter fifteen times and posted the whole lot to sixteen universities the next day without a word to anyone. Three weeks later, answers started to arrive. It was then that my parents realized that my wish to study abroad was not a mere whim that I would outgrow. I started filling out application forms. My unmarried aunt, Batoul al-Malaika, who lived with us and had a long career in the Ministry of Education as a senior inspector of secondary schools, helped me fill out the forms and gave me all the support I needed to make my case.

But I still had to face the most serious and real obstacle. My parents informed me that they could not afford to finance my education in England or the States. This knowledge weighed heavily on me, and I knew that I had to set aside my dream. And although I was sad, I had no bitterness in me. I loved my family too much to expect them to outstretch themselves to give me what I wanted. Even at that early stage of my life, I appreciated having a family who practiced the theory that what a child needed most was to feel loved and respected.

My resignation was deeply felt by Nazik and my Aunt Batoul. They tried first to convince me that people must compromise at times and that I was still luckier than many other girls; that the BCW was, after all, an excellent educational institute; that what I wanted to do with myself later in life would be totally up to me; but I would not listen or be consoled.

It was then, without any consultation with my parents, that Nazik and my Aunt Batoul decided that I should apply for a scholarship to either England or the States. To qualify for a scholarship I needed an average of more than 85 percent in the final secondary education examination. They conspired to transmit to me the knowledge of a right that I possessed and shared with every Iraqi male in my situation. I had not thought of that alternative, but once I knew it existed, all doors seemed once more open to me.

At the end of that year, I got my scholarship to study for my bachelor's degree in England. My parents changed their attitude after the hard work I did to earn the scholarship. I think they realized that it would break my heart to give up my dream.

Unlike my mother's family, which is among the very old Baghdadi families and relatively liberal in their treatment of women, my father's family was on the conservative side. "Are you mad to send your young girl to the West all on her own?" complained my uncle on my father's side, who traveled from another city specifically to discuss the matter with him. "I trust the woman whom we brought up to be a good ambassador for us," answered my father. This statement gave me a great deal of self-confidence and pride at the time. Only later did I understand that to play that role involved a great deal of hard work and responsibility.

My fight to travel to the West was my first real battle with the conventional wisdom of my society, and I know now that I fought it with confidence that I would win. The battle was not easy for a young girl living in Baghdad in the sixties. Winning it did prepare me for the many battles that I had to face, as a woman, later in my life. As a young woman I thought that I fought my battle alone, but I realize now that, had it not been for the strong women close to me, who had always been ready to provide me with support and advice, I might not have been able to follow my dream.

"You are much too strong for your own good." Twenty-five years later, an Egyptian intellectual well known for his progressive views on women issues said to me at a moment of human closeness. I was shocked at the statement and wondered if strength changes its function according to gender or if the statement was a product of the duality that many Arab male intellectuals suffer when dealing closely with women who are intellectually their peers?

During my years in England I was gradually weaned from my strong family attachments, and I began to accumulate lessons and experiences that I did not share with anyone at home. My life was full of new learning that added new dimensions to the person I was. A part of me, however, did not change. I remained an Iraqi to the bone. Western culture was fascinating and offered me great opportunities for learning, but without knowing it on a conscious level, I protected my roots. The way I dealt with the new situation was very different from the norm. In England I met a number of Iraqi women and men who studied in British universities and who were either so totally impressed by Western culture that they felt inferior because they belonged to an East that was considered underdeveloped or who rejected Western culture and could not open up to the endless possibilities of learning because they were basically afraid of looking into a different culture from within.

I think my middle position was the result of Nazik's influence. She was one of the models in my family who showed great tolerance for foreign cultures and foreign people. When I was a child, I often heard her quoting French, English, Latin, and Greek proverbs and explaining their meaning to us. Yet she was also the person who wrote poems about Palestine, Gamal Abdul Nasser, Algeria during its war of independence, and about the 1958 revolution of Iraq.

During my stay in England, I received a letter from Nazik informing me that she was getting married. At the time she was in her early forties and a very famous poet all over the Arab world. My reaction to the news seemed strange to me at the time. I was young and attached to Nazik in more than one way. I also knew that I was a very special "daughter" of hers. Her third collection of poems *Shajarat al-Kamar* was named after a story she improvised for me one summer afternoon, and the last poem in that book was dedicated to me.

As I read the letter, a heavy sense of loss weighed upon my soul. All I could think of was that when I should go to Baghdad for my summer vacation, Nazik would not be in my uncle's house. I started crying. Then I thought that soon Nazik would have a child, a girl maybe, and I felt a terrible jealousy. I got up and went for a walk in an attempt to shake off my thoughts; even then, a "craziness" took hold of me. I tried hard to understand why I was feeling this way when I should be happy that at last Nazik had found a partner worthy of her.

Understanding and accepting the fact that Nazik would no longer be "all there" for me took me a long time. Some months later I went to Baghdad, but even then I dealt with her marriage as "a necessary loss" although Nazik and I kept in very close contact after she was married.

It was only years later that I fully understood that necessary losses are part of life's gifts in one's quest for human wisdom.

The Fundamental Part of Nazik that Remained in Me

"Mother, which do you think is better for a woman, to be happy or to be strong?" my eldest daughter asked me last year as she was preparing a paper on women in the Arab family in a sociology course.

"Why do you formulate your question thus? Why do you imply that it must be one or the other?" I was expressing genuine surprise as I uttered those words. "Because most strong women I know have a hard life, and one cannot be happy if one's life is hard," answered my daughter.

I was speechless. Suddenly, I felt very unhappy. The message I received reflected my daughter's perception of my life, and it upset me tremendously to realize this. Or was it her perception of "our life" she was talking about?

Her father and I divorced when she was eight, her sister two. We were then living as immigrants in Egypt, and although I was jobless at the time, I fought to have custody of my girls. I worked hard to find a decent job and eventually did. I received a loan from the bank, where I worked as an acting research manager, and bought a house that we made into a nice home. Our life was not easy, and we all complained at times. But I assumed that we all evaluated our life as a generally happy one. I worked hard; I looked after them; we shared outings and holidays inside Egypt and abroad. We had a home with lots of music, books, plants, friends, and much love. We had always been very close and shared most of our life. When they were younger, I felt that the possibility of my remarriage worried them, but I was very clear when the matter was raised; I explained that I did not intend to marry again. My refusal to marry was not an act of sacrifice, I explained to them. It was a choice I made for reasons inherent in the institution of marriage.

What shocked me most in my daughter's statement was the implication that if a woman wanted to be happy, she had to be weak. In her mind, I thought, she may see me as an unhappy woman because my life is "hard" compared to the existing "model" of the Arab woman of my economic and social class. Most of this stormed through me as I sat, gazing in shock at my daughter.

She, a very sensitive young lady, realized that I was upset and wanted to change the subject. But I insisted on following it up with her because there seemed to be a number of essential issues that needed clarification. Her younger sister joined us, and we talked well into the night.

What is happiness? What does it imply to be strong? What is the definition of a "hard life" for a woman?

I asked them if they thought of me as a strong woman, and they both answered in the affirmative. Then came the issue of the hard life, and they both said that I led a rather hard life. We then tried to define what makes my life hard and according to what criteria.

During that part of our discussion, I found myself going back to my childhood, to the family and society in which I grew up. My small family now belongs to the same class that my larger family belonged to in Baghdad then. Middle-class values, however, have changed tremendously since then. Hard work and challenge, when I was a child and a teenager, were considered sources of well being and happiness for both men and women. In my children's time, hard work and challenge had become associated with unhappiness. I do not want to dwell in detail on the causes of this change, but I think it is mainly because my generation of Arab women and men had a national dream, the embryo of a huge project to make our part of the world a better place to live in. Our children have no such "luxury." The Arab world has become fragmented and national ties have weakened among Arab countries. Wars, poverty, and unemployment are real threats that impact most classes, albeit in differing degrees. Role models for my generation were people who wanted to create a modern Arab world and who fought hard to achieve their dreams; the children's fight now is merely to be "living and partly living." This is, perhaps, why it seems to them meaningless to quit the easy path and choose otherwise.

During our dialogue, I had to be my most intelligent, perceptive, and convincing self to pass the basic message to the two persons who mattered most to me. Happiness is not a standard formula that applies to everyone. A person chooses her or his own independent path to happiness that is defined by his or her own beliefs and values. During our talk, I explained to my daughters that what mattered most to me throughout my life was to try to live according to my own value system, which was, most of the time, not in complete harmony with my society's conventional wisdom. Yet, once upon a time, I told them, I had had the choice to live and work in Europe where my life could have been easier, but I had decided to remain in my homeland because I knew that I could not be happy if I was uprooted from my culture. My work had meaning to me only if I performed it here, where I belonged, where I wanted to live, and where, finally, I wish to be buried.

Happiness, to me, I told my two young girls, was being as free as one possibly can be to practice one's choices, and it is also to have the grace to pay the price for one's choices. When I went to bed that night the one person I thought of was Nazik. She appeared to give me strength and support, to make me surer of the path I had chosen.

And although I was in my fifth decade, I buried my head in her bosom with tears of gratitude in my eyes for all that she had been to me.

My Sister Isabelle

SCHEHERAZADE

In 1972 I was in Paris on my way back from New York en route to Beirut. It was June and the weather was wintry, the sky was gray, and the whole setting was conducive to melancholy. I started to reflect upon my life, and the desire to know more about myself came over me. I wanted to understand why I was alone, why I had not taken a very conservative route to where I was. I had started painting two years before that time, and painting was not only making me feel very happy but it was reconstructing me in every way. Besides, it was a brand new language and I was learning it with great enthusiasm. Still, I wanted to investigate this feeling of solitude, why it was that I felt so lonely.

I resolved to contact a photographer friend who was now living in Paris but who, when he was living in Beirut, had always expressed the desire to make a film with me. I had seen in New York a wonderful exhibit of autoportraits at the Metropolitan Museum. There, among the great autoportraits of Rembrandt and Van Gogh, were those of lesser-known painters and some photographs that the most contemporary artists had chosen to present. So, I thought, well, why not have this film made of me as an autoportrait? I presented the project to my friend, and he accepted immediately.

He liked the idea very much. He had recently started working in video with another person, and he proposed that they come together to Lebanon with the video equipment and film there in my surroundings.

A month or two later both friends arrived in Beirut. We started to film. My interview took an entire night during which I spoke in front of the camera while the two acted as technicians. They never asked me any questions; I was left to speak at random and in total freedom. The next day we saw the rushes, and because the text concerned mostly my immediate family, we decided that both my friends would interview every member of the family and ask them to talk about me: my mother, my brother, and my two sisters.

The interview with my eldest sister, Isabelle, came to me as a shock. I had no idea at all what her narrative was going to reveal. She expressed an intense involvement with me that I had not previously noticed. I knew, of course, that she had been hovering over me, but what I did not know was that this concern came from an irrepressible jealousy and not from the normal concern an older sister would have for her younger sister. That she had always interfered, that she had always been there to comment, report, fuel all the quarrels I had had with my mother as I was growing up—this hostile behavior had been prompted by jealousy. Now, any older sister can become intensely jealous at the birth of a younger one. What I wanted to understand was how she had gotten away with expressing it and acting upon it consistently ever since we were children. Why were my parents not able to stop her, scold her, or tame her? Why had she gotten away with it all her life?

She got away with it because she knew that no one would contradict her in any sense or try to stop her. She always did as she pleased, talked as she pleased, and most of the time from the top of her head. Suddenly, a whim would come over her, and she would look at me and invent an excuse for a quarrel in an otherwise very peaceful soirée. For example, I had a boyfriend with whom I used to dance so well that we were the talk of the town. My parents wanted the relationship to end, for he had not committed himself to marrying me, and they said, "People know that you are 'going out together,' and so no one would dare come and ask for your hand." He was a medical student, and he thought he could not afford to marry me until much, much later. So I would promise that, indeed, I would break up with him, but my promises would not last very long. My sister was quick to call my mother in Aleppo from Beirut to tell her that I had been seen dancing in the nightclubs with him again. My mother would come running to Beirut. There would be awful scenes, and I would be taken back to Aleppo. Rows were endless. Out of the blue, my sister would look at me and would say: "I hate blondes. How can you love a man who is blond?" Her tone carried such hatred that everyone would be ashamed to hold a different opinion. She would say, "You are badly dressed. You have too much eyebrows."

Once my sister and I were spending the evening at our parents' home.

She had been married for a while and had moved out of the house, but she often came to spend an after dinner soirée with her parents when she had no other social engagement. That evening she suddenly looked at me and cried: "Mummy, Mummy, Look at Scheherazade! How pale she is. She must be pregnant." I must say that in that particular instance my mother behaved very well and said immediately that if I was going to have a child, she was going to take care of it. But usually my sister's interjections had disastrous results. They provoked intense despair in me and drove me out of the house. Little by little as I was more able to do as I wanted, I stopped even attending Christmas lunches. She had turned every family gathering into a little inferno. She had made it impossible for me to be there.

During my last year of high school, my parents decided that I had been unhappy enough being a boarder, and they asked my sister to rent me a room in her apartment so that I could be happier and more comfortable. She had married and lived in Beirut, and my parents were living in Aleppo. She would forage in my room, looking for my personal papers, reading my journal. One day she found *Lady Chatterley's Lover* among my books. After reading the "good" passages with her husband, she called my mother, who came running from Aleppo, and told her about my horrible deed. My mother gave me a good beating, saying, "We thought you were studying philosophy, and all what you were doing was reading dirty books." I did not bother to tell her that I had not read it yet. I still have not read it to this day. My sister knew that accusing me of being more intelligent than the rest of them would be a tremendous success. My mother would react immediately to her instigations. During the family lunch on Sunday, my sister would sit at the end of the table with her children around her as a shield, and she would begin her attacks. My friends were of the lower classes, my clothes were awful, my opinions laughable (for instance, I thought Picasso was a great painter!). Most of all, she said that I had a "bad reputation"; I misbehaved in public for all kinds of reasons. She accused me of being an immoral person and presented herself as highly respectable and irreproachable. It was a shock to me when some of the men who were courting me told me that she had yielded to their passes and that she had had several lovers. The discrepancy between her accusations and her behavior was, in fact, the most harmful to me.

Now when I think of it, I realize that what was reported of her behavior, in public, as they say, was far more unacceptable than anything I had ever done. After a while, the quarrels were so intense that my mother suggested that I attend college in Belgium. Somehow, I accepted, for I thought that maybe I would be able to study there. That had always been my profound desire—to study and pursue knowledge. I went to Belgium, alas, to more nuns and more boarding houses. I hated it and convinced my parents to move me to Paris (which I regret now, for I might have studied had I stayed in Louvain). But I moved to Paris and the difficulties in Paris were of another sort and I didn't attend classes at all.

In Paris I met one of my mother's cousins who worked for UNESCO. He lived in a grand house, a hotel particular on the rue Notre Dame des Champs. He had a salon and three pianos, and we were forever entertaining. There, I met writers and important old ladies. I played the role of hostess for him. When Isabelle saw that we were having a great time, she interfered. She convinced him that he should marry me and that my father would give me a monthly allowance. In fact, he had no desire to remarry because his first marriage had ended in a bitter divorce. But somehow she convinced him and he convinced himself that he was in love. In fact, she had a crush on him and wanted to be part of the relationship. Our engagement did not last very long. I broke it as soon as I realized that it was a real misunderstanding, but, unfortunately, our friendship had been destroyed. Months of aggravation left deep scars on both of us. His love for me turned into hatred. He abandoned his lovely house and adopted a child and left Paris for the suburbs. He later moved back to Egypt. I had lost my best friend in Paris, and my feelings about marriage were forever shattered.

Her behavior could not be explained by the fact that she was the favorite among us, for she was not. I resolved to try to understand what had made it possible. Why had she never been scolded? Why were her passions commands to other people? Why had my parents let her get away with it for so long? The film had become not my autoportrait, as I had intended it to be, but the first portrait of the relationships between members of a family. I was even a model for a friend who lived next door. Years later she brought a filmmaker to Beirut and both had the same idea, a film that was to become, *Beirut, The Last Home Movie,* which was quite a success in the United States and France.

In the final editing of my film we kept Isabelle's portion of the tape in its entirety. She was so perfect. She had always secretly dreamed of being an actress, and the camera presented her with the perfect opportunity. She played her part beautifully. In fact, I also discovered that most people are not hesitant when presented to a camera and will, in most cases, come out with the truth and the whole truth (which explains why most CIA agents use journalism as a cover).

Isabelle's tape started with these words: "She was an enchantment. All the beauty and grace one could find in a little girl, one could find in her." She explained, like no other person had before, in what way my birth had been an event in the family. She also conveyed the sense of a mystery, of a hidden tragedy of which I would have been a victim. I started researching what she meant by this. She said I was a victim of my mother and, although I knew I had great difficulty with my mother at the time, I did not know that I had to look for the causes of my troubles in my early childhood. My sister was six years older than I, and she was old enough to know things that I had only sensed. It seemed to me that both my sisters had memories of that period quite superior to mine.

I was born a third girl in a Christian conservative family in Aleppo. When I use the word *conservative,* I mean it in a very positive way, for my parents had both been educated at foreign schools. My mother had attended a foreign nuns' boarding school in Beirut, the same one we were all later to attend as well, and my father had been sent to the Jesuit boarding school in Lebanon. Later, he went to Austria to attend college before and during the First World War. That education had not altered their deep grounding in their culture and environment. On the contrary, I can say that both my parents were ardent nationalists, and that their education had added to, not destroyed, their appreciation of their own culture. But for my sister, who was born during the French mandate over Syria, the French culture had absolutely destroyed her feeling of belonging in Syria. She admired the French who were living in Syria and identified with them. She had only one desire—to become French.

My father was a very sweet man who hated conflict and unpleasantness. He was from a very old school where politeness governed people's actions. He took his time to think and did not rush to action but pondered about things. His father had been a banker, like many Christian men in those days; my mother's father had been one as well. They acted as the middlemen who borrowed from the foreign banks and loaned money to the Muslim farmers or tradesmen who would not go directly to foreign bankers in those days.

My grandfather was also a dragoman for the German State, which meant he acted as consul in various capacities. He had received in his home the Archduke François-Ferdinand, and his wife the future Empress Zita, and their retinue while they were traveling in the Orient, visiting also Damascus and Jerusalem. My mother had been among the children who lined up in the streets of the old Christian quarter to see the carriages go by on their way to her future husband's house. My grandmother, when asked what the archduchess could do for her in return for her hospitality, asked that her son be educated at a very exclusive school in Austria, the Teresianum, which only the Austrian aristocracy attended.

As a result, my father went to Vienna and spent a few years there. The First World War broke out, and he stayed in Vienna with no means to communicate with his family and no money. He survived by giving Arabic lessons. My mother never believed that he actually gave Arabic lessons, until one day, during their honeymoon, as they were going through the streets of Jerusalem, someone followed my father in the streets calling, "Herr Professor, Herr Professor." My mother was, at last, impressed. My father's comment was, "We taught them the language, and they pulled the rug from under our feet."

During the duration of the honeymoon, when my father realized that my mother was a virgin, he abstained from making love to her. My mother had been previously engaged, and there must have been a doubt in the mind of her fiancé and her future in-laws. My mother tells me that her husband was so thrilled to learn that she was still a virgin that only upon their return to Aleppo did they consummate their marriage. They were to live with his mother, so he wanted his mother to discover the sheets stained with blood in the morning and give her the absolute proof that his wife was a virgin.

My sister Isabelle was born in our grandfather's house. My grandfather had died a while earlier, and the house was inhabited by my grandmother and her unmarried daughter, Adele. My sister was born nine months exactly after the wedding. My mother says she put everything she had in her first child. Isabelle was born the first child of the eldest son in our grandfather's house. My father's younger brother had been married for a few years but had not had children yet; besides, he was living in Beirut and his wife was Lebanese and there was all that distance from the in-laws. But Isabelle was born at home in a house where my mother—and even my father—had no authority whatsoever. She was a gift to our grandmother and our aunt. They both went wild over the firstborn and, I can say, appropriated the baby totally to themselves, as so often happens when it is possible for grandparents to do so. My grandmother, Najla, my Aunt Adele, and the cook, Emilie, took hold of the little girl and gave her more confidence than any other child around us. They had a chant for her that went like this: *"Sabella, tabchi oua emchi, Sabella ma bi-ellek chi,"* which meant "Isabelle stomp and romp, Isabelle, you will never be scolded." She reigned supreme, and she was totally spoiled. I should not use the word *spoiled,* for I do not think it even approximates what she got from that environment. She was the center of attention and she had total confidence and security, security in herself and in her environment. My father was carefree enough in that house to be able to play with her. The only photographs of him playing with any child are with her. Never again did we see him holding a baby. Our parents did not discipline. She was left to do as she pleased; she nearly belonged to our grandmother. Our grandmother, assisted by her daughter and her cook, was unbeatable. Besides, her eldest son would not dream of questioning her authority.

Three years later my parents moved away from the old house and the second daughter was born. Odette was totally rejected by our paternal grandmother. My mother, who loved her parents with a passion, used to go and visit them every day. She would drop off Isabelle with her in-laws and keep the second child with her while visiting her own parents. Her mother-in-law had no wish to see the newborn. My Aunt Adele went so far as to tell Odette that she had been found in the street and was not really her parent's daughter. But that must have happened much later.

Poor Odette. *She* must have had a bad time. The extreme reaction of our grandmother toward Odette, is explained by the fact that when she was born, my uncle in Beirut had had two girls and, therefore, Odette was a fourth girl in the eyes of my grandmother Najla. That was, indeed, too much. Then my uncle had a boy, the firstborn to the two brothers. It was a great joy to the family. Still, because my uncle was only the second son of my grandmother, his son was not given his grandfather's name. Then my mother became pregnant again, and everybody thought that there was a pattern there for nature to follow—two girls followed by a boy. Indeed, everyone prepared for the boy, but I was born, the third girl.

There was extreme disappointment and extreme resignation at the same time. My father was wise; he did not make a fuss, he just said, "Well, she has beautiful dark eyes like black olives, and I always wanted to name a daughter Scheherazade, so let us call this one Scheherazade." My mother said, "Oh, yes, let's! It will stop more girls from coming." But there was a very funny story about my birth that Odette's husband liked to tell. My father had business partners who were called the Khomassiyé. They were five partners among the oldest and richest Damascene Muslim families. They had mills in the outskirts of Damascus. My father used to provide them with threads, weaving materials, and tools from England and Holland. My brother-in-law liked to recall the rumor that when I was born, they came to pay a visit of congratulations to my parents, but apparently one could hear them crying in the staircase, "Ya Latif, Ya Latif!," which is one of the names of Allah one calls during funerals! The disaster of my birth did not affect the relationship my mother had with her mother-in-law because by then, my parents had moved even farther away from the old quarter and my mother had a more assured position in her household. There was also the fact that her second son had a baby boy. Additionally, Syria was undergoing big changes, the Second World War was going on, my father's business started to flourish, and he chose to say that I had brought him good luck.

In fact, we soon were going to have our independence, and Syrian nationals would be able to start running their own country and become prosperous. During the French Mandate over Syria, all businesses were in the hands of the French, and the Syrians were left to misery. My father was a serious nationalist, one of the first to applaud Gamal Abdel Nasser when he nationalized the Suez Canal, saying, "Great, yes, French and English, get out and let the people of the land work in their own country." When Nasser came to visit Damascus after his election as the president of the United Arab Republic, which comprised Egypt and Syria, we came all the way from Aleppo to be part of the crowds who welcomed him.

So although my birth had been a big disappointment, it was offset in the eyes of my father by the growth of his business and his belief that I had brought him good luck. It made me his favorite among the three girls. And I was to remain his favorite, which must have been a terrible shock to Isabelle. Not only was she not his favorite but he thought she was a snob, and he hated that attitude. Having moved to Beirut after her marriage, she became closer to her uncle. The two brothers had long spells of enmity, and her closeness with her uncle was sometimes seen as a betrayal. My father was not a man who would easily talk about his innermost feelings, but Isabelle's opportunism was hateful to him.

Oddly enough, I was to remain his favorite even after the birth of my younger brother three years later. My mother, however, took it badly; her pride had been hurt when she had felt she was less of an asset to the family than her sister-in-law, who had managed to bring a boy into the world. Her mother had consoled her with the words, "Don't you know the saying, 'Happy is the mother of girls.' "? For years, I could not believe this saying was part of Arab wisdom. But there it was, and it meant "Happy is the mother of girls"!

My father was not very talkative, but he loved fun. He had an extraordinary sense of theater, and when we at last were gathered and he happened to be in a good mood, he would invent a little comedy and make us laugh until we were in tears. He had a special way of modulating words and sounds, making one syllable or another much longer, twisting them around. He loved music and dance and was generous of heart. He was extremely generous with me and fair. When I graduated from high school, I was sent to England to learn English and to live with a lady my parents knew. I remember he calculated all the expenses, my possible pocket money and extra money for emergencies, then doubled the whole thing. His philosophy was that women should have all the money they needed, otherwise they would fall into trouble. When I was engaged to my cousin in Paris and this cousin asked him for the promised monthly allowance, my father told him, "I give the money to my daughter, then if she gives it to you, it is her personal choice." He never scolded me, except on important occasions, but he would not stand up to my mother who was the terrifying force at home.

When he came back from the office in the evening and I was working on my homework in the dining-room where the gramophone was, he used to dance with me. I must have been seven. He was very happy then and in love. One of his favorite tunes was a French song about a girl born to a family where there were already two girls; the parents had been waiting for a boy, and "judge, how big was the disappointment." And so we would dance to that tune forever. The song went on to say that whatever the first girl did, so would the second one. And I must say that that is what has happened to Odette over the years; she has followed in Isabelle's footsteps.

We had a happy childhood, all in all. My father's business flourished. He was an important man in Aleppo. We used to go promenading in the afternoon, and I would sit in the middle of the car in the back between my two parents. I felt their importance and felt happy. He had also kept his ties in Austria, which was not the empire anymore. He read German all his life and read German papers that were brought in with the mail everyday. He would sit at his desk in the house, and when he asked me for cold water, I used to go and try every bottle until I found the coldest. That was before he had a heart attack and could not drink cold water anymore. After the heart attack, which was nearly fatal, the laughter and music ceased, and later in the year both my sisters married. The first was eighteen and the second fifteen.

The house was surrounded with a big garden in which four buildings have since been built. It was a lovely garden where we used to search for eggs on Easter days. It was a handsome little building three stories high. My parents had it built and initially lived on the first floor, then eventually on the third. The fourth floor was half-built to follow the rules of urban planning. This was where the children lived. We had three bedrooms and a bath. The rest was a big terrace, and it was our big pleasure to wash it, splashing water and running with brooms. That was much more fun than playing with bicycles and with friends. When we were not playing in it, it was used for drying wheat, tomatoes, olives, and apricots and for cleaning carpets.

We spent the summers in Bloudan in those early days at the Grand Hotel; my mother was still nursing me when I was more than one year old. She had so much milk then that she nursed two other children, sons of friends of hers. I asked her how it happened that she had been asked to do so; she said that her friend wanted to get away and that she simply asked my mother to nurse her child. What freedom! It would not happen today. Bloudan was a resort town, famous for its beautiful dry weather. After a few seasons at the Grand Hotel, my parents rented a villa with a tennis court.

My father used to spend the week in Aleppo, only coming to Bloudan on weekends. My mother spent her days playing tennis with the French officers who were there; they would then spend the evening at home. After a while my father realized that the enormous amounts of beer and tuna he was asked to bring were for those soirées, and he asked his mother-in-law to tell his wife that this was not acceptable. So my grandmother came to spend the weekend with us and explained to her daughter that this could not continue; the whole town had been gossiping, and she had to stop receiving the French officers. My mother could not bring herself to tell them not to come anymore. She was embarrassed, so they closed the house and came back to town early that year.

So we grew up, the first two children making a pair of their own and my brother and I another. My brother and I were "inseparable" as I read on the back of an old photograph. My brother in that photograph was four years old. He used to play at all my games. We played, but I preferred to read all the books I could lay my hands on. One day I was in bed reading when my brother called me. He had invented a very dangerous game. We were to jump from the parapet surrounding the side of the building into the terrace and back from the terrace to the parapet. The neighbors across the piazza called my mother on the telephone to tell her what was happening on the other floor. She vowed to work her entire life for a charity organization if she found us safe. She flew upstairs, and she found us safe. She kept her promise and worked for a charity organization until two years ago when, for the first time, her resignation was accepted.

My mother was a very elegant woman in those days. She bought her hats in Paris, and she looked superb in them. She used to spend three or four months in Europe every year with my father on business trips. She had time to have suits and dresses made for her at Lanvin and Jacques Fath.

After the incident, she became less coquettish and took less care of her appearance. She became a formidable organizer in her charity organization. She was president of it for forty years, first in Aleppo, then in Beirut where she later moved. But since her resignation, she has fallen ill. She withstood fifteen years of civil war with equanimity but not the loss of her position.

So just after I was born, in 1945, Syria fought for its independence and won. Our house was in the middle of three French military outposts. One was a building belonging to an employee of the French administration, an old beau of my mother's who worked for the French for fifty gold pounds a month, reason enough for the French army to occupy his building and shoot from there. Another outpost was installed at the French nuns' school, the Franciscaines Missionaires de Marie, a school my sisters attended.

The surrounding army posts shelled our house because my parents had rented the first two floors to the Syrian administration. When the fighting broke out between the occupiers and the Syrian army, although we slept in the corridors between the bedrooms, we were in great danger. One day, a bomb crossed the house and exploded in the kitchen. My father was on the balcony of that kitchen telling the driver to go home, for we were not to go out that evening after all. My mother thought he had died, for nothing but rubble and fumes were coming from the kitchen. She took us to the cellar underground. My father was safe; it was a miracle. After a few days, she called a French officer she knew to ask him whether it would be possible for her to go to the safety of her parents house in the old quarter. He said no road was safe enough for her to do that, but he could arrange for her to go across the street to the nuns' school. The nuns agreed to take us but refused to take in my father, for he was a man and no man could be in a convent. But my mother asked how come the French army was there, at all! My mother remembers waiting on the top of the stairs to see him enter a friend's house across the street.

I have always been a fierce nationalist like my father, but Isabelle had grown up during the Mandate and she admired the French families around her. She equated their power in the country with the ultimate good and chic, a model to attain. "Bonjour Madame La Comtesse, Bonjour Madame la Duchesse." We used to spend afternoons kissing, pronouncing the magical words, pressing only our cheeks against each other so as to not to destroy the other's makeup. My sister, who had been seri-ously ill, had been given the complete works of Delly (a French romance writer in whose novels the heroine was invariably a poor, sad young woman who married a handsome and rich prince or duke). These books became an absolute model for her until this day.

After independence in 1945, foreign schools in Syria closed for a long time. My parents sent Isabelle to the boarding school in Beirut that my mother had attended. Odette soon followed. I was left at home with my brother. Those were my happiest days. I went to school across the street to the Franciscaines Missionaries de Marie, which reopened after a while with a slight change in the programs. The French nuns later accused me of having only Muslim friends at school, which is an amazing accusation, considering that Syria is predominantly a Muslim country. The majority of the girls attending that school came from the Muslim upper classes. The nuns, with their plebeian origins, would never have dreamed of knowing these families had they not been nuns. It also proves that they had a constant secret agenda never to let the different communities get along with each other. The nuns, in fact, had the same political agenda as the French government from which we had thought we had freed our-selves. Anyway, in my personal life it meant disaster, for my parents sent me to the boarding school in Beirut where I became so ill with hepatitis that I nearly died. I was eleven years old. Both Isabelle and I hated that school whose laws were arbitrary and perverse. I recognized my school when years later I read Michel Foucault's description of French prisons. Odette, however, liked the school. She felt happier there than at home. It was a wide theater for her pranks. Alas, those pranks did not go down too well with the nuns, who expelled her from the school at age fourteen. It led to her marriage at fifteen, which she, of course, regretted all her life.

The perversity of the French nuns was also shown when they scolded Isabelle for having good grades. They were the result, they said, only of her incredible memory and boundless ambition and not of real intelli-gence. I was scolded in the same manner for being the first in my class. My fault was that it was just too easy for me. I did not really suffer in order to learn, I *enjoyed* it. What did they really want? To humiliate the little natives. To break our enthusiasm and character. I can say that the scars left by that education are still with me and Isabelle, and this is the worse part of colonialism. That colonization of the mind is still going on, more than ever.

Isabelle was not at all crushed by the nuns. She had that extraordinary *bagage* that our grandmother had given her at an early age. Her grandmother had told her: "Child, Paradise and Hell are on this earth. Don't look anywhere beyond that. And make the most of it. You make your own Paradise and your own Hell." I must admit that she made good use of that precious information. Our grandmother instilled in her an enormous ambition for power and money with a real tip that she used immediately and constantly. It had certainly helped her reach her goals. At eighteen she married a modest doctor, and together they set out to conquer Lebanese society and the financial establishment. By 1975 they had pretty much succeeded. When the civil war broke out, she immediately saw in the new situation an excuse to move to Paris and turn her efforts to French society. That had been her dream forever. Since her childhood, she had looked up to the elegant French families who flocked to my parents' social parties the way Marguerite Duras's young women dreamt of the elegant ladies from Paris while they led boring and what they felt were second-class citizen lives in the colonies. In Beirut she certainly invited more and more of the diplomatic corps so that she could have connections in Europe. She also thought they were more chic and glamourous than the Lebanese.

I had always considered her with great indulgence for I was seeing a fragility through all this that I pitied. She had invented a way all her own of whining and crying, half to fend off the evil eye, half to express the real fatigue that this constant social climbing provoked. I was her confidante when we were children—half a confidante, I should say, for she never confided everything, being very prudent. She lashed out with part of the story, enough to vent her anxieties. But if I guessed the rest of the proposition, she would cry, "Oh, I never said that." Prudent, calculating, and cunning, she claimed great and noble feelings to be the only motive of her behavior. She seemed to play a game of pretense. She had accumulated all this wealth for *her children only.* She only moved to Paris to give them shelter and safety and to expose them to the salutary effects of Western civilization. Besides, her situation was precarious, (meaning her financial situation); *this wealth was not really hers!* I should worry about her, pray that she can still afford her way of life that gets more and more extravagant all the time. She is all generosity. Her life is a long and strenuous chain of duties. She does not *really* enjoy the parties and the concerts and the musical weekends in Vienna or Venice. These are all social obligations that are killing her and undermining her health. In one word, as she seems to say, we should leave her alone, for this social climbing can in no way be done in company. She has gone as far as to think that my presence in Paris is a threat to it. I would think all that to be laughable had she not constantly pushed me away from herself and our family the way she did earlier by excluding me from the family lunches.

I confess I did not understand the extent of her hostility before I found myself as if by magic here in America. And one day, upon telling a friend a little about her, the friend cried, "But, Scheherazade, this is abuse." I reflected and told myself, maybe she is right. The word *abuse* was unknown to me until then.

This is abuse, my friend said. My sister abused me both physically and mentally. And to tell myself that that abuse came from her jealousy of me did not make it any less painful—a jealousy that did not relent and that had ruined years of my life. When I complain about it to my mother, she says, "No, no, you are the only one she ever loved." But what is love in that case? It is forever mingled with manipulation. Her real love has always been for power—power over people. She has an infinite appetite for authority, an authority that she exercised over children, parents, lovers, and servants.

It is remarkable how much depends on one's relationship to one's sibling. After all, we scarcely lived together in the same house. Isabelle is seven years older than I. By the time I was three she was already at boarding school. She left home for good and was married when I was thirteen. Yet there is such a rivalry and jealousy and, I would say, yearning for the relationship to be smoother. Age did not make anything easier. The pattern of behavior is somewhat the same when we meet now. The authority she was invested with because of her position as the eldest still holds. Of course, we do not obey her, but we respect her position. We do not choose to accept it. If we disagree, we just go away.

PART TWO

Ethnographic and Historical
Excavations of the Self

The Context

In part 2 we excavate the dynamics of intimate selving through ethnographic (Joseph, Hamadeh, Joseph) and historical (Hatem) materials, covering the late nineteenth century to the present. The site for three of the chapters is Lebanon (Joseph, Hamadeh, Joseph) and for one is Egypt (Hatem). Two are written by an anthropologist (Joseph, Joseph), one by a philosopher (Hamadeh), and one by a political scientist (Hatem). The relationships discussed are intimate immediate family relationships—brother-sister relationships (Joseph); mother-son relationships (Joseph); mother-daughter, father-daughter, husband-wife relationships (Hatem)—with the focus in one chapter on the co-wife relationship created through marriage (Hamadeh). Two are urban based (Joseph, Hatem), one on the village (Joseph), and one compares urban and nomadic and sedentary Bedouin settings (Hamadeh). One set of relationships is among the urban working class (Joseph), a second among rural lower-middle and working classes (Joseph), whereas a third includes rural/urban lower, middle, and upper classes (Hamadeh), and the fourth, the urban upper class (Hatem). Educational levels in the relationships discussed vary from illiterate to college educated. In each case, the author is a native of the country of research.

From work in a heterogeneous urban neighborhood of greater Beirut in the 1970s, I argue in my chapter that centrality of the brother-sister relationship to the reproduction of patriarchy and to the socialization of young males and females into their gender and sexuality has been overlooked. Brother and sister mutually shaped each other's gender and sexuality in this neighborhood. The power of that relationship was the cultural mandating of brothers and sisters to love one another and, at the same time, charging the brother with the protection of the sister and the sister with service to the brother. The brother-sister relationship in this Lebanese urban neighborhood helped socialize young males into masculine patriarchal roles and young females into feminine roles, serving the patriarchs. Yet neither brother nor sister moved into their roles seamlessly. Brothers had to learn to assert authority while sisters often resisted and rebelled. Both brothers and sisters took the initiative, actively engaging each other as they contested positionalities within the family. In the process, they mutually contributed to each other's notions of selves while molding their own selfhoods. The brother's power depended on the sister's acceptance of his authority. The sister could offer this acceptance while holding onto a sense of her own agency. The brother-sister relationship, I argue, is a prime example of patriarchal connectivity—the production of fluid, relational selves socialized for gendered hierarchy.

Najla Hamadeh's chapter offers an unusual comparison of the almost unstudied relationships among co-wives in urban and Bedouin (both nomadic and sedentary) settings. She argues that urbanism has generally been associated with the positive outcomes of modernity that result from Westernization, particularly in the transformations of family systems to nuclear forms. In the work of many scholars, the nuclear family is either caused by or the cause of (or both) democracy and higher status for women. The implications of such theorization, Hamadeh argues, are misguided. Finding relationships among co-wives in urban settings to be more deleterious to women and finding these urban co-wives more dependent on their patriarchal husbands, she contends that "reform be pursued in a 'native idiom' " rather than by appropriating patriarchies from other cultures. Bedouin women, Hamadeh discovers, often have very close, mutually respectful, and supportive relationships. They may even mother each other, offering not only household help but emotional nurturance. Patriarchal husbands are determining less of the lives of the Bedouin than of urban wives. Indeed, Hamadeh finds, Bedouin co-wives are less dependent on their husbands than are urban. Both nuclear and extended Arab families, Hamadeh points out, are patriarchal. But urban nuclear patriarchy emerged, in her provocative study, as more oppressive for co-wives than Bedouin extended patriarchal households. The nuclear family, Hamadeh concludes, with its more closely bounded constructs of selfhood may produce individuals with what might be tantamount to "asocial" personalities.

In chapter 7 on mother-son relationships, Joseph explores a case of mother-son love and the son's affinity to the mother's family. This maternal affinity, in a society that is highly patriarchal and patrilineal, directs attention to the complex specificities of family relationalities and suggests a continual need for contextualization of social practices that may diverge considerably from social norms. In this family the son is not only an only son but an only child of late-marrying parents. The family lives in close proximity to both maternal and paternal relatives. Both maternal and paternal families are quite large, offering extensive opportunities for relationships of great depth and breadth. Cultural norms would call upon the son to identify with the father and with the father's family. Yet in this instance, son, mother, and father had minimal contact with the paternal relatives despite living in houses sharing common walls. Although the father in no way acted as if or presented himself as if he had relinquished his authority over his son, yet the son's affinity to the mother and the mother's family was not only clear to everyone but readily articulated by both the son and mother. Contrary to normative expectations of classical psychoanalytic theory, the son did not distance himself from his mother and the mother did not push her son away. Rather, both actively engaged each other in the shaping of each's sense of selfhood. They were each other's fondest companions and confidants, spending more nonwork time with each other than either did with anyone else and looking forward to a lifetime together. Most important, for the purposes of the argument of this chapter, this intimate involvement between mother and son was considered mature, functional, and natural in the eyes of the extended family and community. The social acceptance of this intense mother-son relationship, I argue, is the plausible, although paradoxical, outcome of the patriarchal connectivity I theorize.

Mervat F. Hatem, drawing on Michel Foucault, deconstructs power relationships to uncover the multiple roles women/mothers enact in patriarchal societies. Hatem's focus on historical transformations and use of autobiographical texts offers pioneering analysis of intimate selving in historical Arab family studies. Studying the upper-class family of the nineteenth-century Egyptian feminist 'A'isha Taymur, Hatem contends that mothers, fathers, and children relied simultaneously on "consent, rebellion, coercion, or a combination of these tactics" to produce the patriarchal family dynamics. She argues that studying the microdynamics of power reveals far more contested and complex relationships than might be exposed through the study of structures and normative patterns. Hatem describes how the rebellion of the daughter earned her a literary education, although she, at the same time, acquiesced to her father's insistence on the primacy of marriage in a woman's life. She achieved what Hatem calls a "happy juxtaposition of old and new forms of learning."

The juxtaposition included the daughter taking on her mother's domestic responsibilities, an accommodation that allowed for the continued reproduction of patriarchy while it opened spaces for the novel needs of women, indeed for new forms of femininity. The resultant divided and conflicted "new feminine" self of Taymur, Hatem astutely discerns, did not question the implied oppositionality between the old (feminine) and the new (masculine) interests and orientation—a formula for failure. Hatem's insightful reading of Taymur's autobiographical texts highlights the intricacies of multigenerational and multiple relationalities in the shaping and transformation of their selves. Mother-daughter, father-daughter, husband-wife are cast co-equally as actors inventing each other.

In the chapters in part 2 we draw attention to the need to investigate understudied relationalities and to question the uncritical application of Western theories, Western norms, and Western practices to Arab family dynamics. The authors shed light on transformations over the twentieth century and within the lifetimes of specific persons. The self is not fixed, but constantly contested, and contested with and within intimate familial relationships and structures that, while enduringly patriarchal and relational in general principles, have also shifted and changed in content over time.

5

Brother-Sister Relationships

Connectivity, Love, and Power
in the Reproduction of Patriarchy in Lebanon

SUAD JOSEPH

The Yusifs[1] were a working-class family living in the urban neighborhood of Camp Trad, Borj Hammoud, a part of the Greater Beirut area of Lebanon. Abu Hanna,[2] the Lebanese Maronite father, was a man who, even on the rare occasions when he was angry, spoke with the soft, slow lull of someone who had just awakened from a deep sleep. Um Hanna, the mother and a Palestinian Catholic, graced an abundant figure and a shy yet welcoming smile.[3] A caring family with five boys and two girls, the Yusifs were respected as peace-loving, honorable folks by their neighbors. I lived next door to the Yusifs from 1971 to 1973 and came to know them well over a decade.[4] When I first met them, I sensed a harmony in the family. I never heard a raised voice. I developed close relationships with all members of the family, taking on the role of sister with the parents and aunt with the younger children.[5]

I was particularly close to the oldest son, Hanna. With soft, wavy brown hair and roguish brown eyes that seemed always poised to make an assertion, Hanna, at nineteen, was seen as a highly attractive marriage choice. Very conscious of his grooming and masculine self-presentation, he ritually combed his hair with a comb kept in his back pocket. His medium build and height seemed to expand as he walked with firm yet graceful movements that appeared planned. There were few college students in this street, and Hanna was already in the eleventh grade in 1972.

113

A politically active bridge-builder with friends across ethnic and religious groups, Hanna was viewed as peace loving and conscientious.

I was shocked, therefore, one sunny afternoon to hear Hanna shouting at his sister Flaur and slapping her across her face. Flaur, at twelve, was the oldest daughter and the third oldest child. She seemed to have an opinion on most things, was never shy about speaking her mind, and welcomed guests with boisterous laughter and dancing light brown eyes that invited visitors to wonder what she was up to. With a lively sense of humor and good-natured mischief about her, Flaur was thought, by neighbors, to be a live wire despite the fact that she did not conform to Lebanese ideals of feminine beauty.

Hanna played father to Flaur, even though she helped care for the younger siblings who looked to her for mothering. Hanna repeatedly instructed Flaur to comb her hair, dress attractively, and carry herself with grace. In a local culture in which self-grooming occupied young women, Flaur seemed to pay no attention to her clothing, hair, body, or comportment. Her curls fluttered around her face, her clothes were often wrinkled and worn, and when you hugged her, you could feel a few preadolescent rolls adorning her hips and waist. This irritated Hanna considerably. His ire at her peaked, though, whenever he caught her lingering on the street corner near their apartment building gossiping with other girls. He would forcefully escort her upstairs to their apartment, slap her, and demand that she behave with dignity. No doubt the charge in their relationship came in part because Flaur was entering puberty as Hanna was reaching manhood.

Perhaps because of my special relationship with the family, I was stunned at Hanna's behavior. Flaur sometimes ran crying into my apartment. A few times I heard Flaur screaming, and I ran across the hall. Um Hanna watched. No one, myself included, questioned my right to intervene.

Hanna took it as his right and responsibility to mold and discipline his sister.[6] Neither Um Hanna nor Flaur appeared to appeal to Abu Hanna about Hanna's behavior. Flaur's seventeen-year-old brother, Farid, might have protected her, but he deferred to Hanna. Family members, including Flaur, agreed that Hanna was acting within his brotherly role.

Hanna regarded me as an older sister, consulting me on personal, social, and political matters. I had accepted that role and felt comfortable speaking to him about his behavior. When we talked, he said he knew what the world was like and she did not. It was his brotherly responsibility to train Flaur to be a lady. I suggested he might teach rather than beat her. He responded, with a smile in his eyes, that Flaur could not understand words and he did not hurt her. With authority, he added, he did it *"minshanha, minshan mistakbilha"* (for her, for her future).

When I discussed Hanna's behavior with Um Hanna, she found the matter amusing. I was surprised. She claimed that Hanna was doing his brotherly duty. She continued that Hanna cared deeply about Flaur. Besides, she added, Flaur provoked Hanna and brought his violence upon herself. Maybe, she chuckled, Flaur even liked it.

Flaur, for her part, seemed not unmindful of her own power over Hanna. Although she admired her brother, she teased him about his constant grooming or the romantic interests of neighborhood women in him. She was aware that her behavior would provoke Hanna. There was a willful element to her behavior that I thought was either an attempt to assert her own identity or to involve her brother intimately in her life.

On one occasion when Um Hanna, Flaur, and I were discussing Hanna's behavior, Um Hanna repeated, in Flaur's presence, that Flaur invited and enjoyed Hanna's aggression. With a mischievous smile in her eyes, Flaur laughed and agreed. She added, with bravado, "It doesn't even hurt when Hanna hits me." On another occasion, she indicated that she would like a husband like Hanna.

When I returned to Camp Trad in 1978 during the civil war,[7] I stayed for a couple of days with the Yusifs. Flaur was married and had a one-year-old baby. Although taller, more voluptuous, and womanly, she still seemed a bit disheveled. Her husband was quiet, thin, and pale to the point of seeming unhealthy. Um Hanna asked me what I thought of Flaur's husband. I responded that I thought he was *'akil* (well-mannered). Um Hanna noted that before her marriage, Flaur had lost weight and had become quite pretty. In the pocket-size wedding picture she showed me, Flaur did look beautiful and like a perfect size eight. She had had a number of suitors, Um Hanna went on, and could have gotten a better-looking man. She asserted, *"Wayn Hanna wa wayn hada"* (Where is Hanna and where is this one), implying that the best match for Flaur would have been someone like Hanna.

The relationship between Hanna and Flaur is a prime example of the connective love/power dynamic between brothers and sisters in these Arab families. That dynamic was critical to Hanna's empowerment and masculinization and Flaur's domestication and feminization; Hanna was teaching Flaur to accept male power in the name of love. His family supported his learning that loving his sister meant taking charge of her and that he could discipline her if his action was understood to be in her best interests. Flaur was reinforced in learning that the love of a male could include that male's violent control and that to receive this love involved submission to control. She was learning that her brother was both a loving protector and a controlling power in her life.

Hanna was additionally teaching Flaur how to present her feminine sexuality. She was learning to become a sexual person for her brother. Given Abu Hanna's absence and the interest that Hanna took in her, her brother was the most involved male sexual figure during her puberty. By feminizing Flaur, Hanna was masculinizing himself. Hanna also was using his culturally acceptable control over his sister to challenge his father's authority in the family. By taking charge of his sister, with the blessings of his mother and siblings, he highlighted his father's failures as head of the household. Hanna was learning to become a patriarch by becoming the man of the house in relation to his sister, mother, and younger siblings. Hanna and Flaur's relationship socialized each other into the links between gender, sexuality, love, and power. Their mutual dependency was underwritten by patriarchal connectivity inscribed as love. Their relationship reveals psychodynamic, social structural, and cultural processes through which the brother-sister relationship contributes to the reproduction of Arab patriarchy, a role that scholars of the Arab world have yet to unravel.

Brother-Sister Relationships: Arab Contexts

Although brother-sister relationships have received anthropological attention in the literature on a number of societies,[8] relatively little of the work on Arab societies has considered the centrality of brother-sister relationships to the reproduction of family life and patriarchy. This lacuna comes in part from the relative lack of studies problematizing the internal dynamics of Arab family life. With the "Arab family" becoming increasingly the center of controversy in the literature and popular culture of the Middle East, new efforts have been made to more closely scrutinize the familial issues on both Arab and national bases.[9] Most of the research on family in the Arab world, stressing the cultural ideals of patriarchy, patrilineality, patrilocality, and patrilineal endogamy, has focused on relationships among males.[10] Scholars have paid less attention to brother-sister or other key male-female relationships. Research on Lebanon also offers insights into family life but does not address the brother-sister relationship in detail.[11]

The little work that does exist on brother-sister relationships in the

Arab World tends to regard it as either romantic or patriarchal, focusing respectively on "love" or "power." Scholars who focus on "love" aspects of the relationship are often attuned to psychodynamics but usually do not link them with social structural and cultural process. Scholars identifying the "power" aspects of the relationship tend to be interested not in brother-sister relationships per se but in family structure and culture. These scholars often neglect psychodynamics or inadequately connect them to social structural and cultural processes. Few studies effectively link psychodynamic, social structural, and cultural processes. Most, therefore, do not recognize the connectivity that charges the love/power dynamics underpinning the central role played by the brother-sister relationship in the reproduction of Arab patriarchy.

The Romantic View

In a functionalist vein, the romantic view represents the brother-sister relationship as a kind of safety valve, a relationship of love and mutuality in a presumed cold and authoritarian family system. The approach differentiates the brother-sister relationship from the father-daughter and other familial relationships as the only safe cross-gender relationship in otherwise relatively gender-segregated societies. Given patrilineal endogamy and a family culture in which a woman continues to belong to her natal kin group and her male kin continue to be responsible for her throughout her life, the romantic view valorizes the link to a brother as the woman's lifeline.

One of the best representatives of this romantic view of brother-sister relationships is folklorist Hassan El-Shamy.[12] El-Shamy[12] contends that the brother-sister relationship and its derivative, the ego–maternal uncle relationship, are characterized by a mutual loving not found in other family relationships. All other family relationships (parent-child, spouse, brother-brother, sister-sister, ego–paternal uncle, brother–sister's husband, sister–brother's wife), he claims, are organized around hostility. He asserts[13] that there are incestuous tendencies underlying Arab brother-sister relationships which are unrecognized and untreated in the Arabic psychiatric literature. Basing his analysis of variations of a folktale found in most Arab countries,[14] analysis of selected Egyptian fiction,[15] and a review of some Arab psychiatric literature,[16] he posits a "brother-sister syndrome." This syndrome, is "responsible for the development of a distinctive culture and personality pattern characteristic of the Arab, which transcends religious, regional, and social class differences" and "plays a decisive role in the formation, development, and maintenance of family structure and all other related organizations."[17] El-Shamy, while recognizing significant psychodynamics of the brother-sister relationship, sees little of the hierarchy and so does not link the relationship to Arab patriarchy.

El-Shamy is not alone in casting the cross-sibling relationship in romantic terms, however.[18] Hilma Granqvist, in her classic early studies of Palestinian peasants, contends that for the Palestinian *fellahin* (peasants) of the 1930s the love between sisters and brothers was "more beautiful than the love between wife and husband, because not founded on passion."[19] Granqvist notes that when a woman married, her brother offered himself as her "camel" to carry her burdens.[20] The brother was more responsible for a woman than her husband was: "The husband is only a garment that a woman puts on or throws off again, or she herself can be 'thrown off' by her husband, but the brother is the one who is always there."[21] If a married woman committed a shameful act, the father or brother, not the husband, was responsible.[22] The man's responsibility for his sister had eternal consequences, according to one of Granqvist's informants who asserted: "This is my sister. To-morrow in eternity [at the Judgment Day] she will make me responsible, but not my children and my wife."[23] Although the power between brothers and sisters seems apparent here, Granqvist makes little of it, focusing on the implied love.

Michael Meeker[24] offers an intriguing comparison of Turkish and Arab brother-sister and husband-wife relationships.[25] He contends that among Arabs the disgrace of a woman must be responded to by "those who 'love,' " whereas among Turks it must be responded to by "those who 'control.' " Given that among both the Arabs and the Turks, the brother-sister relationship is one of love and the husband-wife relationship is one of control, then among the Arabs the brother must respond to a sister's disgrace, whereas among the Turks, it is the husband. Meeker, however, does not discuss the connection between love and responsibility. The brother's responsibility of response invests him in controlling the sister's behavior so that he will not have to respond. Responsibility translates into power; love and power become intertwined.

The romantic view of the brother-sister relationship is at times reproduced by scholars in an important attempt to represent Arab persons by respecting their voices. In a portrayal of Egyptian feminist Huda Sha'rawi, Leila Ahmed comments that Sha'rawi's love for her brother was the deepest and most intense of her life.[26] Ahmed quotes Sha'rawi as asserting that when her brother died in her late thirties, " 'all my hopes died,' and but for a sense of duty toward her children, 'I would not have survived him by an instant.' "[27] Offering significant insights into her life, Ahmed views Sha'rawi's relationship with her brother through Sha'rawi's lens of love, even in transactions that also could be interpreted as displays of power. For example, after a period of estrangement, Sha'rawi separated from her husband. According to Sha'rawi's report, her brother refused to proceed with his own marriage until she returned to her husband. Ahmed observes, "Not wanting to stand in the way of her brother's happiness, she agreed to a reconciliation."[28] One could read love/power dynamics here also—the brother using his happiness to control his sister?

The Patriarchal View

Most of the literature on the honor/shame complex focuses on social structural and cultural rather than psychodynamic processes. The scholars interested in psychodynamic aspects of honor/shame rarely apply their analyses systematically to brother-sister relationships and tend to focus on non-Arab Mediterranean societies.[29] Scholars who recognize the hierarchy in the brother-sister relationship tend to be interested in the social structure and culture of the Arab family rather than in psychodynamics or the brother-sister relationship per se.

In this patriarchal view, the brother-sister relationship, as an extension of the father-daughter relationship, is an instrument of the honor/shame complex thought by many scholars to predominate in Mediterranean family culture.[30] Women, through their modesty, are supposed to uphold family honor. Should they bring shame onto the family, their closest male patrilineal relatives must restore family honor by disciplining them or the other culprits involved. Usually the task belongs to fathers or brothers but also might be undertaken by paternal uncles or male cousins.

Most scholars tend not to differentiate conditions under which one or another of the patrilineal males responds. We might wonder whether Arabs differentiate. For example, a Jordanian adage appears to gloss male patrilineal relatives: " 'Deficiency harks back to [patrilineal] origins' but 'the mare belongs to the rider [husband].' "[31] Yet assertions specifying responsibility can also be found. Alois Musil notes that for the Rwala Bedouins:

> The person whom the married woman can most inconvenience is her own brother; hence the proverb: "the brother of a married woman is far re-

moved from any good done by her, but very close to any evil she may be guilty of." [32]

In this view, the father and brother are also responsible for the protection and well-being of the daughter/sister. The father/brother are entrusted with control and protection of the daughter/sister throughout their lives. The brother, then, as a representative of the patrilineal line, exerts patriarchal authority to protect and control the sister in order to maintain family honor. [33] Recognizing the power brothers exert over sisters, scholars adopting this view link the brother-sister relationship with the reproduction of patriarchy. But they tend not to differentiate it from a woman's relationship with her father or her close patrilineal relatives, thereby missing the complexity of the love/power dynamics between brothers and sisters.

Privileging social structural and cultural processes and conflating brother-sister relationships with others, patrilineally distorts the brother-sister relationship. One must unravel the historically and culturally specific dynamics and analyze the codeterminancy of psychodynamic, social structural, and cultural processes.

Connectivity, Love, and Power in the Reproduction of Patriarchy in Lebanon: Psychodynamic, Social Structural, and Cultural Processes

It would be an easy error to assume that if one privileges psychodynamic events in brother-sister relationships, their mutual love is foregrounded and that if one privileges social structural and cultural events, their disparate power is foregrounded. I argue that the patriarchal connectivity of brothers and sisters in love/nurturance and power/violence dynamics was expressed psychodynamically, social structurally, and culturally. It was the interlinking of connectivity, love, and power, throughout, that gave the brother-sister relationship its centrality in the reproduction of Arab patriarchy.

Classical Middle Eastern patriarchy is probably best understood in terms of those pastoral societies in which kinship was coterminous with society and was the key force in organizing politics, economics, religion, and other social processes. The dominance of male elders over kin groups translated into dominance over society. The emergence of state structures transformed classical patriarchy as state leaders competed with kinship leaders for control over individuals and groups, often by coopting kin structures, kin morality, and kin idioms into the state, leading to state patriarchal forms. In many contemporary Middle Eastern societies, kin groups continue to offer effective resistance to state control over their membership. Contemporary patriarchy in the Arab Middle East, therefore, takes many forms. Minimally, then, I use patriarchy here to mean the dominance of males over females and elders over juniors (males and females) and the mobilization of kinship structures, morality, and idioms to institutionalize and legitimate these forms of power. By power, I mean the capacity to direct the behavior of others even against their will.

Contemporary Arab patriarchy takes many forms, leading to variability in brother-sister relationships based on state, class, religion, ethnic, rural/urban, and other differences.[34] I choose, nevertheless, to refer to the phenomenon I am analyzing as "Arab" because of the national, ethnic, and religious heterogeneity of the population of Camp Trad (see below). By using the term "Arab" to refer to the patterns described here, I am signaling the recent origins of the residents of the neighborhood and their heterogeneity.[35] Camp Trad was mostly working class and was, therefore, relatively homogeneous in class terms. As the material below indicates, however, I observed many of the same patterns in other social classes in Lebanon.[36] The national, ethnic, and religious mixture of families, their relative recency in Lebanon and/or Camp Trad, and the observations of similar patterns in other social classes in Lebanon would suggest that the general patterns described were not unique to this urban situation. The meaning of any institution or social practice must be understood in its historically and culturally specific context, however. The implications of the patterns described here for brother-sister relationships in other Arab countries or classes need to be tested empirically.

Pyschodynamic Processes: Connectivity and Love in Patriarchy in Lebanon

I use connectivity to mean psychodynamic processes by which one person comes to see himself or herself as part of another. Boundaries between persons are relatively fluid so that each needs the other to complete the sense of selfhood. One's sense of self is intimately linked with the self of another so that the security, identity, integrity, dignity, and self-worth of one is tied to the actions of the other. Connective persons are not separate or autonomous. They are open to and require the involvement of others in shaping their emotions, desires, attitudes, and identities. Like Catherine Keller, I use connective, rather than connected, to indicate an activity or intention rather than a state of being.[37]

The concept of connectivity is useful in characterizing the social production of relational selves with diffuse boundaries who require continuous interaction with significant others for a sense of completion. Defined as such, it is a nonculturally specific concept. I use connectivity to depart from Western-centric notions of relationality that are associated with judgments of dysfunctionality. The leading theorist of dysfunctional notions of relationality, Salvador Minuchin,[38] offered the concept of enmeshment to describe constructs of self that resonated with my observations in Camp Trad. His insights, although powerful, are limited by his Western-based assumptions that individuation, autonomy, and separateness are psychodynamically necessary for healthy maturation. This judgment emerges from evaluations of persons in Western, industrialized, market, and contract-based societies organized around the expectation of mobile and autonomous selves. Minuchin's family systems theory is also limited by its functionalism and his neglect of patriarchy.[39]

Rather, I employ connectivity in the context of a culture in which the family is valued over and above the person or society and in which "individuation," "autonomy," "separateness," and "boundedness" as understood in the American psychotherapeutic literature are less valued than bonding with and commitment to family.[40] It is in the context of the primacy of the family over the person and society that the love/power dynamics of the brother-sister relationship makes sense and contributes to the reproduction of Arab patriarchy.[41] This is not to say, however, that there were no individuated, autonomous, separate, bounded selves in Camp Trad. Rather, I argue that such bounded selfhood was relatively unsupported, whereas connective selfhood was both supported and valorized.

In Camp Trad, brothers and sisters were expected to love one another. I use "love" here to mean deep "feelings" of caring. Current research has significantly contributed to culturally sensitizing emotion words.[42] Although I do not employ a literary usage of "love" as does Lila Abu-Lughod in her important work, I agree with her that emotion words can signal culturally significant values that "contribute to the representations of the self, representations that are tied to morality, which in turn is untimely tied to politics in its broadest sense."[43] Meanings of emotion words must be understood in the context of local cultures, the value systems they signal, and the culturally specific notions of selfhood that they represent.

Connective relationships could be loving or hostile. Connective relationships were considered loving when persons anticipated each other's needs, attended to, and acted in each other's interests, took on each other's concerns, pains, and joys as theirs. In Camp Trad, love was understood as an enactment of connective relationships. Brothers and sisters were called upon to develop such loving relationships. Their senses of self, identity, and future called for their mutual involvement with each other. They saw themselves reflected in each other's eyes and lives. A brother was responsible for his sister's behavior. A sister was expected to embrace a brother's wishes as her own. The boundaries between them were fluid. They were to read each other, anticipate needs, and fulfill expectations unasked. Figuring out what was his, what was hers, were not central preoccupations. They were to share, care, and commit to each other.

Connectivity was poignant among Camp Trad brothers and sisters because the expectation of love and nurturance was coupled with gendered dominance supported by familial structure and culture. Through the brother-sister relationship, men learned that loving women entailed controlling them and women learned that loving men entailed submitting to them. Sisters also had some power over brothers. Women had numerous avenues for involving their brothers in their lives. Because a woman's behavior immediately reflected on her brothers' honor, dignity, and sense of self, she could enhance or detract from her brothers' status by her actions and potentially compel her brothers into action. Connectivity was a double-ended hook joining the lives of brothers and sisters.

As a result, the brother-sister relationship became a critical vehicle for the socialization of males and females into culturally appropriate gender roles, thus helping to reproduce patriarchy. That is, I am arguing that, in Camp Trad, contrary to much of Western psychodynamic theory that places almost exclusive stress on the parent-child relationship for modeling of appropriate gender roles, sibling relationships were also significant vehicles of gender socialization. Cross-siblings used their relationships to learn and practice socially acceptable notions of masculinity and femininity, dominance and submission, and commitment to patrilineal kinship structures, morality, and idioms—processes mediated through connectivity.

Social Structural Processes:
Family, Marriage, and Inheritance

A number of features of Arab family social structure contributed to the dependence of Camp Trad women on their brothers. First, women were considered to belong to their natal families even after marriage. Their natal families were ultimately responsible for their behavior and well being, and in the long course of lives, such responsibility fell most heavily on brothers.

Second, Muslim men could marry up to four wives, and divorce, although uncommon in practice, was primarily a male privilege. Legally, Muslim men could divorce their wives easily and/or marry additional wives. Thus, a Muslim marriage left women structurally vulnerable. For the same reasons, reliance on a father could be problematical.[44] Muslim fathers could become involved with the children of other wives and even abandon children by previous marriages. Full siblings, however, shared the same set of family ties. Because of the structural possibility of abandonment by the father, the brother-sister relationship also could be a locus of contestation between sons and fathers about control over the family. Brothers could use their rights over their sisters to challenge the authority of their fathers, thus preparing to become patriarchs in their own right.

Third, the cultural ideal of marriage between the children of brothers (FaBrSo/Da marriage), according to most scholars,[45] bolsters both patrilineality and patriarchy, that is, reinforces the natal kin ties of both men and women. For men, FaBrSo/Da marriages meant that their sisters could marry the men they considered their closest allies after their own brothers and the ones most bound to protect their sisters. For sisters it meant that their brothers could marry the women closest to being their own sisters. And each could marry the person closest to the role of their cross sibling.[46] Endogamy also meant brothers and sisters could live near each other, facilitating the fulfillment of the cultural expectation that brothers remained responsible for sisters throughout their lives.

Regardless of whether siblings married relatives, there seemed to be an edge in their relationships with each other's spouses. Structural strains in marriages could develop from the continued claims of brothers and sisters on each other's love and loyalty. Men and women expected their spouses to live up to their idealized images of their cross-siblings and often negatively compared their spouses to these images. El-Shamy found that Arabic folktales depict the sister's relationship with the brother's wife as one of jealousy and hostility,[47] whereas the brother's relationship with the sister's husband is depicted as mainly neutral, although at times "potentially negative."[48]

Siblings could offer protections to each other's children, even against parental authority. The brother as *khal* (maternal uncle) played an important structural role as nurturer of his sister's children. El-Shamy,[49] quoting an Arab adage, "*'al-khal walid'* (the maternal uncle is a father [literally, 'birth-giver'])," argues that the affection of the khal for his sister's children was an expression of brother/sister love.[50] Similarly, the sister as *'amta* (paternal aunt) was seen as nurturer. This role of the *'amta* was reflected in the popular Lebanese saying: *"al 'ammi bit 'imm matrah al um"* (the father's sister can take the place of the mother).

Structural tensions from competing obligations could constrain the brother-sister relationship. Aging parents expected to be cared for by sons, even though in reality many were cared for by daughters. Men's obligations to their families of procreation increased as their families matured. Thus, a man's duties to his sister were always competing with claims on him by his parents, wife, and children. As a result, brothers often could not fulfill their sisters' or the culture's expectations.[51] Women were also structurally caught between competing loyalties. Husbands demanded loyalty from their wives. Children expected the undivided involvement of their mothers. Women often felt torn between families of origin and of procreation as they matured.

For sisters, another social structural source of limitations developed from the asymmetrical expectations engendered early. Brothers were socialized to receive more than to give service to sisters. Throughout their growing years, sisters did for brothers much more than brothers did for sisters. As adults, brothers expected the same. Women at times felt frustrated by the asymmetry.

Tensions were also built into the structure of inheritance. Many women left their patrimony with their brothers as insurance against future need. This could lead to tensions with husbands who wanted to claim their wives' inheritances. Additionally, a woman's children, as they matured, might lay claims on their mother's inheritance.

The issue addressed implicitly by these observations is the preservation of patriarchy in the context of a segmentary patrilineal system. In such systems the boundary of the kin unit could change in keeping with what was contested. Depending upon where the line was drawn around the family at a particular time, preservation of patriarchy might require opposition to siblings' spouses (in FaBrSo/Da marriages, the cousin) and at other times alliance. Although these were Muslim patterns, the values surrounding them permeated Camp Trad culture across religious lines. In the Camp Trad cultural ideal, the structure of family, marriage, and inheritance reinforced sisters' dependence on brothers and brothers' responsibility for sisters despite these variable conditions.[52]

Cultural Processes: Honor and Shame

For both brothers and sisters in Camp Trad, connective identities and mutual love were linked to family honor. The ideal of brother-sister relationships in Camp Trad was based on a cultural promise: a brother will protect his sister; a sister will uphold her family's honor. Men saw themselves as their sisters' protectors.[57] Invested in their sisters' behavior, their sense of their own dignity and honor was tied to their sisters' comportment. They were permitted by their parents and the culture to see sisters as extensions of themselves and, thus, to be molded to fit their sense of self. This included the cultural sanction to discipline their sisters when their behavior was considered improper.

Sisters identified with their brothers as their security. A woman without a brother was seen as somewhat naked in the world. A brother's achievements opened opportunities for his sisters, just as his failures closed doors. Sisters understood that to receive the protection and support of brothers they had to address their brothers' expectations.[54] They were socialized to accept their brothers' authority over their lives and to see it in their own interests to accept that authority. Even when they might have disagreed with their brothers, sisters acknowledged their brothers' "rights" over them as a central vehicle for maintaining family honor.

Thus, connectivity was an underlying psychodynamic process supporting the enactment of the cultural practices entailed in maintaining family honor. It is, I argue, because their connectivity encouraged brothers and sisters to view love and power as parts of the same dynamic that their relationship was so critical an instrument of the reproduction of Arab patriarchy. It is also because love and power were experienced as part of the same dynamic that these patriarchal relations had such hold on the members of Arab families. That is, patriarchy seated in love may be much more difficult to unseat than patriarchy in which loving and nurturance are not so explicitly mandated and supported.[55]

My data is presented around three sets of processes. After describing the local community, I first discuss psychodynamic processes in brother-sister relationships focusing on the love and power dimensions of connectivity. Second, I analyze social structural processes of family, marriage, and inheritance, drawing out the implications for cross-sibling mutual dependence and responsibility. Finally, I consider how cultural processes, working through notions of honor and shame, linked brothers' and sisters' senses of self. The processes I discuss below did not characterize all brother-sister relationships at all times in Camp Trad. Yet they constituted such a significant pattern of relationality in discourse and in practice that one could see, and I demonstrate, a fundamental intertwining of connectivity, love, and power in psychodynamic, and social structural, and cultural processes.

Local Community

Borj Hammoud is an urban working-class municipality in the Greater Beirut area. In the early 1970s almost all of the religious sects and ethnic groups of both Lebanon and the neighboring Arab countries were represented in Borj Hammoud. About 40 percent of the population were Lebanese Shi'a. Forty percent were Armenian Orthodox, Armenian Catholic, or Armenian Protestant. The remaining 20 percent were Maronite, Roman Catholic, Greek Orthodox, Greek Catholic, Arab Protestant, Syrian Orthodox, Syrian Catholic, Sunni, Druze, 'Alawite.[56] The population included Lebanese, Syrians, Palestinians, Greeks, Jordanians, and Egyptians.

My fieldwork in the Camp Trad neighborhood of Borj Hammoud just before the outbreak of the civil war in 1975 captured a unique moment in modern Lebanese history. It was a period of change, escalating tensions, and potentials.[57] Camp Trad experienced an unprecedented high degree of heterogeneous relationships among peoples of different religious sects, ethnic groups, and nationalities. Its residents, primarily Arab, included members of all of the communities mentioned above. Many shared patterns of family life developed across religious, ethnic, and national lines.[58]

Most of the families in Camp Trad were recent migrants to the area.[59] A Lebanese Maronite agricultural area at the turn of the twentieth century, the neighborhood became gradually urbanized, particularly in the 1940s with the influx of Armenian refugees. Palestinians entered the area after the creation of Israel in 1948. Syrians and rural Lebanese began settling in the 1950s for economic opportunities or to escape political insecurities. In the early 1970s few household heads had been born in Camp Trad or Borj Hammoud. Almost all the residents had come from rural backgrounds where extended families ties remained vital. Some, like the Palestinians and Armenians, were cut off from their places of origin, whereas others, like the Lebanese, Syrians, Jordanians, and Egyptians, had access to natal family and village ties. A number of the residents had managed to reconstitute parts of their extended families within Camp Trad and Borj Hammoud. Sociologically, there were many household forms: nuclear families, joint, extended, duo-focal, single parent, single individual. Yet, culturally, Arab family ideals of patrilineality, patriarchy, and patrilocality were relatively strong for most residents.

In the early 1970s, when I began fieldwork, Lebanon was in the midst of economic, political, and social crisises. Banking, trade, and tourism were being undermined by the Arab-Israeli conflict fought on Lebanese soil. Inflation, unemployment and underemployment, and worker strikes fueled the sense of economic crisis. Rapid urbanization had left the infrastructure of Greater Beirut ill equipped to respond to the mass demand for basic services. A "ring of poverty" circled Beirut.

The Lebanese state system was being challenged from within and without. Lebanon had become the primary site for attacks by Israel against the Palestinians and vice versa. Political minorities, such as the Shiʿa, were organizing to demand equitable representation in government. Bribery and brokerage became necessary for most political transactions.[60] Stalemated, the minimalist Lebanese state could not provide the services and protection citizens wanted.[61]

In this economic, political, and social pressure cooker, individuals were thrown onto their families for help finding jobs, financial assistance, political protection, and emotional support.[62] Family had always been central to social, economic, and political life in Lebanon. Ruling elites recruited followings and distributed services to their clienteles on the basis of kinship.[63] Non-elite individuals relied on their families for brokerage and protection in a state that was perceived as untrustworthy and inefficient.[64] Although it was not new for individuals to rely on their families, such dependence was precarious because the same pressures were limiting the avenues through which family members lived out their obligations. So although individuals needed, turned to, and believed in their families as the repositories of their identities and securities, family members found it increasingly difficult to carry out familial obligations.

The conditions of the early 1970s in urban Lebanon, therefore, in many ways were undermining the foundations of patriarchy. It was a struggle for brothers and sisters to live out the roles and responsibilities for which they were socialized. Under these pressures, it is remarkable that brother-sister relationships remained powerful. It is only by linking psychodynamic, social structural, and cultural processes that one can understand the ongoing struggle to live out brother-sister relationships even under conditions that were undermining the family system that gave them meaning.

Psychodynamics of Connectivity

Connectivity as Love

In Camp Trad, connectivity was taken to be an expression of love. Brothers and sisters were taught to bond with each other and to see themselves mirrored in each other. Brothers saw their identities and sense of self wrapped up with their sisters' attributes and behavior. Sisters saw their dignity and security tied to their brothers' character and fortunes. Brothers and sisters were expected to love and look out for each other through adulthood.[65] Parents and other relatives encouraged brothers and sisters to idealize and romanticize each other. They supported their using each other as standards for judging potential spouses. I had a sense that something precious was undermined by the marriage of either.[66] Um Hanna's (above) concern that Flaur's husband was not as handsome as Flaur's brother was, in cultural terms, an acceptable criticism of Flaur's husband. Idealization of the brothers and sisters was expressed through sayings that children learned. *"Al-ikt hanuni"* (the sister is sympathetic) was a frequently repeated saying in Camp Trad. Sisters referred to their brothers as *"akh al-hanun," "al-'atuf," "al-'aziz," "al-habib,"* and *"al-ghali,"* (the brother is sympathetic, sensitive, dear, beloved, and priceless). The idealization of cross-siblings continued after marriage. Brothers and sisters named their children after each other at times. Nimr Zahr, a seventy-three-year old Lebanese Shi'i from Kfar Dunin in Southern Lebanon, had had a sister who died when she was about twenty. Five years later, when he had his own firstborn child, a girl, he named her after the deceased sister. His second son was named after his wife's brother.

Sonia Fraij was a thirty-five-year-old Lebanese Maronite married to a thirty-six-year-old Greek Orthodox bus driver's aide. Two of her brothers lived next door to her. She had named her oldest son after the younger of these two brothers and her youngest son after her youngest brother, who was living in Australia. A strong-willed and outspoken woman, she continually praised her brothers, described them lovingly, and compared them favorably to her husband. In interviews she subtly, in his presence, put her husband down in relation to her brothers. The older brother traveled frequently. The younger, John, a strikingly handsome twenty-six-year-old, was a chronically unemployed construction worker. Sonia had a loving relationship with John. As his apartment was right across the hall from hers, he spent much of his leisure time with her in one of their apartments. John spoke in the most affectionate terms of Sonia, gazed on her lovingly, and seemed to hang on her words. The expressions of devotion were among the most pronounced in the neighborhood. They were together all the time. She both served him and took charge of his life in some ways. She cooked for him, washed his clothes, went shopping with him, received her house visitors with him, and at times took him with her when she paid some of her formal calls. In some ways, John acted as a husband in the absence of her husband, who worked long hours. Having a brother nearby whom she loved, served, and to some degree managed, and who also protected her, empowered her.

A number of neighborhood women seemed to compare their husbands to their brothers. Yasmin Unis, a forty-seven-year-old Lebanese Shi'i, married for love, yet said her brothers *"bi nawru hiyyati"* (light up my life). Her sense of identity came from her natal family. She and her children referred to her brothers repeatedly when speaking of themselves. Her marriage was relatively stable, yet she spoke of her husband as *maskin* (poor, humble), a mixed compliment and criticism.

I found this idealization/romanticization of brother-sister relationships in other social classes in Lebanon, particularly the Beirut middle classes. Among the families I observed, married and unmarried brothers and sisters talked of each other affectionately. Middle-class brothers and sisters went together to parties, movies, theaters, and other social occasions. They danced together, escorted each other in cohort group events, traveled together, and often walked arm in arm in the streets. Brothers, by accompanying their sisters, might have been giving them access to activities they might not have had otherwise. In playing the dual role of sister's protector and partner, they contributed to the romanticization of the relationship.

Unmarried women often devoted themselves to their brothers and their brothers' children. Unmarried men often relied on their sisters to provide emotional support and household service. Unmarried adults usually lived with their natal families, so unmarried brothers and sisters often became each other's primary caretakers.[67] In one case, a married Maronite woman with no children had raised her brother's two children while he was working in West Africa with his wife. The children called their aunt "Mama" and her husband, "Baba" (father).

Although there is little research on sexuality in brother-sister relationships in Arab societies, my own fieldwork indicates that the brother-sister relationship was sexually charged.[68] Boys and girls in Camp Trad practiced sexual presentation with each other in socially approved ways. They seemed to groom themselves as much, if not more, for each other as for other opposite-gender individuals. Brothers paid attention to and commented on sisters' clothing, hair styling, and makeup. Sisters sought their brothers' approval for their self-presentations and offered their own evaluations of their brothers' presentation. Brothers defined their sexuality in part by asserting control over and lavishing attention on sisters. Sisters defined their sexuality in part by acceding to their brothers and/or by affording resistance.

Among a number of middle-class Beiruti families, also, I noticed that brothers and sisters were very involved in each other's attire and comportment. Brothers in these families often participated in purchasing their sisters' wardrobes. Sisters, although not having similar control over the brothers, often, nevertheless, significantly influenced their style by their evaluations.

On festive occasions, when Camp Trad young people dressed up and could engage in sexual play-acting, brothers and sisters seemed particularly involved with each other. Few families had much in the way of fancy attire. Going to church on Sunday or the mosque on Fridays, visiting neighbors and family on Christian and Muslim holidays, and attending weddings and funerals were among the few occasions during which Camp Trad youth could parade themselves. On these occasions brothers and sisters often escorted each other or went in the company of their families. On such occasions they usually spent more time in the company of each other than with nonfamily individuals. Brothers and sisters, besides the rest of the family, were on display to each other and seemed to take great interest in the opportunity for expression that such occasions provided.

I noticed in other parts of Beirut and surrounding suburbs that festive occasions were similarly occasions for constructing sexualities. Here, too, brothers and sisters seemed to use each other for role playing. For example, in family gatherings brothers and sisters danced with each other from a young age. On one occasion I observed two preadolescent middle-class siblings (children of a Syrian Christian mother and an Italian father) dancing together in their home in a suburb of Beirut during a festive gathering. The boy was advancing toward his younger sister. With roars of approval and great laughter the men and the women in the room (all Arab, except the father) shouted, *"bi hajim, bi hajim"* (he attacks, he attacks). The little boy, appearing somewhat confused, accelerated the behavior. The little girl, seemingly as confused, was ignored and continued dancing. Such occasions were prime times for learning culturally appropriate sexual behavior.

The romanticization/sexualization of the brother-sister relationship appeared to have had concrete expression at times. There was one half-sibling marriage reported by Camp Trad informants.[69] Sa'da Hamid was a fifty-five-year-old Lebanese Shi'i from Bint Jbeil in Southern Lebanon. Both her parents had been married twice. She reported a marriage between her sister by her mother and her full brother, that is, the couple shared a mother, but had different fathers. In 1972 Sa'da's brother, eighty-two, and his wife/half-sister, seventy-eight, were living in their village of birth.[70] In a more ambiguous case, Yasmin Unis, a Lebanese Shi'i, reported a marriage between her step-siblings, who did not share a parent.

Connectivity as Power

Romanticization and sexualization differentiated the brother-sister relationship from other familial cross-gender relationships. The relationship was differentiated, also, in terms of its role in gender socialization. Training for relationships of power organized around gender: brothers and sisters were used in the family system and used each other to learn culturally appropriate hierarchal masculine and feminine roles and identities. Additionally, young males emerging into their manhood might compete with their fathers for control over the family, using relationships with their sisters as a base of power—at times with the cooperation of their sisters and mothers.

Brothers and sisters learned early that love and power were parts of the same dynamic. Love meant acceptance of the power asymmetry and culturally approved assertions of the asymmetry were taken as expressions of love. Parents taught daughters that loving their brothers included serving them and taught brothers that loving their sisters included some control over them. Families may have preferred brothers to fathers as sisters' protectors because their secondary positions relative to fathers would burden them with less responsibility should violence occur.[71] Little girls practiced modesty, seductiveness, and serving authoritative males with their brothers, thereby learning how to be feminine. Brothers practiced sexual assertion, receiving feminine nurturances, and protecting and take charge of the life and sexuality of females. Although connective love/power dynamics were enacted in parent-child and other family relationships, the mutual gender socialization distinguished the brother-sister relationships.[72]

Young men also distinguished themselves from their fathers in relation to sisters by being physically present in the house. Fathers were often absent, working long hours six days a week. Brothers usually did not work if they were still in school and spent much of their nonschool time at home. When they did work, they often spent more time at home or around the neighborhood than did their fathers. Married brothers could play their cultural roles toward their sisters more effectively if they lived in proximity to their sisters. A remarkable number of Camp Trad adults indicated that they did have siblings in other parts of Borj Hammoud or neighboring districts. Those whose cross-siblings lived further away still expressed similar attitudes toward their siblings.

For young males living with their families, adolescence was the period to shape their manhood. Taking charge of the lives of their sisters and, at times, those of their mothers and younger brothers, was an avenue of empowerment for some males. Mothers often deferred to their older sons' control over younger children.[73] Some fathers deferred to their sons, whereas others resisted. The degree of power the brothers took, then, was affected by how much power the father asserted. The more controlling the fathers, the less power the brothers could assert. In the case of the Dawuds, a Palestinian Catholic family (discussed below), the eldest son exerted considerable authority, including defying his parents to help his sister marry the man she loved. In the case of the Rafik family, Abu Mufid,[74] a Syrian Sunni, exerted patriarchal control to such a degree that the oldest son could assert little.

Differences in the brother's view and the sister's view of their relationship or in their reading their own and each other's needs could create spaces for resistance.[75] Yet when resistance occurred, the challenge most often was not to the basic premises (love/power) of the brother-sister relationship. Rather, it usually centered on whether the sibling was acting on those premises properly, or it was understood as miscommunication or was explained away as flukes of character. Flaur's persistence in her behavior, despite Hanna's response, might be seen as resistance, except for the fact that she did not challenge his right to have authority over her or that he loved her and that she loved him. Instead, she and her family brushed it off as the consequence of her feistiness.

Structure of Family, Marriage, and Inheritance

Family and Marriage

Some of my informants stated a preference for non-kin marriage. The cultural norm of marriage between relatives, however, was still valued as an ideal by most of my Muslim informants.[76] Although expressed as an ideal less frequently by Christians, endogamy was nevertheless practiced among them as well. Saʿda Hamid, the Lebanese Shiʿi whose brother and half-sister had married (above), was herself married to her father's brother's son. Five of her seven married children were married to relatives, including two sons who had married two sisters. Two other sons had not married relatives, but their wives were related to each other. All but one of her children lived in Borj Hammoud and were very involved in each other's lives. Four of Saʿda's siblings had married relatives and two of them (a brother and sister) lived in Camp Trad.

Brothers and sisters were involved also with each other's children. The father's brother (ʿam) was viewed as a formal authority often feared second only to the father, but the khal, (maternal uncle) was seen to be affectionate, loving, warm, and playful. He could become a substitute father in the absence of the father. The khal could also shelter the sister's children from their father. In one incident a young Camp Trad Maronite man had a heated dispute with his father after which the son took refuge in the home of his khal. The children of the khal, both sons and daughters, were also sources of emotional support and compassion, at times in contrast to the children of the father's siblings. In the cultural ideal a similar relationship was expressed with the mother's sister (*khalta*) and her children. The sister as the ʿamta (paternal aunt) was expected to be affectionate to her brother's children. A common saying in Camp Trad depicted this relationship: *"ya ʿamti ya ikt bayyi hamm min ummi ʿaliyyi"* (my aunt, my father's sister, worries for me more than my mother). At the same time, as a member of the patriline, the ʿamta also occupied a position of authority vis-à-vis her brother's children. Hanan, a Lebanese Shiʿi, lived two stories below her brother's daughter, Dalal. Visiting each other daily, more than they each visited anyone else, Hanan helped Dalal by watching the three children (the oldest of which was four), shopping for her, and cooking with her.

Inheritance

Inheritance and property issues impacted the brother-sister and the husband–brother-in-law relationship.[77] Women often did not take their inheritances from their natal families. Leaving their inheritance with their brothers could offer them insurance should they need protection from their families of origin.[78] A woman's attitude toward inheritance could change as she and her family of procreation matured. She might want the inheritance to help support her children. As her sons grew older, she might rely more on them than on her brothers.[79] Husbands and brothers could compete over a woman's inheritance.[80]

Najat, a thirty-two-year-old Lebanese Sunni married to a forty-one-year-old Lebanese Sunni (son of a Tunisian Sunni), had three brothers between twenty-six and thirty-six years old. Najat's siblings (married, divorced, and single) all lived with their mother in nearby Sin il Fil except for a married sister in Aley. Her father had died earlier in 1972, shortly before my interview. Najat claimed that she had refused to take any inheritance from her father's property. She had left it with her brothers. As she said, "My brothers' and mine are the same. It will always be there for me."

Family Culture: Honor and Shame

Ideally, brothers continued to be responsible for their sisters' behavior and welfare throughout their lives, even after marriage[81] although the practice was often contradictory in the 1970s. Should a woman commit a shameful act or be compromised in any way her brothers shared responsibility with her father in disciplining or avenging her.[82] The range and limits of brotherly responsibility for protecting and controlling adult sisters can be seen in the following example. The whole neighborhood street became involved in this dramatic enactment of the brothers' roles as protectors of their sisters' and families' honor. The key actors included the Dawuds, a Palestinian Catholic family, Amira Antun, a recently widowed Lebanese Chaldean Catholic of Syrian origins, Amira's son Edward and brother Francis; Abu Mufid, a Syrian Sunni discussed above; and Abu Mufid's brother's son, Adnan.

The Dawuds were a close family. The parents and sisters were bonded in devout admiration of their sons/brothers. They saw the sons/brothers, especially the oldest, Antoine, as heroes (*abtal*).[83] The parents and sisters outdid each other in superlatives describing Antoine. They emphasized his strength and courage. Active in the Fateh wing of the Palestine Liberation Organization, Antoine was frequently armed, which no doubt added to the family's sense of his fearsomeness.

Antoine had helped his sister Antoinette elope against their parent's opposition. Antoine was 19 when Antoinette, 18, decided she wanted to marry their mother's father's sister's son. Their parents opposed the marriage because Fadi was poor. Antoine was interested in marrying Fadi's sister. Overriding his parents, Antoine had helped his sister elope with the intention that Fadi would then help arrange Antoine's marriage to his sister. Later, Antoine decided that Fadi's sister was too demanding and did not marry her. Antoinette's marriage was still intact, however. Antoine and Antoinette had a close relationship, and she continued to think of him as her protector.[94]

Antoine and his brothers appeared to derive pleasure and personal pride from the beauty and comportment of their sisters. The sisters also felt their security and dignity were linked to their brother's involvement with them. The Dawud sisters boasted continually about their brothers. Twenty-one-year-old Therese often said that if she could only find a man like her brothers, she would marry instantly.

In the spring of 1973 Adnan, a young Sunni, had his eyes on an unidentified young woman living on the street. Neighbors thought it was Therese. In a manner considered inappropriate, Adnan drove repeatedly in front of her house. He sped his car screeching through the street. Given the narrow streets and the fact that small children usually played outside unsupervised, neighbors complained. Adding to this concern was the fact that although intermarriages did occur in the neighborhood, they were usually arranged in a more discrete manner. It was a breach of etiquette for courting to take place in this manner, particularly given the intersectarian character of the relationship. Therese's brothers (Antoine, twenty-four, Jacque, nineteen, and Michel, fourteen) discussed the matter with several male friends living on the street, including Edward Antun (the twenty-year-old son of Amira Antun), Rafik Abdullah (the eighteen-year-old son of a Maronite woman divorced from her Shi'i husband), and Hanna and Farid Yusif (Hanna's seventeen-year-old brother). They decided to stop Adnan.

One afternoon late in March, Adnan sped through the street several times. Michel Dawud and Edward Antun were at home. During his next pass, they stopped his car and told him they did not want him to drive through the street because there were children playing. Adnan had a friend with him. He replied that he was free to come and go as he wished and, furthermore, that they were not to speak with him but could speak with his friend. The friend had a long knife and made "teasing" or "threatening" looks at the young men. Michel Dawud became irritated and hit Adnan's friend in the face. Adnan sped away.

The commotion attracted the attention of a number of residents. Rafik Abdullah was home ill but came down to the street in his pajamas. Farid Yusif was coming down the stairs from his apartment and went to join his friends. Abu Antoine (Therese and Michel's father) had overheard the conversation and had come to try to make peace. ʿAdil and Zaynab, close Shiʿa friends of Amira Antun (Edward's mother), stepped out as well. Within a few minutes, more than fifty people had gathered in the street, and many stood on their balconies or rooftops watching.

Adnan, in the meantime, had collected his friends and relatives from the predominately Shiʿi neighborhood of Nabʿa. They returned to the street in two cars. At an apparently prearranged whistle, the two cars drove through the narrow street at top speed, aiming right at the crowd. Most of the people jumped out of the way, but Edward Antun was slightly injured. A car parked at the end of the street blocked Adnan's escape. Neighbors began beating the cars and breaking the windows. Within a few minutes, though, the two cars sped away.

It was early evening by this time, and I heard the commotion at my end of the street. I had been helping Um Hanna who was ill. I went down the street to find members of nearly every household talking excitedly. Um Antoine was arguing with Zaynab. Um Antoine shrieked, "This is the fault of the Muslims. The Muslims are coming to get us!" Zaynab, a Shiʿi, shouted, "Don't make this sectarian!" Hanna Yusif told me that his brother Farid had noticed that one of the two cars had been that of Mufid (the son of the Syrian Sunni, Abu Mufid) and that he thought he had seen Mufid with them, but he could not be sure.

Edward Antun was rushed to the hospital by ʿAdil, Zaynab's husband and Amira Antun's good friend. Amira became hysterical, tearing at her clothes and screaming uncontrollably. Amira was a forty-one-year-old mother of ten children ranging in age from five to twenty-two. Her husband had died in 1971 just as I was beginning my fieldwork. She had six sons (her four oldest children were all male), including a married son, but she turned to her second oldest brother, Francis, as a father-substitute for her children. Francis, thirty-four, married with no children, owned a pinball arcade two short blocks away from Amira's apartment.

When Edward was injured, Amira's neighbors gathered around her, particularly her good friends, Zaynab[85] and ʿAdil. Amira had excellent friends in the neighborhood; however, the primacy of the brother was apparent. Francis was informed of the incident and came quickly. When he arrived on the street, the crowds parted to let him through. I vividly remember the hushed silence as he approached his sister and embraced her. There was a stirring sense among the neighbors that Amira was now in the care of the most honorable of protectors—her brother. The silence among the neighbors added to the drama and the authoritative voice with which he spoke. He turned to the people and demanded to know what had happened to his nephew. As her brother stood there next to her, there seemed to be a feeling that now justice would be done.

Abu Antoine sent for his son, Antoine. The tension noticeably increased as Antoine arrived almost immediately with a motorcade of armed Palestinian guerrillas dressed in civilian clothes. The neighbors now felt bold and invincible. The presence of Therease's brother Antoine, backed by the Palestinian guerrillas, and Amira's brother Francis, along with nearly all the men of the neighborhood, enhanced the incredible sense of neighborhood solidarity.[86]

The crowd gathered around to tell the story of the incident. Some of the young men of the neighborhood had run after the car. Later, a couple of the culprits were found in a shop near Francis's pin-ball machine store. Francis was among the neighborhood men who found them. They beat the culprits and called the police. The families of the Shi'a young men were mistakenly told that one of their sons had been killed. Several cars from the Shi'i neighborhood of Nab'a, filled with men and guns, came immediately to Camp Trad. The Nab'a families arrived just as the police pulled in, so they drove away. The one person who was still in custody was taken to the police station. Within minutes, a phone call came from a *za'im* (political leader), and he was released.

Adnan's paternal uncle (FaBr), Abu Mufid, deflated the conflict. He lived on the same street as the Dawuds and was highly respected. Abu Mufid told me that he thought his nephew was a bit wild and he would rather not have gotten involved. He felt he had no choice but to intervene for the sake of neighborly good will and to protect his own name. Arranging a meeting between Adnan and the Dawuds and Antuns, Abu Mufid forced his nephew to apologize.

The incident provoked a neighborhood crisis. Across religious, ethnic, and national lines, neighborhood people supported the brothers' actions. It was uniformly discussed in terms of the brothers protecting the honor of their sisters and families. Men and women seemed to agree that the incident was primarily about honor, not religion. Therese and her parents extravagantly praised Michel and Antoine while Amira heaped praise on her son Edward and brother Francis. The men were described as abtal (heroes). The neighborhood men, in general, appeared to take great pride in their manly display of solidarity. And the women glowed in admiration of the men. In the immediate days after the incident, there was a noticeable swagger in the walk of the men directly involved. Displays of boasting by both men and women created a sense of possession: they owned this street. Brothers had protected their sisters and men had protected their women—the ultimate social boundary of the community. The community was reminded of the importance sisters had in their brothers' lives. For all the participants the incident reinforced the cultural belief that brothers were the foundation of sisters' security. The culture had been supremely upheld in a most honorable manner.

Arab Brothers and Sisters: Connectivity, Love, and Power in the Reproduction of Patriarchy

Granqvist[87] reports a story about brother-sister relations cited among Palestinian fellahin. She indicates that fellahin women, given a choice as to whom they would prefer to free from military service (which was equated with death), would choose to free their brothers rather than their husbands or sons.[88] The reasoning reported was: "A husband may [always] be had; a son can [also] be born; but a beloved brother, from where shall he come back [when he is once dead]?"[89] This is a story about brother-sister love for Granqvist.[90] But it is also about the centrality of the brother-sister relationship to the reproduction of patrilineality and patriarchy. Arab sisters, committed to preserving their patrilineages, invested in their brothers, for it was only through their brothers that they ensured the continuity of their patrilines and security.[91]

In Camp Trad the brother-sister relationship was central to the reproduction of patriarchy. It contributed to socializing young males and females into appropriate gender roles. Young females learned feminine roles by submitting to brothers. Young males learned to be patriarchs by practicing first on their sisters and younger brothers. Brothers could also use their relationships with their sisters to contest their fathers' authority and attempt to build a sphere of influence from which they would mature as patriarchs.

The sister paid a price for the protection of the brother. She served the brother, to some degree shaped herself into his image, at times put her brother before her husband. Sisters had some power in this relationship because their conduct directly affected their brothers' and families' standing. The tensions around the issues of honor, protection, and control at times led to violence.

At the same time, the brother-sister relationship was one of love. Brothers and sisters reported deep caring and concern for each other. They were expected by others and expected themselves to protect and nurture each other for all their lives. Brother-sister love was romanticized. Their masculinity and femininity were defined and practiced in a connective relationship that was often sexually charged.

Complexity is missing in much of the literature. As my analysis suggests, the brother-sister relationship was a connective relationship built on the duality of love and power expressed psychodynamically, social structurally, and culturally. It was second only to the mother son relation in evoking love, and yet it was premised on a power asymmetry—the subordination of the sister to the brother. The intense involvement of brothers and sisters in each other's lives invested each in their natal family and its reproduction. Life-long connectivity organized around love and power gave the brother-sister relationship a forceful role in the reproduction of Arab patriarchy. By the early 1970s, Camp Trad brothers and sisters were living with external stresses that made achievement of cultural prescriptions concerning their relationships more difficult. The instability of family life; the economic, political, and social uncertainty; and the limitations of the Lebanese state in providing services and protections thrust people onto their families for support at a time when it was increasingly difficult for family members to help each other. It is striking that, under these conditions, men and women, nevertheless, still made the effort to embrace their cross-siblings and the patriarchy and patrilineality their siblingship supported.

Wives or Daughters

Structural Differences Between Urban
and Bedouin Lebanese Co-wives

NAJLA S. HAMADEH

Polygyny has ancient roots in Arab society, having existed alongside monogamy and other types of marriage since pre-Islamic times.[1] Because polygyny is still permissible in contemporary Islamic communities of the Arab World, many Muslim Arab women have to deal with the possibility, if not the actuality, of having to cope with a co-wife (or co-wives)[2] despite the fact that nowadays households that include more than one wife for a husband are far from the prevalent norm.[3] Analysis of the women's ways of coping when they do find themselves in such a situation may yield significant insights concerning the vulnerabilities or strengths in the women's psychosocial baggage. A comparative study of the variation of such relationships between communities with different social norms enables an assessment of the impact of each type of society on the construct of the selves of women and on the efficacy of the type of subjectivity exhibited by these selves.

In Arabic the co-wife is referred to as *al-durrah,* "the one who harms." The popular saying is *"al-durrah murrah"* (the co-wife is a bitter taste). Both usages suggest that popular opinion expects the relationship between co-wives to be one of resentment and antagonism. Moreover, most writers about polygyny record mainly the discord between co-wives and

I am grateful to Jean Makdisi, Suad Joseph, Huda Zureik, Tarif Khalidi, and Basim Mussallam for their insightful suggestions and their editorial comments.

141

the misery that a woman experiences as she finds herself obliged to share her husband with another, and sometimes with more than one, woman.[4]

I was enticed to study the relationship between co-wives by the discrepancy between the way such relationships are depicted in popular attitudes and in the vast majority of literature and what I have sometimes observed. I have sometimes witnessed in my patrilocality, in the Bekaa' valley, co-wives who maintain friendly, and occasionally affectionate, relationships with one another. One can surmise that popular sayings and stories neglect friendly relations between co-wives because it is the unfriendly ones that are colorful, problematic, and good material for rich plots. Because popular wisdom tends to promote the moral and the beneficent, it is understandable that it tends to portray the perils of polygyny to deter people from practicing it. Moreover, the neglect in books and studies of friendly relations among co-wives results from the fact that urban life receives the most interest and is more easily accessed by writers, and such friendly relations, as confirmed by the current study, are rarely found in urban society.

I briefly describe my fieldwork and recount my findings, giving a detailed account of three cases that represent a variety of the most typical findings. I then analyze what the gathered data and the described case studies reveal concerning structural differences in the self-constructs of urban and Bedouin Lebanese women and their relevance to a study of Arab women or to the specificity of women's self-constructs in general.

I aim at objectivity, as much as possible. But I do not pretend that my affiliation and background do not influence my point of view, at least where aesthetic preference and sympathy are involved. To a certain extent, because most writers come from urban backgrounds, my nonurban 'bias' maybe an asset insofar as it presents the other side of the picture and thus may ultimately lead to a more complete portrayal.

The Field Study

The area I come from in the Bekaa' valley is frequented during the summer season by Bedouin tribes who spend the rest of the year in the Syrian Desert. A considerable proportion of the sedentary population of the area are of Bedouin origin. The latter call themselves asha'ir[5] and take pride in their Arab (Bedouin) ancestry.[6] They are careful to preserve many of their Bedouin traditions and values although their houses and their economic means of survival and some other aspects of their practical lives, such as electricity, television, and motorized transportation, are akin to those of other peasants in the area.[7] Because my study is concerned primarily with psychological variations influenced by social traditions, I consider the nomads and sedentary *asha'ir* as one group, referring to them as Bedouin. These peoples I compare to a sample of urban co-wives that I interviewed in Lebanese cities. Limited by time and scope and the specific aims of the present study, I exclude the peasants of the Bekaa' who are not considered to be descendants of known Bedouin tribes. The peasants are considered to be of "inferior" lineage, and their social norms and values differ from those of the Bedouins.

Aside from the data gathered by the field study, my analysis draws from earlier observations. I live simultaneously in two types of environment. I was born and have lived most of my life in the city of Beirut; at the same time, I have always had access to the Bedouin and peasant-Bedouin communities in my patrilocality in the Bekaa' valley where I have frequently visited and sometimes spent summer holidays. This situation gave me the opportunity to witness relationships between urban, as well as Bedouin, co-wives.

I began conducting my survey of Bedouin co-wives in the summer of 1992 and continued the fieldwork in the summer of 1993. For that purpose I spent most of these two summers in the Bekaa' valley. During the interval between the two summers and in the winter of 1995, I interviewed a number of urban co-wives in the cities of Beirut and Tripoli and in the town of Baalbeck. My research covered eighty-five women, each of whose husbands had either one or two other wives. Twenty-eight of these were Bedouin, thirty-five were sedentary of Bedouin origin, and twenty-two were urban. The main reason for the restricted number of subjects was the scarcity of polygynous households, especially in the cities.

One of the case-studies I include comes from outside the survey. It is an account of the relationship between my late paternal grandmother and her co-wife, also deceased. I include this case because it coincides with several characteristics of some relationships between Bedouin co-wives and because this case provides, within the scope of my experience, a unique example of polygyny in a higher social class. My account is based on direct observation that predates this study by many years and on what was recounted to me, recently, by people who had lived in my grandfather's house.

Each co-wife covered by the survey was interviewed alone, often several times.[8] Sometimes, I also talked to the husbands or other family members. During the fieldwork, some husbands insisted that I include their points of view. One urban husband of three young wives told me:

"Why do you talk to them?" indicating his wives. He added: "They will only tell you lies. If you want the truth, you can only get it from me." This husband, and other husbands, seemed to want to talk to vindicate a condition that caused them a measure of shame or, perhaps, of guilt. Several, like the afore-mentioned husband of three, seemed to feel a mixture of pride and shame about their multiple marriages. The shame or guilt is understandable: polygyny is infrequent, and the Kor'an discourages polygyny even in the very verses that permit it.[9]

I interviewed forty-one first wives and forty-four second or third wives. Approximately one-third of the women lived in the same household with their co-wives. When asked how they felt about their co-wife (or co-wives), 26 percent said that they loved and/or had friendly feelings toward her (or them), 14 percent said that they had neutral feelings, and 59 percent said that they hated, were jealous of, or felt both hatred and jealousy toward their co-wife (or co-wives). Those who claimed to have friendly or neutral feelings toward their co-wives were mostly Bedouin (51 percent of the Bedouins and 5 percent of the urban). As might be expected, second or third wives seemed to be more kindly disposed toward their co-wives than were first wives. One significant finding was that the first wife tended to feel less hatred for, and/or jealousy of, the subsequent wife (or wives) when she believed that her husband took another wife for reasons other than love.[10] When the husband married again in order to have offspring or because his first wife had borne only daughters or because his counterpart in an exchange-marriage (*muqayada*)[11] took another wife, the wife took more kindly to the new wife. Even when she believed that the husband married another woman because of an excessive sexual drive, she tolerated the co-wife much better than when she thought that love propelled him toward the new marriage.

To illustrate the types of relations that exist among the co-wives, I portray three sets: urban, nomadic Bedouin, and sedentary rural of Bedouin origin. In line with the collected data, the chosen illustrations depict antagonistic relations between urban co-wives and neutral to friendly relations between Bedouin co-wives. The three portraits are drawn from a middle-class, a lower-class, and an upper-class set of co-wives, respectively.

Wadad and Lama (Urban Co-wives Living in Beirut)

Wadad is the only daughter among five brothers of a well-to-do textile merchant. She finished high school and oscillated for a few years between helping her father and brothers in the shop and idling around, waiting for an appropriate husband. She was physically unattractive but probably had expected that her father's wealth and social position would help her procure a husband. At twenty-five, she married Mounir, a self-made man who had recently earned a Ph.D. Soon after their marriage, he was appointed to teach at a university. The marriage produced three children. When I met her, Wadad was in her late forties.

Lama, the co-wife of Wadad, was fifteen years younger than she. She was a tall, black-eyed beauty, who had grown up fatherless. Her mother had worked as a housekeeper to support her and her one sister and two brothers. The mother had instilled in her children the value of education as their only means to rise from the state of squalid poverty they were reared in to a more comfortable and respectable station. Lama and her siblings, who seemed to have been endowed with high levels of intelligence and vitality, had fulfilled their mother's dreams by acquiring university educations. As a student at the Lebanese University, Lama had taken courses taught by Mounir. She had found herself drawn to discuss with him some of her emotional and financial problems. Eventually, a love relationship had developed between them, which had led to their marriage. Soon after their marriage, Mounir installed Lama in a separate house, and weeks later, he broke the news of his new marriage to Wadad.

Lama believed that Mounir kept his first wife because he hoped to benefit from what she would eventually inherit. She also believed that her husband did not appreciate her enough because of her poverty. She tried to get around her co-wife's advantage and her own weak position by becoming economically productive. Thus, she worked as a teacher and later as a school administrator. She did not seem, however, to be motivated as a careerwoman. She spoke of her job as a burden added to the load of housework. For the latter she expressed unalloyed loathing. She also did not exhibit much interest in her job. When I attempted to discuss with her conditions, or methods, of education, she showed little enthusiasm. The only ideas she expressed that were in harmony with what she was doing were socialist views that criticized idleness and emphasized the practical and moral necessity that each able person join the work force.

I visited the two households. The ways each of the two women dressed and decorated her home were noticeably informative about her view of herself and her mode of relating to life. Wadad's house gave the impression of a poorly organized antique shop. In the small apartment, in a fairly respectable neighborhood, the imitation Louis XV armchairs looked out of place. On shelves and on tables stood several silver frames containing family photographs and many other silver ornaments. Several hand-stitched *aubusson* (embroidery on canvas) pieces, portraying little girls and wild animals, were displayed on the walls. She insisted on treating me to juice, cookies, nuts, coffee, and chocolate every time I visited her. The cups she served coffee in were gold-rimmed with an elaborate design. She had dyed her hair an unbecoming yellowish blond and was once wearing what appeared to be an expensive designer dress, a size or two too tight for her.

Lama's apartment was in a newer building in a modest and populous neighborhood. The furniture in the living room included formica tables and other cheap, practical items. The overall impression was that of a temporary residence. The colors were dark. Tin pots containing wilted plants stood on the window sill and on tables in the living room. It was probably the impact of Lama's story that made me see that everything looked sad and longing to be elsewhere. Lama was dressed in the extremely plain "Islamic costume," which has recently become popular among women of some pious Muslim groups. The costume consisted of a shapeless gray suit and a white scarf that enveloped the head and covered part of the forehead.

Wadad related to me that when her husband told her of his new marriage, she felt as though the walls of her house were closing in on her. She fell to the floor and for three days refused to get up or to eat. (She must have been exaggerating.) When her husband attempted to reason with her, she drove him out of the house with her hysterical shouting. Later, she thought that if she allowed her grief to overwhelm her, she would die, and that would please the couple whose happiness was being built on her ruin. She thought that her death would hurt only her children. From then on, she decided to do whatever she could to hurt Mounir and Lama while fighting to keep Mounir as father for her children. Thus, when he proposed to divide his time equally between the two households, she accepted. She even accepted resuming sexual relations with him "although I hated him like the devil. But I wanted to do anything that would spite her," Wadad said.

At one point during the Lebanese civil war (1975–91), Lama's house was destroyed; thereupon, she moved into Wadad's house. Wadad had asked her eldest brother to demand of Mounir that he not infringe on her legal right to have a separate house. The brother had said that he would talk to him, but never did. She could not take the matter to court because the war had suspended judiciary action and because the house was registered in Mounir's name. Wadad described the ensuing period as "hell." She confessed, "When the two of them stayed in their room, with the door closed, I felt I was losing my sanity." She said that Lama kept teasing her and invading all her space. She added: "She kept peering into my closets and criticizing my clothes. She made fun of my style in setting the table, saying that I wasted all my time doing elaborate things that are totally useless." To illustrate the difference between her manners and those of her belligerent co-wife, she added, "When one day I bought a rag doll for Lama's little girl, Lama snatched the doll from the girl and tore it to pieces."

In 1984, during a round of fighting, a piece of shrapnel entered through the living-room window and hit Lama's five-year-old daughter in the head. The child was reduced to a vegetablelike state, and there was no hope her condition would improve. "After the injury to her daughter," continued Wadad about Lama, "she was transformed. She quit her coquettish ways, started praying five times a day, and tried to be civil to me and to my children. But sometimes I feel that it was better the other way. When she visits me with my husband, I feel awkward and humiliated. When somebody refers to her as 'Mrs. Mounir,' I feel that she is erasing my very existence."

When I talked to Lama, she sounded like one who considered her life shattered. She shed many tears as she recounted her story. She explained that she had always wanted to live a great love. She added that when she and Mounir became attached to one another, she thought that she was going to live the love for which she had always yearned. She was not much bothered by his being already married because she was sure that the true and strong feeling that bound them together would lead him to divorce his first wife. When time passed and he did not divorce Wadad, Lama felt that the love between them was being smothered. "But all that became unimportant," added Lama, "after my daughter's accident. Seeing her with me only in body, without being able to reach her spirit, caused me to lose all attachment to life. I became certain that God was punishing me for having wronged Wadad and her children. I tried to evoke God's forgiveness by becoming a good Muslim. I also tried to compensate Wadad by going to her house and doing her housework. But she understood this to be a comment on her cleanliness. She insulted me, saying that my house was as dirty as a pig-sty." Lama's religious scruples did not stop her, however, from criticizing Wadad's way of dressing and of carrying on as "unbecoming to a mother and an elderly woman." Indeed, the one time I saw Lama smile was when she talked of her co-wife turning blond in her old age!

Um Hussein and Amira (Nomadic Bedouins)

Um Hussein (the mother of Hussein) and Amira are co-wives in a no-madic tribe that spends most of the year in the steppe areas adjoining the Syrian Desert and the summers in the Bekaa' valley. During the summer season, the women work in the fields as day laborers. They also tend live-stock and attend to the usual housework. I was told that they consider their sojourn in the desert as an easier time during which they are freed from working as farmhands.

Their Bekaa' abode, in which I visited them, consisted of three tents: one for receiving guests, one for cooking and washing, and one for sleep-ing. The woman with whom the husband was spending the night would sleep in the tent allotted to receiving guests. The other wife would sleep in another tent with Abu Hussein's (the father of Hussein) sister Ghaza-leh and the teen-age daughters of Um Hussein and Abu Hussein. The area around their tents was kept clean. The guests' tent was the best fur-nished, with imitation Persian rugs, a huge copper coffee maker, and em-broidered cushions used to seat visitors or as back supports. That tent was referred to as Um Hussein's.

The women wore long, loose robes and very attractive headgear that made their eyes and the bone structure of their faces appear to advantage. Um Hussein was plainly and soberly dressed in dark colors; and Amira wore colorful fabrics, an embroidered vest and a great deal of makeup and jewelry. Ghazaleh, the independent businesswoman (she made and sold cheese), wore a more practical shorter dress with long pants underneath. She was the first to engage me in conversation about her life, comment-ing on the treachery of men: "If you trust the love of a man, you are like one who entrusts a sieve with holding water." She had married for love against the wishes of her family. She had worked hard before successfully convincing her father and brothers to break her engagement to her cousin and to accept her marriage to the man she loved. After a few years of happiness, her husband married another woman from a neighboring tribe. He married the girl against her family's wishes, fleeing with her on horseback (white?) from her family's quarters to his own. Ghazaleh re-acted by asking for a divorce, which the husband refused to grant. But Ghazaleh went back to her family[12] "to live *mu'azzazah mukarramah*" (loved and respected). Having told her story, she went off to attend to her business, leaving me to interview her brother's wives. As she was re-counting her story, I was struck by the good taste with which she could string together her words and sentences. In fact, most of the Bedouins interviewed were impressive conversationalists.

Um Hussein, a high cheek-boned classical beauty, was thirty-five when I met her in 1992. Her father used to be a sheep merchant. She had three brothers and two sisters. She described her family as "a respectable one, whose members did not blaspheme and did not slander other people." She illustrated the high moral caliber of her kin by telling me that although one of her sisters had been dead for ten years, her husband still refused to remarry, saying that he could never find another woman like his late wife.

Um Hussein had married at the age of nineteen. She and her husband had had three daughters and one son. Her youngest child and only son, Hussein, had drowned in a pond when eight years of age. About one year before the death of Hussein, her husband expressed a desire to take another wife "in order that the daughters will have more than one brother to protect them when their father is no longer there for them." A few months after the boy's death, Um Hussein proposed that she herself find a new wife for her husband.

She visited a family that had three daughters of marriageable age and chose the youngest, Amira, a beautiful girl of seventeen. When the family of Amira set as a condition for their consent that one of the daughters of Um Hussein be given in an exchange marriage (muqayada) to Amira's brother, Um Hussein consented despite her daughter's aversion to the young man.[13] The arrangement concluded, Um Hussein took Amira to the town of Baalbek to buy her trousseau. When Amira expressed her desire to wear an urban white bridal gown rather than the usual Bedouin wedding costume, Um Hussein bought her one.

On the wedding day Um Hussein, still in mourning for her son, baked and cooked for the wedding feast. When she noticed that the neighbors were boycotting the celebration out of respect for her mourning, she changed her black garments and made a round of the neighbors, asking them to join in the festivities. In the evening, she spread carpets, a mattress, and cushions for the newlyweds in a separate tent. She adorned the tent with flowers, filled a plate with fruits and a pitcher with fruit juice. As she described all these details, I sensed in her, alongside the suppressed pain, a feeling of pride similar to the one conveyed as she told me of her brother-in-law's refusal to replace her dead sister. For her, both accounts reflected how respectable, self-denying, and generally good people the members of her family were.

Amira is the third daughter in a family of six boys and eight girls. Her father also is a sheep merchant. When I asked her whether she could read and write, she answered with a surprised laugh that added charm to her reddish-haired sunny-faced beauty. She laughed further: "The whole family is illiterate. The only exception is my father, who taught himself, although he has never been to school." She said the last phrase with pride, still smiling broadly.

Amira looked perfectly happy. Before and after my interviews with her and her co-wife, she sat close to Um Hussein, a little behind her. She seemed unquestioningly willing to do her bidding and be guided by her. When I asked her why she had agreed to marry Abu Hussein, she answered, "Because they liked me and chose me from among my sisters, I also liked them." Because the choice referred to was made by Um Hussein and not by her husband, it was not clear whom the girl liked and whom she accepted. When I pressed her about why she had consented to marry a man old enough to be her father, she repeated that he was respectable and that she felt that Um Hussein (Um Hussein again!) could make of her a better person. She also said that she liked the company of Um Hussein's daughters. From fragments of phrases punctuated by much giggling, I gathered that she was enjoying her sexual encounters with Abu Hussein and that she did not feel guilty or awkward toward Um Hussein on that account. She seemed to feel that her youth and her co-wife's maturer age entitled her to be preferred sexually and entitled Um Hussein to take precedence over her in other domains.

Um Hussein expressed regrets about her new situation: "Who would like to see her husband in the arms of a girl of seventeen!" she asked. She added: "The new wife is like a new dress. Nobody likes to wear an old garment when one has acquired a new one." Yet, despite that, she treated her co-wife with maternal affection. She appeared to take Abu Hussein's new marriage as destiny, dictated by circumstances for which nobody could be blamed. She said that her faith in God remained a great solace and that what she really hoped for were God's grace and the respect of the community. It was obvious that she had, at least, the latter. The men treated her with affectionate respect, and the women sought her company and were counseled by her. The general attitude toward her implied that self-denying individuals like her, who uphold the norms of society regardless of the cost to themselves, are the pillars and the pride of their small community.

When I revisited them in the summer of 1993, I found some change in the attitude of Um Hussein toward Amira. I was told that during the winter Abu Hussein had divorced Amira and that he had taken her back only after much pleading from Um Hussein. The older co-wife explained, "Respectable people like us do not take other people's daughters, impregnate them, and send them back to their folks." When I asked Abu Hussein about the reason for the divorce, I was told that Amira's mother had caused it by urging her daughter to demand that he divorce his first wife. This made Abu Hussein so angry that he divorced Amira instead. He added, "I respect all the family, but Um Hussein has in my esteem a special position, before everyone else, because she sacrificed for the sake of the family and because she is the mother of my daughters and bears the name of my late son."

Um Hussein admitted that although she still considered Amira a good girl, relations between them had changed: "I no longer draw her to me and kiss her cheeks as I would my own daughters," she said. Amira, however, pleased to be carrying her newborn daughter in her arms, insisted that she still loved, respected, and obeyed Um Hussein. I witnessed Um Hussein giving her orders concerning what to do for the baby and saw that Amira was prompt in doing her co-wife's bidding. Yet, Um Hussein had during this last interview the attitude of a chastising, rather than of an approving and encouraging elder, which she had had the summer before. Amira seemed to respond by trying her best to regain the affection and confidence of her co-wife although her main effort was directed toward tending the precious bundle that she carried about on her back, held in a cloth-basket dangling from her shoulders. Probably the lack of anxiety in her attempts to appease her co-wife resulted from the deep satisfaction that she appeared to feel because of the little one in the basket.

Almaza and Ward (Sedentary of Bedouin Origin)

Almaza was my paternal grandmother, who passed away at the age of one hundred and four in 1964, and Ward was her co-wife, the second wife of my paternal grandfather. She passed away in her mid-nineties in 1988. Although the families of both women, the Hamadehs and the Harfoushes, respectively, have been well known in Lebanon for several centuries, the two families identified with their ancient Bedouin descent. They were very proud of their origin and maintained many of the old Bedouin traditions and values.

Almaza was a tall blonde, daughter of a *pasha* (*"pasha"* is an Ottoman title bestowed by the sultanate on some politically influential individuals) who, in her early twenties, married her paternal first cousin. Her father was proud of her, believing her to be of exceptional intelligence. Encouraged by her marked interest in politics, he used to discuss with her political matters that the other women knew only generally and vaguely. This interest and her habit of conversing with politically active kinsmen about issues related to their work remained with Almaza all her life. Strongly identifying with the family's political role, she did not seem to be bothered by the fact that being a woman prevented her from engaging in politics directly. She had a poetic talent by means of which she sublimated her need to express herself in the field of her interest by composing songs and poems about events happening on the political scene.

Rivalry over political leadership existed between Almaza's father and, later, her brother, on the one hand, and her husband and, later, her son, on the other. Almaza always took the side of her family of birth (father and brother). She became eager for the advancement of her son's political career only after the death of her brother. Almaza showed the same type of preference when she undertook to use what she inherited from her parents to educate the children of one of her brothers, who had died young, depriving her own children.

When Almaza's brother, who was married to her husband's sister, took another wife, Almaza's husband retaliated by taking another wife, a traditional retaliation in such circumstances, to avenge his sister. The second wife, Ward, was a short, dark-eyed, lively, and intelligent woman. Even in her old age, she had a knack for saying things that made people laugh, regardless of how solemn the occasion might be. She often joked about the contrast between the title of her family of birth (she had the title of princess) and their extreme poverty. Before her birth her family had lost the wealth and political affluence that they had had in the past. She was orphaned before her teens and grew up with her sisters and young brothers in a household run in harmonious collaboration between her mother and her mother's co-wife. Growing up among women and little boys, Ward probably yearned for the security that the presence of a man in the house brings, for, when she married, she lavished on her husband more explicit appreciation than the traditions of their community permitted.

Ward was not discreet in her efforts to please her husband. She used to wear kohl (this, for some reason probably having to do with class, was not customary in her entourage although very usual, even for men, among other Bedouin groups), rouge her cheeks, and get all dressed up when it was time for her husband to return to the house. She also cooked special dishes for him and insisted on serving them herself. Such behavior shocked the women of her husband's family, whose traditions required that a woman show no sign of affection, but only respect, for her husband. For them, even uttering the husband's name was considered a shameless act. Thus, in the early period of her marriage, Ward was criticized and picked upon. She was nicknamed *muhammarah* (the rouged one). Her co-wife felt that she had to defend her although she also was shocked by her "shamelessness." Thus, a bond, as between protector and protected, developed between the two women.

Before Ward's inclusion into the family, Almaza used to supervise the household, including care of the children. Afterward, however, she gladly relinquished such tasks to her co-wife. Ward took over, adding some sophistication in housework that she had learned as she grew up closer to the town of Baalbek. She taught the women ironing and the use of certain utensils. Ward was also the one to manage finances. She used to set aside the money required for housekeeping and give the rest to Almaza to spend as she deemed fit. One family ritual, called "the blessing," required that whenever a new harvest was brought home, Ward would take the first token to Almaza for good luck. This ritual, vaguely reminiscent of pagan beliefs that associated fertility and plenty with femininity, was meant to be a prayer for abundance and for the preservation of the mother of the family (Almaza) until the next harvest.

Ward had no children, yet her maternal love added warmth to the lives of several generations of her husband's family. She lavished care and attention on Almaza's children. Her stepdaughter grew to love her more than she did her own mother. Later, when the wife of one of her stepsons died in childbirth, she took care of his numerous children. She also saw to it that what she inherited from her husband would go, upon her death, to her husband's children and not to her nephews and nieces, who were her legal heirs by Muslim law. The community appreciated Ward lavishing attention on the children. She became very popular. Her small 'failings' faded from sight. Her rouge (which she continued to use way into her old age) and her "shamelessness" were no longer considered moral defects, and everybody came to appreciate and admire her generosity of heart and action.

The house they lived in was a large, airy mansion that combined the Ottoman and the Mount Lebanon styles of architecture. It featured a large hexagonal reception area, wide balconies in the background of which stood arcades partially covered by colorful tainted glass, and a red brick roof. Except for the men's reception area, where the seating arrangement was in divan style, the house was furnished like the inside of some Bedouin tents: rugs and cushions spread on the floor and big wooden chests adorned with oriental designs that functioned as closets for clothes and other items. The women wore clothes that also combined Bedouin, Lebanese, and Ottoman elements, choosing from those what were more becoming and more convenient for their various purposes. The young women kept an eye on fashion in Istanbul, and the older ones maintained the fixed traditions of Bedouin and Lebanese female attires.

Almaza and Ward openly communicated to each other, in word and action, their thoughts and feelings, including their occasional jealousies of each other as co-wives. I was told that when once their husband, upon returning from a trip, went directly to Ward's room, Almaza expressed her anger by staying up all night, keeping a fire ablaze in the open court. After that he always greeted her first before going to see Ward. As a child, I often heard them bickering about whom their late husband had favored. Sometimes, they laughingly teased each other over who was going to die first and thus gain the privilege of lying in the grave closest to their husband. They also used to express their fondness of each other, each telling the other how lost she felt when the other was away for a day or more.

During their husband's lifetime and after his death, they used to sit in the afternoons for long hours on the same cushion, smoking the *narguila* (water pipe) and discussing various issues. They often slipped into competitive discussions of the history of their respective families. Yet, behind each other's backs, each used to remind the younger folk not to overlook their duties to the other. They also attended to each other in times of sickness and confided in each other their innermost thoughts and feelings. Ward used to repeat the songs that Almaza composed, and Almaza's eyes used to glitter, as her face became wrinkled with merriment, upon hearing Ward's witticisms.

Structural Differences in the Attitudes of Urban and Bedouin Women Toward Co-wives

As revealed by the statistics cited in the field study section above, the vast majority of urban co-wives feel hatred toward one another, whereas Bedouin co-wives exhibit a variety of affective connections to their respective co-wives. The feelings toward one another explicitly voiced in the interviews were, to a great extent, corroborated by observation of behavior and conversations heard outside the scope of the interviews. Urban women's claims were generally of hatred toward co-wives, and their behavior, even when the perpetrators seemed to think that they were being neutral, polite, or even humane, conveyed the enmity they professed. For example, Wadad emphasizing her genteel origin in the fashion in which she decorated her home and her exaggerated insistence on the rituals of hospitality were, at least partially, strategies aimed at offsetting her co-wife's "common" background. Her desperate attempts to look attractive were an endeavor to beat her co-wife at her own game because she believed that Lama had seduced Mounir with her physical charms (she resisted admitting that Mounir had fallen in love with Lama). The accounts that Wadad gave of Lama's ill-treatment of her while Lama stayed in Wadad's house during the war and of her buying a rag doll for Lama's daughter were clearly meant to portray herself as the innocent victim, "the heroine," and Lama as the insolent and unfriendly "villain."

Likewise, Lama seemed to have chosen to become economically productive mainly because she wanted to be on a par with Wadad. It also appeared highly probable that a major incentive for her adoption of socialist and anti-bourgeois ideas was the fact that, judged by such ideas, Wadad fared very poorly. Even religious commitment may have acquired an additional attraction in Lama's eyes as another basis for feeling superior to her co-wife, who had absolutely no interest in spiritual matters. Because of the type of relationship that existed between the two women, one may suspect that Wadad's insistence on trying to look attractive and her valorization of the mundane and the materialistic were major incentives for Lama's choice of plain clothes and of her apparent loss of interest in the contest over feminine appeal and in worldly matters in general. Both women appeared to be motivated in many of their choices by an impotent hatred of each other that, when expressed, caused more inconvenience to themselves than to their co-wife.

By contrast, the Bedouin women expressed, when questioned, and exhibited in their behavior toward their co-wives a variety of feelings that ranged between the extremes of hatred and love. The ones who did not hate their respective co-wives seemed to attempt to adjust to their polygynous marriages by taking into account the co-wife's (or co-wives') disposition and preference. In the case studies above, not only Almaza and Ward, who happened to have different attitudes and preferences, could leave each other space to be what they chose without significant antagonism or interference but also Um Hussein and Amira, each of whom coveted the other's role, sacrificed in order not to trespass on a territory judged to be more appropriate for her co-wife. Um Hussein sacrificed in the domain of sexual satisfaction, relinquishing the role of the young and attractive wife, which she herself was clearly still equipped to play, and Amira's sacrifice was to be content with a status equivalent to that of an unmarried daughter (although daughters are much more secure in the love and the permanent acceptance within the family than second wives can ever hope to be), who had to defer to the authority of the older woman (or women because Ghazaleh, too, had her share of ordering Amira about).

Bedouin women who claimed in the interviews to hate each other tended to justify the hatred by referring it to the actions or the character of the co-wife. In so doing they appeared not to believe that her being the co-wife was enough justification for hating her. This was evidenced by Bedouin women's tendency to give reasons for any antagonism that they professed to feel toward their co-wives. They would say that they hated her because "She is a liar"; or because "she is a hypocrite"; or because "she is greedy, always trying to get more than her share." A frequent cause of the declared hatred was laziness. Two of the Bedouin co-wives claimed to hate a co-wife who "fakes sickness every time we have an over-load of work." Urban women were comparatively less prone to give such explanations, frequently appearing surprised when asked for reasons for their hatred. Their attitudes indicated that partaking of a woman's hus-band was clearly a sufficient and very good reason for the woman to hate her co-wife.

The prevalence of enmity in the relationships between urban co-wives and the failure to see anything in the co-wife other than a threat indicate the existence of structural factors in urban women's lives and/or psycho-logical formation that lead to their view of their role as a wife as the cor-nerstone of their existence and the most central determinant of their identity. The fact that Bedouin co-wives exhibited more variety in their outlooks toward their co-wives indicates that such a structure is absent, as a pervasive trend, from the lives and personalities of Bedouin women. Moreover, the fact that Bedouin co-wives seemed more aware of the indi-viduality of their respective co-wives, even when they hated them, indi-cates that their judgement (objectivity) is not completely obstructed by a marital threat. This fact also reflects a view of themselves that is, compara-tively, more individualistic and more conducive to their functioning freely and independently.

In the following two sections I argue that (1) the basis of this struc-tural difference lies in the fact that the husband occupies a more central position in the practical and social lives of urban women than in those of Bedouin women and (2) the self-construct of urban girls is built around their future roles as wives, whereas that of Bedouin girls is more en-meshed with their situation as daughters of their families (or tribes or *ashirahs*).

Reasons Why Husbands Are More Central in the Lives of Urban Women than in Those of Bedouin Women

Economic and Social Factors

The economic factor in Bedouin life displaces the husband from the center of his wife's life. Community of possessions among large tribal groups impede the couple from forming an economic unit. The woman's assured claim on support by her consanguine close relatives gives her a measure of economic security apart from her husband. Moreover, the Bedouin woman's work on the land and in tending livestock and in weaving tents and blankets, all of which are basic for the survival of the group, give her a sense of economic worth and as such enhance her psychological independence.[14]

In contradistinction, the usual family unit in urban localities is nuclear. Nuclear families are economically self-contained units. They do not usually expect or receive external financial help. This situation makes a wife who does not have her own economic resources totally dependent on her husband, and often when she does work, her earnings are recognized as secondary and are frequently used for items that the family can dispense with rather than for the basics. It is interesting to note, in this connection, that urban husbands are pressured by the community to be the main breadwinners, whereas among Bedouins a competition between husband and wife over productivity is nearly unheard of, a fact supported by the great numbers of "male Bedouins of leisure" who spend their days making coffee and chatting with guests while the women and children attend to matters of livelihood. Indeed, until quite recently (the early 1990s), urban husbands were discouraged from allowing their wives to engage in salaried occupations. Popular sayings that denounce husbands who live off their wives and the great number of women who fill their time by joining charitable or other organizations testify to this tendency.

Even when city women are economically independent, as in the cases of Wadad and Lama, their independence from the husband remains thwarted by the fact that a woman on her own in an Arab city is an uncommon and an ill-tolerated phenomenon. Had these two women been Bedouin, their kinsmen would have claimed them away from an unhappy marital situation. Had they been in an American or European social setting, they could have led an independent life. Whether they were Bedouin or Western women, it would have been much easier for them to get a divorce and probably remarry, but, living in a Lebanese (or Arab) city, they found that their choices were between an unhappy marital situation and the loss in social prestige, and they preferred to persevere in the former.

The urban woman's choice is restricted because although Arab tradition and Islamic law dictate that unmarried or divorced females should be financially supported by their closely related kinsmen, conditions of life in the city, including small apartments and the difficulty of coping financially in a consumer society, make the practice of such a tradition and law cumbersome for both sides. Women often are pressed to get married or to stay married because they feel that they cannot rely on their brothers for support or because they fear they will inconvenience their brothers' families. Brothers are usually too busy with their own lives to take their obligations toward their sisters seriously. In the urban case mentioned above, Wadad's brother failed to render her a small service that she asked of him. Her position as one daughter among five brothers gave her little advantage aside from, at most, moral support that she learned not to test at the actual level.

In this volume Suad Joseph writes of how Burj-Hammoud sisters frequently value their brothers more than they value their husbands, considering brothers to be their continuous security anchors and their unfailing protectors. Such expectation, I would argue, comes from the indigenous Bedouin-tribal origins in Lebanese society. Based on this study, the fulfillment of expectations seems to dwindle as Arab families move away from their Bedouin origins and toward urbanization. Although attachment between brothers and sisters in the Lebanese cities remains stronger than that found in other communities in which the impact of modernity has been more pervasive, the trend under the impact of urbanization and modernization is for these attachments to fade into a one-way commitment from the sister to the brother.

Why do sisters remain more, or longer, attached to their brothers than the other way around? If I were to venture an emotional analysis of this phenomenon, I would say that because the girl is wounded by losing her original identity-location-kin, she yearns to keep the bonds with her past-childhood roots more than does the boy for whom such a forced loss is out of the question. On a more practical note, perhaps the tradition of brother/sister cherishing dwindles more quickly for brothers than for sisters because brothers, especially in cities, are raised to be centers of authority and loci of the family's pride and prestige. The assignment of this role to sons is particularly required in cities, like those of Lebanon, where the wider-scope patriarchal authority of elders is lost but not effectively replaced by the authority of a modern state as it is in the industrialized

world. It is ironical, if this analysis is correct, that the patriarchy of brothers (effectively, of all males), which is encouraged in order to fulfill a social
need created by civil society failing to carry out its duty, gets often to
copy the tyranny and inefficacy of the rulers whose failings it is supposed
to cover.

In traditional Bedouin communities it is usual for brothers to repay the
sister's husband with violence if he is violent with her, and in mugayada,
which is a far from infrequent form of marriage among Bedouins, when a
husband divorces a man's sister or brings home another wife, the brother
retaliates by divorcing the sister of that husband or by marrying another
wife in order to get even with the brother of his wife for hurting his sister.
Even a woman's disgrace, according to Bedouin tradition, is punished
and otherwise borne by her family of birth (and later by her children) and
not by her husband or his family. All this changes with urbanization, tying
the woman more closely to her husband and loosening her ties to her
family of birth.

For companionship and emotional exchange Bedouin women often
rely a great deal on other women. The lifestyle of the Bedouins causes
them to spend most of their time with members of their own sex. The
women, especially when young (because the older matrons often join the
men's gatherings during meals and for social interaction), share work and
amusement with other women. Friendships are exclusively with members
of their own sex. This makes the co-wife, sometimes, a more likely candidate for enriching and sharing a woman's life than the husband is. This
was apparent in the Bedouin case studies recorded above and especially in
reasons given by Amira to justify her consent to marry Abu Hussein.
Bedouin men live in their own separate world. Their presence is felt in big
decisions and in gaining or losing wealth and/or status for the community, but not in the actual everyday life of the women. Toward kinsmen
and husbands Bedouin women extend obedience and loyalty, where traditions so require, but men as individuals remain abstract entities that rarely
form part of the daily transactions.

Romantic love, as is implicit in the rich and detailed portrayal of Lila
Abu-Lughod,[15] is, in Bedouin society, mainly an adolescent revolt with
little knowledge by the lovers of each other. Yet even this form of love is
fiercely fought by the whole social set-up, which tries to prevent romantic
attachments even within marriage.[16] Moreover, Bedouin social pressure
structures exchanges between the couple to express emotional indifference and nonchalance.[17] They often preempt the kind of exchanges that
can quench the thirst for emotional interaction from taking place between

couples, even married ones. To satisfy needs for affective exchange, Bedouin women have to rely mainly on each other.

By comparison, women in the city rely heavily on their husbands for companionship and emotional exchange and support. City life limits the woman's daily contact, to a large extent, to members of her nuclear family or to her work associates if she happens to work outside the home. Life in the city is often too fast and too busy to permit spending much time with friends or relatives. Moreover, love-marriages tend to be more frequent in urban settings, raising the couple's expectations of each other in quantity and in quality. Love-based marriages are certainly more emotionally fulfilling, but within such marriages women, having few rights to protect them emotionally and otherwise, are much more vulnerable. The rate of divorce in modern communities, where love-exchange between marriage partners is expected, leads one to question the wisdom of counting on marriage partners for continued emotional support. In societies in which divorce and multiple marriages are easily accessible to husbands, the emotional reliance on marriage places women in a precarious position that causes even loved and cherished wives to feel insecure. Indeed, aside from the fact that relatives cannot be divorced, in general, blood relations are not only more enduring but they tend to carry a steadier and a more reliable affective connection than that between marriage partners.

The Difference in Value Systems

The most crucial value, in Lebanese urban society, is material success. For the vast majority of Lebanese urban women, the way to such success is via a rich husband. The few women who manage to achieve political (usually through a male relative, often one who has suffered a violent death) or intellectual prominence often suffer from not being taken seriously as professionals and from being blocked from reaching the truly satisfying elevated levels of success, which society seems to collaborate in allocating only to men.[18]

Where social status is concerned, the main value according to which women in Lebanese urban society are measured is their marital status. Professional or not, a woman is judged by whether or not she has achieved the status of wife and mother. Condescending smiles and sometimes suppressed giggles are often seen or heard when an older woman, although professionally successful, is introduced as "Miss." When professional women miss out on the roles of wife and mother on the way to professional achievement, they often suffer from a feeling of inadequacy caused by prevalent social values.[19]

The more "modern" urban women's need to express individual talents and choices, added to the internalized social values that emphasize marriage as a necessary condition for women's recognition and acceptability, results in women having to juggle the two roles—professional person and mother, who has to bear, often unaided, the sole responsibility for housework and child care. This leads to the devaluation of women's right to enjoy a free space in which they can recharge their spirits and unleash aspects of their need for the artistic and the playful.

By comparison, Bedouin women (and men) derive their social status and value primarily from their lineage. In fact, a Bedouin woman with a nonprestigious lineage would not experience a significant change in her social status, even if she were to marry into an old and powerful tribe. Apart from lineage, the achieved worth of the individual, in Bedouin society, is determined by the larger community, especially the elders in that community. The elders' criteria usually have to do with moral uprightness and usefulness to the community. In the cases mentioned above, both Um Hussein and Ward received reinforcement and were rewarded with much appreciation by their respective communities for their moral and socially beneficial attitudes and actions. Um Hussein did not lose in social prestige when her husband took another wife. On the contrary, she gained a great deal of respect for the wisdom and self-denial with which she handled the situation.

In this context my observations are at variance with Abu Lughod's claims that the virtues that society values in Bedouin women are passive ones, *hasham* (modesty) being the ultimate Bedouin feminine virtue, and that the reward Bedouin women get for living according to moral precepts is neutral.[20] My observation of Bedouin society indicates that although the passive virtue of hasham is valued, mainly in young girls, bestowing on them, when present, a measure of social approval or acceptability, for Bedouin women in general, a higher degree of reinforcement exists for active virtues such as caring, sacrificing for the benefit of the group, and wisdom (*agl*). The more highly valued agl is other than the agl that Abu-Lughod mentions as a correlate of hasham. Agl linked to hasham is a virtue that indicates a passive disposition that causes the girl to accept traditional behavior, and agl as wisdom indicates an ability to assess situations actively and to make practical and rational choices expressed in words and deeds that sometimes surpass, or may be at variance with, social norms. For wisdom, and for the other positive and active virtues, the reward in Bedouin society is not neutral but is generous and positively felt. Such virtues are capable of elevating the social status of the Bedouin woman and of giving her recognition and a form of power as was apparent in the cases of Um Hussein and Ward. In fact, Ward achieved social recognition and was cherished by her community for of her active qualities of caring and loving despite criticism for her lack of hasham.

Moreover, shared household responsibilities and seasonal variation in work loads coupled with a value system still not totally consumed by materialistic criteria of wealth and success leave the Bedouin women time and scope to attach value to the enjoyment of the playful and artistic aspects of life.

Comparing urban and Bedouin basic values, one finds that they are divisible into three categories: (1) value outside the woman's control, mainly marriage for urban women and lineage for bedouins; (2) value within the woman's control, consisting of possible careers for urban women and room for morally appreciated conduct for Bedouins; (3) value attached by the woman to her personal happiness, which is seen by urban women to be a function of love-based marriage, whereas bedouin women view happiness as deriving from play, art, and friendship and not solely from matrimonial bliss. Where values 2 and 3 are concerned, Bedouin women have more control over factors that impact their happiness and factors that lead to the acquisition of society's appreciation.

Development of the Self in Urban and Bedouin Women

The conditions and values in urban Lebanese society cause the woman's self-construct to be structured around the axis of her future role as a wife. The psychosocialization process continues to be affected by social pressure and by practical aspects of a quotidian life that push the woman to identify herself primarily as a wife. Unlike the urban ways, lifestyle among and values of Bedouin groups cause the woman's self-construct to be based on her continued identification as the daughter of her family of birth. The husband's position in a Bedouin woman's life is comparatively less pivotal because socioeconomic factors keep her strongly connected to consanguine relatives and to other women, even after marriage.

The difference in the two groups' sense of identity is verified by the fact that the vast majority of wives in Lebanese cities such as Beirut, Tripoli, and Sidon socially assume, when they get married, the family names of their husbands. They add the husband's family name to, or substitute it for, that of their own families, whereas rural and Bedouin wives continue to call themselves by their maiden family names. This variation, which may partially be concomitant with the desire to copy Western trends, must also derive from a socially ingrained psychological predisposition to identify with the husband. Indeed, urban Lebanese women must have a very strong urge to follow this practice, which in their case is against practicality and against religious recommendations. Lebanese law recognizes women only by their maiden names (it is the only name that appears on all legal documents, degrees, etc., until the final death certificate), and, thus, by assuming socially the husband's name, they end up with two names, which goes against the original practical purpose behind naming. This urban practice is also contrary to the Kor'anic command (33:5) to call people after their fathers and to the Tradition (*Hadith*) of the prophet, which commands: "Name girls after the names of their fathers. This is more dignified for them" (my translation).

The urban tendency to psychosocially identify women as wives rather than daughters entails, especially in communities that permit divorce and polygyny, that urban women feel vulnerable at the very source of their self-construct. This tendency causes a growing urban girl to fear that she may fail to acquire, in the future, this necessary ingredient to complete her identity. The urban girl grows as a plant with no fixed roots. She waits to acquire, in the future, perhaps, a vulnerable anchor (a husband) and can consider that she has developed fixed roots only when she has children, grown and male, a factor that comes too late in life to help her secure a psychologically integrated sense of self. What adds to the psychological misery that comes as a package deal with the urban type of female self-identity or self-construct is the fact that although becoming, or staying, a wife is a psychosocial necessity for these women, initiating and keeping the marriage are totally dependent on the men. Moreover, the prerequisites for being sought after as a wife are often qualities that are outside the woman's control, such as beauty, youth, a rich father, or a prestigious lineage. She usually has to wait passively or maybe pray or use magic (two "activities" that spring from the recognition of her lack of power to control her destiny), hoping that this effort may procure a husband for her.

It is quite likely that it is the female's identification with her role of a wife that leads the urban woman's personality to grow to be dependent and passive, verifying Freud's theoretical general model of femininity. It is quite possible that Freud derived his model from his observation and psy-

choanalytic practice in a conservative city environment (the Victorian society of Vienna at the beginning of the twentieth century) that represses
or forecloses in women every personality trait that does not coincide with
what is desirable in a wife. Probably, if Freud's female subjects came from
other types of society, such as either contemporary postmodern Western
societies or traditional Bedouin communities, he would have found the
"nature" of femininity to be something else. This question may be worth
pursuing in some other work that attempts to isolate "feminine" characteristics induced by socialization.

In the present study, the urban women overlooking the personhood
and individuality of their co-wives, which was apparent in the structured
attitude of the women to their respective co-wives, regardless of co-wives'
qualities and actions, reflects their own views of themselves as lacking
autonomous being. This diminished self-concept is exhibited as lack of
courage in facing reality, a lack that impedes the ability to deal with problems. In the above-mentioned example of Wadad and Lama, instead of
doing something to change situations that caused them great suffering,
the two urban women tended to indulge in self-mystification and in activities that led nowhere. Such misguided and wasted efforts are recogniz-
able in Wadad's futile and costly attempts to look attractive and
sophisticated and in Lama punishing herself by working hard at home and
outside without enjoying either of those time-consuming, indeed life-
consuming, activities. Lama's later endeavor to withdraw into another
world, by means of religion, was equally incapable of solving her problem.
Both women stayed with Mounir although Wadad claimed that she had
come to hate him and Lama said that she had lost her love for him somewhere during their tumultuous marriage. The two women were economically capable of living on their own, but neither of them managed either
to walk out of a situation that brought her a great deal of unhappiness or
to do something to change it or to learn to accept it. Their actions and attitude seemed to spring from a sociopsychologically instilled lack of self-
dependence, which expresses itself as lack of initiative and as a groping
emotionally based type of judgement incapable of enabling them to assume mastery over their lives.

Because urban women's selves are constructed around their role as
wives, which places the husband in the central position of what is required
to make them feel whole and adequate, a competitor for the husband is
seen as a colossal and devastating threat. The person embodying such a
threat, namely the co-wife, can only be met with aggression and hatred.
Hatred or aggression can be effective, however, only if the one driven by

them possesses a measure of autonomy and recognizes the availability of some space for the manipulation or transformation of reality in accordance with one's desires. The urban women of this study seemed helpless, behaving as though, for them, the scope for decisively effective action was nonexistent. This may be referred either to the fact that the Lebanese urban woman's self-concept is structured in a way that collapses, in her view, the space between her and her husband so that there is no space separating her from him in which she can act; or to the fact that such structuring, which situates the woman in a passive position from the source of her psychosocial identity and worth (the husband), causes her to be passive in general and, hence, to fail to recognize any effective mobility within her reach as a free subject. The lack of this efficacy as a subject is apparent in the fact that the efforts of the urban women surveyed were not geared to changing anything in the actual situation. The women faced their problem, as Wadad and Lama did, by trying to get temporary relief by appeasing their own hurt feelings rather than by changing the actual aspects of their lives that caused these feelings. Their manner of coping was similar to that of people who drown their problems in alcohol or other drugs, thus reducing further their problem-solving potential.

In comparison, the Bedouin women relating to, or identifying with, their respective families of birth holds the advantages of continuity and unalterability. It guarantees a sense of belonging that structures their self-construct from the very beginning to have firm and secure roots. Moreover, Bedouin women's more accessible control over what decides their mobile or achieved social status, which in Bedouin communities derives from their evaluation in terms of moral uprightness or social contribution, gives them a stronger sense of self-determination. The feeling of security and of having a measure of control over their social image create in Bedouin women a greater efficiency in dealing with situations realistically and in solving problems. In this study Bedouin women were more capable of adjusting to their marriages and of relating to their co-wives. They were also more likely to leave the marriage when staying in it made them unhappy. For example, although, as mentioned earlier, urban and Bedouin women found it most difficult to love or to be neutral toward their respective co-wives when the marriage, their own or that of their co-wife, was based on romantic love, when the husband had a new marriage based on love, urban first wives tended to bear their pain without doing anything effective to change the state of affairs (as in the case of Wadad),[21] and Bedouin women tended either to separate (Ghazaleh is an example) or to divorce a husband who was in love with another wife.

That Bedouin women see themselves as effectively autonomous is reflected in their outlook toward their co-wives as persons and not just as rivals. This is evident in the lack of uniformity in their feelings toward the co-wife and in the fact that Bedouin co-wives' feelings toward one another were subject to change in accordance with the behavior of the one toward the other, more so than the feelings of urban co-wives. For example, Um Hussein declared that she did not love Amira in the summer of 1993 the way she had in the previous summer. What Amira did changed Um Hussein's feelings for her. In contrast, Wadad resented Lama equally at the beginning, when Lama was saucy and aggressive, and later, when she changed and tried to appease Wadad and even to serve her. Lama, also, treated Wadad at first only as a rival for Mounir and later as a means to acquire God's forgiveness. Wadad, the human individual, and her actions had nothing to do with Lama's earlier or later behavior toward Wadad. Furthermore, although Lama's behavior toward Wadad changed dramatically, her feelings, as she herself admitted, remained the same: pure hatred and resentment despite the attacks of guilt that occurred after her daughter's accident. All this evidence indicates that urban women do not see their co-wives (or themselves) as independent individuals.

Although the urban women in the survey exhibited individuality in choices pertaining to education and work, and even in their selection of certain values from among what society supplies (bourgeois, or socialist standards; religious commitment or an agnostic outlook), yet their choices sprang from a subjectivity that did not exhibit great conviction in its independent individuality. Their "independence" seemed to be another social value that they unquestioningly embraced. As subjects they were incapable, as the above example of Wadad and Lama illustrates, of breaking loose from the materialistic values to which their choices of occupation and "ideology" appeared to be subservient. Although Lama criticized the bourgeois materialism of her co-wife, her belief that Mounir kept Wadad for the sake of her money indicates valorization focused on the material aspect, an indication that makes the genuineness of her opting to lead an ascetic existence questionable. The study indicates that urban Lebanese women choose their roles from the available restricted spectrum and that few make choices that spring from individual preferences that seek the woman's comfort or joy rather than social prestige and respectability, whether it is a broad choice (political or religious) or a less-crucial one (clothes, art objects).

Indeed, I venture to claim that although urban women have much more of a say in the choice of a husband, yet, with so much conditioning, their choices tend to be largely society induced. The Bedouin women often succumb to arranged marriage, yet they can maneuver other aspects of their lives to place more emphasis on what they enjoy from a few choices of occupation and a wider range of recreational activities. Indeed, if linguistic expression is considered a possible means of genuine self-expression or a surrogate desire fulfillment, Bedouin women's constant recourse to poetry[22] and to songs and to imagination-enriched tales and legends is expected to give them a considerable scope for cathecting urges and desires.

The urban women lack initiative in the pursuit of free, individually determined, sources of enjoyment of life such as friendships, nature, play, and art. By comparison, the Bedouin women's choices arise from a deeper relating to the self and its desires. Maybe the latters' closeness to nature is a factor. Because Bedouin women are more secure in their identity, they are more capable of acting freely, and because they are more deeply and genuinely integrated into the community into which they are born, the structurally permeable boundaries of their selves enable them to be more capable of identifying with the joys and miseries of others.

The Bedouin identification with the tribe is deeply ingrained, exhibiting a high degree of affective investment and of genuine concern exemplified by Um Hussein's readiness to sacrifice for what she considered to be good for her husband and Ward deriving joy from the happiness and care she provided for children who were not her own. That urban woman's selves are more solidly bound is indicated by the fact that despite their dependence on their husbands they do not seem to be particularly capable of experiencing joy and pain vicariously through his joy or pain.

In the case studies Bedouin women's connectivity to their tribes did not seem to exercise much inhibition of their initiative as individuals.[23] They were able to choose the roles they preferred from among those, albeit limited, available to women in their community. In so doing they were, sometimes, less-conforming to traditions than urban women. Almaza not bothering to hide her lack of interest in mothering is one example of this nonconformity and Ward's "shameless" behavior and her preference for people who were not her blood-relatives over others who were are other examples. Helped by the practical fact that Bedouin women share and divide the traditional chores, which leaves the women time and scope for roles that spring from personal preference, such as poetry (Almaza) or making and selling cheese (Ghazaleh) or adopting the role of a mother even without the assistance of biology (Ward), they had more scope for exercising their comparatively more powerful subjectivity in choosing to engage in, or to neglect, traditional occupations and values.

Where the internalization of moral codes into the self is concerned, Bedouin women, whose psychological identification with society is via unalterable consanguine relating usually reinforced by affective ties that are less subject to fluctuation than those with the husband and his family, appeared to more authentically integrate society's moral standards. The Bedouin women's good will toward society was apparent, in the survey, in having aims that were greatly aligned with those of society,[24] sometimes against their personal interests (e.g., Um Hussein working to patch up the marriage of Abu Hussein and Amira for the sake of propriety and the good name of the family). Such good will also expressed itself as society-serving activities (e.g., Ward's life-long nurturing of the descendants of her husband and co-wife).

Urban women relate much more superficially to the traditions and norms on which their society is based. Identified and evaluated on the basis of criteria external to their origin and control, they become socialized to look at themselves as "other" and as a being not capable of transcendence, as Simone de Beauvoir notices about women (urban Western women of the 1940s). In fact, the basic structure of a society that treats them as valued objects for a husband rather than as cherished children of a tribe, or ashirah, requires of them decorum rather than commitment, passive conformity rather than active involvement. When psychological identification with society is based on the marriage connection, a connection that is neither originally present nor usually secure and reliable, relating to society is more likely be as an outsider and a passive entity (immanent being, *an in-itself*, rather than as a being who attempts transcendence, *a for-itself*).[25] Self-conscious freedom in women living in such societies is discouraged. It is a trait that the woman herself fights or hides as part of her effort to be accepted socially.

Freud's observing in women a comparative moral laxity, or a weaker superego, is understandably true of women adjusted to, and living in, a society that identifies them mainly as wives. In such a society, where women's sense of identity rests on precarious and changing grounds and on grounds in which the woman's emotional investment is usually comparatively weaker than that with her family of birth, it is expected that women exhibit a less-authentic internalization of the norms and rules of society. Societies, like that of the Bedouins, and unlike that in which Freud lived or the present-day Lebanese urban society, may exhibit a different basic structure of female morality, as this study illustrates. Indeed Bedouin societies' decrees that the major source of the tribe's honor depends on the chastity of its women, is a sign of the expectation, which experience must have verified, of a high degree of commitment by Bedouin women to their society's moral ideals.

The urban prevalent norm that valorizes success, material possessions and marital respectability, creates an additional and powerful barrier not only to the conscience-based type of internalized morality but also to the free pursuit of happiness in the fulfillment of personal desires. Material values are more demanding of time, effort, and mental involvement than, say, moral values. Thus, the urban woman is pushed to sacrifice peace of mind and natural needs for the sake of affluence and respectability, which are often linked to being married. For the sake of keeping a husband, she may sacrifice integrity and indulge in hypocrisy (as was seen in the behavior of Wadad and Lama toward each other and toward Mounir). When let down by a husband who has left her or who has married another wife, she may even forego the attempt to pursue comfort and harmony. This was evident in the houses and clothes of the surveyed urban co-wives, which often appeared more directed to convey statements related to status and/or vanquishing an enemy (a co-wife) than to satisfy the desire for comfort, self-expression, or aesthetic enjoyment. The artistic dimension in these women's lives appeared to be minimal, and where it existed, as in the aubusson pieces hanging on the walls of Wadad's house and the silver ornaments on her tables, it tended to be stereotypical and impersonal, indicating that the woman's psychological dependence on a husband and identification as a wife diminish her ability actively to integrate her personal preference into the elements of her own life.

The physical surroundings of Bedouin women showed a greater harmony between their own desires and what was considered proper by their community. Probably because of their positive affective connection that goes both ways to the source of their social identity, they seemed to be more capable of managing to secure their comfort and to maintain their enjoyment of life while obeying the norms of their community. This harmony was indicated, in this study, in Bedouins' dress and in their living quarters, poor or rich. It was also apparent in the Bedouin co-wives' greater attunement to the artistic,[26] which was seen in their embroidery, their constant use of poetry (Almaza),[27] and in the great emphasis they laid on perfecting the art of conversation.

Conclusions

In the Arab world Bedouin norms are generally the origin, or the past, which is being infiltrated, to varying degrees, especially in the Middle East and North Africa, by Western norms. Because this infiltration is taking place to a greater extent in the urban centers, the positive valorization of urbanity is often reflected as looking favorably on the imported changes. Moreover, because the West is the nest of power and the source of the most pervasive media transmission, its ways are gaining ground and appeal in various regions of the world. A hasty consideration of urban as positive and desirable and of the Western impact as positive and desirable seem to cause an oversimplification in the light of which the impact of imported changes on an Arab or Islamic world with certain characteristics that remain unchanged (multiple marriages, restrictions on women, a closely controlling patriarchy) is taken to be a move in the right direction. The findings of this study encourage a more holistic scrutiny under which the above-mentioned infiltration may be better judged with respect to the impact of its outcome on the status and happiness of women.

For example, in the light of these findings, Hisham Sharabi's call on Arab society to move toward the nuclear type of family in order to achieve democratic relations and to discourage patriarchy[28] does not appear to embody unquestionable good advice. In addition, such findings make the claim of Edwin Terry Prothro and Lutfy Diab that the mandate by leading to the emulation of Western family patterns effected a move away from patriarchy[29] and the claim of Beth Baron that the last two centuries, which witnessed a modernization of the Egyptian family, also weakened patriarchy[30] highly debatable. The thrust of my argument is in line with Leila Ahmed's recommendation that reform be pursued in a "native idiom" and not in one appropriated from other patriarchies found in other cultures.[31] It is essential to avoid biases and generalizations; for example, the fact that urbanity or Western ways holds many desirable traits should not lead to the assumption that any motion in their direction is desirable and completely positive.

Whether Arab women live in extended or in nuclear families, they remain under patriarchal hegemonies. The surveyed women living within a nuclear Arab family seemed to fall under a more oppressive form of patriarchy than the tribal one, insofar as patriarchal power in the tribe concentrates decision making and the assessment of individuals in a few elders who are usually chosen for their wisdom and their superior moral standing. Such power to make decisions and to pass judgment on women accrues, within a nuclear family, to every husband, regardless of his moral or mental caliber. In Bedouin communities, the authority of the elders, or *sheikhs,* together with the watch that tribes keep on the behavior of their members, ensure some rights for women and a measure of fairness in the way they are treated, whereas under urban patriarchies women's sense of security has to depend on civil society and its willingness to afford women a measure of protection.

Unless civil society in each Arab country becomes a deterrent to the "nuclear" patriarch, the conditions of the life of an Arab woman under such absolute patriarchy are very precarious. Often, neither religious laws—*shariʿa* often depart from the word and spirit of the Korʾan as a result of self-serving biases of the patriarchs who draft religious law[32]—nor civil laws effectively protect the interests of women or safeguard their dignity.[33] In Lebanon the sectarian regime is incapable or fearful of implementing change or of adequately enforcing rules. Such a regime prevents imported or locally devised new social ways from being woven into the fixed social realities to form a more efficient or more equitable society.[34] Indeed the variety of political regimes in the Arab world is expected to create a variety of outcomes of the Western infiltration.[35] Where the state unifies society and is effective in replacing the old tribal patriarchy with a form of central power more capable of keeping men (and women) in line, Arab society may be capable of improvising new formulas that replace the old ways or of integrating the new into the old in workable fashions. This integration may happen even under totalitarian regimes, provided these are strong, secular, fair and effective. A weak government that is either not interested in or incapable of organizing and controlling its civil society, however, may harbor some imported characteristics alongside some indigenous ones, giving birth to a mélange that causes women to suffer on both accounts. This was demonstrated *to be the case* with the conditions that had structured the selves of the surveyed Lebanese urban co-wives. A woman does not have to be persecuted to develop the personality of a victim. When society is organized in a fashion that allocates to its women a precarious and mobile position with no guarantees of a measure of autonomy and/or rights, their self-constructs will reflect this position. This self-image is not expected to undergo much change even if a woman happens to be pampered by circumstances as in marrying a loving and gentle husband who shares his authority with her and respects and appreciates her position in their nuclear family.

At the level of the discussion of the psychosocial conditions under which women in general live, and not just in Lebanon or the Arab world, the above investigates the problematic of women having to shift families between the ones of birth and those of marriage. A man is identified with one family, one locale, and one name from birth to death. But a woman's self-construct has to prepare her to live as a "nomad," not only in the geographic sense but also where her psychological identity and social adjustment are concerned. This "nomadic" existence may be the cause behind several of the so-called "feminine" characteristics that are detrimental to women's status and to women's ability to hold the reins of their lives and to steer them in directions advantageous to themselves and/or promoting the fulfillment of their desires. It is ironical that my investigation reveals that in Lebanon Bedouin women have a more "settled" self-construct than that of urban women!

Psychology has demonstrated the importance of every detail of the "family drama" in the formation of the child's personality. The tone and type of the family drama determine whether the child is expected to grow to be more individualistic with more strictly defined borders between self and others or whether it is socialized to be more caring for others and more dependent on them. This study indicates that Lebanese urban women seemed to be lost between the two patterns.

At an even more general level that embraces women and men, this study questions the wisdom of attaching value to items that are not related to, or that have a negative impact on, happiness, whether it is happiness of the individual and/or that of society. Valorization of success and of material achievement, which reinforces a closely bound construct of the self is shown by the above portrayal and arguments to obstruct allocating space for the enjoyment of pursuits that favor the individual's happiness and obstruct higher moral commitment where the latter often leads to bestowing happiness on others. Indeed, because socialization in any form of upbringing is geared to form social individuals, a socialization that creates individuals with closely-bound self-constructs[36] is one that, in a sense, is not in harmony with its own purpose. For to produce individuals with clearly demarcated and closely guarded boundaries is, in some senses, tantamount to creating asocial personalities. Clearly, such individuals would be more likely to interact with others superficially, in a socially acceptable and functional fashion, without becoming socially committed at the deeper or more affective, and perhaps more effective, levels.

People with closely bound self-constructs ruled by material values may carry a latent threat for social and global aims, owing to their lack of social integration and commitment. They also have a type of self-construct that sabotages its own access to happiness in play, in friendship, and in deriving joy vicariously by means of contributing to the happiness of others. It seems, from the types recorded and analyzed here, that by shutting out others from the self one tends to shut out access to the pulse of the general vital force, which is the more reliable source for attuning to the world and for seeking, and finding, happiness.

My Son/Myself, My Mother/Myself
Paradoxical Relationalities of Patriarchal Connectivity

SUAD JOSEPH

Ad Dunia Um (The mother is the world)

"*Sibhan Allah* (Praise the Lord)! *Tub al-asl* (She looks just like her roots [her father])," Um George[1] joyfully exclaimed to Nada and Na'im, the parents of eighteen-month-old Dani, as they stood outside Nada and Na'im's summer home in the Christian village of Yusfiyyi, a suburb of Beirut, Lebanon.[2] A small group had gathered in the narrow winding street lined with front doors that opened directly into cars flying by at autostrat speed but which invited neighbors and relatives into constant communication and contact with one another.

"Why? She looks just like *me!*" protested the robust Nada, who at around 5'5" weighed nearly twice as much as her slight and slightly shorter husband. Picking up Dani and holding her daughter close to her face, she indignantly continued, "She couldn't be more like me!"

"But I was paying you a compliment," explained Um George, a bit stunned.

"It's not a compliment. She looks exactly like me," Nada insisted, her voice rising so that those indoors could easily hear the escalating difference.

"You should feel proud if I say she looks like her father," reprimanded the now indignant Um George in a shriller voice mixed with mischief and criticism.

The conversation expanded as neighbors, relatives of one or more of the group, joined in from their balconies and windows. "Haqq ma' Nada

(Nada is right)," Wahid insisted, standing bare-chested in his undershorts on the balcony of his second-story apartment, the only child of his late-marrying parents. "Btishbah 'umha. Shu fiha? (She looks like her mother. What's wrong with that?" added Sitt Salma,[3] leaning over the balcony shoulder to shoulder with her son, Wahid.

"*Ma'lash* (Never mind). Um George meant only to say something nice. She looks like her father; she looks like her mother. It doesn't matter," offered the always conciliatory Um Kheir, sister of Sitt Salma.

"No, she should compliment me that Dani looks like me!" Nada dug in her heels.

The uncharacteristic conversation continued for several more minutes until peace was forged by some acceptance that Dani resembled her mother. Throughout the exchange, Na'im stood silently smiling at his wife and daughter. Much more characteristic was another conversation that was repeated so many times that I stopped keeping record of when and where and who said it to whom. It was repeated so often that I, like my fellow Lebanese, not only naturalized it, but found myself reciting it whether or not it was true.

"*Shu btishbah bieyya!*" (How she resembles her father!), Jocelyn remarked to Hanini and Butros about the younger of their two daughters. "Photocopy," smiled Butros, proudly beaming at three-year-old Samira at play with her five-year-old sister Samra. "She walks like him, she talks like him, and all she wants to do is follow him around," chimed in Jocelyn as delighted as Butros in the reproduction of a true clone of her husband.

Patriarchal Paradoxes

Children in Lebanon have been generally expected to follow their fathers. Parents and extended relatives have expected children, especially sons, to look like their fathers. In the two families discussed above, there were no sons at the time of the conversation. In each case, a daughter was said to look just like the father. Similarly, newborns, regardless of how unclear their features might be, have been routinely said to resemble their fathers or at least their fathers' lines. Children generally are members of the father's family in this patrilineal society, take on his religion, his citizenship, his ethnic and national identity, his political loyalties, and his local and familial allegiances. Women reproduce children, especially sons, for their husbands' genealogical lines. Children belong to their fathers and, in some respects, are properties of their fathers.

Yet, paradoxically, despite (or maybe because of) the legally and socially sanctioned continuities between father and child, Lebanese have expected mutually unconditional love and adoration between a mother and her children of both sexes. Most children in Lebanon have grown up with the *matal* (proverb), *ad dunia um* (the mother is the world). Songs praising the mother, poems romanticizing the mother, and love lyrics of all genres valorizing the unadulterated love children have for their mothers and mothers for their children have been part of every child's growing experience. Thus, although children, especially sons, are to be like their fathers, they are unconditionally to love and be loved by their mothers.

The question that drew my attention to the scenes described above is the less-common situation in which there is not only unconditional love between mother and son but the son, with social acceptance, identifies with and follows the mother and the mother's line. It could be that the unbounded exaltation of the mother figure in Lebanese culture is so expansive that it can admit the occasions when a son identifies far more with the mother's family than with the father's. It could also be that patriarchy and patrilineality are so firmly in place that occasions of maternal affinity offer no serious challenge to the grounding assumptions of Lebanese social organization. It is this relationship of mother-son love and son's affinity to mother's family as rejection of father-son continuity in a highly patriarchal and patrilineal society that I explore in this chapter, using the case study of Wahid and Sitt Salma.

Wahid and Sitt Selma lived in the small Christian village I call Yusfiyyi in the Mount Lebanon province of Lebanon. Village elders claim the village is about three hundred years old, having been founded by three or four families who have remained and peopled the village over the years. Although there has been no official census in Lebanon since 1932, village leaders suggest the current population is about four to five thousand, a tenfold increase in the past half-century. Divided primarily between Greek Orthodox and Maronite Catholics, until recently, the village housed only those born there or married into local families. Its relative proximity to the Greater Beirut area has attracted "outsiders" who are buying property. Almost everyone owns property, however, with renters being very scarce in this village. It is largely a "face-to-face" community, with most people knowing everyone in the village and a large percentage related to each other.

Wahid, Sitt Salma in the Bosom of Family

Wahid was the unmarried only child of Sitt Salma and Abu Wahid. Aged twenty-three in 1994 when I began research in the village, he lived at home with his parents in their two-story building. The plan had been for Wahid to occupy one floor when he married, with his parents remaining on the other floor. Wahid worked full time with his maternal uncle *khalu* while studying civil engineering in a branch of the Lebanese University.

Abu Wahid, sixty-nine years old in 1974, was one of seven children, all born, married, and living in Yusfiyyi. He and his four brothers had built a series of adjoining houses with common walls, making a long L-shape on the family property. The family property remained undivided. Wahid had been raised in the immediate environment of his paternal uncles and cousins with his father's sisters and their children also close by. There were a number of marriages among Wahid's paternal cousins.

Sitt Salma and her parents, three brothers, and three sisters similarly were all born, married, and lived in Yusfiyyi. Other than one sister, though, they did not live in Sitt Salma's immediate neighborhood. Sixty-five when I began my work in 1994, Sitt Salma daily spent time with her sister, Um Kheir, who lived immediately across the street. Despite her proximity to Um Kheir, Sitt Salma expressed closer affinity to another one of her sisters and her brothers whom she visited quite regularly.

All the houses abutting Wahid's contained his paternal relatives; all the houses in the immediate vicinity contained paternal or maternal relatives. Many, if not most, of the people in the immediate neighborhood could be traced as Wahid's relatives in one line or the other. Thus, Wahid grew up in the womb of his extended family, immediately ensconced among patrilineal relatives with maternal relatives close by.

Absent Presence of Abu Wahid

Abu Wahid was retired and chronically ill when I first met him in 1994. During a five-month period that year, he had two short hospital stays. He was always around the house but was almost entirely ignored. I was struck by how little Wahid and Sitt Salma seemed to engage Abu Wahid in conversation even though he boisterously interjected himself constantly. I found myself, at times, slipping into an unawareness of his presence in the apartment and occasionally, similarly bypassing him in conversation. When visitors came, Abu Wahid often remained in his room or downstairs sitting alone on a chair in front of the house—door to door with his deceased brother's family.

Rarely, however, did he visit his next-door brother's children or the brothers and their families who lived in the adjacent sections of their commonly owned building. Some years earlier, there had been a dispute between Abu Wahid and his brothers. From that time, Abu Wahid and his family did not visit any of Abu Wahid's brothers and their families even though they all lived door to door.

Abu Wahid was not a passive soul, however. Indeed, both he and Sitt Salma cultivated his image as a violently uncompromising man. He was known to have a volatile temper and a bit of a mean streak. Sitt Salma, at times, posed him as the "bad guy" when she negotiated financial or other transactions. "I would compromise or agree," she would protest, "but Abu Wahid would not let me."

Abu Wahid seemed like an absent presence. He ate by himself except when there was company for dinner. He slept in a room of his own. Few people engaged him in conversation or seemed to come particularly to visit him.

Sitt Salma and Wahid

Sitt Salma woke up between 4:00 and 5:00 A.M. daily.[4] Putting on a robe over her nightgown, she almost daily went across the street for coffee with her sister, Um Kheir, and/or next door with the elderly Um Shakir (Um Kheir's husband's maternal aunt). I often joined those early morning gatherings where gossip, information sharing, and analysis of each day's events were often coupled with jokes, card playing, and story telling. Sitt Salma usually refused to have more than one cup of the strong Arabic coffee, regularly reminding us that she liked to have a cup with Wahid. She was almost always the first to leave the intimate gathering, rushing home before 6:00 A.M. to wake up Wahid. As he prepared to go to work, she made breakfast for the two of them.

During the day she meticulously did her cooking, cleaning, and other housework and tailored clothes commissioned by other villagers. Sitt Salma waited for Wahid to come home for his dinner, usually around 3:00 P.M. In preparation, she always lighted the *azn* (wood-burning hot water heater) enough ahead of time so the water would be just right for his bath when he arrived. Sitt Salma and Wahid, by themselves, ate dinner in his bedroom or in the living room on a tray. While Wahid napped after dinner, Sitt Salma kept everyone away and the house quiet. She appeared to organize all her life and work around Wahid, saving the water, always in short supply, for his baths, washing his clothes, cooking his favorite foods and spending many hours talking with him about family and neighborhood events. Wahid was Sitt Salma's primary companion.

Not only did they have their early morning coffee and eat all their meals together, they also slept in the same bedroom. Sitt Salma complained that she could not sleep with Abu Wahid's snoring and moaning. In the two bedroom apartment, she slept with Wahid, who also at times woke her up at night to ask her to stop snoring. With small apartments and houses, multiple family members sleeping in one room and parents sleeping in rooms with adult children was not uncommon in the neighborhood although it was decreasing in practice as families expanded their houses and married children moved out.

Sitt Salma also did most of her formal and informal visiting with Wahid. Almost always Abu Wahid remained at home alone, complaining that he was too ill to go out. Most of her social calls were to her sisters and brothers. Wahid not only accompanied her on these visits but actively relished the time with his maternal aunts and uncles. Similarly, when the maternal aunts or uncles paid a visit, Wahid remained at home, entertaining them with his mother. Wahid also accompanied his mother on other social calls. As the only person who could drive a car in the family, accompanying his mother might appear to have been a necessity, but he genuinely enjoyed and wanted to go with his mother on most of these calls, he indicated to me. When Sitt Salma had callers, it was Wahid who received them with her, not her husband. Similarly, Sitt Salma would wait for Wahid to take her shopping for groceries or other errands she might need to run.

Wahid felt strongly about his responsibilities as an only son. "I grew up as an only child. My parents were very attached to me. Because they loved me very much, I would like to have children," he offered as his reasoning for wanting children himself. When I asked him what he thought the characteristics of a good boy were, he answered: "He should respect his parents, accept their view. He does not leave them when they are old. He must be honorable."

Khawwal (Became like his maternal uncle)

"*Khawwal* Wahid," Sitt Salma said proudly. As I had not heard that expression before, she explained to me that *khawwal* meant that he had followed in the footsteps of his maternal uncles. "*Bi oolu innu khawwalt*

(They say I followed my maternal uncles)," Wahid proudly exclaimed to me in a long interview about family. Sitt Salma and Wahid were both quite explicit and verbal about the fact that Wahid had not followed his father or father's line but had patterned himself after his maternal uncles.

I had asked Wahid what *amthal* (proverbs) had guided his upbringing and would guide how he raised his children. He volunteered, "*Al walad louw bar, bi yitla' tiltine lil khal* (if nothing comes of the boy, he will still be two-thirds like his maternal uncle)." Sitt Salma had repeated the same matal (sing.) to me a number of times. Wahid explained, "The mother always raises her children like her brothers were raised. A boy will take from his khal. They tell me I took a lot from khali. I am a lot like *akhwali* (pl. of *khal*), even my behavior is like them. I see it a lot that a son comes up like the khal. I see most young men are like their akhwal. It is natural because the mother raises the son like her brothers."

Wahid explained that he did not like his father's family and had nothing to do with them. An incident had occurred in the early 1990s in which his paternal relatives had turned against them. His father had responded by telling him the matal, *rubbi kalbak, bi yu'kuh jambak* (You raise your dog and he'll bite your leg). Wahid said that his father had raised his brothers and they had turned against him. This experience had a fatal impact on Wahid's relationship with his paternal relatives.

One of Wahid's maternal uncles, however, had given him his car. He worked for one of his maternal uncles to pay his way through school and to help support his parents. After he completed civil engineering, he started working full time with this khal. Wahid also felt much closer to his mother's sisters than he did to his father's sister. One sister, living at the edge of Yusfiyyi, visited very frequently. Wahid delighted in her visits, prioritized spending time with her at his home or hers, and saved relished morsels of information to share with her. He highly valued her opinion of events, often actively seeking her advice.

Similarly, Sitt Salma always praised her brothers and sisters. She referred to any brother when she mentioned his name as *habib albi* (sweetheart). She rarely made direct comparisons between her brothers and her husband's, but the indirect comparison was quite evident to listeners of her matrilineal praise. She also admired all her sisters, particularly the one who visited most frequently. Numerous times, she lauded this sister's quick wit, capacity to remember amthal and sharp mind. She and her sister Um Kheir, at their daily coffees, often talked in the most approving terms of their brothers and sisters to each other and to other visitors.

Although there were status differences between his mother and father's line, perhaps it was less the status per se that led Wahid to follow his maternal line than it was the general nature of his and his father's relationship with his patriline. That his father had felt betrayed by his brothers and their children over an earlier incident contributed to Wahid's rejection of his father's family. The rather volatile temper of one of the brothers and of Wahid's own father also may have done little to endear Wahid to his patriline. His matriline, however, Wahid experienced and portrayed as stable and honorable.

In local terms Sitt Salma's family might have been of slightly higher status than his father's family. One of her brothers had an important position in the local municipality, one was a secondary school teacher, and one owned a construction company. Abu Wahid's brothers had done adequately by local standards. One owned a small lumber shop, and another was a fisherman. Their statuses, however, in terms of local regard, were slightly lower than that achieved by Sitt Salma's family.

This was particularly interesting because Sitt Salma and Abu Wahid were distantly related. Sitt Salma could not tell me precisely how, but she knew there was a kinship connection. Although Sitt Salma accepted that her son could marry outside the family and even outside the religious sect, she claimed that she would have forbidden him to marry a Muslim or a non-Lebanese Arab. She explained, "*Min akhad min gheir miltu, rikib 'illi gheir 'iltu* (whoever marries outside his community bears problems that are not his problems)." It is always better to marry within the known community, she cautioned.

My Mother/Myself

Mother-son relationships were generally close in the local culture as were mother-daughter relationships. One Yusfiyyi mother, for example, after her son married and moved into the apartment she and her husband had built over their summer home for him and his wife, began spending winter nights in their summer apartment in order to be close to their son. The summer and winter apartments where technically in the same village, only a ten-minute car drive away. She complained that she missed him too much, even though they had and continued to spend their weekends in the village as well. It was too hard not to have him directly in her house, she said, despite the fact that she saw him daily, their houses operated functionally as one house, and they spent almost all their weekend leisure time together.

That Wahid and Sitt Salma should be so close was normal and natural in the village—and in much of Lebanese and Arab culture. That he was both an only child and an only son no doubt intensified their intimacy. Building on cultural norms, Wahid felt that his mother had been the single most important influence in his life. "My mother would sew all night. I would be home and wash the dishes, put things away for her. My mother taught me many things of life. My father had no time for me. My mother had the *fadil kabir* (big role)," Wahid explained to me. He congratulated his mother on her discipline and childrearing. "I grew up an only child as if I were not an only child. I was not spoiled. She taught me to be solid, strong in life. My mother is strong. She is very able. She is the only one who taught me, not my father." For Wahid, his mother was so crucial and important that his best metaphor to understanding the Lebanese state was to liken it to a mother. "*Ad dawli um attani*" (the state is a second mother), he proclaimed. "The state teaches the people. The state is responsible to make good programs for the children, and so forth. The state is the mother of all."

Wahid added that "with the father, one is more hidden. With the mother, I am more honest. I am more harsh toward my father than my mother. It is natural. Both are suffering for me, but it is natural to have this difference." To clarify, he continued, "The feelings of the mother are not different from the father's toward the son. The father may be harsher or even swear at the son. But the mother never, never will swear. But the feelings are the same."

Asked to describe the ideal mother, Wahid answered, "The ideal mother is my mother. She is able. She knows how to run her house. She knows how to do everything. She knows how to raise her son a good way, to teach her son everything in life. She doesn't speak bad about people. She is well mannered." He added definitively, "She made me into a man."

Wahid offered a description of the ideal father but did not volunteer that his father fit this description: "The ideal father listens to his children and solves their problems logically. He knows how to treat his wife in front of his children so he and his wife are one person. He respects his wife and children. He teaches his children the difficulties of life."

For Wahid, the ideal son (or daughter) was one who never forgot *fadil ahlu* (the role, contribution of his parents). It was especially important to him that daughters not forget the *fadil* of their mothers. What a parent does for a child, he pointed out, stays with a child all his life.

When I asked Wahid whether he would raise his children any differently from the way he had been raised, he answered that he would raise them as his mother had raised him. He added that his parents, especially his mother, would be the most significant people in helping him raise his children because he expected his parents to live with him in the house. He said that he expected that his children would listen to their mother more than anyone else, explaining that for him, "I have my mother before everything. My father was distant. My mother was close. She raised me, so I listen to her more." Beyond their mother and his parents, he thought that his children would be most influenced by their mother's siblings. He said this not because he had no siblings, however, but because he believed that mother's siblings are more involved than father's siblings in the rearing of children in general.

Nevertheless, he was careful to assert that no one has "rights" over a child other than the parents—not even the grandparents. "It is not the old days when if someone made a mistake, everyone gathered to take account," he explained. Children, now, had no specific responsibilities to their grandparents nor did grandparents have specific responsibilities for the grandchildren, he insisted. It was all on the parents. Having said that, he added that neither his daughter nor his son would have a right to disagree with their grandparents (or parents) if the grandparents are teaching them the important principles of life.

My Son/Myself

That Sitt Salma was so invested in Wahid was most natural in the eyes of her family and community. Not only was he an only child but he was a son. Sons, by cultural norms, are considered to be responsible for parents in their old age despite the reality that daughters often take more responsibilities for their aging parents than do sons. One afternoon, in the summer of 1996, a group of village women gathered for coffee at the home of Um Kheir, Sitt Salma's older sister. They were commenting on how the daughters of Um Shakir, an elderly village woman, had all gathered around to take care of their mother when she fell ill. Each day one or more daughters came by to cook, clean, run errands for their elderly parents, visit with them and take them places if they needed an escort. All of the women seated under Um Kheir's grapevine, except Sitt Salma, had daughters and sons. Sitt Salma made a point that sons were important, but several quickly chimed in that in the end nothing was like having a daughter for your ending days. To this, Sitt Salma quipped with obvious sarcasm, "Poor me, then I will be all alone when I age! I have only a son!" Quickly, all the women asserted that of course a son was first and foremost.

It was a dialogue against the grain of the predominately verbalized cultural norms that offer the son as the uncontested pride of his parents and as the undisputed first authority with regard to his parents. Almost all villagers recognize the more complex reality in which daughters not only take responsibility toward their parents but parents often feel more comfortable asking of their daughters than asking of their sons. Yet the palatable relief when a wife produces a son for her husband is testimony to the yet relatively unchallenged centrality of the son to the family.

For Sitt Salma, having children was the most important thing in life. She wanted more, but had married late. When Wahid turned out to be a difficult child, she postponed having a second, and then it was too late, she explained. "Children are good for your end (*akhirtik*). If you have no children, it is like having nothing. If you have no children, your memory dies. If you have a child, they will say, 'This is the child of so and so.' "

Sitt Salma had strong beliefs about childrearing and was a rather disciplined parent by local standards. Her view of the ideal son was that he was good in society, respected, valued, and knew how to talk. "He listens to his family. If he is not raised well, he gets angry and leaves when his parents talk to him. A well-raised son, when his parents talk to him, he says, *'Tikrami, ana be amrik* (You are welcome, I am in your command)." The most important thing to teach a son is respect for his parents, she observed.

Sitt Salma was especially good at remembering and using proverbs. Very much like the older generation, but unlike the younger generation of parents, she liberally used proverbs in raising Wahid and continued to pepper her speech with proverbs as occasions arose. When I asked Sitt Salma what proverbs had been important in her own upbringing and her parenting of Wahid, she, in her interview conducted two years before my interview with Wahid, responded with exactly the same proverb that he offered as crucial in his upbringing—that two-thirds of the son follows the mother's brother. She stated that Wahid had khawwal, adding that she had wanted him to be like her brothers because they had good reputations and wealth. Like Wahid, she said that her mother had been the most important influence in her life. And in 1994, she offered the proverb that Wahid had volunteered in my 1996 interview with him as his key guide in choosing his wife: *Tub al jarra 'ala timma, titla' al bint la umma* (Tilt a jar to its mouth and the daughter will turn out like the mother). She added another proverb, *Talli' 'ala um wa lim* (Look at the mother and gather). She contended that she had always taught Wahid to find out about the mother before he chose his wife. Indeed, two years later, when I interviewed him on this subject and he had become engaged, Wahid recited this proverb and explained that he had first met his fiancée's sister, then her mother. Only then did he feel comfortable about courting her. When he came to like the mother and sisters, he felt confident that the fiancée would be a good wife.

Sitt Salma said that she always tried to speak calmly to Wahid so that he would listen to her words. She would tell him, *"Haza jaza' la yisma' kalam ummu"* (This consequence comes to the one who does not listen to the words of his mother), a proverb mothers at times liked to recite. Abu Wahid, Sitt Salma observed, was narrow-minded. If Wahid did not agree with him, he would swear at him right away. He had no patience with Wahid because that was the way he had been raised.

She said that she had raised Wahid by herself. Abu Wahid would come home only after 6:00 P.M. by which time she had done everything. "If his father said anything [bad] to him, I didn't like it. If the father says anything [bad] to the son, the son won't respect him." She claimed that she and only she was responsible for raising Wahid. "No one else—not even the father—is responsible," she contended.

She felt strongly that a child should agree with the mother on all the guidance she gives him. "A mother does not guide in the wrong way. The child should obey the mother. Whatever the mother says, the child should obey," she insisted. "Refusal is forbidden. If you permit a child, he'll repeat it each time." But she pointed out that Wahid had told her that she was not right in everything. This reminded her that the child has a right to try to persuade the parent. "If the mother finds out that the child is right, the mother will give him his right." She claimed that whatever she said, Wahid always followed her words. She extended this to add that a child does not have a right to disagree with his elders.

After Wahid grew older she qualified, "Now the most important person when he grew older is his khal (maternal uncle). His khal forced him to go back to school and he employed him." Sitt Salma proudly recalled to me that Wahid had often said to her, "God give me time to live to be able to be like khali (maternal uncle) and to let me help you live even better than khali let his wife live."

Marriage

Wahid and his parents expected him to live in the same building with them after he married. For that reason they had built two stories to their house, each a complete two-bedroom apartment. This was a common pattern in Yusfiyyi. Parents often either added floors to their buildings for their married sons or built, on family or purchased land, a building with a complete apartment (usually a full floor) for each of their sons. In cases in which parents could not afford the costs, the brothers often collectively built these multiapartment buildings for each other. The general assumption, following patrilocal customs, was that the son brought his wife to his family and that daughters moved out. Some parents built even for their daughters, however. Often married sons lived in the same apartment or house as their parents until they could afford to add a story or build another building.

When Wahid married in 1996, he and his wife moved into the same apartment with his parents. His mother had rented the other floor for a three-year-period that did not expire for another year. The plan was that either Wahid or his parents would move into that apartment once the tenant's lease had expired. Wahid and his wife busily refurbished his parents' apartment during the summer of 1996. They changed light fixtures, repainted the house inside and out, transformed the hallway entrance into an additional sitting room, and remodeled the kitchen. Abu Wahid had moved out of his bedroom to share bedrooms once again with Sitt Salma. Wahid had taken Abu Wahid's bedroom and remodeled it to add a half-bath.

Wahid's fiancée came frequently during the summer of 1996 to spend time with Sitt Salma and Abu Wahid and to help make decisions on the refurbishing of the house. Sitt Salma tried to accommodate their desires although she clearly did not like some of their tastes. An excellent cook, Sitt Salma made fine meals for when her future daughter-in-law visited, often inviting her sisters, brothers, or others, including me and my daughter, to join in. A proper hostess, she insisted on everyone eating their fill.

At one point in such a meal, Wahid protested to his mother that she should leave his fiancée alone if she did not want to eat. Sitt Salma explained that she just wanted to make sure that her daughter-in-law was not shy and was eating properly. Rather curtly, Wahid repeated to leave his fiancée alone and that she could decide for herself what she wanted to eat.

It was clear that there would be some jostling around boundary setting between the new couple and the old family. Yet the situation was not fractious. Sitt Salma accepted it although apparently she was a bit embarrassed. Having lived with a temperamentally volatile husband, Sitt Salma knew how to let minor outbursts pass and to return later to deal with issues.

The fiancée remained quiet and accomodating throughout the exchange and throughout all the interactions I observed over the summer of 1996. Wahid had told me that he had chosen her in part because she came from a large family and seemed accomodating. He said it was important to him that his wife knew how to get along with his parents because he planned to live with them and to take care of them as they aged. His wife would have major responsibilities for his parents under their living arrangements. Sitt Salma seemed quite pleased with his choice of wife. Indeed, it seemed as if her best-laid plans had all gone aright.

Conclusion

Mother-son relationships have been widely recognized as strong in Arab societies in general. Many explanations have been offered. Some have argued that the mother has only her son to rely upon in the long run in the predominately Muslim Arab cultures because the Muslim man can marry up to four wives and has the right and ease of divorce without his wife's consent. Although divorce is extremely difficult for Arab Christians like Sitt Salma and Abu Wahid, the norms of Muslim communities have influenced the minority Arab Christian communities. Arab culture in general, being patriarchal and patrilineal, valorizes the son as the prime offspring of his parents. Even though many parts of the Arab world are rapidly changing, in most Arab societies it is by birthing a son that a woman makes her claim to status. In this regard, Sitt Salma and Wahid's closeness clearly fits the cultural norm.

Some scholars, however, have suggested that the closeness of the mother-son relationship may be problematical or even dysfunctional. Halim Barakat has been concerned that the deep attachment to family, especially in the mother-son relationship is close to morbidity.[5] Hisham Sharabi and Mukhtar Ali[6] have faulted Arab mothers for coddling sons too much. Andrea Rugh,[7] writing on Egyptian families, has argued that the mother experiences the son as "her own personal ego extension." She observed that mothers compete with fathers for the affection of their sons, with the mother's "unrestrained love and affection" being driven by an "urgency" because her only security, if her husband divorces her, is her son's willingness to stay with her and care for her.[8]

Such competition between mothers and fathers for sons and the strength of the mother-son bond, when it occurs, might appear to threaten patriarchy, in addition to the judgment of dysfunctionality offered by some scholars. That a son may follow his mother's brother (khal) rather than his father or father's brother might appear to be an even greater threat to patriarchy in this highly patriarchal culture. Although there may be problems in particular relationships and in the long run as social changes transform local societies and these changes may spell problems for patriarchy, in the context in which I observed these mother-son dynamics in Yusfiyyi I suggest close mother-son relationships were not only functional but a plausible, although paradoxical, outcome of this patriarchal, patrilineal, endogamous society.

The Christian village of Yusfiyyi, although surrounded by other Christian villages in Mount Lebanon, has existed in the otherwise predominately Muslim environment of the Arab world for centuries. Although there is no uniform, homogeneous "Muslim" culture in the Arab world, some basic principles are generally supported. Patriarchy, patrilineage, and endogamy are among these. Arab cultures, Muslim or Christian, generally are patriarchal. I have elsewhere[9] defined patriarchy as a gendered and aged domination—the privileging of males and seniors (including senior women)—which is justified and supported in kinship structures, moralities, and idioms. Patriarchy is also supported by religious, political, and economic institutions in much of the Arab world.[10] Patrilineage, reckoning descent through the male line, has taken on a specific form in Arab cultures because of endogamy. The cultural preference (often not followed) among Muslims, has been for marriage in the patriline. The cultural ideal for many Muslims has been the marriage of the children of two brothers. As Murphy and Kasdan[11] observed, this would give the patrilineal system, paradoxically, a bilineal slant because mother's and father's relatives would be the same in such endogamous marriages. A strong connection with a mother's brother, in endogamous marriages, would reinforce the same larger family unit as would a strong connection with a father's brother.[12]

Christians were formally admonished against close cousin marriages. In practice, however, Lebanese Christians often married close cousins on either the patrilineal or matrilineal side. In Yusfiyyi, a small village with a long history of endogamy, people often joked that if you scratched deep enough, everyone was related. Patrilineality in Yusfiyyi, although upheld, was perhaps not as dominant as normatively prescribed in Muslim cultures. And in any case, the authority of the maternal uncle still vested power in a familial male, reinforcing the general principles of patriarchy.

Neither Abu Wahid, Sitt Salma, Wahid, or any of their family members or neighbors ever commented to me that Wahid was unusual in his attachment to his mother and her family. The hypervalorization of the mother, indeed, could be compensatory to the mother's subordination to father and son and brother and husband. This valorization of the mother, paradoxically, gave her a considerable degree of power and autonomy, particularly in relation to her children. That Sitt Salma's family was of slightly higher status may also have moved Wahid toward his maternal line. Abu Wahid's break with his brothers and their children also installed a boundary between him and his family that Wahid did not cross.

Whether the intensity of closeness between Sitt Salma and Wahid is dysfunctional is yet another matter. Counter to the claims of some scholars, I argue that in the context of such small, face-to-face communities in which children expect to live in close proximity to their families all their lives and sons are expected to care for their aging parents and mothers are expected to give and love their children, especially their sons, unconditionally, this closeness is quite functional. To conceptualize the functionality of such close relationships, I developed a relational theory of selfhood[13] that I call connectivity.

By connectivity I mean relationships in which a person's boundaries are relatively fluid so that persons feel a part of significant others. Connective selves do not experience themselves as bounded, separate, or autonomous. They may read each other's minds, answer for each other, anticipate each other's needs, expect their needs to be anticipated by significant others, and often shape their likes and dislikes in accordance with the likes and dislikes of others. Maturity may be signaled in part by the successful enactment of a myriad of connective relationships.

Connectivity exists side by side with individualism in the same culture and perhaps even in the same person. These are not oppositional polarities. They often partake of each other, being applied situationally or, at times, leading to tensions within and between persons. In a culture in which the family is valued over and above the person, identity is defined in familial terms, and kin idioms and relationships pervade public and private spheres, connective relationships may be not only functional but also necessary for successful social existence.

Among Arab families connectivity is often embedded in patriarchy to produce what I call *patriarchal connectivity.* I use patriarchal connectivity to mean the production of selves with fluid boundaries organized for gendered and aged domination in a culture valorizing kin structures, morality, and idioms. Patriarchy entails cultural constructs and structural relations that privilege the initiative of males and elders in directing the lives of others. Connectivity entails cultural constructs and structural relations in which persons invite, require, and initiate involvement with others in shaping the self. In patriarchal societies, then, connectivity can support patriarchal power by crafting selves responding to, requiring, and socialized to initiate involvement with others in shaping the self, and patriarchy can help reproduce connectivity by crafting males and seniors prepared to direct the lives of females and juniors and females and juniors prepared to respond to the direction of males and seniors.

Sitt Salma, Abu Wahid, and Wahid displayed aspects of this construct of patriarchal connectivity. Sitt Salma appeared to be a contented and fulfilled woman. Although she had chilly relations with some family members and neighbors (some of whom regarded her rather ill), in general she maintained a congenial surface with almost everyone, even members of her husband's family whom she clearly did not like (and who did not like her). Wahid appeared to be a proud son. To the degree he may have not been liked or respected by his relatives, this had nothing to do with his closeness to his mother, his plan to live in the same apartment or house, or his devaluing of his father. Wahid was held in very high regard by his mother's family, who routinely praised his work habits, his discipline, and his dedication to his mother.

Abu Wahid did not appear threatened by Sitt Salma and Wahid's relationship per se. Chronically ill and bedridden in 1994, he seemed more vigorous in 1996 and 1997. Whether he felt fulfilled was difficult to say, particularly in 1994, given that he was generally thought of as cranky. Yet in 1996 and 1997, he expressed enthusiasm for life, exhibited energy and humor, and seemed more active than in 1994. Obviously pleased that his son was about to complete his university degree and to be married, he appeared to relish the moments in front of him.

How such relationships between mothers and sons will fare in the dramatic transformations occurring throughout Lebanon and in Yusfiyyi in the future is difficult to predict. In the short run, the civil war in Lebanon, which lasted from 1975 to 1991, appears to have drawn families closer to each other in many ways while, perhaps, in other ways it has undermined some of the principles of family life. During this study, however, it was clear that Sitt Salma and Wahid's close relationship was viewed and experienced as not only functional but mature. It is, perhaps, one of the paradoxes of patriarchy and patriarchal connectivity that powerful mother-son relationships not only exist but thrive, are normalized and naturalized, and are highly valorized in this yet familial culture.

8

The Microdynamics of Patriarchal Change in Egypt and the Development of an Alternative Discourse on Mother-Daughter Relations

The Case of ʿAʾisha Taymur

MERVAT F. HATEM

Introduction

Marxian and radical feminist discourses on women, power, and powerlessness have contributed conflicting claims regarding the relationship between patriarchy and mothering that are difficult to settle theoretically. For some, mothering is the primary justification for the sexual division of labor that restricts women to the private sphere as dependents of men.[1] For others, it is the basis of a particular social status from which women derive some power in patriarchal societies.[2] For a third group, mothering enlists women's complicity in the social reproduction of gender inequality.[3]

In this chapter, I use Michel Foucault's deconstruction of the meaning and the praxis of power to develop an alternative discourse that explains how the interest in the exercise and the execution of power illuminates the complex dynamics of mother-daughter relationships and the role that they play in the change of patriarchal societies. Toward that goal, I critique the historical discourse that draws upon the experiences of ʿAʾisha Taymur's upper-class family in nineteenth-century Egypt to shape an understanding of the familial dynamics behind social change. Modernist historians[4] and feminist writers[5] offer the same dominant discursive narrative on Taymur's life. They contrast Taymur's struggle with her mother over the pursuit of a literary education with her father's support of those aspirations. Their analyses usually suggest that women/mothers in Egypt were the traditional opponents of change, whereas men/fathers were important catalysts for its introduction.[6]

In place of the above discourse, which has had a powerful hold on the historical memory of women and their understanding of their relationship to change, I present a different reading of Taymur's struggles that is more evenhanded in its discussion of the contributions of her mother and father to the introduction of change. I pay special attention to the microdynamics of power in mother-daughter relationships (which included Taymur's relationship with her mother and then her relationship with her own daughter) and how both showed women's contribution to the development of complex forms of consciousness that simultaneously resisted and facilitated change.

Mothers, Fathers, Daughters: The Microdynamics of Power in Egyptian Families

The advantage of taking the microdynamics of power as the basis for the development of an alternative discourse is that it focuses attention on the detailed roles that women, men, and children played within patriarchal families that the macro debates on patriarchy are seldom able to capture. Within Middle East studies, the discussions of the patriarchal/Muslim family have recently taken on an eclectic tone. Some still maintain that in Arab/Muslim families men monopolize "power" and that women and children do without it.[7] In contrast, feminists have argued that Middle Eastern women have successfully used the private world of the family to augment their power.[8] Some have documented women's resistance to patriarchal rules governing marriage, divorce, custody of children, and inheritance through the court system.[9]

Although these divergent approaches to the study of the roles women play in the family were successful in challenging their presumed passivity, they were silent on the conscious and unconscious psychodynamics of gender inequality within patriarchal families. Taymur's autobiographical texts captured this dimension in their discussion of the intrafamily dynamics. They showed the complex social and emotional character of patriarchal power and its heavy reliance on a combination of consent (persuasion) and the threat of coercion, which included emotional pressure. The dominant narrative reversed the power relations that exist in patriarchal families. It highlighted the role that women played as the primary caretakers who were also the powerful enforcers of the rules and the social embodiments of femininity. In contrast, it presented the father as a detached bystander not responsible for the rules or interested in their enforcement. His intervention in support of his daughter was given a naïve benevolent spin that overlooked how his interests as a patriarch were served by his actions.

Yet rebellion against the mother sent an important warning signal to the father, whose social power within and outside the household depended on compliance of his womenfolk. Both parents had clear but different interests in the outcome of any reorganization of gender roles. Mothers received societal approval and respect when they successfully socialized their children into existing gendered roles. Failure in this task exposed mothers to censure from the patriarch and their social and familial networks. Socially, small rebellions by daughters were looked on as having spillover and spin-off effects on other sexual and/or marital rules associated with the family's honor. These threatened to emasculate the father, whose exercise of power within his most immediate domain depended, to a very large extent, on compliance. A challenge of a mother's authority could easily be followed by a challenge of his authority within the family. This conflict would undermine the familial basis of the social power he enjoyed in public arenas.

Finally, female children emerged in these accounts as active participants, who in some specific contexts, were able to question existing rules, including the definition of their gender roles. Their compliance with these rules could not be assumed but had to be secured either through consent, coercion, or a combination of both. One could not, however, exaggerate their autonomy and/or power. Children were totally dependent on their parents for care and protection. At an impressionable age, they were also susceptible to the direct or the indirect pressure/influence of the parents.

This influence was demonstrated during the less-well-known second phase of Taymur's struggle against the prevailing patriarchal rules of her time. Her adult attempt to address the serious dilemma of reconciling her domestic preoccupations with her literary interests and ambitions led to an unequal arrangement with her daughter, Tawhida. She transferred her domestic responsibilities to her daughter and denied her daughter's desire to pursue literary study and training. Through this arrangement, Taymur reproduced the indigenous and modern repudiation of the feminine in favor of masculine models of literary training and production. She eventually realized that there was a high emotional cost to this arrangement. Her preoccupation with literary and other public activities led to her inability as a mother to detect the early signs of Tawhida's deteriorating health. Taymur lost her eldest daughter at the age of eighteen.

The Patriarchal Narrative on Mother-Daughter Relations During 'A'isha Taymur's Childhood

The dominant narrative on 'A'isha Taymur's struggle with her mother over the pursuit of a literary education highlighted their conflicting views, interests, and aspirations. In contrast, it emphasized the common interests of father and daughter and the power of their alliance to bring about a change in women's gender roles. It exaggerated the social changes that 'A'isha Taymur's education was to represent. It also overlooked how the father's long-term social expectations for his daughter did not question the primacy of marriage and children. In fact, even though much is made of the differences between the life of 'A'isha Taymur, the poet, and that of her mother, both spent their adult lives as the primary caretakers of men and children.

Most discussion of Taymur's childhood experiences emphasized her upbringing in an upper-class family whose openness to nonreligious education established its modernist credentials. To understand her social milieu, I offer some general and brief comments on the ruling class that Muhammad 'Ali (1805–1848) relied on to build a modern nation-state in Egypt and of which Taymur's father and husband were members. Muhammad 'Ali, who was born in Kavala, Macedonia (in the Balkans),[10] developed a new Turkish ruling class of trained soldiers and bureaucrats to consolidate his hold on political power. Because he ruled over Egypt's ethnically distinct population in the name of Islam, the new state and his ruling class were not likely to question Islamic social practices or customs, including those that related to the education of women. According to historical sources, women in the Egyptian middle and upper classes have had some access to education since the fifteenth century.[11] This was not a social practice or an innovation that could be credited to this new ruling class.

This class enjoyed clear bureaucratic, economic, and political privilege. Their wealth, ethnic roots, and access to power were inherited. As a result, members of this class were identified with aristocratic/conservative social privilege and support for another hereditary institution that is, the monarchy of the dynasty that continued to rule Egypt until 1952.

As a member of this class, Ismail Taymur Pasha, 'A'isha's father, traced his paternal and maternal grandfathers to Turkey and Kurdish Mosul in Iraq. One was a high-ranking officer, who eventually rose to the position of governor, and the other was a high-ranking bureaucrat. Although Taymur's grandparents and great-grandparents were born outside Egypt, they lived their adult lives in Egypt and were, therefore, shaped by that experience. Ismail Taymur, who was born in Egypt, rose to important positions in the foreign department and the Royal Council.[12]

'A'isha Taymur's mother was a Circassian slave. Like her husbands' parents and grandparents, she was born somewhere else (in the Caucuses). When she bore Ismail children, he freed her to avoid his children being born into slavery.[13]

'A'isha Taymur was born into this household in 1840. Her parents had three daughters. There was also a son who was born much later, one year before his father died in 1872. Contrary to what most discussions of the harem (women in sexually segregated households) during this period suggest, this one was preoccupied with its daughters because of the absence of male offspring. If this household like many others during the nineteenth century was extended, then 'A'isha Taymur's account only referred indirectly to this aspect of its structure. It highlighted the power that both parents had over the important decisions in their daughter's life. Although it was possible that the parents' decisions were influenced by others in the household and that 'A'isha was unaware of it, her texts clearly asserted the authority that the parents had over their children and that this was not contested by other members of the family. Taymur's mother decided what her daughter should learn. The only other participant in this discussion was the father.

Taymur wrote several accounts of the childhood experiences that led her to poetry in the introductions to her Arabic, Persian, and Turkish anthologies. As a member of the aristocratic class, she was more restrained in her description of these experiences to her Arabic readers. In the Turkish and Persian accounts that addressed other members of her class, she shared more of her feelings, the intimate details of the negotiations between her mother and father, and the agreement they finally reached regarding her education. For these reasons, I begin with the Arabic description of her rebellion against her mother's attempt to teach her the feminine occupations of her class. This narrative is followed by more details from the Turkish and Persian accounts, which added other layers to an understanding of the complex negotiations regarding her education.

> [Ever since] I . . . began to move around, to distinguish the sources of temptation from those of rationality and to be aware of what is forbidden by my father and grandfather, I have found myself fondly preoccupied with suckling the histories of ancient nations. My maturing energy tended toward investigating the accounts of those who preceded us. I was enamored of the nightly chats of elderly women [in my family] who recounted the best stories/histories. I was fascinated by the strange twists of fate. To the best of my abilities, I contemplated their meaning whether it was serious or funny. I also selected and committed the best of them to memory. At that age, I had no other capability but listening. I [also] had no other access to other forms of enjoyment and entertainment.
>
> When my mind was ready to develop and my capabilities receptive, my mother, the goddess of compassion and virtue and the arsenal of knowledge and wonder, may God shelter her with his grace and forgive her, approached me with the tools of weaving and embroidery. She was diligent in teaching me. She worked hard to explain things clearly and cleverly, but I was not receptive. I was not willing to improve in these feminine crafts. I used to flee from her like a prey seeking to escape the net.
>
> [At the same time], I would look forward to attending the gatherings of prominent writers without any awkwardness. I found the sound of the pen on the paper to be the most beautiful . . . and I became convinced that membership in this group was the most abundant blessing. To satisfy my longing, I would collect any sheets of paper and small pencils, then, I would go to a place away from everyone and imitate the writers as they wrote. Hearing that sound [of pencil on paper] made me happy.
>
> When my mother would find me, she would scold and threaten me. This only increased my rejection of and inadequacy at embroidery.[14]

The dominant reading of the above account only focused on Taymur's desire to learn how to read and write and her mother's opposition. In this discussion I give equal attention to other forms of learning that 'A'isha received at the hands of other women in her family whose standing she did not specify. It was here that the extended character of the family was made evident. From these women Taymur learned important rules of conduct, that is, the sources of temptation, the taboos—what her father and grandfather forbade—and rationality. Through storytelling, they embarked on the informal education and the entertainment of children. Taymur described herself as "suckling" (almost instinctively and unconsciously) these stories and the social lessons they outlined. Not only were the women skillful narrators of amusing stories but they also passed on oral histories of families and nations in the process. This knowledge of history, both personal and social, was the reason why a young Taymur identified these women as the cultural reservoir of wisdom and foresight. Through her interaction with them, Taymur reported learning to reflect and to contemplate the meaning behind their stories.

As Taymur advanced in age and consciousness, she was exposed to other types of learning. The system of sexual segregation that functioned at midcentury did not start at a very young age. She mingled freely, until the age of seven to nine years, with men from within and outside the family in the literary gatherings that took place in her father's house. This gave her access to a different type of learning—formal and literate associated with maleness. It belonged to the writers who visited and entertained her father. When she developed an interest in this type of literary learning, she discovered that her family deemed it inappropriate for female children.

Instead, Taymur's Circassian mother took over the task of initiating her into the feminine occupations of embroidery and weaving. Through them, discipline and concentration were learned. Even though Taymur described her mother as the goddess of compassion, her mother demanded obedience and compliance. The scolding and the threats by her mother conformed to the clichéd image of the Circassian mother as strict, rigid, and prone to discipline. Her mother's persistence in teaching her embroidery and weaving probably reflected her knowledge of the importance of these skills for the definition of aristocratic domesticity. In this family, learning to read and write was clearly less important.

In Taymur's account feminine learning within the aristocracy combined in complex ways the oral learning of history, social rules, and the aesthetics of color and coordination learned through embroidery and weaving. In contrast, masculinity was identified with formal high culture with emphasis on reading and writing and interest in literary production. If the former was viewed as traditional, it was only because it was different from the masculine in its reliance on informality, oral transmission, and manual skills. Whereas the Islamic literary traditions gave importance to oral transmission of the sacred word (e.g., the Quran and the *Hadith*), the oral transmission of ordinary experience, manual skills, culture, and history, which women storytellers performed within different families, did not enjoy the same prestige. The major exception to this cultural attitude toward women storytellers was Scheherazade in *The Thousand and One Nights*. This literary work highlighted the skills of the learned storyteller and the important contribution she made to her family and society.[15] Her tales helped heal the emotional wounds Shahrayar suffered after the discovery of his wife's infidelity.[16] By teaching him to be more reflective, Scheherazade saved the realm and womankind from his violent rage. This ideal had resonance in Taymur's description of how enamored she was by these women and their stories. The skills of reflection and knowledge of the personal/social dynamics of their world lay at the heart of this cultural model of femininity. The emphasis on the manual skills of weaving and embroidery represented another aristocratic feminine ideal associated with the expectation that slave women demonstrate their skills through the production of embroidery and weaving. Both of these indigenous definitions of femininity existed alongside one another within the aristocratic class.

Because 'A'isha Taymur's rejection of embroidery in favor of learning how to read and write was interpreted as questioning the boundaries separating feminine and masculine forms of learning, the father was eventually called upon to settle this conflict, which had significant implications for the socialization of his other daughters. This was how Taymur described her complex feelings about the painful struggle with her mother and the parallel struggle between her mother and father as they debated what needed to be done.

> Even though I was genuinely inclined toward [literate] learning, I also tried to win my mother's approval. But I continued to dislike the feminine occupations. I used to go out to the reception area [*slamlik*] past the writers who happened to be there and listen to their melodious verse. My mother—may God rest her in the heavenly gardens—was hurt by my actions. She would reprimand, threaten, warn, and promise to punish. She also appealed to me with friendly promises of jewelry and pretty costumes.
>
> [Finally], my father reasoned with her, quoting the Turkish poet who said: The heart is not led, through force, to the desired path. So do not torment another soul if you can spare it! He also cautioned: Beware of breaking the heart of this young girl and tainting her purity with violence. If our daughter is inclined to the pen and paper, do not obstruct her desire. Let us share our daughters: You take 'Afat and give me 'Asmat [another of 'A'isha's names]. If I make a writer out of her, then this will bring me mercy after my death.
>
> My father, then, said: Come with me 'Asmat! Starting tomorrow I will bring you two instructors who will teach you Turkish, Persian, *fiqh* [jurisprudence] and Arabic grammar. Do well in your studies and obey my instructions and beware of shaming me before your mother.[17]

The above was a complex account of the emotional conflict between mother and daughter and how the father negotiated an agreement with the mother regarding the education of their eldest daughter. First, the rebellion of the daughter was not free from the simultaneous desire to find a way to please her mother. The mother could not compromise, however, on the issue of the boundaries that separated femaleness from maleness. The shame the mother experienced stemmed from the feeling that she had failed to elicit obedience from her daughter, who seemed determined in her challenge of existing rules. As a slave who obeyed others, the disobedience of the daughter was experienced as a personal rejection. It also alarmed the mother, who seemed to identify the learning of embroidery with the esteemed domestic status and aristocratic privilege she wanted for her daughters. Understandably, she was invested in securing for her daughter this prized status. This explained why she proceeded cleverly to use all the emotional weapons in her arsenal. She reprimanded, threatened, and promised her daughter different types of rewards. She did this on her own without soliciting the help of the father, who at this stage remained a bystander. It was clear that the socialization of young girls was the established responsibility of the mother and that a father did not usually intervene between mother and daughter.

When he did intervene, it was clear from the way he approached his wife that this was done with care and affection. He proceeded to persuade, not order, his wife to let him take a different route. This was a touching scene. He quoted her verses from Turkish poems, which might be closer to her Circassian heart. In the end, he negotiated a complicated arrangement for the education of two of his girls. Of the two daughters who were old enough to go through feminine training, he would guide the education of the rebellious 'A'isha while the mother took care of 'Afat's. In this bargain it was understood that he would bear the blame if his eldest daughter turned out badly. This agreement exonerated the mother from any blame and placed that responsibility squarely on his shoulders.

What led the father to contemplate this unusual arrangement? One can only speculate. As mentioned previously, at this point Taymur's father had three daughters and no son. With one daughter showing interest in what would have been the proper education for a son, the father may have taken some vicarious satisfaction from this unexpected turn of events. He was willing to put some family resources into 'A'isha's literary education as a surrogate son. For those who read into the above account the feminist credentials of Ismail Taymur Pasha, there are serious problems with this interpretation. He did not want all of his daughters to have a literary education. The agreement reached with the mother stipulated that the other daughters would be brought up in the usual conventional ways.

Emotional motives and intentions aside, the father was clearly worried about the ominous effects of a prolonged confrontation between mother and daughter. He indirectly alluded to this concern in the exchange with his wife. He suggested that in dealing harshly with the daughter's unorthodox interests, the mother might break the girl's heart and drive her to a more serious challenge of the rules, that is, those which would taint her sexual purity (*tuhr*). This stood as the more awful prospect. He was afraid that this small rebellion would develop into a more serious challenge of patriarchal expectations. It was this fear that led to his unusual intervention on behalf of his daughter. His support for change was designed to contain its subversive effects. He was willing to make concessions to this limited rebellion to avoid a potentially major one. After securing his wife's cooperation, the first thing he made 'A'isha promise was to obey his instructions and not to shame him before others.

In an interesting aside, Taymur Pasha stated an Islamic belief that his success in making a writer (by implication a virtuous person) out of his daughter would be rewarded by mercy from God after his death. This indicated that Islam was represented in the mid-nineteenth century as rewarding parents who through education raised virtuous daughters knowledgeable in religious/literary pursuits. During this period, the idea of women versed in literary learning was also not an unusual one. There were three such well-known women who claimed that status. An adult Taymur called upon them later to tutor her in poetic meters and Arabic grammar.

For the education of the young 'A'isha, the father brought his daughter two male tutors to instruct her in Turkish, Persian, fiqh (Islamic jurisprudence), and, finally, Arabic grammar. The fact that Taymur recruited male teachers to assist his daughter in learning Turkish and Persian confirmed the observation that sexual segregation was not strictly enforced upon young girls. The custom was, however, that the male teachers recruited to teach young girls were advanced in age. The study of fiqh was designed to put this new type of learning into a socioreligious framework.

Analysts have assumed that the father's provision of the above resources contributed all the necessary conditions for Taymur's successful initiation into literary education. Absent from this discussion was her mother's cooperation and how it provided a hospitable climate for change. If the mother had continued her overt or hidden opposition, then the efforts of father and daughter could have been easily undermined. There was no evidence of either in Taymur's accounts. As a result, 'A'isha's education proceeded smoothly. Despite early opposition Taymur's mother was not willing to subvert her daughter's success in her new accomplishments. She chose to be protective of her daughter's accomplishments whether she agreed with them or not.

Even though Taymur excelled in her studies, this stage, with its unique experiences for the daughters of this family, ultimately ended with her marriage a few years later. 'A'isha did not question her early marriage or her domestic responsibilities as a wife and a mother. Both made it difficult to pursue her literary interests. As her father had predicted, the containment of her modest challenge of patriarchal rules regarding what young girls should or should not learn contributed to Taymur's acquiescence to the prevailing dominant definitions of femininity.

Although much is made of 'A'isha Taymur's novel education and how her father's support contributed to the rise of a new generation of women whose options and social standing were different from those that preceded them, Taymur's adult experiences were not different from those of other free women of her class. Only her roles as wife and then mother were socially valorized during this period. They provided her with rights and privileges of which her slave mother was conscious. Yet in the end 'A'isha's adult preoccupations and those of her mother were not that different. Both spent their adult lives as the primary caretakers of men and children in their families.

Patriarchal Silence on the Sacrifices that Taymur and Her Daughter Made to Secure Her Status as a Poet

Most discussions of Taymur's life are silent on the very special relationship Taymur had with her daughter, Tawhida, who realized her mother's desire to complete her literary education. This was a curious omission. Taymur's different accounts stressed that the alliance with her daughter was behind the completion of her literary studies. In this section I examine the reasons behind this discursive silence, the generational changes it showed in the education of female children, and how these intersected with Taymur's struggles as a wife and mother who had literary aspirations.

Taymur was married at the age of fourteen to fifteen to Muhammid Bek Tewfik Zadeh, the son of the governor of the Sudan at the time.[18]

Marriage brought on domestic responsibilities and motherhood. For the next thirteen years Taymur's personal and familial history was not very different from that of her contemporaries. It was not clear how many children she had. There were references to three of her children in her poems: a daughter, and two other sons. There could have been more. In addition to children, wealthy households sometimes included other close and distant members of the family besides slaves, which made the management of these households a very demanding task.[19] It presented a very serious hurdle for someone with other interests at heart. In response, Taymur turned to her eldest daughter, Tawhida, for help.

According to Taymur, Tawhida was an exceptional young girl. This was how her mother described her.

> After ten years [of marriage], the first fruit of my heart—Tawhida, who is part of my self and the spirit of my joy, reached the age of nine. I enjoyed watching her spending her days from morning till noon between the pens and the ink bottles, and during the rest of the day and evening, she wove the most beautiful crafts. I prayed for her success, feeling my own sadness regarding what I missed when I was her age and repulsed by these activities.
>
> When my daughter was twelve years of age, she began to serve her mother and father. In addition, she managed the household, including all of the servants and the dependents. It was then that I was able to find areas [zwaya] of relaxation.[20]
>
> At this point, it occurred to me to resume what I missed as a youngster—learning poetic meters. I brought a woman instructor to teach me. . . . But she passed away six months later. My daughter, who had attended these lessons, was able because of her youth and sharp intellect to excel in this art more than I did.[21]

From the above description, Taymur was clearly a good, but tormented mother. Because she did not put undue pressure on Tawhida to learn a particular set of skills, Tawhida took equal delight in the learning of languages and in the feminine crafts. Through her daughter Taymur even began to enjoy the crafts she originally had rejected. She regretted the fact that she had been unable to appreciate them in the past.

In describing the transfer of her domestic duties to Tawhida, she suggested that this was her daughter's decision. This comment raised the question of how Tawhida reached that decision. Did she make that decision on her own? Was she pressured into it? And what would constitute coercion or consent in this case? Judging by Taymur's family history, there was no familial and/or social expectation for a twelve-year-old girl to take on such a huge responsibility as the management of a large household. Before her marriage, Taymur spent these youthful years resisting the learning of embroidery and then pursuing the study of reading and writing.

If this was not part of a young girl's preparation for marriage, why did Tawhida volunteer to do it? Before the switch of roles between mother and daughter, Taymur described a happy Tawhida enjoying learning to write and to embroider. Taking on household tasks would have interfered with Tawhida's own pursuit of literary interests, which she clearly enjoyed. Did she volunteer her services because she could see her mother's intense disappointment at not being able to pursue her own literary interests? Even if the talented twelve year old had illusions that she could take on her mother's duties and still pursue these other interests, it was a mother's role to correct that misconception. Taymur's allusion to competitive feelings with her daughter, whose youth and intellect made her a better student, could have complicated Taymur's feelings and decision. In contrast to Taymur's struggle with her own mother, Tawhida emerged in this tale as a child eager to please her mother. As part of this effort, she assumed the role of a surrogate mother in the Taymur household.

Because her father was by then a prominent public figure, one can safely assume his minimal involvement in the affairs of the household. Although he must have noted how Tawhida had taken over her mother's duties in the household, he chose not to intervene between mother and daughter and passively consented to this arrangement. It was not much later that he passed away. Although other female members of the household could not have shared Taymur's unconventional interests, they failed to intervene possibly because they expected the plan to fail.

With more free time on her hands, Taymur recruited three women instructors who helped to polish her literary skills. An old instructor passed away after six months. In her place Taymur recruited Fatima al-Azhariya and Setita al-Tablawiya to teach her Arabic grammar and poetic meter.[22] The first was a writer; the second was a poet. They worked for a living by tutoring other women. This occupation set them apart from Taymur, who wanted to learn the tools of their trade to establish herself as a literary aristocratic woman. Under their guidance, she began to compose long verse and the lighter literary form of *Zagal*.

In her literary training Taymur behaved very much like a man would, devoting all her energy to the formal learning it required. She ceased to be available to the needs of others. Through this repudiation of femininity, Taymur reinforced the connection between masculinity (identified emotionally with the ability to satisfy one's individual needs unencumbered by the needs of others) and literary learning as a nondomestic preoccupation. In this way she was able to complete her literary training and to satisfy her desire to be a poet.

In addition, Taymur began to experiment with other social roles. As a member of the aristocracy who knew many languages, she became a valuable resource for the Royal Court. "I was invited by her royal highness . . . the mother of the *khedive* [the title of the Egyptian ruler at the time] Ismail to the palace whenever the relatives of the Persian king visited. . . . I stayed with them during the visit, entertained them, and inquired about their customs and their moral habits."[23]

In addition to spending considerable time learning the tools of literary production, Taymur's language skills took her away from home to serve as a court translator and companion. As a result, her availability for the needs of others within the family diminished further.

In increasingly disconnecting herself from the affairs of the household, Taymur's emerging social persona became more individualistic and distant from the immediate needs of others, that is, very similar to those of her male counterparts. It explained her late discovery of Tawhida's fatal illness. The situation was complicated by Tawhida's attempt to hide signs of her illness from her mother. Could it be that Taymur's new literary persona made her seem less of a mother figure in the eyes of her own daughter? It is also possible that Tawhida's frustrated literary aspiration found some vicarious satisfaction in her mother's success, which she was invested in protecting. Whatever it was, Taymur's late and frantic efforts to save her beloved Tawhida did not succeed. She died at the age of eighteen.

Conclusion

In the above, I have presented a different reading of the dominant narrative on 'A'isha Taymur's emotional and social development in a patriarchal family. Her early struggle to pursue a literary education was only partially successful. It was consciously interrupted by the patriarchal expectation that she marry at a young age. The effects of this experience stayed with the adult Taymur and affected the education of her daughter. For a while her daughter could equally enjoy the old and new types of feminine education. Taymur's desire to continue her adult education without challenging the existing patriarchal rules regarding the legitimate social occupations of a wife and mother were consistent with the lessons she learned during her childhood struggles.

The dominant patriarchal discourse paid little attention to the lessons it taught Taymur regarding patriarchal change and the rights and definitions of femininity. It is clear that the "new" femininity continued to be identified with contested social and emotional boundaries for women. Only Taymur's father and her husband had relatively clear and well-defined boundaries that were respected by all. As upper-class men in a changing modern society, their needs had changed to include women's education. In any negotiations of change the centrality of the needs of men were not in question. It was understood that Taymur's education before marriage and its completion after marriage were not to affect the patriarchal expectation that she consider the needs of men as her primary concern. So although Taymur's needs changed as a result of her literary interests, her life continued to be organized around servicing the needs of men: first those of her father and later those of her husband.

Consciously or unconsciously, the young Taymur learned that the demand for change was more likely to succeed from the comfortable position of identifying with the patriarch. She gained access to the literary domain of men through her father's support, not his displeasure. If the expansion of the educational possibilities of women undermined the restrictive patriarchal definition of femininity, these effects were quickly contained by the father, who demanded her obedience. It explained why Taymur did not eventually challenge her father's view of her literary interests as secondary to her primary role as wife and mother. It also foreclosed the possibility of a future rebellion against the subordination of her adult needs to those of husband and children. Instead of proving the enlightenment of modernity and its patriarchs, it showed how men were actively engaged in minimizing the subversive aspects of women's demands for change. Equally significant was their development of a patriarchal discourse that represented their role in this process as benevolent, liberal, and even feminist.

Given the above, it is not surprising that the change in women's education did not contribute to any challenge of their roles as wives and mothers. They continued to be the primary caretakers of the needs of men and children. As proof, Taymur's long-term literary aspirations were quickly sacrificed to accommodate her father's and the social expectations for Taymur to marry and to have children. During the first ten years of marriage when the clash between Taymur's needs and those of her husband's and children's occurred, hers gave way.

It was this valuation and the respect of the needs of men that were at the base of their privileged social status in modern society. It translated into relatively clear boundaries. In contrast, the subordination of women's needs and/or their valuation only when they overlapped with those of men explained their continued subordinate status. The internalization of these very different definitions of "self" represented a form of gender inequality that was seldom examined in the reproduction of patriarchal societies or the discussion of the strategies for its change.

The contestation of women's emotional and social boundaries was not only evident in their unequal relations with men but also included the blurring of boundaries among women. It provided a psychodynamic explanation of the conflictual relations that women had with one another in patriarchal society. Its clearest and most intimate manifestation occurred in the relations between mother and daughter. Taymur's mother and even Taymur herself did not see their daughters' needs as separate from their own. As a result, their needs as mothers' were constantly confused with those of their daughters. Taymur's mother wanted her daughter to enjoy the privileged status of an aristocratic girl, a status that was closed to her as a freed slave. 'A'isha's needs as a young girl with unusual interests in literature were discounted by her mother, who feared that they were going to undermine her daughter's proper socialization as an aristocratic young girl whose skills in embroidery and weaving confirmed her domestic pursuits.

Taymur reproduced this psychodrama in her relations with her daughter. Noting her daughter's dual interest in literary production and feminine occupations, Taymur developed a curious interpretation of how her daughter's versatility related to her own needs. In transferring her domestic responsibilities to her daughter, Taymur seems to have decided that her daughter would either take equal pleasure in the completion of her mother's literary study and/or that her daughter could easily enjoy a feminine occupation like the management of the household. This provided evidence that Taymur, like her mother before her, confused her needs with those of her daughter's. In both instances, this confusion of boundaries contributed to conflictual relations between mothers and daughters.

In an earlier article on the psychodynamics of mothering and gender in Egyptian families, I argued that the fluid boundaries among women allowed them to "make use of group resources and supports provided by other women."[24] The result was an enhanced agency and a less-urgent need to challenge the existing definitions of femininity.[25] Taymur's biography showed another side to this blurring of boundaries among women. It contributed to their complicity in the exploitation of other women and the high human cost in the preservation of the patriarchal status quo. Taymur and her mother selected the paths of least resistance to change.

Taymur's slave mother did not rebel against her master. Rather, she relied on the well-known strategy of improving one's status by bearing the master-children. In this way, she gained her freedom and the social status of a mother of free aristocratic women who had a right to inherit a share of their father's wealth and through marriage, a life of social and economic privilege. In her well-intentioned attempt to secure aristocratic status for her daughter, Taymur's mother was willing to stifle and to repress her daughter's unusual needs.

After becoming a wife and mother, Taymur's decision to resume her education, consciously or unconsciously, sacrificed her daughter's needs. In transferring her domestic responsibilities to her daughter, Taymur chose the path of least resistance. She did not consider asking for her husband's help and/or his increased involvement in the affairs of the family. There was precedent of such male involvement in the traditional domain of women in Taymur's own personal history. Her father took over her education, which had been the primary responsibility of her mother. Yet Taymur must have reasoned that asking for her husband's help could provide a source of opposition to her plans. Instead, she devised the arrangement with her daughter that would elicit the least opposition from her husband. Her assessment proved correct. There was no record of the arrangement between mother and daughter provoking any opposition from her husband, who apparently did not care who took care of his needs (his wife or his daughter) as long as they were properly met.

Although this conservative strategy of change allowed Taymur to complete her education and to emerge as a prominent poet in the 1870s, it was not without costs. It pitted the needs of the mother against those of her daughter. Tawhida's happy juxtaposition of old and new forms of learning had to be sacrificed to satisfy the needs of the mother. By taking over her mother's domestic responsibilities, both daughter and mother made it possible for the patriarchal system not to change to accommodate the novel needs of women. The sacrifice of the needs of one woman to satisfy the needs of another other showed the complicity of both in preserving the existing unequal relation among women and between them and the different patriarchs. The result was paradoxical: despite the changes in the status of women, patriarchal social expectations of women's obligations in the family went unquestioned.

For Taymur, the personal cost of her decision not to challenge patriarchal expectations by transferring her domestic obligations to her daughter was tragic. The sacrifice of Tawhida's needs, magnified by her death at an early age, provoked enormous feelings of guilt within Taymur. It led her to begin seven years of mourning for the death of her daughter. Implicit in this prolonged mourning was the realization of her complicity in the repudiation of femininity/mothering that had made her less available to fulfill her daughter's needs. By embracing the masculine social model, whose strategy was to sacrifice the needs of women to satisfy their own, she ended up putting the burden of satisfying her changing role on the shoulders of her daughter. In many ways, both the model and strategy set up Taymur for major emotional conflicts. Being a mother was premised on the repudiation of her literary interests. Excellence in the new activities required the abandonment of motherly responsibilities for children. Not only did these new rules produce enormous levels of frustration among women but they pitted the needs of mothers and daughters and their interests in education against one another

Finally, I am encouraged that this dominant discourse that posits the conflicting needs of mothers and daughters (and the sacrifice of one to serve the other) in the pursuit of an education is being challenged in the intellectual strategies developed by feminist women educators[26] to overcome the problem of high attrition rates for young girls enrolled in state schools in upper Egypt. The development of community schools in that underdeveloped part of the country is premised on the conviction that for the education of young peasant girls to succeed one needs to take into account the needs of overstretched peasant mothers who rely on their daughters to manage their heavy work loads. Instruction in those schools takes into account this class experience and work obligations without sacrificing these young girls' desire for education. Creative scheduling and integrating these work experiences and their frustrations into the classroom discussions[27] show that these young girls are encouraged to develop a sense of themselves as different yet connected to their mothers. Instead of conflicting interests and needs, greater attention is given to facilitating the constructive intersection of the needs of mothers and daughters in rural working-class settings.

PART THREE

Literary Imaginings of Intimate Selving

The Context

Part 3 consists of two chapters with analyses of the dynamics of intimate selving as represented in literary imaginations. Both authors focus on Egyptian writers (Altorki on Naguib Mahfouz, Al-Nowaihi on 'Abd al-Hakim Qasim and Mahmud Diyab), among the most influential in the Arab world. Both focus on male authors and on how Egyptian male novelists construct Egyptian masculinity. The novels discussed in the two chapters are all semi-autobiographical. Each chronicles the making of selfhood of specific men in their familial contexts over the span of their lives. The gendering of the male child into boys and men occurs within patriarchal family structures in both chapters. In both chapters the narrative is one of contestation, of the struggle of male children for identity and selfhood. Masculinity is documented as achieved, not implying that femininity is not achieved but that gender and sexuality for both male and female children is an active construction of active agents working within and against social and cultural institutions, norms, and idioms. For both Altorki and Al-Nowaihi these novels are not only a form of autobiography but also a kind of ethnography, a sociology of the society from the perspective of the novelist.

Soraya Altorki reads Najib Mahfouz's Nobel Prize-winning the Cairo trilogy as arguing for neither the generality nor exceptionalism of the Egyptian family and the relationships described. Yet, Altorki points out, the novel successfully captures many of the values and crises of Egyptian society in the early twentieth century. Colonialism, the national struggle, regime autocracy, economic instability, wars, and the intense contradictions between Western and indigenous cultures—hallmarks of this historical period—impinge on family relationalities and transform them. Family relationalities, in Altorki's reading of Mahfouz, cannot be explained outside the context of these national, regional, and global dynamics. Indeed, that seems to be the point of Mahfouz's rendering of his semi-autobiographical main character, according to Altorki. Mahfouz describes family life as patriarchal. Focusing on the father-son relationships in the Cairo trilogy, Altorki argues that patriarchy is not timeless, but is socially constructed, and constructed differently depending on time period, personalities, and cultural dynamics. The early relationships between fathers and sons seem to approximate the notion of patriarchal connectivity although later dynamics appear to shift away from this construct. Although the structure and content of patriarchy changes over the course of the novel, yet patriarchy appears to endure, leaving the reader in doubt as to whether Mahfouz meant to imply the possibility or impossibility of overcoming gendered and aged domination. Intimate selving in father-son relationships, therefore, has different outcomes with different personas under different conditions. Sons struggle with each other, with their fathers, and with their selves as they co-construct each other. Yet the overpowering love of the main characters for each other links them in enduring relationships. This provocative reading reveals the changing and complex character of patriarchy over time and within any one period of time. It is a compelling argument for a more nuanced view of the social construction of father-son relationships in shifting patriarchal systems of relational selving.

Magda Al-Nowaihi's analysis of the construction of masculinity in the novels of 'Abd al-Hakim Qasim and Mahmud Diyab opens to public scrutiny the often hidden, forbidden grounds of family life. These semi-autobiographical accounts allow the novelists to examine their own lives while protecting themselves from the charges of betrayal that often accompany public exposure. As Al-Nowaihi points out, fear of charges of betrayal have frequently led to the cloaking of family secrets in many societies, not only in Arab societies. The novelists detail the dynamics of identity formation and address the fundamental question of how one becomes a man. The protagonists, young boys, construct their masculinity through contestations with and against the acceptable "feminine." Masculinity is a set of relationalities that engage with femininity. The relational self that emerges is relational both in the sense of the masculine being constructed in relationship to the feminine and in the sense of the development of a notion of self that, as Al-Nowaihi argues, "derives its sense of worth and well-being with others, from being part of, rather than apart from, a collective entity" (chapter 10). Al-Nowaihi offers profound insights into the inventions of masculinity not only in son-parent relationalities but in multiple sites and multiple relationalities.

In the chapters in part 3 one's attention is drawn to the importance of literature as a source of theory and data for understanding the construction of selves in intimate relationalities. The line between literature and ethnography is particularly thin in these semi-autobiographical accounts. Altorki and Al-Nowaihi render the novel as a crucial source of knowledge and information, as self-reflective narratives that expose the interiority that is often concealed in what might artificially be considered more scientific accounts, thereby offering rare and rich insights into the process of intimate selving.

Patriarchy and Imperialism

*Father-Son and British-Egyptian Relations
in Najib Mahfuz's Trilogy*

SORAYA ALTORKI

Najib Mahfuz's novels richly depict the social reality of everyday existence in Egypt, earning him a comparison to Dickens, Balzac, and Dostoevsky. Masterful portrayals of Egyptian family life and society, the novels also serve as a laboratory for a comparative study of patriarchy and imperialism.[1] In his masterpiece, the trilogy—*Palace Walk, Palace of Desire,* and *Sugar Street*[2]—the relationships between the patriarch, Al-Sayyid Ahmad, and his three sons, Yasin, Fahmy, and Kamal, are central, with the relationships with grandsons later playing an evolving role.

A sociopsychological analysis of these familial relationships is clarified when seen in the light of Egyptian historical developments—primarily the British Occupation—during this time period. Mahfuz tells a story that centers on family relationships and the changes they undergo in their historical context. The theoretical framework that I offer here, one that uses in-depth case studies to identify issues that have broader societal significance, seeks to render explicit that which is implicit in this masterful treatment of Egyptian family life.

I thank the following individuals for reading and commenting on earlier drafts of this paper: Mary Arnett, Suad Joseph, Deniz Kandiyoti, and Huda Zurayk. I have incorporated many of their suggestions but, of course, I alone am responsible for any errors that it contains.

Because this paper deals mainly with father-son relations, for convenience, masculine pronouns are used when referring to individuals, regardless of gender.

Neither Mahfuz nor I claim that the family is somehow "typical" of all Egyptians. Because a society is composed of a rich variety of individuals, it would be misleading to suggest that the experiences of one particular family are representative of them all. These characters, however, do reflect many of the values of their social world and do undergo the crises of Egyptian society in the early twentieth century. Among these crises are the nationalist struggle against colonialism, the autocracy of the regime, economic hardships associated with wartime and the great depression, and the contradictions between Western and indigenous culture.

To analyze the trilogy I refer to a number of recurring themes, which underpin various developments in the novel. They are presented here as dichotomously conflicting ideal types, that is, as heuristic devices designed to uncover various layers of meaning inherent in Mahfuz's novel. These themes basically derive from a theory of patriarchy I develop here and include (1) patriarchy and polyarchy; (2) mistrust and trust; (3) dependence and autonomy; (4) inequity and justice; (5) dissimulation and truth. In their interactions the father and his three sons try to negotiate their way through the conflicts illustrated by these themes.

At the same time, national politics are evolving in ways that also involve these themes. Mahfuz articulates the changing relationships between father and sons with the evolving relationship between Britain and Egypt. Although it would be an oversimplification to equate Britain with Al-Sayyid Ahmad as paternalistic symbols and Egypt and the sons as filial rebels, Mahfuz does make the analogy between family and national-level tendencies and developments and links them dialectically to one another in the presentation of his story.

Analytical Themes

Egyptian family life during the time under review may be characterized as patriarchal.[3] Although the concept of patriarchy must not be treated in some essentialist way, as Kandiyoti reminds us,[4] for the purposes of the analysis here, I discuss some of its general features. Patriarchy literally means rule by the father. In a patriarchal system authority in the household is based on generally unqualified obedience to its master, the father. Suad Joseph, somewhat broadening the conceptualization, notes that "the kinship structure, its morality, and its idioms privilege males and elders."[5] Such households could be very large, containing several generations of family members.

In the ideal type of classical Arab patriarchy, this extended family would usually be characterized as patrilineal, patrilocal, and patriarchal. In his controversial book, which is too rigidly argued, Sharabi implies that the vertical, top-down authority patterns featured in these arrangements range from the seemingly most innocuous matters to those of life and death. The head of the household's absolute will, capriciousness, arbitrary rule—his veritable aura of infallibility—is sanctioned, nay ritualized, by immemorial custom. Sharabi argues that in such settings knowledge is rooted in myth and belief, truth in religion and allegory, language in rhetoric, and rule in monocracy.[6]

These views are misleading. I present an alternative view of patriarchy and, consequently, an alternative view of the implications of patriarchy on father-son relations. I maintain that, reproduced in every generation, patriarchy is not a timeless concept but is socially constructed.[7] Differences in fathers' personalities, the fact that moral codes are open to interpretation, the gradual diffusion of foreign cultural influences, and changing social conditions all impact the scope and magnitude of patriarchal domination. Furthermore, different sets of parents may have varying intensities of patriarchal influence over their different sets of children. Additionally, the fact that misdeeds by family members could call into question the patriarch's honor means that he depends upon them in ways that undercuts the unidimensional view of patriarchal authority.

Moreover, it is intriguing that the role of the mother is generally not considered in characterizing such systems. The assumption is made that because authority rests with the patriarch, mother and daughters appear in the shadow of men. Modern psychology would, of course, underscore the impact of the mother-son relationship. This relationship has been examined only sporadically in some Middle East settings, as for example in the writings of Abdelwahab Bouhdiba.[8]

Related to these considerations about the variability of patriarchy is what Joseph, based on her empirical research among Lebanese, calls "patriarchal connectivity."[9] She maintains that patriarchal systems in reality may diverge considerably from the ideal type. This is because patriarchs are in dynamic, not static, relationships with others in the household. A patriarch's personality may not only be influenced by household members but he may even actively seek to involve himself with them for the purpose of helping to shape that personality. In this case, the patriarch sees himself as an extension of others in his household, just as they see themselves as extensions of him—an intriguing modification of the standard view of classical patriarchy, a view that maintains that connectivity is one-sided. This more nuanced view of patriarchy provides scope for considering the role of the mother, and others, in influencing patterns of family relationships. Because of space limitations, these considerations on the mother's role cannot be pursued further here.

As a socially constructed phenomenon, patriarchy may be characterized by certain attitudes and behavioral traits of people in society. It is incorrect, therefore, to maintain that these attitudes and behavioral traits are impervious to modification as social conditions vary. In the first volume of the trilogy, Mahfuz leads one to believe that he has a rigid view of patriarchy, one that stresses that the father (1) mistrusts the ability of members of his family to wield power to make decisions; (2) fosters dependency among these family members upon himself; (3) enjoys unequal relations with them that privilege him and promote inequities; and (4) unwittingly encourages dissimulation and deception on the part of the family members. As the trilogy develops, however, he unfolds the more complex and changing character of patriarchy.

On what grounds may Mahfuz draw such a rigid picture of patriarchy? The central idea seems to be that the patriarch insists on control over his household. If this premise is accepted, then it follows logically that he mistrusts the ability of others within his nuclear household to wield any of his power to promote the family's good; that he promotes their dependence upon him as a technique of control; that the rules he hands down contain punitive sanctions against the family members to prevent them from harming the family's interests as he sees them; that his censorship of their actions becomes so pervasive that they devise various strategies of avoidance as a way of carrying on, thus minimizing the chances of confrontation and conflict with the father.

These points represent an ideal type that is scarcely realized in real life situations. It must be stressed that in different contexts patriarchal families exhibit different degrees of mistrust, dependence, inequity, and dissimulation, or perhaps some of these elements may be missing entirely. Certain contingencies always cause patriarchs to diverge from the above-listed patterns. For example, a dominant matriarch in the household could prove to be a check upon the father. Or perhaps he had had a particularly accommodating father as a role model, which might lead him to adopt a diluted version of authoritarian patriarchalism. Or maybe, despite being head of the household, he did not control its entire budget and, hence, did not exercise the total control that would be necessary to dominate his family. Others in the household may contest, even rebel, against the patriarch's totalitarian control, leading to incremental modification and even drastic change in his authority and the expected obedience of his male and female dependents.

Taking these considerations even further, family interests are not a given but are continuously created and recreated by its members. Consensus may not exist as to what constitutes family interests because family members have differing notions of what they are. These differing notions, in turn, are the result of the fact that human beings interpret things in ways that are influenced by their own experiences, which necessarily vary from individual to individual. This is in contrast to the notion that family interests are fixed in time and place.

Because patriarchy is socially constructed, it is the product of relations between men and women, women and women, and men and other men. In the early twentieth century Arab-Muslim society—Egypt—with which the trilogy is concerned, women to a great extent are valued insofar as they are the bearers of male children. Kandiyoti[10] argues that male children are powerless vis-à-vis patriarchs in ways that are similar to the powerlessness of women. She maintains that, as toddlers, these youngsters see and feel the tension among the womenfolk when the father reenters the house. They thus come to harbor a certain awe and fear of this man, especially as they become old enough to receive corporal punishment at his hands. Worse still, they learn that he can instantly repudiate their beloved mother.

It is possible, as Kandiyoti argues, that such experiences "mutilate the male psyche." Thus traumatized, a son could go as far as to vow not to behave like his father. Yet, social customs validating the patriarchal system exert their powerful influence, and such an individual could become quite conflicted. Meanwhile, the young son is suddenly thrown into the company of other males because he has reached the age when he can no longer be permitted in the women's quarters. In the men's world he is at the bottom of the hierarchy of power, fending for himself as best he can. He will also get involved in arguments and even violent altercations with other men. But men's company also contains inducements: he will be expected to take part in their gatherings and to share experiences, conviviality, and ideas with them. Thus, he will be socialized in patterns of male behavior. Moreover, as these things are unfolding, his father continues to "rule the roost" in ways that maintains the son's distinctly subordinate status. Although the father-son patriarchal relationship may remain intact (in some cases, without any alteration), some sons could—under conditions already outlined—move to change it. After all, sons do not all share the same status. Age is relevant to the pecking order along which they array themselves, such that an older son could himself be a "patriarch" vis-à-vis his siblings.

To elaborate somewhat on the remaining themes, the dichotomous opposite of patriarchy is *polyarchy,* which literally means rule by the many in a political community (rather than a family). Nonetheless, I employ it here as the antithesis of patriarchy for want of a more exact term. As employed here, polyarchy tolerates individuation and autonomy of dependents from the master. Because it is being used as an ideal type, the same caveats about not essentializing patriarchy apply to polyarchy.

In the case of mistrust versus trust, some patriarchs may view their dependents as children who do not know how to take care of selves. Indeed, a patriarch may be so mistrustful and aloof that he exhibits what Joseph refers to as "cold connectivity," that is, whereas he may be subject to the influence of household members, he still remains outwardly aloof.[11] Specifically relevant to this essay is Joseph's comment that the patriarch in Mahfuz's trilogy is a classic example of a "cold connective patriarch."[12] Yet although he may mistrust his family members' ability to execute important decisions affecting the family's welfare, the mother might wield a countervailing influence upon them. That is, her nurturing and affection could cause them to build up their self-confidence even if or as her husband may undermine it. Sons also may acquire a modicum of trust in themselves through extra-household experiences (such as at school or work). Such developments could even derogate somewhat from their exclusive trust in their own father as they learn he is not infallible and they are not without resources of their own. Yet the seeds of mistrust that "cold connective patriarchs" likely have planted in them earlier could hinder their efforts to trust in their own abilities as mature males.

Turning now to dependency versus autonomy, the aloof patriarch treats his household as his assets. He makes them depend upon his wisdom, experience, and judgment. The "cold connective patriarch" causes his sons to see themselves as extensions of his personality. As they try to reappropriate their identities from him, they may have varying degrees of success but probably cannot, in any case, escape severe chastisement and self-doubt.

The conflict between inequity and justice may be factored into the analysis of patriarchy along the following lines. The "cold connective patriarch" hands down unilateral judgments that restrict people's movements. Although he does not necessarily reject the desires and goals of others in principle, he does believe he knows what is in their best interest.

He is not an arbiter but an arbitrary *deus ex machina*. His sanctions are meant to censor and punish challenges to his authority.

"Cold connective patriarchs" insist on obedience. In so doing, they may cause their dependents to adopt desperate measures to escape the tyranny of their rule. Thus arises the conflict between dissimulation and truth. In withholding information from him, in manipulating information regarding their activities, their desires, and their thoughts, they are heeding their own requirements and thereby belying his requirement that they follow his instructions to the letter.

Synopsis of the Novel

The trilogy spans the period 1917–44. It focuses upon the 'Abd al-Jawad family, which lives in Cairo's Coppersmith Bazaar quarter, near the great mosque of Al-Azhar. Al-Sayyid Ahmad is a prosperous shopkeeper who spends his days in his shop, his nights carousing with friends, and one or two hours a day with his family. His first wife left him to escape his tyranny and to pursue her own life. By this wife, the patriarch had a son, Yasin, his oldest. He then remarried a dutiful, religious, uneducated, and loving woman, Amina, the mother of Al-Sayyid Ahmad's two other sons: Fahmy and Kamal. At the family's daily coffee hour, held in the patriarch's absence and presided over by Amina, the mother and children (including two daughters) gossip and discuss politics. It is at these sessions that the love and affection that dwells in this home are made manifest.

The patriarch is well known in the city quarter where he lives. Women are attracted to him, and he has had many mistresses. He is gregarious, generous, and successful, the sort of person everyone wants to be with and a natural center of attention. At home, though, he is distant, authoritarian, smug, and outwardly contemptuous of his family members' abilities.

His sons are repressed in various ways. Yasin is the prodigal son who, like his father, is a sociable and well-liked person but unlike him cannot control his lust. Thus, he is constantly involved in scandalous behavior. When he spies on his father's love-making in a brothel, he is overwhelmed with relief, as though his father's conduct validates his own erotic drives.

Fahmy is an intellectual who confers honor upon the family by his success in his studies. He is an idealistic nationalist, naïve and puritanical in matters of sex and suffers from exaggerated moral rectitude. Kamal is shown initially as a boy with a "normal" appetite for mischief and a carefree attitude, the darling of the family and bold in his ways.

All three brothers are terrified of their father's wrath but nurtured by their mother's loving and stable stewardship over the household. Both sisters marry and move out of the house, and Fahmy is killed by British troops during a political march, a fact that deeply traumatizes the family. Yasin is forced to move out of the house after he proposes to the woman whom Fahmy had wanted to marry, an act that outrages his stepmother. It is the only time in the whole story that the darker side of Amina is revealed. The patriarch, who had suffered a stroke in the wake of Fahmy's death, recovers some of his health and returns to his partying ways despite his doctor's admonitions. Yasin, like his father, cannot stay away from taverns and continues to search for lusty sex, laughter, and good company.

Kamal, who had earlier harbored thoughts of love for an aristocratic girl, avows his feelings for her and is rejected. Deeply wounded, he calls into question many ideas about life, love, and happiness that had not troubled him before. He loses his bold manner and tries to compensate for his grief by throwing his energies into his books, his articles, and his intellectual discussions with friends. Mahfuz is quoted as having said: "Kamal reflects my intellectual crisis. It was a generational crisis, I think."[13] In contrast, until the nationalist agitation, Al-Sayyid Ahmad had lived in more secure times in the absence of an atmosphere of crisis.[14]

Al-Sayyid Ahmad suffers a relapse and is forced sharply to restrict his movements. Meanwhile, his grandsons approach adolescence with the boldness that Kamal had lost. Yasin's son, Ridwan, who had been his grandfather's favorite, advances spectacularly as a high-ranking official in the same ministry that employs his father in a lowly job. Yasin, himself, has settled down under the influence of his third wife, a former mistress of his father's, and he transfers his dependence on the patriarch onto Ridwan. As Kamal grows older, he chooses to attend the Teacher's College, much to Al-Sayyid Ahmad's disgust. His teaching and books do not bring him the solace he is looking for, and so Kamal is shown visiting bars and frequenting prostitutes but with a sensibility that is very different from that of his older brother and father. Whereas he is searching for temporary comfort from a lonely existence, they are looking for a good time, pure and simple. Kamal does flirt with the idea of marriage but rejects it, presumably because he does not want to make lasting commitments.

As Al-Sayyid Ahmad grows older and weaker, he is confined to his bed. The book's very symbol of masculinity thus becomes progressively more helpless, like an infant who must depend upon others. During a World War II air raid, he is forced to seek shelter outside the house, but the effort is too much for him, and he finally dies.

Two of his grandsons become revolutionaries, and their conviction, determination, and unequivocal views about religion, politics, career choices, and marriage partners contrast markedly with the ambivalences of Kamal and Yasin. At the novel's conclusion, the skeptic, Kamal, embraces the credo of one of his nephews—to be true to what seem to be the highest ideals of the people.

It is important to note that political incidents pervade the novel. They affect the lives of its characters in important ways. Egyptian nationalism is brought out in references to the Ahmad 'Urabi rebellion of 1881–82, the meeting of the Wafd with Reginald Wingate in 1918, the revolutionary events of 1919, British and Allied soldiers occupying the streets and terrorizing the local population, the exiling of Zaghlul, the competition among the politicians and their harsh autocratic rule, the fickleness of the king, the corruption of officials, the suppression of the Egyptian constitutions of 1923 and 1930, Nahhas Pasha's revolutionary speech of 1935, the Palace Incident of 1942, and World War II air raids. The oppression that most of these events bespeak and the rebellion that they engender are mirrored by the oppressive rule of the patriarch in the 'Abd al-Jawad household and efforts by the sons to escape it.

The Patriarch and His Sons

In this section I apply my theory of patriarchy, elaborated earlier, to the relationships between Al-Sayyid Ahmad and his sons. According to my approach, which focuses upon the social construction of patriarchy, the set of relationships between the household head and the family members is subject to change as a result of intrafamily and societal factors. To recall, the five dichotomous themes to be examined are patriarchy and polyarchy, mistrust and trust, dependence and autonomy, inequity and justice, and dissimulation and truth.

Al-Sayyid Ahmad is an upstanding member of the Egyptian middle class. Fastidious in his habits at home and in his shop, his bourgeois tastes are reflected in his desire for security and stability. A social lion in society, he becomes a rigid disciplinarian at home. Al-Sayyid Ahmad saw himself mainly as a manager of his family's domestic relationships rather than a participant in them. Life was a matter of keeping situations from unraveling, of holding off the chaos that was lurking outside the house. Although he loved each of his sons, Al-Sayyid Ahmad's "Hanbali puritanism" (1:219) fosters a consuming need to establish control over his family and to dampen their emotional behavior. Mahfuz puts it this way:

"Everything in the house yielded to a higher will with a limitless authority almost like that of religion. Within these walls even love itself had to creep into their hearts timidly, hesitantly, and diffidently" (1:236).

Although a patriot, the father fears being enmeshed in politics and wants to devote his personal energies to his family and his friends. This grand patriarch realizes that his family's prestige depends in part upon his having dutiful sons. He seeks to imbue each of them with his own traits and values, and, indeed, his pleasure-seeking and sociability are seen in Yasin; his heroics and reflectiveness in Fahmy; and his dutifulness and a desire to be loved by everyone in Kamal.

The sons, however, in several ways, rebel against their father. Yasin's attempts to satisfy his lust bring on repeated crises with his father that he vaguely knows in advance will occur but which he hopes somehow to ward off. Yasin sees his rebellions as natural expressions of his lust for life, not as a desire to take over the patriarchal mantle.

Fahmy is the old man's "best son," dutiful, an excellent student with brilliant future prospects. His rebellion against the British has ramifications of disobedience to his father. Fahmy saw the leader of the nationalist movement, Sa'd Zaghlul, as a second father. An observer's comments about him when Zaghlul was exiled: "why was Fahmy so insanely angry, as though Sa'd [Zaghlul] were his father" (1:353).

Kamal's rebellion is more interiorized, criticizing his father in soliloquies. Toward the end of volume 2, Kamal, addressing his father *in absentia,* says: "What have you done besides hurt and punish us with an ignorance your good intentions do nothing to excuse? . . . We've known you as a tyrannical dictator, a petulant despot" (2:372–73).

Mahfuz's portrait of Al-Sayyid Ahmad does depict the man's unspoken love for his sons and his concern that they not harm themselves in the decisions they make. The problem, though, is that he always covers his feelings with an autocratic and censoring demeanor. In the relationship between Al-Sayyid Ahmad and Yasin the father's mistrust is not in the son's extraordinarily developed lust for life but in his failure to control it. The father grieves for Yasin when the latter brings harm to himself, and he tries to shield his son from the injuries the behavior of Yasin's courtesan mother inflicts on him. Yet, outwardly, he mainly rages against his prodigal son's behavior, and Yasin, although a giant of a man, feels tiny in his father's presence, "choked" and "stifled" at the thought of crossing him (1:205). His father frequently calls him an "ox" and a "mule," and just as beasts will thrash around when others seek to restrain them, there is a certain animal wildness to Yasin that resonates with his father's "customary violence" (1:68). Even so, Yasin does have a canny ability to penetrate to the truth of his father's and brothers' self-delusions, and, thus, some of his observations about their character are accurate and trustworthy.

Al-Sayyid Ahmad esteems Fahmy because he is both obedient and a good student, but nonetheless he mistrusts his passion for political involvement. Unlike Yasin, whom the father mistrusts for his unregulated appetites, Fahmy earns paternal mistrust because the patriarch fears his emotional commitments, which, in his case, might even endanger his life and may jeopardize the whole family. Despite the anxiety of living under the cloud of his father's constant anger, Fahmy implicitly trusts his father's moral rectitude, rejecting intimations to the contrary as inconsistent with the latter's prudence and piety.

As for his youngest son, Kamal, Al-Sayyid Ahmad suspects his judgment in choosing to become a teacher instead of a lawyer and his commitment to science over religion. Kamal perceives Al-Sayyid Ahmad as "not one of those stupid people. . . . He was simply the victim of his time, place, and companions" (2:52). Times had changed, but his father had not. His mother, however, had responded that teaching was an honorable profession. No doubt, Kamal had drawn strength from her quiet support despite Al-Sayyid Ahmad ridiculing his choice. Yet, was Kamal right about making such a commitment to science and philosophy? Yasin had once chastised him: "You shrug off commitments so that nothing will distract you from the truth, but truth lies in these commitments. You won't learn about life in a library. Truth is to be found at home and in the street" (3:24).

Kamal's trust in Egypt, in Sa'd Zaghlul and the other nationalist leaders, and in the Egyptian people was deep and unshakable. Despite this, though, Kamal seemed in general to become less and less trusting and more and more skeptical. By the end of the novel, he is portrayed as looking for a meaning to his life and forced to acknowledge continued ambiguity in matters of love, truth, and justice.

Yasin is so dependent on his father, spiritually and materially, that he feels helpless. His attempts to gain autonomy only succeed in conferring shame on the patriarch and his family although he himself seems somewhat impervious to this, feeling it only transiently. When he discovers his father cavorting in a brothel, however, he is immensely relieved, taking it as a sign of self-confirmation. Even after leaving home upon his second marriage, though, he never feels self-assured and asks himself repeatedly why he has failed where his father has succeeded.

Eventually, Yasin's dependency is transferred to his own son, Ridwan. This dependency brings him greater happiness and peace of mind as he experiences pride in his son's accomplishments, convincing himself that this is in some measure because of his own influence.

As for Fahmy, although a self-contained person able to take care of himself, he had never contravened his father's wishes, including the man's instant rejection of his desire to marry the woman he loved. Yet, he secretly joined the nationalist movement and refused to abandon it when discovered. When he later asked forgiveness (without having yielded, however), his father was moved but remained adamant lest Fahmy be tempted to breach the rules anew. As Mahfuz writes regarding the father in a different context but with direct relevance to the current situation: "What [Al-Sayyid Ahmad] hated most of all was for any of them to see him lapse from the stern dignity to which they were accustomed" (1:253–54). Although Fahmy dies without having gained his father's blessing, and his death is ever after a source of grief for the patriarch, his determination to stay loyal to the cause of Egyptian independence in the face of patriarchal anger and ridicule is the sterling act of self-assertion on the part of the three sons in the entire novel.

Although one might hold that at the intellectual level Kamal was an autonomous individual, he was emotionally less so and endlessly agonized by the "eternal questions" of life, dissatisfied with the world as it was and refusing to meet it on its own terms. Questioning everything, including authority, he would not accept received wisdom from the past.

Kamal never married and did not physically leave his father's abode. He continued to depend on his parents even while rejecting their values. In an effort to escape the home's stultifying atmosphere, he chose "internal" flight, turning to his books as a way to escape.

The conflict between inequity and justice is a crucial theme in the trilogy. The patriarch is caught in a dilemma between the harshness of his verdicts and the realization that they can produce inequities. Indeed, such harshness was the measure of the man he was. Consider the following passage in which he is contemplating how to respond to his wife's having visited a religious shrine in violation of his orders never to go out of the house.

> He convinced himself that if he forgave her and yielded to the appeal of affection, which he longed to do, then his prestige, honor, personal standards, and set of values would all be compromised. He would lose control of his family, and the bonds holding it together would dissolve. He could

not lead them unless he did so with firmness and rigor. In short, if he forgave her, he would no longer be Ahmad 'Abd al-Jawad but some other person he could never agree to become. (1:194)

This "cold connective" patriarch longs to be more just, but his entire character depends on behavior that fosters injustice. As Amina once told Fahmy: "Your father's a strange man. . . . What others take for granted, he considers a crime" (1:117).

The tension between inequity and justice affects the sons in various ways. Yasin believes his situation is unjust both because his mother had abandoned him to pursue her own life of self-fulfillment and because his father treats him in manifestly unfair ways. With his own children, however, he is determined to deal justly and never to subject them to the inequities he suffered at his parents hands: "Al-Sayyid Ahmad's oldest son never wished to play the cruel role with [his children] that his own father had with him. The idea of creating in Ridwan's heart the feelings of terror and fear he had felt for his own father was deeply abhorrent to Yasin" (3:53).

Fahmy, for his part, appears to have dedicated his life to the cause of justice. In his eventful interview with his father, Fahmy scarcely realizes it, but the old man silently admits to himself that justice is on his son's side. It is because he has been disobeyed and also because he sincerely believes that Fahmy's actions endanger all the members of his family that he is so bitterly opposed to his son's actions. He recognizes, however, that Fahmy's invocation of the Qur'anic imperative to "struggle for the sake of God" was applicable to the nationalist struggle: "Al-Sayyid Ahmad privately agreed with this statement, but his agreement itself and the feeling of insecurity it occasioned when he was debating with his son made him fall back on anger" (1:423).

Kamal had felt the injustices of his father's oppressive ways as much as his brothers had. In his soliloquy he says: "I vow that if ever a father I'll be more a friend to my children than a disciplinarian. . . . I've decided to limit your despotism . . . by fleeing (2:372–73). But, as already noted, Kamal does not flee and tries to find solace in his studies.

From the many confounding situations created by the demands of the patriarch, there seems to be little reasonable means of escape. Reason encounters only a stone wall. This results in frustration, inaction, or the humiliation of trying to dissemble: "Lying was not considered contemptible or shameful in this household. Living in their father's shadow, none of them would have been able to enjoy any peace without the protection of a lie. They openly admitted this to themselves" (1:424).

Yasin dissimulated for the sake of liberty, both his own and that of others. He was chiefly responsible for encouraging his stepmother to make an unauthorized pilgrimage in defiance of her husband's irrational commands. When her trip is discovered, Yasin conspires to lie to his father to escape his wrath. For the whole family the circumstances surrounding the "offense" take on enormous proportions, and they place huge store in their concocted story to avert the man's punishment.

Notwithstanding his trust in himself, Fahmy was also not above dissembling to his father. He never admitted to his father the major role he played in the nationalist cause. When, as a result of Fahmy's influence, Al-Sayyid Ahmad and his sons are rescued from an ugly mob and it dawns on him that Fahmy is more than peripheral to the movement, he becomes enraged. Yet, Fahmy's withholding information had been a tactical necessity in a situation where reasoned discussion would have been impossible. A strong connection is depicted, thus, between a patriarchal system that produces irrational expectations and conditions and the need to devise various strategies of manipulating facts to escape the patriarch's wrath when those expectations are inevitably breached.

Belittling the initiative that his son had shown in participating in the nationalist movement against the hated British, the father shouts that "he alone would set [his children's] course for them, not the revolution, the times, or the rest of humanity" (1:398). Despite his bravery in the revolution, Fahmy "was terrified and felt reduced to nothing. He concentrated his attention on skirting this wrath and trying to escape" (1:420).

Trapped by his unwillingness to take an oath on the Qur'an that he will withdraw from political action (note that he was unable to lie outright, even though he did withhold the truth), Fahmy tearfully begs his father to excuse him. Al-Sayyid Ahmad loses control, vilifies him, and sneers that "the only word that counts around here is mine, mine, mine" (1:425).

Such dilemmas also faced Kamal. Earlier in his life, as a young boy: "[Kamal] would not have been able to obey that haughty, tyrannical will. He furtively took his fun behind his father's back whenever he felt like it, at home or on the street" (1:49).

Later, when Al-Sayyid Ahmad had softened toward him and adopted a more gracious tone, the father continued to condemn his son's ignorance and folly, and Kamal's reaction was to lie to escape his wrath. His father found out about an article on Darwinism that he had written and became furious:

"What sect does this Darwin belong to? He's an atheist, his words are blas-phemous, and reporting his theory's a reckless act. Tell me: Is he one of your professors at the college? . . . Do you study this theory in school?" Kamal grabbed for this safety rope suddenly thrown to him. Hiding behind a lie, he said, "Yes." . . . Kamal lacked the courage to tell his father that he believed in the theory as scientific truth and for this reason had felt he could rely on it to create a general philosophy for existence reaching far beyond science. (2:335, 337–38)

Ironically, despite his commitment to science and reason and despite his rebellion against the patriarchal system, Kamal has internalized its ele-ments so thoroughly at the hands of his father that he is unable to escape its consequences. This was especially so in regard to the conflict between revelation and science and in matters of sex. He could never resolve his internal struggles, and he remained throughout his life a deeply conflicted individual despite occasional flashes of insight. For example, at one point he wondered, "Perhaps it's a mistake for us to look for meaning in this world precisely because our primary mission here is to create this mean-ing" (3:198).

Patriarchy and National Politics

The linkages between the psychosocial and the political factors are implic-itly established in Mahfuz's trilogy. National developments are greatly rel-evant for the evolution of father-son relations.

The "patriarchal" domination of the British over Egypt is reflected in the paternalistic sentiments of British consuls and high commissioners. Lord Cromer (consul-general from 1883 to 1907), for example, felt "that 'subject races' were totally incapable of self-government, that in fact they did not really want or need self-government, and that what they really needed was a 'full belly' policy which fed the population."[15]

Such general sentiments drove British conduct "on the ground" in Egypt. When Egyptians refused to accept passively their "full belly pol-icy," the British retaliated with repression. Sometimes, Egyptian national-ist leaders openly advocated revolution against the British as was the case with Zaghlul's successor, Nahhas, in 1935. Kamal, who had gone to hear the popular nationalist, somewhat timidly joined the demonstrators in a confrontation that was bloodily crushed (3:30–33). In a similar manner Al-Sayyid Ahmad crushed the hopes of his sons for greater freedom from his control.

Not only are such calls for independence suppressed by the British, but the same rebellious leaders are also shown bowing to British actions as Nahhas did in accepting the prime ministership in the famous Palace Incident in 1942. Kamal attacks Nahhas this time, saying, "[W]hen he yielded to the British ultimatum our independence was reduced to a legal fiction" (3:221). Yet Kamal, himself, often bowed to his own father's diktat at home, and his defiance was highly inconsistent.

But the Egyptian people are more consistent in revolting against patriarchy than were Al-Sayyid Ahmad's sons. The following example is representative of Mahfuz's depiction of the struggle of the masses in the trilogy. On the eighth anniversary of Jihad Day (November 13, 1935)[16] Kamal attended a Wafdist rally and overheard someone in the crowd condemn the British policy of repressing demands for freedom: " 'Commemoration of our past struggle is a struggle in every sense of the word this year'. . . . Another observed, 'it should provide a response to Foreign Secretary Hoare and his sinister declaration.' . . . A third shouted, 'the son of a bitch said, "We have advised against the reenactment of the constitutions of 1923 and 1930." Why is our constitution any business of his?' " (3:27).

At the level of national politics, the motif of mistrust versus trust is also pervasive. An excellent example of the mistrust-trust theme is shown in the fraternization between Yasin and Kamal with British soldiers encamped on their street. Yasin engages in small talk and smokes cigarettes with them and derives a certain satisfaction from this, whereas Kamal sings for the appreciative soldiers, especially one called Julian. But Egyptians resented the occupation of their country, and British troops had developed a reputation for harsh behavior toward them. Accordingly, fraternization by Yasin and Kamal with soldiers in their own street is taken by anti-British Egyptian nationalists for collaboration. A nasty scene ensues from which the 'Abd al-Jawad males are rescued only by chance from the clutches of an angry mob. Trusting Julian and his fellow British officers on their street to be good, kind, and decent had led to a crisis for the family, just as trusting them to be ethical at the national level flew in the face of the atrocities committed by them throughout the occupation.

The conflict between dependence and autonomy is especially pertinent at the national level in the trilogy. One sees cycles of demands for political autonomy and repression. The 'Urabists rebelled in 1881–82 and were suppressed. The Egyptians demanded independence in 1918, and their leaders were exiled. The people rose up en masse in 1919 and were crushed. Zaghlul, the nationalist leader, was released from exile and then rebanished. The British granted a constitution in 1923 and let Zaghlul serve as prime minister in 1924, but they forced him out and suspended the constitution when challenges to their rule increased. Similarly, the sons periodically probe for greater independence from their father and are rebuffed by him. The issues range from greater freedom to move outside the house, to marriage, to career choice. But every time a move is made for great autonomy, the patriarch does his best to prevent its realization.

In a revealing passage, Mahfuz writes that Zaghlul and Egyptian politics have a distinct bearing on Kamal's own personal life, with both trying to rebel against the system: "Kamal found that the political activities of the day presented an enlarged version of his life. When he read about developments in the newspaper, he could have been reading about the events at Palace Walk. . . . Like Kamal, Sa'd Zaghlul was as good as imprisoned. . . . Kamal felt the same emotion and passion about the political situation as he did about his own personal condition" (2:227).

Rebellion by Egyptians against the British has its obvious implications and parallels for Al-Sayyid Ahmad's sons' opposition to him. Alarmed by Fahmy's involvement in the anti-British nationalist movement, the father tries to sort out his feelings: "News about the strike, acts of sabotage, and the battles filled [Al-Sayyid Ahmad] with hope and admiration, but it was a totally different matter for any of these deeds to be performed by a son of his. . . . The revolution should rage on outside. But the house was his and his alone. Any member of his household who talked himself into participating in the revolution was in rebellion against him, not against the English" (1:422).

Elsewhere, Mahfuz again makes explicit the implications of Egyptians seeking independence from the British for the sons seeking autonomy from their father when he has Fahmy reflect on Zaghlul's meeting with Wingate. Fahmy was elated by the potential that this meeting had for Egypt's future, in stark contrast to the repressive atmosphere he found in his father's house. He even imagined that Egyptian independence would somehow create a liberating set of conditions in the 'Abd al-Jawad household: "Talk of national liberation exited great dreams in him. In that magical universe he could visualize a new world, a new nation, a new home. . . . The moment his mind returned to this stifling atmosphere of lassitude, ignorance, and indifference [in his father's house] he felt a blazing fire of distress and pain that desire released from its confinement" (1:326).

One of the most telling incidents in which rebellion against the British is likened to rebellion against their father comes when Yasin and Kamal are returning home after a night of drinking and worry about their father's certain anger at finding them coming back so late:

> Kamal feared [Al-Sayyid Ahmad's] despotic power more than anything else. . . . Why should that be? Al-Sayyid Ahmad was just a man. . . . Why did Kamal fear him and feel intimidated by this fear? . . . His hands had pounded on the gate of "Abdin Palace during a great demonstration in which people had defiantly challenged the king: 'Sa'd or revolution!' Then the king had backed down. . . . Faced by his father, though, Kamal was reduced to nothing. (2:371–72)

His father would not back down. He was more intimidating than the king of Egypt himself!

As for the theme of inequity and justice, it, too, may be tracked at the national level. In one fascinating sequence, when Al-Sayyid Ahmad is partying on a houseboat with his friends, he proclaims that the age of the great Egyptian singers had ended with the death of a great artist of song:

> Muhammad Iffat teased his friend, "You're a reactionary. You always try to cling to the past. . . . Don't you insist on ruling your home by fiat and force, even in the age of democracy and parliament?" Al-Sayyid Ahmad replied scornfully, "Democracy's for the people, not the family. . . . Do you really want me to assemble Kamal, his mother, and Yasin to let them vote before I deal with a problem?" . . . Ibrahim al-Far said, "If the revolution's the cause for the problems our children are causing us, may God forgive Sa'd Zaghlul." (2:398)

In short, the temper of the times, the demand for democracy and justice has caused serious problems for fathers trying to manage their families' affairs.

In the interplay between family circumstances and Egyptian national politics one can see the struggle between dissimulation and truth variously presented. For example, at one point Kamal reflects upon the betrayal of promises made by dissimulating politicians to the people of Egypt:

> I experienced the reign of Muhammad Mahmud, who suspended the constitution for three years in the name of modernization. . . . I lived through the years of terror and political shame that Isma'il Sidqi imposed on the nation. The people placed their confidence in these men and sought their leadership, only to find them odious executioners; protected by the truncheons and bullets of English constables . . . their message for the

Egyptian people has been: "You're minors. We are your guardians."
(3:27–28)

At the very end of the novel, Kamal is reflecting on his nephews, who
have been arrested and interned for seditious activities. Unless they rise
up in arms, Kamal suggests, the people must resort to hypocrisy to be
even a little happy: "You must worship the government first and foremost
if you wish your life to be free of problems. . . . But when will this afflic-
tion be removed? When will martial law be lifted? When will the rule of
natural law and the constitution be restored? When will the Egyptians be
treated like human beings again?" (3:306).

Yet dissimulation will not have the final word. Mulling over the beliefs
of his Marxist nephew, Kamal appropriates them as his own:

> I believe in life and in people. I feel obliged to advocate their highest ideals
> as long as I believe them to be true because shrinking from that would be a
> cowardly evasion of duty. I also see myself compelled to revolt against ideals
> I believe to be false because recoiling from this rebellion would be a form of
> treason. This is the meaning of perpetual revolution. (3:306)

Conclusions

I have examined the structure of patriarchy in Najib Mahfuz's most important novel, the trilogy. Recent work on patriarchy and the general
thrust of social science over the last generation has stressed the social construction of human relationships rather than their essentialization. Accordingly, I have emphasized the variations that are possible within
patriarchy, rather than its uniformity across historical time and place. Over
the span of twenty-seven years patriarchy evolved from the father's hegemonic control to his acceptance of the dilution of his power. In the first
volume Mahfuz's portrait of Ahmad 'Abd al-Jawad is more strictly drawn.
There, patriarchy denotes the father's overweening authority, his suspi-
ciousness of efforts by his family members to make decisions, their reliance upon him, alone, to guard the family's honor, his arbitrary, unfair
rulings affecting even the most innocuous matters of their existence, and
their turning to dissimulation to deal with the pressures that such a system has visited upon them. Although Mahfuz certainly has not shown the
father to be a monster, he is depicted as a dictator and tyrant—a fact that
is attested to both by members of his family and his friends.

But later, Al-Sayyid Ahmad is shown to have changed his rules somewhat (despite saying at one point that he would never do so!). For example, by the mid-1930s, his wife has permission to leave the house, and he greets his schoolteacher son, Kamal, with a "gracious affectionate tone" (3:8) instead of mercilessly attacking him for coming home late. Yasin, who has moved out of his house, and Kamal, who continues to live with him, still fear their father's wrath, but this fear is tempered by Al-Sayyid Ahmad's growing infirmity.

His grandsons, moreover, are not enmeshed at all in his "Hanbali puritanism." They go their own way with remarkable boldness. Note that their own father treated them in ways that differed markedly from Al-Sayyid Ahmad's dealings with Yasin, Fahmy, and Kamal. This difference might be the result of the reaction of the grandsons' father to the old patriarch's severe treatment of his own sons, which he had an opportunity to observe. But as important is that the father of these grandsons was raised by his mother because his own father had died when he was very young. This would suggest that mothers have influence not only in their sons' upbringing but also in their interpretation of their own roles as fathers later in life.

In the same vein, a major development in the book is the displacement of Yasin's dependence upon his father onto his own son. Why this occurs is related to the overall changes that are taking place in society. Equally important, however, is the influence upon Yasin of his wife, who has succeeded in taming his extravagant behavior in ways his father never managed to do. Yasin, now calmer and less enmeshed in his relationship with Al-Sayyid Ahmad, comes to esteem Ridwan and even relies upon him for emotional and material support.

In both these cases—that of the grandsons and Yasin—one sees changes in father-son relationships taking place, in contrast to an invariant model of patriarchy that is engendered when the latter is essentialized. Intriguingly, these changes are mediated by women. One cannot help asking the question: Is Mahfuz hinting that women help to shape men's conduct as patriarchs?

Beyond these considerations is another important finding of this study, namely, the parallels that Mahfuz draws between family connections and the ties between the rulers of Egypt and the masses. These trends clearly underscore the asymmetrical relationships that exist at both the family and national levels. If the sons in the trilogy rebel against their father, they do so at most mainly in their own minds, rather than in some open confrontational way. Even Fahmy's rebellion is agonizing in the remorse it creates in him as he barely holds his own in the face of paternal rage.

But this is not the case for the Egyptian masses. Their rebellions are full-blooded, even though unsuccessful in the short run.

Mahfuz's trilogy has an epic scale, and its characters run the gamut of life's experiences. The struggle between family patriarch and his sons for esteem and love occurs against the backdrop of a conflict between colonialism and the Egyptian people for the right to control public affairs. The pervasiveness of inequity generates a search for justice while miscarriages of justice reinforce patterns of domination and submission. Forces of repression vie with those seeking freedom. In the process of struggle the pressures of irrational behavior and dissembling one's intent compete with the exigencies of truth, reason, and analysis. These are grand themes, indeed, and they go to the very heart of the human condition.

A compelling feature of the trilogy is the obvious love that the four major characters have for one another. Their battles are sometimes exasperating and hurtful, but at other times they seem to yield clarifications. The interactions of father and sons reflect some specific crises in Egyptian society during the early twentieth century: economic security, legitimacy of authority, search for sovereignty, and the achievement of cultural authenticity. Although there is much in the novel to suggest that the conflicts outlined here would end in a dispirited resignation and acceptance of one's place in the larger scheme of things, Mahfuz finishes his story on a distinct note of optimism. It is true that the clarity with which the grandsons see things contrasts with the ambiguities and the ambivalences of the first and second generations of the 'Abd al-Jawad family. But Mahfuz seems to be suggesting that such clarity was really only made possible by the antecedent struggles of the old patriarch and his three sons. Those struggles revolved around such issues as family honor, career choice, marriage, and involvement in national politics. It, therefore, was left to the third generation to choose unequivocally among alternatives that had been as crystallized as they could become under the existing circumstances. Yet whether the third generation would be able to escape the structures of patriarchy altogether is left in doubt.

10

Constructions of Masculinity in Two Egyptian Novels

MAGDA M. AL-NOWAIHI

In recent years various critical schools have reaffirmed the view that the literary text does not exist separately from the world that creates it and that it in turn helps recreate, that literature is both a central cultural production and a participant in the creation of culture.[1] Moreover, the fictionality of literature does not invalidate it as a source of knowledge and understanding. For one thing, the issue of fictionality and truth in texts has been immensely complicated in recent years. A great deal of discussion has been given to the narrative devices and representational modes of history,[2] the almost inherent fictionality of seemingly referential genres such as autobiography,[3] and even the limitations of language itself as a system of signs attempting, but often proving inadequate, to transcribe the world.[4] Moreover, gender, which is my focus here and which is no longer seen as an inherent and inescapable biological condition but as a cultural construction or constructions, is very much, as Teresa De Lauretis puts it, "a representation . . . the representation of gender *is* its construction."[5] The study of gender representations is, therefore, as valid as, if not a prerequisite to, actual case histories, statistics, and so forth.

Literature as a medium of knowledge in the interaction between different cultures—of which this volume, written in English and published in the West, is a part—has the potential to replace, or at least balance, description from the outside with exposition from inside. One counters paradigms with a contextual multiplicity that is closer to the real and moves beyond unitary concepts and rigid dichotomies to explore the encounters between specific personalities and social forms, the exchanges between dominant cultural structures and private feelings. Literature reminds one, as Nina Auerbach puts it, of how "our diverse ideologies have been soaked from the beginning in the impurities of experience."[6] Moreover, one sees identities that are not a given and, in this case, masculinities that are not fixed categories. One sees persons in the process of being constructed and defined; one sees them, both in what is written and in the act of writing itself, in negotiation with their world. Instead of viewing culture as fixed, stagnant, almost immutable, one sees it as a process that is organic, experimental, and constantly evolving. Culture, after all, has the power to simultaneously "shape the individual and yet to endow him with a mode of self-creation that seeks to transcend cultural and linguistic determinism."[7] The text becomes an important element in this view, for it is, as Edward Said puts it, itself an "event" that exposes, examines, and rewrites the world. Literature is, therefore, not simply a document but also an agent of history.[8]

'Abd al-Hakim Qasim's *Ayyam al-insan al-sab'a* (The seven days [ages] of man) (1969, English translation 1996) and Mahmud Diyab's *Ahzan madina: Tifl fi al-hayy al-'Arabi* (A city's sorrows: A child in the Arab quarter) (1971) are semi-autobiographical Egyptian novels in which family life takes center stage. Although neither author explicitly states within the text that his work is an autobiography, or *sira dhatiyya,* both works are widely held to be autobiographical. My concern here will not be with the degree of correspondence between the events in these works and the lives of their authors. Yet the autobiographical nature of the works, and the fact that it is not explicitly mentioned, is interesting for another reason, for the difficulties associated with writing about one's family in a public forum cannot be undermined. Leila Ahmed comments that "much has been written about the Middle Eastern family in its externals . . . but there are no accounts, not even imaginative or fictional ones, by women of how in practice these social structures affected individual interiority."[9] Indeed, many autobiographies written by men are also amazingly devoid of any intimate details about the family.[10] This code of silence when it comes to one's family is by no means limited to Arab culture. There is no dearth of examples from the writings of various ethnic groups. Nancy K. Miller[11] admits that it is only after her father can no longer read that she can write about intimate family details: "By going public with the details of domestic arrangements on Riverside Drive, I was flying in the face of the parental injunction not to 'tell' that had haunted my adolescence and continued well into my adult years; the panic my parents felt that they would be exposed by us; the shame over family secrets."[12] Male writers are not immune either. Many of them become aware from early on that "family life was not a possible subject in public discourse."[13] The injunction to silence when it comes to family matters seems almost universal, and one way to escape it is not to admit openly that one is writing about one's own family.

Within the family, and ultimately against the family as an embodiment of prevailing social norms, an ethics of identity is being played out by the two protagonists: the nameless narrator of *Ahzan madina* (A city's sorrows) and ʿAbd al-ʿAziz in *Ayyam al-insan al-sabʿa* (The seven days). Both works begin with the protagonists as very young children, and end at a point where they perceive themselves to have become, through very difficult and painful paths, men. In *Ahzan madina* this occurs as the narrator is on the verge of, or in the initial stages, of puberty, and *Ayyam al-insan al-sabʿa* ends with ʿAbd al-ʿAziz as a college student, or in late adolescence. The movement of the two is not a straight path leading simply to an initiation or entry into the adult world of manhood, into becoming one of the men of their respective communities. In other words, these narratives are not traditional Bildungsroman. This process of identity formation involves attempting to answer two central and related questions: What does it mean to be, and how does one become, a man? The answers are open-ended and still in the process of being negotiated, for manhood is not a given but is a concept that is being explored and defined. This manhood cannot be separated from the structures of gender provided, and often enforced, by society, and a sense of self has to be formulated within the cultural constructions of masculinity available to these two boys. Indeed, although gender, or being masculine as a category of being that is different from being feminine, is not the only parameter within which the ethics of identity are played out, it does become a crucial category of self-definition, one that intersects with and parallels the other parameters that contribute to the construction of personhood. Two of these parameters that are central to both novels are the organization and gendering of space or spheres, and the perceived tension between individualism and relationality. In both works questioning and rejecting gender roles prescribed by society is deeply tied in with a rejection of the cultural and ideological organization of space along gender lines, and this translates into an ability to interrogate and rebel against the dominant culture in almost all its aspects. Through contesting the construction of acceptable femininity and "appropriate" female space, these boys are redefining their conceptions of masculinity and taking their first steps toward remapping the relations between self and others. Moreover, if one examines these two works against the background of the Arabic novel, one sees that a new twist has been added to the previously dominant storyline of an individual subject facing a hostile, uncomprehending un-differentiated collective, with a positive outcome being the triumph of the individual in the face of this homogeneous collective. The more typical storyline is here subverted in the sense that this reconfiguration of man-hood and rebellion against the social norms is not pure gain, for individu-ation and the loss of easy identification with the group are not necessarily a cause for celebration. In both works there is a perceived tension be-tween two opposing models of the self; the individual self who values au-tonomy, independence, and being unique, and a more relational self who derives its sense of worth and well-being from affiliation with others, from being part of, rather than apart from, a collective entity. In the ten-sion between these two models of the self, which is central to the ethics of identity, gender may not be the only issue, but it is neither a peripheral nor a separate one either. Rejecting socially sanctioned gender roles in-volves a movement away from the relational self, which is looked upon with great nostalgia by both narrators because it included feelings of root-edness, security, stability, and continuity. In the case of *Ahzan madina* (A city's sorrows), there is an important added dimension, for the narra-tor is convinced that a more communal or collective mode of existence is superior to a society pervaded by the values of individualism, both morally and practically. I add here that neither work and neither narrator totally resolves the tension between the individual and the relational self.

Although I take the son/parents relationship as a point of focus in my analysis, it is important to note that in these two novels the masculine self is negotiated within and against multiple sites and multiple relationalities. The son/parents relationship is certainly a central site for constructing identity, but it is the convergence and divergence of this core relationship with other crucial relationalities that determine the sense of self articu-lated within these texts. Relations with siblings and playmates, neighbors and relatives, and with figures who are distinctly different from or even in opposition to the parents play a major role in the construction of mas-culinity. One must take into account the fact that these relationships are played out within families that inhabit spaces that are very different from the space characteristic of the Western nuclear family. Western sociologi-cal and psychological theories attempting to explicate identity formation and gender differences have assumed the nuclear family as normative. In these theories the major categories of space are the private and the public, with sharp distinctions and demarcations between the two.[14] I have found it useful to employ these two categories in some instances but have also found that they do need some modification in the current context. To take one example, the absence of the father, and the almost exclusive parenting of the child by the mother in an isolated space that they inhabit away from others, is at the core of Nancy Chodorow's explanations of many of the differences between men and women.[15] According to her, the female self is more relational, with fluid boundaries between self and others, because formulating a sense of self for a female does not involve the rift with and differentiation from the primary caretaker, the mother, that it does for the male child, whose sense of self is, therefore, more autonomous and with fixed boundaries and a hierarchical mode of operation. Chodorow's theories have been extremely influential, but they would have to be modified in the cases of these two protagonists, indeed in the cases of many Arab families where the process of socialization and the patterns of relations within which the self is constructed are fundamentally different from the Western-based models.[16] In *Ahzan madina* (A city's sorrows) the narrator is growing up in a lower middle-class family living in the Arab section—as opposed to the affluent European section—of the Egyptian coastal city of Ismailiyya in the 1930s and 1940s. Yet his nuclear family is expanded to include the eight families who live on the same street where all the women and men become aunts and uncles and all the children become cousins. In fact, the narrator usually refers to the men and women as "our fathers" and "our mothers," and the narration itself is often dominated by the plural "we." The space the children grow in may not be public, but it is communal. Major and minor events are celebrated together, and decisions are never made without collective discussion and deliberation. In *Ayyam al-insan al-sabʿa* (The seven days) ʿAbd al-ʿAziz lives in a small Egyptian village not far from the city of Tanta, in the northern part of the Delta, probably from the late 1930s to the 1950s. Here also the children are being raised in a space that is communal, where the family itself includes two wives and many children and where relatives, neighbors, and friends are deeply involved in the daily activities and decision making. They cook, bake, plant, celebrate feasts, and even travel in a group. The children are not simply observing and learning from the parents but are doing so in a multimembered group. ʿAbd al-ʿAziz's half-sisters, for example, learn cooking and baking from their stepmother, and he finds comfort and safety in the arms of various maternal figures, including his stepmother, an older married half-sister, and a number of family friends. One is very far from Chodorow's world of the absent father and isolated suburban housewife and children.[17] Perhaps that is why in both works the male self has aspects of personality that would be considered primarily feminine in the West, such as a tendency toward relationality and a resistance to autonomy.[18]

The growing awareness by the two narrators that these communal spaces of men and women are separate, and the extent to which their separateness is a statement of the perceived differences between men and women, is an important thread in both novels. Both protagonists, and the readers, gradually realize that the allocated spaces are also ideological constructions, concrete enactments of social views on propriety and on the abilities and duties of each sex, and both gradually come to reject their societies' views on the proper spaces of men and women. In *Ahzan madina* (A city's sorrows) this rejection is primarily prompted by the feeling that the organization of space is inherently unfair to girls and women, whereas in *Ayyam al-insan al-sabʿa* (The seven days) the separation of the spheres becomes a symptom, if not a cause, of the perceived backwardness and lack of civilization of ʿAbd al-ʿAziz's community. In both cases the relationship between the narrator and his parents is a good predictor, and reflector, of his attitude toward the gendering of spheres and its implications for society, and can be used as a window through which to analyze the different outcomes to the moral dilemma posed by the opposition between the individual and the relational self.

Most of the events in *Ayyam al-insan al-sabʿa* (The seven days) revolve around the villagers' annual visit to the nearby city of Tanta to attend the *muwlid*, or religious celebration, commemorating the birth of Al-Sayyid al-Badawi. The novel's first six chapters are mapped out progressively according to the stages of this physical and spiritual journey: preparing for it, undergoing the trip, and the actual celebration in the city of Tanta. But the reader is also involved in a parallel although not concurrent journey, the growing up of ʿAbd al-ʿAziz. Although there is no overt mention of the lapse of time other than the sequence of the trip to Tanta, it slowly but surely becomes clear that ʿAbd al-ʿAziz is viewing his world in new and changing ways. The narration is in the third person, yet we are very much into the mind and heart of ʿAbd al-ʿAziz, and it is his shifting perception interspersed with passages belonging to an earlier time in his life that make the change in him even more defined, that dominates the relating of events. His inner journey becomes as much the focus of our attention as the journey to Tanta so that we are observing a pilgrimage to site and a pilgrimage to self.

In this village community the worlds of the father and the mother, or men and women, are fairly separate and self-contained. ʿAbd al-ʿAziz has easy access to both worlds and can be a part of women's congregations because he is a child and as such enjoys an ambivalent, almost nongendered status. On one occasion, before the women shed most of their clothes in the heat of baking, one woman looks toward him, warning teasingly, "Do not trust the male even if he is little," but this is clearly treated as a joke by everyone, including the joker herself (73). In the earlier chapters, coinciding with the early stages of preparing for the trip and when ʿAbd al-ʿAziz is still a young child, he does not seem to notice this separation of the two worlds or, at least, sees no reason to question or comment upon it. The reader, however, may be aware of this separation earlier than the child, for the reading experience is not equivalent to the experience being narrated. The structuring of the narrative itself clearly reflects the spatial and ideological separation of the two worlds, so that the first chapter is devoted almost exclusively to the world of the father, Hajj Karim, and his friends, and the second to that of the mother and her daughters, stepdaughters, women neighbors, and so on. In the first, entitled *Al-Hadra,* which I call "The session," or "The religious gathering," we see the men preparing for the approaching festival of Al-Sayyid al-Badawi by reading and reciting popular religious texts and poems and doing the *dhikr,* a sufi form of reciting certain formulas in praise of God to the accompaniment of music and rhythmic body movements. Only one woman is present in this *hadra,* the black wife of Al-Sanhuti, whose color is apparently a marker for her marginality, or at least difference (42). But although the men, and ʿAbd al-ʿAziz, do not seem consciously to be aware of the absence of the women, at least not as an absence worth thinking about or a situation worth remedying, their absence is made more tangible to the reader by their presence on the margins, for they only appear on the unlit edges "as a far-off, mysterious frame for the evening hadra" (40). Their curious observation of the event indicates their interest and marks their absence as the unjust exclusion that it is. The next chapter, "The Baking," is the mother's version of preparing for the festival, and it is a world where men appear only in passing. The women sit around the oven, baking the bread and pastries that will be consumed and distributed to the poor during the festival. Baking for them serves purposes similar to the religious gatherings for the men, for it is not simply a functional occasion but also one with spiritual and social dimensions. It not only fulfills their duty to produce food but is an opportunity to exchange information, tell jokes and stories, console one another, and even dance and sing.

A few points are worth making here. First, the modes of interaction within both groups are not significantly different, for the men are interacting in what could be termed a "relational" way in which there is a deliberate merging of selves into a community of the faithful. They are referred to as "the friends" (*al-sihab*) or "the brothers" (*al-ikhwan*). It is not really possible to claim that the women are more relational. In fact, one might even be able to argue the opposite, for what brings the women together, the baking, is immediately functional although, as I mentioned, the original purpose of the occasion is transcended and expanded in the actual enactment. One could also say that the men socialize primarily for the pleasure and comfort of being together even though, again, from their point of view the dhikr has a functional purpose. At any rate, the popular religious celebration is both a cause and an opportunity for group socialization for men and women alike. Second, what is already clearly different in these two chapters is the relationship of ʿAbd al-ʿAziz to each parent. ʿAbd al-ʿAziz perceives each parent as the leader of his or her group, the sovereign of his or her world. He views his father as a spiritual leader, a source not simply of knowledge but also of warmth, laughter, and generosity. There is genuine caring between Hajj Karim and the other men and between him and his son. His mother is also considered by ʿAbd al-ʿAziz to be knowledgeable and strong, but the warmth and laughter in the women's gathering occurs in spite of, rather than because of her. In other words, for this couple it is the man who is more relational than the woman. During the baking, ʿAbd al-ʿAziz is aware of and notices his mother's actions, but he is not emotionally focused on her, and she is excluded from his emotional attention, which is directed toward other women in the group. Two women in particular evoke strong filial feelings in him: the family friend Hajja Shawq and his older half-sister Rashida. This is a child who, from early on, has more exclusive emotional ties to his father. The other men in the hadra may be liked and admired by ʿAbd al-ʿAziz, but none of them replace or even duplicate the feelings he has for Hajj Karim, who is *his* father. Rashida and Hajja Shawq, by contrast, treat him in a more "motherly" fashion than does his mother and in turn become emotional substitutes for her.

As the narration progresses to describe the trip to the city of Tanta, ʿAbd al-ʿAziz has reached a stage in which he is more aware of the separation of these two worlds and of the inherent unfairness to the women, who always seem to be getting second best. In the third chapter both men and women make "The Trip," and ʿAbd al-ʿAziz notes that even the traveling is undertaken separately. The women watch the men as they set out on their trip the first day, whereas "they will travel tomorrow, but what a trip. They will go out dressed in black and covered up and will not go by this paved street to the station. They will be led to a path deep in the fields, avoiding the paths of people, tripping in their garments. . . . That is how their trip will be. They wish that they were men, but the worst trips are better than staying home" (96–97). And in the following chapter ʿAbd al-ʿAziz will question even that final statement, for when they get to their rented rooms in Tanta, again each group has its own allotted space, which coincides with its responsibilities. The men's usually take them out of the house, whereas the women, for the most part, are in the kitchen preparing the food: "ʿAbd al-ʿAziz looked at the face of Rashida (his older half-sister) bending over the pot and encircled with steam. Is that why she came from the village? To remain a prisoner in the kitchen and from there immediately to the train? Is that all her pleasure? She looked up. Her withered eyes whispered to him tenderly. She put the serving spoon into the pot and came out with it, offering him a greasy piece of meat. He refused it, disgusted. She returned the meat to the pot with weeping hands" (152). This passage exemplifies a point I made earlier, which is that issues of gender parallel and become intertwined with other aspects of identity formation. One device that Qasim uses repeatedly in *Ayyam al-insan al-sabʿa* (The seven days) is focusing on ʿAbd al-ʿAziz's growing disgust with the physical aspects of the villagers' life, the dirt, insects, odors, and so on, that he is oblivious to early on, but which gradually absorb and repel him. This physical repugnance is associated with a growing criticism of other aspects of the villagers' life so that here, for example, we see how his disgust is directed both at the greasy meat, and other unsavory details of the kitchen, and at the position relegated to Rashida and the other women. Part of ʿAbd al-ʿAziz's disgust seems also to be directed at his sister's easy acceptance of her role. His feelings are not unambivalent, though, for the image of her weeping hands indicates a feeling of guilt over the wounding effects of his rejection, a rejection of the tenderness in Rashida's eyes, which he still needs and appreciates.

Yet the separation of the spheres of men and women in *Ayyam al-insanal-sabʿa* (The seven days) is more complicated—messier, and more difficult to ascribe to a specific reason, theorize, or generalize about than might appear to be the case so far. On the one hand, this separateness is an indicator that this community holds certain beliefs regarding the duties and abilities of each sex and the value it ascribes to these abilities. Yet

there seem to be many examples of women who cross over the boundaries, who assume roles that are traditionally thought of as men's, and
who are, nonetheless, respected and admired. Perhaps the main general-
ization that one can safely make about the novel's portrayal of gender
roles in this community is that abstract values, or notions of the way
things are supposed to be, are constantly modified and challenged for the
reader by the details of actual personalities and relationships. How things
should be does not always coincide with how they actually are. For example, one can glean how relationships between men and women are ideally
imagined in this community from a number of statements that the narrator makes before any actual women or real couples come on the scene. In
referring to the father of ʿAbd al-ʿAziz, and his relationship to the land,
one gets an image taken from the world of marriage: "and Hajj Karim is a
master farmer, the land is his obedient wife, and he is her stern (cruel)
lord" (11). One reads that the men "worked all day in the land until their
hands became cracked, and they yelled and screamed at the children and
the women and flogged the animals." Later, when they calm down and
no longer feel exhausted, "they smile and regret their angry storming at
the women and children and animals" (10). In both of these last quota-
tions, and in a number of other statements, women are put in a category
comparable to children and even animals. There is a perceived hierarchy
of power and authority behind these statements—one in which the men
are at the top of the scale. One also receives hints regarding the crucial
importance of motherhood as a determinant of social value and esteem
for a woman. For example, a childless "barren" woman "walks broken,
heavy with guilt" (15) and is almost always silent and withdrawn.

But as the novel progresses, we see that there are actually few women
or families who fit the stereotypes, and we also see that those who defy
them, or at least do not adhere to them, are often happier than those who
do. There are women who exist in nontraditional positions outside both
worlds, such as the village theif or the Gypsy, and Sanhuti's black, huge
wife, the musician who participates in the dhikr with the men. But it is
not only marginal or unusual women who do not fit into the prescribed
spheres, for there are others who move freely between the two worlds.
Notable among these are ʿAbd al-ʿAziz's two mother substitutes. The
widow Hajja Shawq works hard inside the house and out on the fields and
"is both father and mother to her children" (60). The Hajja is not a freak.
On the contrary, she is liked and admired by everyone in the village and
serves as a role model to the younger women: "When the girls talk about
Hajja Shawq, they are fascinated, their eyes wide with admiration, and

hovering on their lips are happy, sly smiles" (90). One could, of course, argue that widows often enjoy a nontraditional status in many traditional societies, their widowhood having liberated them from rigid gender expectations. Yet it is not only widows whose lived reality contradicts, or does not conform to, the models or ideologies. Rashida bears full responsibility for her family, whereas her husband is a lazy weakling (200). Nor is this the only example of a marriage that does not conform to the stereotype of the powerful husband and the passive and compliant wife. We see other husbands who are like helpless children, whose wives have to provide them with support and strength, almost like mothers (64), and men who are totally devastated and unable to cope after the death of wives (180, 225). We see wives farming side by side with their husbands in the fields (57, 214), taking control of the money (33), and nearly ruling their husbands (214). We also see a number of childless women who lead unconventional but apparently fulfilled lives and men regretting their determined quest for fatherhood at any expense.

But perhaps most important for ʿAbd al-ʿAziz in this respect is the relationship between his parents as observed by him. His mother is far from being Hajj Karim's "obedient wife" and he "her stern (cruel) lord." She often disagrees with her husband and resists him by withdrawing, voicing dissent, or refusing to comply. When, for example, Hajj Karim attempts to convince her of the importance of giving to the poor in honor of al-Sayyid al-Badawi, which she believes stretches the family income beyond reason, she is "stubborn, and does not soften, making dry, terse comments. . . . In the old times he used to storm at her when she objected to what he wanted, and their fighting used to terrify him [ʿAbd al-ʿAziz], so he would scream in terror, and people would carry him off until the fighting was over. The traces of this fear are still in his soul, like the marks of a healed wound. He is a little sorry for his father; he no longer storms at her as he used to in the past. His fierceness has softened before her stubbornness or her forced giving in which awaits a chance to express its refusal" (53). The wording of the last two sentences, in which we are told that ʿAbd al-ʿAziz feels sorry for his father for no longer storming at his mother, and so on, confirms ʿAbd al-ʿAziz's weaker attachment to his mother and the stronger bonds he shares with his father. At the same time, the fear, indeed terror, he used to feel and still bears the scars of must have been on behalf of the mother or, at the very least, indicates the child's desire that the union between the parents not be ruptured. One can only guess at whether the tension between the parents was a source of ʿAbd al-ʿAziz's estrangement from his mother.

This does not mean, however, that the women enjoy full equal rights or have as much control over their lives as do the men. I mentioned previously the women's exclusion from the spiritual life represented by the dhikr and their having to take second best in the entertainment offered by the trip to Tanta. Another crucial difference between men and women is the degree of choice they have over their personal lives as expressed in issues of marriage, divorce, and remarriage. In such a community marriage does not conform to the Western model of two individuals who have decided, primarily on their own and for their own needs and desires, to be together. Here it is a merging of two families, sometimes even communities, in which individual preferences are subordinated to the interests of the group. Yet even within this framework there still is a distinction across gender lines, for men certainly have more choices and opportunities to at the very least reject certain arrangements. But *Ayyam al-insan al-sab'a* (The seven days) has at least one instance in which a woman is being coerced into marriage and one instance in which a woman is divorced against her wishes. If one focuses again on 'Abd al-'Aziz's parents, one also finds an instance of polygamy that 'Abd al-'Aziz himself finds painful and unjust. 'Abd al-'Aziz's mother is Hajj Karim's second wife, and the two wives live in the same house. 'Abd al-'Aziz has a great deal of sympathy for his stepmother, and he realizes that when his father married his mother, the space and power of the first wife in her own home was severely reduced. It is clear that Hajj Karim no longer has any sexual or emotional relationships with this first wife so that it could be said that he is married to her in name only. Yet her silence and oppression in the household cause one to rethink polygamy and its discontents, for it becomes clear that sexual jealousy, at least in its very limited definition, is not the only, or even the primary source of injustice in polygamy. For even though the first wife still harbors secret desires to resume a full relationship with Hajj Karim, an even more palpable source of pain is the usurpation of her status. Polygamy involves a battle for power over the household, over control of the available goods and services, so to speak. Yet here again 'Abd al-'Aziz's sympathy for his stepmother does not translate into a criticism of his father, who is responsible for creating this situation. Rather, 'Abd al-'Aziz feels vaguely hostile toward his own mother, whom he sees as controlling and domineering. Hajj Karim in effect withdraws and lets the two women battle it out with the result that the stronger personality, 'Abd al-'Aziz's mother, becomes the head of the household. Thus, 'Abd al-'Aziz never actually observes his father being outwardly harsh or cruel to his first wife, but he does see his own mother

behave unkindly to his stepmother. It is possible that this hostility between the two mothers, so to speak, is another source for the weakness of
the bonds between the mother and son and the fact that Rashida and
Hajja Shawq become to a great extent mother substitutes.[19]

'Abd al-'Aziz's relationship with his mother is an important key to understanding how his reaction to the village women figures in his later rebellion against his community and his reworking of his identity. We see
that whereas 'Abd al-'Aziz reserves most of his love and sympathy for his
father, the narrator of *Ahzan madina* (A city's sorrows) identifies strongly
with his mother and at times feels a current of hostility toward his father
on her behalf. 'Abd al-'Aziz's problem with his mother does not seem to
be her strength, for both Rashida and Hajja Shawq are strong and have a
great deal of influence over his father, but that she does not conform to
his sentimental vision of a woman as warm, tender, and nurturing. In his
own family the common stereotype of the level-headed practical father
and the loving but not very firm or sensible mother is reversed, for
whereas his father is the source of affection, imagination, and spirituality,
his mother is practically oriented, concerned with the welfare of the family purely from the materialistic point of view and has no time for displays
of affection (210). He is, in fact, amazed at what unites her and his father,
who seem to be such different personalities with very little in common.
The following description is significant. She is constantly

> doing battle with her short, solid body and her white, round, sullen face
> and her narrow eyes that are always staring at the ground. She is doing bat-
> tle against something, a certain ruin that she imagines approaching. She ex-
> presses it in her words and stern orders to the girls and her warning them
> against carelessness and disorder and throwing away crumbs. And she ex-
> presses it in the quick glances of her observant eyes, searching in every cor-
> ner, looking for mistakes or shortcomings. And she hurls her anticipation
> every now and then in the face of Hajj Karim, threatening. But he smiles
> and shakes his head securely. He has an unbounded faith in what is coming.
> The hand that gives never becomes empty, and the home in which guests
> eat is never ruined. Two separate worlds, two estranged spouses, how then
> do they steal hours together in this house full of children and animals to
> sleep together and crowd the world with children every year nonstop? (53)

But although Hajj Karim depends on his friends, not his wife, to fulfill
his emotional and spiritual needs,[20] he seems to respect these same practical abilities that cause most of the problems between them and to have an
emotional, and not just a physical, need for her. Perhaps he is able to dis-

cern what 'Abd al-'Aziz cannot, which is that this woman's obsession with the material well-being of the family is her mode of expressing her genuine concern for its members. This, in effect, prevents her from developing a broader vision of community, for outside interests are seen by her as competing with rather than complementing the welfare of her family. Even at the end of the novel, when 'Abd al-'Aziz is older and more mature, he is unable to develop anything but fleeting sympathy for his mother when she tries to protect him from pain and disappointment by concealing their financial hardships from him. This momentary awareness of her attempt to shield him from harsh reality is quickly countered by his perception of her as a rather coarse person, lacking in fine feelings or thoughts and consuming her waking hours with mundane activities then falling instantly asleep. The limitations of 'Abd al 'Aziz's vision of his mother are not problematized or counterbalanced in the novel by any distancing or irony and are not shown to be the product of a rather idealized conceptualization of womanhood, therefore, verging on a misogyny that is fortunately avoided in the descriptions of the other female characters.

'Abd al-'Aziz's growing ambivalence and internally conflicted attitude toward both the village and city women plays a significant role in his struggles to formulate a sense of identity. As he grows older, he increasingly compares his village to the city of Tanta with unfavorable results for the village that are displayed, at least momentarily, in a growing aversion to the women of the village in general although it later transpires that his attitude toward city women is not unproblematic either. Women become a category by which he can judge and condemn his community. In fact, the city itself acquires the symbol of a woman, and all positive dealings in the city are dealings with women, whereas unpleasant situations are reserved almost exclusively for dealing with city men, who are rough policemen, condescending bureaucrats, or corrupt petty businessmen. The differences between city and village women are both physical and related to character and, as I mentioned previously, physical details merge and become symbolic of nonphysical aspects in 'Abd al-'Aziz's imagination. City women are soft, elegant, sophisticated, and assertive, whereas those of the village, like everyone else in it, seem more and more like animals to him, hardworking but crude and inelegant as epitomized by his own mother. Moreover, the issue of space becomes symbolic of the differences between the two groups. City women, from his point of view, are not restricted to enclosed areas and enjoy access to the outside world, and this translates into an appealing openness in their demeanor: "The woman of Tanta never leaves the window, but in the village she descends from the street to the pit of the house through the door, and in the bottoms of the houses you find women like cows. But here they call to one another and laugh long, coquettish laughs" (118).[21]

'Abd al-'Aziz's ambivalence toward the women, which is symptomatic of his growing disenchantment with the village, displays itself in his troubled sexuality. In his village sexuality is not the taboo subject that it is in the community where *Ahzan madina* (A city's sorrows) takes place. The men proudly and lightheartedly joke about their sexual achievements in front of him, and the women also talk and laugh about sex freely with one another. They are not embarrassed to express their desire for one of those attractive men of Tanta (74). It is perhaps ironic, although probably true to life, that the educated and urbanely mobile 'Abd al-'Aziz is more repressed and more disturbed about his growing sexuality than any of his fellow villagers. What disturbs him is the strength and intensity of his sexual desires, for whereas the older men seem to him to be always in control of their sexuality, he feels constantly frustrated and angry, "nothing ever satisfies his hunger, a hunger that makes him cry, wanting a kiss or an embrace" (77). His sexual instinct is a force in and of itself and is not tied down to one female in particular. He desires several women simultaneously, and it is the desire more than any specific woman that is moving him: "Samira, Sabah, Hajja Shawq. There is a thirst in his chest that a whole river can not quench" (74). Thus, *Ayyam al-insan al-sab'a* (The seven days) does not present us with a romanticized love story in which the protagonist pursues one great and desperate love affair against all odds but offers a truer to life picture of the sexual and romantic floundering of an adolescent who is in the process of coming to terms with his own sexuality. Yet 'Abd al-'Aziz himself is not ideologically innocent and seems to ascribe to a more romantic notion of love as is evidenced by the self-hatred caused by his inability to restrict his desires to one woman.

In later adolescence his growing attraction to Tanta is also echoed in his sexuality. He tells himself that he is no longer attracted to the village women, who do not have "the pungency of the girls of Tanta, nor their effect." (138). Yet, as I mentioned above, his feelings about city women are not unambivalent. The very assertiveness that makes them so attractive in his eyes creates a certain barrier against possessing them sexually so that he asks about a businesswoman: "How bold are her eyes, how could a man ride her?" (132). When he makes love to a girl from Tanta, he thinks of "her erring body, hot with sinfulness" (159). He is even more distressed when he sees another man from the village with a woman in the stairwell, performing the exact motions that he has just completed: "He ran before 'Ayiq caught him, having sex in a group like rabbits" (159). His growing aspirations toward romantic individualism are shocked by the fact that his sexuality equates him with the other village men, making him part of the group from which he is struggling so hard to separate himself. So far he has lived within this group where relationality is the primary method of interaction for the two sexes and where the individual self is subordinated to the community, yet now this group seems to him to be like a herd of animals, unchanging over the ages, living by tradition and instinct rather than by imagination and creativity. He no longer wants to be a part of this "animal of imaginary proportions and strange shape, its body extending in the streets of the city, moving yet not aiming anywhere, wide-eyed with stupidity, unquestioning, its mowing coming from unknown depths, shaking the vicinities monotonously, moving toward an unknown goal" (160). And the unsavory physical details escalate and merge in 'Abd al-'Aziz's imagination to an extent that makes identification with this group unbearable. His repugnance at their food and the hunger that drives it becomes a repugnance at their sexual instincts, which then become associated with their religious instinct, and he imagines this animal that is the villagers sexually assaulting the woman-city (168). Thus, 'Abd al-'Aziz transforms the pilgrimage into an aberration of the literary topos with which he is no doubt familiar through his education. The celebrated erotic quest in which the land is the beautiful beloved for which the lover yearns is turned upside down so that the city is now the ravished woman succumbing to the unwanted attentions and brute force of the male/villagers.

Yet the city and its attractive women also frustrate him and brings violent thoughts to his mind, for he can never really belong to it nor it to him: "the high houses on both sides with dark fronts, divided by the squares of lit windows where the women are crowded. Those laughs exuding sexuality. He would like to squeeze the soft necks to the point of suffocation. The sly city, soft with flirtation and adornment" (160). In spite of 'Abd al-'Aziz's growing aversion to his native community, he cannot easily abandon the relational self that is inextricably wound up in it. Although he believes that he wants to separate from this community, to individuate fully, he still has a strong need to "fuse with the huge body" of the villagers (169). His childhood experiences, his memories of its intense pleasures and warm feelings, bind him to these people and keep his need for them alive or, to put it differently, keeps alive in him the need to belong to a larger entity, to be part of a community. After all, 'Abd al-'Aziz's role model as a child, his father, is a man who consistently sacri-

fices his own interests for the welfare of the group. It is these very qualities of deep commitment to others, generosity, and self-effacement that
ʿAbd al-ʿAziz loves and admires, and it is the perceived lack of them in his
mother that is responsible for the weak ties he has with her. At the end of
Ayyam al-insan al-sabʿa (The seven days), ʿAbd al-ʿAziz, primarily because of his father's sickness and senility, is forced to return to the village
from Tanta where he had been attending school. The sorrow and pity
that he feels for his father's changed position curiously neutralizes the
threads of contempt that he had been harboring, particularly because his
father's impending mortality forces him to assume the "man of the family" role or, in other words, to take over the father's position. As he faces
this prospect, he chooses to follow in his father's footsteps and become
part of the community. Yet there are major differences. The older group
of the brothers (ikhwan) has now dispersed, and in their place is a more
practical, materially oriented village leadership who would deem the dhikr
and the spirituality of the older generation old-fashioned and obsolete.
The new group replaces the fusion of selves that took place during the
dhikr and the deep merging of beliefs and interests that occurred between
his father and the ikhwan with gatherings in a café, a neutral place, to listen to the radio, an activity that is not fully interactive. One sees that the
community itself, and not simply ʿAbd al-ʿAziz, has begun a process of
change, at least partly because of the encroachment of technology as sym-
bolized by the radio. As ʿAbd al-ʿAziz sits in that café, he feels doubly impoverished, for he can neither recapture the communal warmth and
spirituality of the ikhwan, partly because it no longer exists, nor can he
become the independent, autonomous individual he had aspired to be.

I turn to *Ahzan madina* (A city's sorrows) and that street in urban Ismailiyya during the late 1930s and 1940s where the eight families among
which the narrator grows live. We saw that ʿAbd al-ʿAziz's age is crucial in
his observation of and reaction against the separate spheres of men and
women. In *Ahzan madina* age takes an almost center-stage position in
the very process of separating the sexes. Within the private/collective
space that the eight families inhabit and in the interactions of this extended clan with the outside world, the narrator notes the intersections of
constructions of age with constructions of gender, and this allows us to
see gender in the making, to witness the very creation of difference between the sexes. Younger children in this community are neither separate
nor particularly different according to sex, but older children and, in particular, adolescents are kept almost totally segregated from one another.
Adults are not as segregated according to sex as adolescents, for their

worlds intersect and separate, yet the child is keenly aware of men and women as different categories of being. The juxtaposition of these three age groups, with particular focus on issues of gender, allows us to perceive these differences as the results of an intense process of indoctrination beginning in the middle childhood years. In fact, one of the strongest preoccupations of this child is to observe and attempt to understand the ways in which the worlds of males and females are separate and different and the perceived reasons behind this. The events recollected start with this child around the age of three or four, and there is a strong attempt to transcribe his feelings and thoughts, the very texture of his experience as it actually happened, with minimum interference by the adult whom he has become. In early childhood he often lacks the information necessary for following the subject matter of adult discussions and, perhaps, that is why he is an acute observer of nonverbal phenomena—facial expressions, bodily gestures, tones of voice—that are his clues to navigating the adult world. For example, he is with his mother in the street and he says something funny, "and a loud laugh escaped my mother, which she soon stifled with her hand, looking around her in embarrassment." (29). Without fully understanding what is happening, he is beginning to note and internalize the demands made on women for modesty in the public sphere and how they often involve an unnecessary and absurd repression of spontaneity.

Much of this child's powers of observation are directed toward the relationship between his parents and the power dynamics between them. He believes that his mother usually concedes to the father's opinions, "for matters in our house ran as follows, God wills first, then my father makes the decisions, then my mother agrees, and matters are carried out. And we [the children] had to carry them out if we had a role in the game" (31). His perception of family relationships, indeed of how his world functions, is a hierarchical one, with the mother occupying an intermediate position between the father and the children. Yet the novel is full of instances where the mother does not agree with the father. Most of the fights, or at least most of those noticed by the narrator, revolve around the children, and she is quick to disagree with her husband when she feels that they are not being treated fairly. When he is being chastised by his father for some misbehavior, the mother intervenes: "and my mother cut in to save me, but my father did not pay any attention to her defense, and asked me bitterly . . . and my mother objected, but he continued his speech, without paying attention to her objection." (54).[22] On another occasion, "the argument between them heightened and branched out, and turned into a fight, and like every fight between them it ended with my father's victory and my mother's bursting into tears" (39). Although the child thinks that the mother loses the battles and the father is victorious, it seems that she only loses the verbal battles. In the end, her opinions are usually carried out, at least in matters related to the children. According to the child's perception, however, it appears that he does not notice this fact, and he comes to identify strongly with his mother's victimization and believes that her powerlessness parallels his own.

Are women different from men, and how? The narrator observes that his mother and her friends have different areas of interest from the fathers': "I think that the women of our street, my mother and my seven aunts, had reached a stage of boredom from their repeated talks about pregnancy and childbirth and the dreams they had and their repeated stories about husbands and children and their similar memories of death and their dead relatives. They searched for a common pleasure and only found it in sorrow. For in most of their meetings, they exchanged conversations about death and the dead. . . . The women of our street did not concern themselves with politics. Sorrow was for them, and politics were for men" (85). The war, and Egypt's increasing involvement in it, changes that, but even though his mother becomes more interested in politics, her approach to it is different from that of his father. Whereas the latter is concerned with the personalities of leaders and various military strategies and configurations of global power, the mother looks at a map of the world detailing the war and asks the simple, but to her enormously important question, "And where are we here?" (116). She is more interested in how the war will affect her family and neighborhood than in its more abstract aspects. Her interest seems to confirm the view that the female self is less concerned with hierarchies and general notions of power, or with abstract moral schemes and definitions of right and wrong, and more focused on community and significant others, on interpersonal relations and the actual feelings of well-being of those around them.[23]

The war also forces the mothers to switch from covert to overt decision making. His mother reaches a point where she decides and carries out her decision without reverting to tears and what would be stereotypically called feminine wiles, but openly and without even the pretense of consultation with the father. This happens after a heavy raid that occurs while all the men are absent, attending a funeral in a different city. The mothers take the children to the area where they are used to hiding, but feel more vulnerable and powerless without the men, "as if the presence of the men alone could prevent the disaster from happening and force life to continue" (132). But perversely, this very feeling of powerlessness and vulnerability, or perhaps the realization of the absurdity of believing that the men could actually protect them against death, also leads them to make their first major decision without consulting the men first: "We will migrate. A decision that was made by the women of our street. I do not think that they had ever united in making a decision before and without consulting the men. A miracle produced by the disaster" (141–142). Later, his mother also makes the decision to return on her own. When she does, the men make fun of her, "but in the end they bestowed upon her the title of 'the martyr' and 'the heroine' " (182). Although his mother is almost forcibly thrown into the role of primary decision maker, she appears to be glad and capable of assuming it, for it is made clear that her decision to both leave and return were the appropriate ones for her family at these two different points in time. A question that does come to mind is whether this woman's newfound assertiveness will extend beyond the war and to other areas of interaction with her husband, but *Ahzan madina* does not offer an answer to this question.

Yet these differences that the child observes between the worlds of his father and mother are balanced by his own world of siblings and playmates, where we see gender differences being created and inscribed, almost forcefully and unnaturally at times. Some of the most critical observations and questions that he has about sex differences emerge during his interaction with his playmates. One particular girl causes him to ask questions about appropriate, or even natural, behavior for girls: "I often asked myself, why was Zaynab created a girl and not a boy, for she had a boy's heart and abilities. She preferred to play with boys and competed with them and won over them, and she usually hit them and scratched them with her nails until she bloodied their faces. At any rate, up to that time I did not know the difference between a boy and a girl, except that a girl had let-down hair and a dress with tree leaves and flowers on it and that grownups consider her to be the weaker and the gentler and the closer to tears. And none of that was in Zaynab, except for the dress with leaves and the let-down hair" (59–60). Part of this child's conception of the differences between girls and boys is the result of his own observations, and it appears that, up to a certain age, these were limited to differences of dress and hair styles, and those are, of course, social conventions. The other part, dealing with a girl's personality and behavior, has been transmitted by the adult world. He seems more confused about this part, especially because his observation of Zaynab contradicts it. At this stage there are no clear basic differences between the sexes that he actually observes or experiences. In fact, the novel is full of descriptions of games and activities in which boys and girls are playing side by side in much the same manner and style of interaction, activity, thought process, moral judgments, and so forth.

But as the children grow older, the values and traditions of the adult world increasingly infringe on their own. In fact, it appears that the rules of behavior applied by the parents to older children and adolescents are much more rigid than those applied to either adults or younger children. This boy is particularly fond of a girl called Karima, and as they grow older, he notices that she no longer plays outside with the group of children and asks her about it:

> "My father forbids me."
> "Forbids you? Why? All the children play."
> "But I am a girl."
> "And why shouldn't a girl play?"
> "My father says that it is *'ayb* for a girl to play with boys."
> What I heard bewildered me and brought a lot of questions into my head, so I said, "Zaynab plays with us."
> She thought a little bit, biting her thumb with her small teeth, as she used to when a problem confused her, then said, "My father forbids me to play with Zaynab."
> "Why? Nawal also plays with us."
> "Your sister does not play with you."
> And I suddenly realized that my sister did not play with us, and I was amazed. I thought for a moment, trying to find an explanation, and then I looked at her and found her smiling as though it pleased her to confuse me. (69)

Several interesting facts emerge in this conversation. First, the children do not understand the reasons for the father's prohibition (there is no mention here of the mother's view). In fact, they are confused by it because it does not appear to be universally applied, yet Karima accepts it without any attempt at defiance. This neither means that all girls are similarly prohibited at this stage nor that they all accept adult prohibitions unquestioningly. Zaynab, for example, continues to play with the boys outside and even objects to one of the fathers, who is trying to control her behavior: "Whenever he sees me playing, he says to me, 'Don't play with the boys,' and that is not his business" (94). Indeed, many of the females in this work voice dissent and refuse to comply. Second, the word *'ayb,* meaning something shameful, disgraceful, or dishonorable, appears for the first time in conjunction with inappropriate female behavior. The conjunction between women's appropriation of, or even presence in, public space and the concept of honor, between their bodies and the power of the male is beginning to be inscribed. *'Ayb* is a word whose implications the children do not yet completely understand but which will become more and more significant in their lives and in the novel, and the children will have fully understood it and at least one of them will attempt to redefine it by the end of the novel. The fact that the boy fails to notice that his own sister has stopped playing with them is also important. It is as if what happens in this child's family seems natural and beyond questioning to him, and an outsider is needed to direct his attention to its problematic nature. This points to the instrumentality of the other in the understanding, even recognizing, of the self, of the outsider illuminating the world of the insider.

It transpires that at this stage the prohibition against Karima is not really directed against playing with boys as an overall category, but against her presence in the public space; it is against her playing with the boys in the streets.[24] She invites the narrator to play in her house, and they have another, for him confusing, conversation about the differences between girls and boys and the limitations on their behavior although here Karima and the boy reverse the roles they held in the previous discussion, for it is now he who assumes too much unquestioningly. He is surprised when she tells him that she will start school soon, for he had concluded, without giving the matter much thought, that because girls did not attend his religious school, they were prohibited from memorizing the Quran. When Karima points out that her mother prays, he concedes that his mother does too and realizes that he has made a false assumption. He again displays an ignorance regarding his own sister, who would also be starting school with the rest of the girls (70–71). This boy has moved along the path of unconsciously internalizing some of the assumptions that go into gender discrimination. From questioning the difference between the sexes and the idea that they should not have equal access to public space or play the same games, he has now internalized the idea that the sexes are different and should be treated differently, that boys will have access to experiences that will be closed to girls. This internalization is of such strength that he is generalizing and assuming even when no explicit rules have been given by adults. In fact, in this case his assumption involved overlooking a fact that is part of his experience, which is that his mother prays and, therefore, recites the Quran.

As the war changes the interaction between the father and the mother, it also changes the interaction among the children. When they congregate during the air raids, girls and boys are allowed to play with each other freely, "for this prohibition undoubtedly lost any meaningfulness in the face of the thought of quick joint death, which forced its shadow on the minds" (126). But this is only a temporary hiatus, for when the war ends, and this coincides with the children moving into adolescence, the segregation between boys and girls becomes almost total, and the changes promoted by the war end: "The girls were totally separated from us, windows and doors were closed on them, even Zaynab was separated from us" (206). Thus, the space available to the females has narrowed further, even for those of them with fairly liberal parents, such as Zaynab, and their condition is akin to incarceration. Their access to males and their worlds is even more restricted and now includes the boys of the extended clan. This ban will only be lifted in this type of community when the girl is married and the danger of her damaging the family honor by having premarital sex is over, for it becomes increasingly clear that at the basis of this segregation is the intense fear of the ʿayb. At this stage of life, which is commonly viewed as a time when the sexual drive is uncontrollable, the females are isolated to minimize the potential for damage. The intersections between women's bodies and access to them and the honor of the family and the clan, and the control of female sexuality as a guarantor of good reputation and high standing within the community has been well established, not simply for Middle Eastern societies, for it cuts across different regions and eras.[25] *Ahzan madina* abounds with small details indicating the assimilation of the notion of the inviolability of the female body that growing up necessarily involves. Even before the narrator learns all the details of sexuality from a slightly older and precocious friend named Ali, he has already absorbed this notion as one can see in little gestures he makes. For example, on one occasion when the eight families spend the entire night together in the shelter during an air raid, he says: "The dress of my oldest sister had rolled up to show her thighs, so I pulled it down. . . . It is not proper to look at women's bodies while they are sleeping, Ali" (138). He also learns about the neighborhood of the prostitutes, females whose bodies are easily accessible and who are, therefore, involved in the ʿayb. He does not recall how and when they learned, but they surely did, that going into this neighborhood was a big crime, which God would not forgive and which would make a Muslim lose his honor (196–97). In other words, these women could contaminate the men who associated with them, and involve them in the 'ayb. It is precisely around this issue of the intersections between sexuality and honor and against space as an ideological construction that the narrator will rebel and assert himself. The acculturation of the children regarding gender-appropriate behavior extends to nonsexual matters, with the notion of manhood being tied to an ability to repress or at least mask emotions, particularly when they indicate certain vulnerabilities. For example, when the boy's dog dies and his mother sees him crying, she says: "Are you crying because of a dog? Men do not cry over dogs" (247).

The understanding of the relationship of female sexuality to the concept of 'ayb, plays a major role in the child's growing individuation, for his questioning and ultimate rebellion against the moral code of his parents and community is brought about by his encounters with two women, each marginal in her own way. On the surface these two women, a prostitute condemned by his parents and standing in extreme defiance of their world, and a virtuous wife called Basima, who is approved of and described as an angel by his mother, seem opposites. But the narrator comes to the realization that they are both victims of the rules of 'ayb that govern women and that much unites them and, at least to some extent, unites all females whose freedom and access to space is seriously curtailed by the laws of 'ayb. To put it differently, these two women who are seemingly so different from his own mother also have much in common with her. The narrator's awareness of sexuality dates from, or perhaps coincides with, the arrival of the young and attractive Basima and her husband as newlyweds to the neighborhood. A few weeks later the children notice that the adults are secretively whispering and that their big secret has something to do with the new couple. They overhear that the bridegroom is not a man, a concept that the child, and even his relatively sophisticated older friend Ali, finds problematic and causes him to probe the very concept of manhood: "What does it mean for a human being to be a man, Ali? Why did God divide his creatures into men and women? And how can there be a man who is not a man?" (100). His uncle explains that a man is not a man when he cannot have children, an answer that momentarily satisfies the child. In a community where everyone is open and friendly to one another, the new couple's habits of keeping all the windows and doors closed and not associating with their neighbors are rather strange, indeed offensive. The adults speculate that the bridegroom feels inferior because of his sexual impotence and is afraid that his wife might fall in love with a "real man" and betray him. The child already understands that betrayal is ʿayb, "even though the ʿayb itself was an obscure term in my mind at that time" (109).

A friendship develops between Basima, who is always symbolically appearing behind bars, and the child, but she is afraid that her husband will discover this friendship. Her fear excites the child, who still does not know what the ʿayb is but does know that to be a part of it one has to be a "real man": "Is it possible that her speaking to me is ʿayb? The kind of ʿayb that our street hates? My heart would tremble with mysterious throbbing over this idea. Then I would smile in surprise, imagining myself the protagonist of a ʿayb story, a story whose hero is a boy who hasn't turned ten yet" (175). A few months later his friend Ali tells him all the details concerning sexuality, which he now understands to be the ʿayb he had heard of so often. Although he finds the sexual details fascinating and cannot help dreaming about them at night, they are already linked in his mind with the shameful ʿayb, and he, therefore, deliberately separates Basima from these thoughts and falls into a form of sexual schizophrenia: "I distanced the image of Basima from my head while I was listening to him. I hated for her image to become mingled with the phrases he was pronouncing and the pictures he was presenting" (190). But Ali brings her up in the conversation, finally clarifying that obscure concept of her husband not being a "real man." This knowledge makes the narrator even more uncomfortable and ambivalent about his friendship with Basima.

The second problematic female to appear on the scene is a prostitute who moves into their own neighborhood at the end of the war and of whom his parents strongly disapprove, for "ʿayb is personified in her in a glaring way, in her looks and turns, her walk, in every particle of her being" (217). In contrast to his mother, who modestly covers her mouth when a giggle escapes her in the street, this is a woman who laughs loudly and brazenly in public. In contrast to Basima, who is always behind bars, this woman insists on access to public space. The children quickly catch on to the fact that their parents, particularly the fathers, are morally outraged and consider her presence in their neighborhood a blow to their honor. They, therefore, start throwing stones at the woman's house and car, and their parents turn a blind eye to this behavior. One day, at her wits end, she runs into the street, tearing out her clothes and hair, and her tears and words have a powerful impact on the narrator:

> The woman plunged into the middle of the street in a black transparent shirt and started turning around herself, screaming in a crazy way: "Hit me, here I am in front of you; hit me if you want to. Hit me, you children of re-

spectable people; why don't you hit me? If this pleases your mothers' hearts, then do not stop throwing stones; come on, hit me." But the hands of the children were paralyzed; not one stone was aimed at her. The children stood staring at her, bewildered, while she continued her screaming, facing them, one after the other, with her uncovered chest. Then she suddenly collapsed and started crying and covered her face with her hands and went to her house and disappeared in it, leaving her door open. Her tears touched my heart. I felt pain for her, the demon of our parents had collapsed before us, the young . . . this woman is not worse than the other new residents of our street. She is even better than some in a way. She cries at least. I screamed at the children suddenly: "Stop it kids, stop it. Find yourselves another game." (236–37)

The pity, sympathy, and even respect that he feels for this woman, despite her "black transparent shirt" and "uncovered chest," are his first conscious rebellion against the world of his parents and their codes of acceptable behavior. Although he had previously failed to understand, and had even questioned, some of the distinctions that the adult world made between girls and boys, the questioning this time is of a different nature. It is not simply an inability to understand or agree with a certain set of values imposed by "respectable people," as the prostitute sarcastically calls them, but an awareness that these values are, in fact, cruel and unfair, marginalizing and victimizing human beings who are basically "not worse" and "even better" than those whose behavior is considered appropriate by the community. The reference the prostitute makes to pleasing their mothers' hearts is also interesting, for it appears that she is making a subliminal appeal to the women, establishing a connection with them somehow. Freudians and proponents of object relations theories have discussed the importance of the prostitute as a focus or object of sexual attention in the early development of male sexuality after the oedipal stage because of the fact that she is Other than, or a figure as different and unlike the mother as possible.[26] What is significant here is that the narrator goes well beyond this duality of mother/prostitute. He sees the prostitute not as an object for sexual desire but as someone akin to the mother, a symbol for oppressed womanhood.

The narrator's questioning of and rebellion against his parents' values is further confirmed by an encounter with Basima, the other alienated woman in the neighborhood, although her alienation is a result of adhering closely to, rather than defying, the rules of the 'ayb. He goes to Basima's house seeking sympathy and comfort for the sudden death of his dog, but instead the lonely, frustrated, almost desperate woman tries to seduce him. When Basima sees his fear and discomfort, she feels extremely guilty and asks him to leave and never come near her again, but before he does, she gives him some information that explodes his world:

> "Do you see this window? I do a filthy thing behind it. I spy on people. I spy on that woman whom you all hate. I watch her door all the time. And in the nights when my husband is absent, I don't sleep until the light disappears from her windows. I respect this woman. Do you hear me? I respect her because she is a strong woman. She knows how to win. Her victory over all your men gladdened me. She tore my husband's heart up. I laughed silently when I saw him writhing. And I also love her because she is the only honest person in this street. She is honest with herself and with others. Shall I tell you a secret? Listen well and do not forget what I say. A man from your street, one of the men who fought her and spit on her, goes to her house. Twice a week at least. Do you hear me? I see him sneaking to her in the dark, and leaving in the dark, without his noticing me. And I know his face as well as I know your face, and I know who he is, but I will not tell you his name. Do you know why? You will not understand if I tell you; you are nothing but a stupid child. Are you crying?"
>
> I was crying. My tears were falling copiously, and mixing with the sweat on my face. I said in a weeping voice, "I want to get out of here." (256)

Basima's words lead the narrator to reject his parents' morality and beliefs, for it is not only that his community had misjudged and mistreated the prostitute, who is not the demon, but it transpires that apparently respectable, religious people are hypocritical sinners. Strict enforcers of the rules of 'ayb themselves commit the 'ayb in secret. He thinks that it might be his own father who visits the prostitute, which causes him to doubt his budding manhood: "I am nothing but a stupid child. I cry over a dog, tremble in the presence of a woman, cling to my father's purity as if he were God, and do not understand anything" (258). Later, there is a strong implication that it is the strictest and most conservative of the fathers who is the prostitute's secret guest, perhaps not surprisingly. Furthermore, Basima's secret admiration and love for the prostitute points to the affinity of the two women who on the surface are such opposites. The prostitute becomes Basima's alter ego, and secretly observing her is Basima's only source of pleasure and feeling of power as a woman. The similarity between the two women is further emphasized in the novel's final pages in a scene that parallels that of the prostitute running out into the street, that public space in which women's presence is strictly regulated, to confront her harassers. This time it is Basima who runs out into the street to confront the neighborhood about their unfair values and fla-grant hypocrisy. She is wild and uncontrollable in her white wedding dress, which is meant to symbolize her purity and angelic status and thus, perhaps, contrast with the prostitute's transparent, low-cut black shirt, but which also ironically points to her persistent virginity, which is an aberration of the "normal" yet is celebrated by the community as a sym-bol of decency and morality.

The narrator, in deciding to break away from the values of his parents and community, to assert his readiness to explore and determine matters on his own, to formulate his own set of values rather than simply accept what is being handed down to him by others—in short, to become a "man," makes a bold decision to break the taboo of space and himself visit the neighborhood of prostitutes. This breakaway from respectable space, space that has been ideologically sanctioned by his parents, be-comes a symbolic act of extreme defiance and rebellion. It is a rebellion against spatial demarcations as a concrete manifestation of the privileging of males and disenfranchisement of females. It becomes a statement against the child Karima being forbidden from playing in the street, the adolescent Zaynab being locked up behind windows and doors, his mother having to cover her face in embarrassment because she laughed in the street, the prostitute's quest for acceptance and respectability ending in harassment and marginalization, and Basima's socially admired virtue, which culminates in madness.[27] The narrator comes out of this visit ex-cited, yet unhappy and burdened by his secrets. His decision to become an individual, to break away from the community and with it to lose his own relational self, is a very painful one, one that he is willing to accept but that brings him little joy. Becoming an individual, although necessary, is cause for mourning rather than celebration, and the novel poignantly closes on him watching and envying his younger brother who is still inno-cently firmly entrenched in his group—who is still, in the words of the children's song that he is chanting with his friends and which the narrator himself used to participate in just a short while before, a green leaf on a firmly rooted, engulfing tree.[28]

Both of these semi-autobiographical novels offer a wealth of details on family life in their respective communities, and one can no doubt make some valid generalizations and draw some comparisons between rural life and lower middle-class urban communities. But what is more interesting to me is that both works show the tenuous waters that a person must nav-igate with and against the family to create the self. Within this ethics of identity, two interrelated points emerge: the tension between the individual and the relational self and the crucial importance of gender as a category of self-definition. For both protagonists, the quest for individuation parallels an inability to accept socially sanctioned beliefs about female space, power, and identity, and sexuality plays a critical role in this rejection of patriarchal societal norms. In *Ayyam al-insan al-sabʿa* (The seven days) it is not patently clear whether it is the desire to separate from the group that fuels rejection of village female models or vice versa, whereas in *Ahzan madina* (A city's sorrows) there is no doubt that patriarchal values and their inherent unfairness to women drive the need to individuate. The points at which they conclude are slightly different, for whereas ʿAbd al-ʿAziz decides to reinstate, although somewhat modify, a relational self, the nameless narrator decides to accept the individuation. Both decisions are tinged with anger and sorrow, however, and show that the tension has not been entirely resolved, which is perhaps ultimately for the best. This marks a significant development in the history of the Arabic novel in that there is a reexamination of the novel's founding story of an individual self in conflict with an unsympathetic collective, for here the very process by which the self individuates and the losses involved in this individuation are exposed. Finally, one could ask whether the not atypical experiences that have led these two growing boys, in their journey towards manhood, to interrogate and reject patriarchy so forcefully would produce the same reactions for everyone, or whether the protagonists are unique. I would say that although the narrators are certainly exceptional, they are not unique, and perhaps more important, both Qasim and Diyab, by creating these two works, are attempting to contaminate average readers and cause them to question the shared worlds of the writer and readers.

Notes

References

Index

Notes

Preface

1. Notable exceptions were Hamid Ammar, *Growing Up in an Egyptian Village, Silwa, Province of Aswan* (London: Routledge and Kegan Paul, 1954); Sania Hamady, *Temperament and Character of the Arabs* (New York: Twayne Publishers, 1960); Edwin Terry Prothro, *Child Rearing in Lebanon,* Harvard Middle Eastern Monographs, no. 8 (Cambridge, Mass.: Harvard Univ. Press, 1961); L. Carl Brown and Norman Itzkowitz, eds., *Psychological Dimensions of Near Eastern Societies* (Princeton, N.J.: Darwin Press, 1977).

2. Daniel Lerner, *The Passing of Traditional Society: Modernizing the Middle East* (Glencoe, Ill.: Free Press, 1958).

Introduction

1. Michelle Rosaldo; *Knowledge and Passion: Ilongot Notions of Self and Social Life* (Cambridge, Eng.: Cambridge Univ. Press, 1980); Catherine Lutz, *Unnatural Emotions: Everyday Sentiments on a Micronesian Atoll and Their Challenge to Western Theory* (Chicago, Univ. of Chicago Press, 1988); Catherine Lutz and Lila Abu-Lughod, eds., *Language and the Politics of Emotion* (Cambridge, Eng.: Cambridge Univ. Press, 1990); T. Minh-ha Trinh, *Woman, Native, Other: Writing, Postcoloniality and Feminism* (Bloomington: Indiana Univ. Press, 1989); Michael Taussig, *Shamanism, Colonialism and the Wild Man: A Study in Terror and Healing* (Chicago: Univ. of Chicago Press, 1986); Gloria Anzaldua, *Borderlands/La Frontera* (San Francisco, Calif.: Spinsters/Aunt Lute Press, 1987); Judith Butler, *Gender Trouble: Feminism and the Subversion of Identity* (London: Routledge, 1990); Deborah Gewertz, "The Tchambuli View of Persons: A Critique of Individualism in the Works of Mead and Chodorow," *American Anthropologist* 86 (1984): 615–29; Henrietta Moore, *A Passion for Difference* (Bloomington: Indiana Univ. Press, 1994); Dorinne Kondo, *Crafting Selves: Power, Gender and Discourses of Identity in a Japanese Workplace* (Chicago: Univ. of Chicago Press, 1990); Jane Flax, *Thinking Fragments: Psychoanalysis, Feminism, and Postmodernism in the Contemporary West* (Berkeley and Los Angeles: Univ. of California Press, 1990); Catherine Keller, *From a Broken Web: Separation, Sexism, and Self* (Boston: Beacon Press, 1986); Kenneth J. Gergen, *The Saturated Self: Dilemmas of Identity in Contemporary Life* (New York: Basic Books, 1991).

2. Moore, *Passion for Differences,* 33.

3. Salvador Minuchin, Bernice L. Rosman, and Lester Baker, *Psychosomatic Families. Anorexia Nervosa in Context* (Cambridge, Mass.: Harvard Univ. Press, 1978).

4. Deborah Anna Luepnitz, *The Family Interpreted, Feminist Theory in Clinical Practice* (New York: Basic Books, 1988), 68.

5. Ibid., 67.

6. Alan Roland, *In Search of Self in India and Japan* (Princeton, N.J.: Princeton Univ. Press, 1988), xvii.

7. Ibid., 10.

8. Ibid., 11–12.

9. Ibid., 8 n.

10. Kenneth Gergen, "Social Understanding and the Inscription of the Self," in *Cultural Psychology: Essays on Comparative Human Development,* ed. James Stigler, Richard Shweder, and Gilbert Herdt (Cambridge, Eng.: Cambridge Univ. Press, 1990), 583.

11. Ibid., 585.

12. Ibid.

13. Nancy Chodorow, *The Reproduction of Mothering* (Berkeley and Los Angeles: Univ. of California Press, 1978).

14. Ibid., 169.

15. In "What Is the Relation Between Psychoanalytic Feminism and the Psychoanalytic Psychology of Women?" in *Theoretical Perspectives on Sexual Difference,* ed. Deborah L. Rhode (New Haven, Conn.: Yale Univ. Press, 1990), 122, Chodorow argues gender identity is the conscious recognition of one's masculinity or femininity; whereas, gender personality is a developmental product resulting in the construction of masculine and feminine selves. Females experience self in relationship not because they know they are females but because of developmental relationship to the mother. Male denial of relationship, Chodorow conjectures, may, however, result from their sense of masculinity.

16. Carol Gilligan, *In a Different Voice, Psychological Theory and Women's Development* (Cambridge, Mass.: Harvard Univ. Press, 1982).

17. Evelyn Fox Keller, "Science and Gender," *Signs. Journal of Women in Culture and Society* 7 (1982): 589–602.

18. Nancy Hartsock, *Money, Sex and Power, Toward a Feminist Historical Materialism* (New York: Longman, 1983).

19. Hartsock, *Money, Sex and Power,* Fox Keller, "Science and Gender"; Jane Flax, *Thinking Fragments: Psychoanalysis, Feminism and Postmodernism in the Contemporary West* (Berkeley and Los Angeles: Univ. of California Press, 1990).

20. Sandra Harding, "What Is the Real Material Base of Patriarchy and Capital?" in *Women and Revolution,* ed. Lydia Sargent (Boston: South End Press, 1981), 135–64.

21. Nancy Chodorow and Susan Contratto, "The Fantasy of the Perfect Mother," in *Rethinking the Family: Some Feminist Questions,* ed. Barrie Thorne and Maryland Lalom (New York: Longmans, 1982, 55–75); Jane Liebman Jacobs, "Reassessing Mother Blame in Incest," *Signs* 15, no. 3 (1990): 500–514.

22. Chodorow, *Reproduction of Mothering*; Nancy Chodorow, "Family Structure and Feminine Personality," in *Women, Culture, and Society,* ed. Michelle Zimbalist Rosaldo and Louise Lamphere (Stanford, Calif.: Stanford Univ. Press, 1974).

23. Luepnitz, *Family Interpreted.*

24. Lillian B. Rubin, *Intimate Strangers: Men and Women Together* (New York: Harper, 1983).

25. Debra Nails, "Social-Scientific Sexism: Gilligan's Mismeasure of Man," *Social Research* 50, no. 3 (summer 1983): 643–65; John Broughton, "Women's Rationality and Men's Virtues," *Social Research* 50, no. 3 (summer 1983): 587–642; Hester Eisenstein, *Contemporary Feminist Thought* (Boston: G. K. Hall, 1983); Iris Marion Young, "Is Male Gender Identity the Cause of Male Domination?" in *Mothering, Essays in Feminist Theory*, ed. Joyce Trebilcot (Totowa, N.J.: Rowman and Allanheld, 1983), 129–46; Elizabeth Spelman, *Inessential Woman, Problems of Exclusion in Feminist Thought* (Boston: Beacon Press, 1988); Pauline Bart, "Review of Chodorow's 'The Reproduction of Mothering,' " in *Mothering: Essays in Feminist Theory*, ed. Joyce Trebilcot (Totowa, N.J.: Rowman and Allanheld, 1983); Ann Ferguson, "On Conceiving Motherhood and Sexuality: A Feminist Materialist Approach," in *Mothering: Essays in Feminist Theory*, ed. Joyce Trebilcot (Totowa, N.J.: Rowman and Allanheld, 1983).

26. Spelman, *Inessential Woman*, 188.

27. Ibid.

28. Chodorow, "What Is the Relation?"

29. Deborah Rhode, "Theoretical Perspectives on Sexual Difference," in *Theoretical Perspectives on Sexual Difference*, ed. Deborah Rhode (New Haven, Conn.: Yale Univ. Press, 1990); Chodorow, "What Is the Relation?" 129, observed that all psychoanalytic theories of gender, including feminist, neglect or are unable to conceptualize gender salience and called for questioning whether gender is always a dominant identity or feature of personality.

30. Barrie Thorne, "Children and Gender: Constructions of Difference," in *Theoretical Perspectives on Sexual Difference*, ed. Deborah L. Rhode (New Haven, Conn.: Yale Univ. Press, 1990), 106.

31. Marilyn Frye, "The Possibility of Feminist Theory," in *Theoretical Perspectives on Sexual Difference*, ed. Deborah L. Rhode (New Haven, Conn.: Yale Univ. Press, 1990).

32. Roland, *In Search of Self*, xvi.

33. Moore, *Passion for Difference*, 34.

34. Sylvia J. Yanagisako and Jane F. Collier, "The Mode of Reproduction in Anthropology," in *Theoretical Persectives on Sexual Difference*, edited by Deborah L. Rhode (New Haven, Conn.: Yale Univ. Press, 1990).

35. See Chodorow and Contratto, "Fantasy of the Perfect Mother," and *Signs* 15, no. 3 (1990) special issue on mothering, particularly the exchange between Raquel Portilla Bauman and Susan Rubin Suleiman. See also Seyla Benhabib, "The Generalized and the Concrete Other. The Kohlberg-Gilligan Controversy and Feminist Theory," in *Feminism as Critique*, ed. Syla Renhabib and Drucilla Cornell (Minneapolis: Univ. of Minnesota Press, 1987), 77–95; Elizabeth Abel, "Race, Class and Psychoanalysis? Opening Questions," in *Conflicts in Feminism*," ed. Marianne Hirsch and Evelyn Fox Keller (New York: Routledge, 1990); Spelman, *Inessential Woman; Flax, Thinking Fragment;* Carol Stack, "Different Voices, Different Visions: Gender, Culture and Moral Reasoning," in *Uncertain Terms, Negotiating Gender in American Culture*, ed. Faye Ginsburg and Anna Lowenhaupt Tsing (Boston: Beacon Press, 1990), 19–27.

36. Mervat Hatem, "Toward the Study of the Psychodynamics of Mothering and Gender in Egyptian Families," *International Journal of Middle East Studies* 19 (1987): 287–306.

37. Stack, "Different Voices"; Patricia Hill Collins, "The Social Construction of Black Feminist Thought." *Signs* 14, no. 4 (1989): 745–73.

38. Deniz Kandiyoti, "Islam and Patriarchy: A Comparative Perspective," in *Women in Middle Eastern History,* ed. Nikki R. Keddie and Beth Baron (New Haven, Conn.: Yale Univ. Press, 1991).

39. Michelle Rosaldo, "Toward an Anthropology of Self and Feeling," in *Culture Theory, Essays on Mind, Self and Emotion,* ed. Richard Shweder and Robert LeVine (Cambridge, Eng.: Cambridge Univ. Press, 1984), 137–57; Trinh, *Woman, Native, Other;* Lutz, *Unnatural Emotions;* Kondo, *Crafting Selves;* Hatem, "Psychodynamics."

40. Brown and Itzkowitz, *Psychological Dimensions;* Hatem, "Psychodynamics"; Hisham Sharabi, *Neopatriarchy: A Theory of Distorted Change in Arab Society* (New York: Oxford Univ. Press, 1988).

41. See Andrea Rugh, *Family in Contemporary Egypt* (Syracuse, N.Y.: Syracuse Univ. Press, 1984), and idem, *Within the Circle: Parents and Children in an Arab Village* (New York: Columbia Univ. Press, 1997); Anne Meneley, *Tournaments of Value: Sociability and Hierarchy in a Yemeni Town* (Toronto: Univ. of Toronto Press, 1966); Majid al-Haj, *Social Change and Family Processes, Arab Communities in Shefar-A'm* (Boulder, Colo.: Westview Press, 1987); Hatem, "Psychodynamics"; Mervat Hatem, "Underdevelopment, Mothering, and Gender Within the Egyptian Family," *Arab Studies Quarterly* 8, no. 1 (1986): 45–61; Susan Schaefer Davis and Douglas A. Davis, *Adolescence in a Moroccan Town, Making Social Sense* (New Brunswick, N.J.: Rutgers Univ. Press, 1989); Sharabi, *Neopatriarchy;* Halim Barakat, "The Arab Family and the Challenge of Social Transformation," in *Women and the Family in the Middle East, New Voices of Change,* ed. Elizbeth Warnock Fernea (Austin: Univ. of Texas, 1985), 27–48. For Lebanese family studies see Nura S. Alamuddin and Paul D. Starr, *Crucial Bonds, Marriage among the Lebanese Druze* (Delmar, N.Y.: Caravan Books, 1980); Samir Khalaf, "Primordial ties and Politics in Lebanon," *Middle Eastern Studies* 4, no. 3 (1968): 243–69; idem, "Changing Forms of Political Patronage in Lebanon," in *Patrons and Clients in Mediterranean Societies,* ed. Ernest Gellner and John Waterbury (London: Duckworth, 1977), 185–206; Prothro, *Child Rearing in Lebanon;* Edwin Terry Prothro and Lutfy Najib Diab, *Changing Family Patterns in the Arab East* (Beirut: American Univ. of Beiruit Press, 1974); Judith Williams, *The Youth of Haouch El Harimi: A Lebanese Village* (Cambridge: Center for Middle East Studies, Harvard Univ. Press, 1968).

42. See Hatem "Underdevelopment"; idem, "Psychodynamics," for an application of Chodorow's work to Egyptian families; Sharabi, *Neopatriarchy,* for a political psychology treatise; Fouad Moughrabi, "The Arab Basic Personality: A Critical Survey of the Literature," *International Journal of Middle Eastern Studies* 9 (1978): 99–112; and idem, "A Political Technology of the Soul," *Arab Studies Quarterly* 3, no. 1 (1981): 68–89, for a critical analysis of the political uses and abuses of social-psychological studies of Arabs. See, also, Ammar, *Growing Up;* Davis and Davis, *Adolescense;* Vincent Crapanzano, *The Hamadsha: A Study in Moroccan Ethnopsychiatry* (Berkeley and Los Angeles: Univ. of California Press, 1973); and idem, *Tuhami: Portrait of a Moroccan* (Chicago: Univ. of Chicago Press, 1980).

43. John Gulick, *The Middle East: An Anthropological Perspective* (Pacific Palisades, Calif.: Goodyear Publishing, 1976), 30.

44. Ibid., 31.

45. Clifford Geertz, Hildred Geertz, and Lawrence Rosen, *Order in Moroccan Society* (New York: Cambridge Univ. Press, 1979); Michael Johnson, "Political Bosses and Their

Gangs: Zu'ama and Qabadayat in the Sunni Muslim Quarters of Beirut," in *Patrons and Clients,* ed. Ernest Gellner and John Waterbury (London: Duckworth, 1977), 207–24.

46. George Hakim, "The Economic Basis of Lebanese Polity," in *Politics in Lebanon,* ed. Leonard Binder (New York: John Wiley and Sons, 1966), 60.

47. Michael Gilsenan, "Against Patron-Client Relations," in *Patrons and Clients in Mediterranean Societies,* ed. Ernest Gellner and John Waterbury (London: Duckworth, 1977), 167–84: Khalaf, "Changing Forms"; Halim Barakat, *The Arab World: Society, Culture and State* (Berkeley and Los Angeles: Univ. of California Press, 1993).

48. Sharabi, *Neopatriarchy;* Barakat, *Arab World.*

49. Barakat, "Arab Family," 28.

50. Hisham Sharabi and Mukhtar Ali, "The Impact of Class and Culture on Social Behavior: The Feudal-Bourgeois Family in Arab Society," in *Psychological Dimensions of Near Eastern Studies,* ed. L. Carl Brown and Norman Itzkowitz (Princeton, N.J.: Darwin Press, 1977), 240–56; idem, *Neopatriarchy.*

51. Juliette Minces, *The House of Obedience. Women in Arab Society* (London: Zed Press, 1982), 43.

52. Rugh, *Family,* 32.

53. Rugh, *Within the Circle.*

54. Cynthia Nelson and Virginia Olesen, "Veil of Illusion: A Critique of the Concept of Equality in Western Thought," *Catalyst* 10, no. 11 (1977): 8–36.

55. Khalaf "Primordial Ties"; idem, "Changing Forms."

56. Lila Abu-Lughod, *Veiled Sentiments: Honor and Poetry in a Bedouin Society* (Berkeley and Los Angeles: Univ. of California Press, 1986); Leila Ahmed, "Between Two Worlds: The Formation of a Turn-of-the-Century Egyptian Feminist," in *Life/Lines: Theorizing Women's Autobiography,* ed. Bella Brodzki and Celeste Schenck (Ithaca, N.Y.: Cornell Univ. Press, 1989); Soraya Altorki, *Women in Saudi Arabia: Ideology and Behavior among the Elite* (New York: Columbia Univ. Press, 1986); Hatem, "Psychodynamics"; Suad Joseph, "Brother/Sister Relationships: Connectivity, Love, and Power in the Reproduction of Arab Patriarchy," *American Ethnologist* 21, no. 1 (Feb. 1994): 50–73.

57. Keller, *Broken Web,* 9.

58. Khalaf, "Primordial Ties"; "Brother/Sister Relationships"; Joseph, and idem, "The Family as Security and Bondage: A Political Strategy of the Lebanese Urban Working Class," in *Towards a Political Economy of Urbanization in Third World Countries,* ed. Helen Safa (New Delhi: Oxford Univ. Press, 1982), 151–71.

1. Teta, Mother, and I

1. The fruit of this resolve is a book manuscript, "Inside History: Three Generations of Arab Women," nearing completion.

2. As I prepared to write the biographies of my grandmother and mother, I read widely in general histories of the area. I found the following standard texts: particularly useful Albert Hourani, *A History of the Arab Peoples* (London: Faber and Faber, 1991); and Kamal Salibi, *The Modern History of Lebanon* (London: Weidenfeld and Nicolson, 1965). On the specific subject of the missions, I found particularly useful A. L. Tibawi, *British Interests in Palestine, 1800–1901* (London: Oxford Univ. Press, 1961); and idem, *American Interests in Syria 1800–1901* (Oxford, Eng.: Clarendon Press, 1966). Henry Harris Jessup,

Fifty-Three Years in Syria, 2 vols. (New York: Fleming H. Revell, 1910), a missionary classic, was important among the many missionary books and journals I read.

3. An account of Mrs. Bowen-Thompson's life and career is contained in Rev. H. B. Tristram, ed., *Daughters of Syria* (London: Seeley, Jackson, and Halliday, 1872).

4. The present headmaster of the school's successor, the Lebanon Evangelical School for Boys and Girls, was kind enough to offer me access to the only records available from those days. Most of the school's old records were lost during the Lebanon war that began in 1975, but luckily a single book of "Examination Marks" was found. It covered the period from 1893 to 1912, and in it I found my grandmother's and two of her sisters' names and marks. The book includes much valuable information, such as syllabi, prizes, punishments, lists of names and patrons, and hints of social attitudes.

5. Letters exchanged between my parents at the time of their engagement during the autumn of 1932 were carefully preserved by my mother. I found them after her death. From them and from her notebook comes the account of the quarrel about the wedding. From them, also, comes the certainty of his passion for her and her shy but growing love for him.

6. As the scramble for new papers took place in neighboring Arab countries, she complained indignantly to her sons—both my uncles record this in their memoirs—that although she of all of them was an authentic Lebanese, both her parents having been natives of Mount Lebanon, she was not allowed Lebanese papers, let alone to provide her children with them. The nation imposed by the French included the prejudices of the French against women, and to this day the women's movement has been fighting this legacy of "modernism." Eventually, as a dependent of her eldest son, Teta was given a Jordanian passport.

7. See "Contradictions, or Mirrors: A Self Portrait," in Jean Said Makdisi, *Beirut Fragments: A War Memoir* (New York: Persea Books, 1990).

8. Tristram, *Daughters of Syria,* 27.

9. Jessup, *Fifty-Three Years in Syria,* vol. 1, 224.

10. Leila Ahmed, *Women and Gender in Islam* (New Haven, Conn.: Yale Univ. Press, 1992), 152ff.

11. Tristram, *Daughters of Syria,* 192.

12. Frances E. Scott, *Dare and Persevere* (London: Lebanon Evangelical Mission, 1960), 29.

13. Tristram, *Daughters of Syria,* 190–1.

14. Makdisi, *Beirut Fragments.*

2. Searching for Baba

1. Suad Joseph, "Connectivity and Patriarchy among Urban Working Class Arab Families in Lebanon," *Ethos* 21, no. 4 (Dec. 1993): 452–84; and idem, "Gender and Relationality among Arab families in Lebanon," *Feminist Studies* 19, no. 3 (fall 1993): 465–86.

2. Cortland, N.Y.

3. Like many born in the Ottoman Empire, my father was not registered at birth with the Ottoman state. The Maronite Church also did not keep systematic records of births or baptismals.

4. Mama knew her age, but not precisely when her parents died.

5. *Sito* is colloquial Lebanese for "grandmother."

6. *Gido* is colloquial Lebanese for "grandfather."

7. A *dirbakki* is a drum made of clay and sheepskin. It is a central instrument in popular Arabic music.

8. *Hind* means "Indian" (*Hinoud*, pl.) in Arabic.

9. Lebanon's foremost female vocalist.

10. *Mughtaribin* is Arabic for "immigrants," Lebanese who have gone literally to the West.

3. The Poet Who Helped Shape My Childhood

1. Bitter lemon trees.

2. An Arab poetess, linguist, and critic, who has published several collections in Arabic. Some of her work has been translated into English and French. She has several books on issues concerning Arab poetry and literature.

3. A two-thousand-year-old system organizing the linguistic structure of all Arabic poetry.

5. Brother-Sister Relationships

1. The names of all Camp Trad residents have been changed.

2. Abu Hanna means "father of Hanna." Adults with children were referred to by the name of their oldest male child. Thus, Hanna's mother was called Um Hanna, the "mother of Hanna."

3. It was not uncommon among urban working classes in Lebanon for women to be overweight during and after their childbearing years.

4. Fieldwork was carried out from 1971 to 1973 under a National Institute for Mental Health (NIMH) predoctoral research grant. Briefer follow-up research was undertaken in 1974, 1976, 1978, 1980, and each year from 1993 to 1997. Unless otherwise indicated, the argument in this paper refers to the period just before the outbreak of the Lebanese civil war in 1975.

5. The dynamics of these families resonated with me. Having been born in a village not far from Camp Trad and raised as an Arab-American, my relationships with these families and my analysis in this chapter have been shaped and informed partly by my own family experiences.

6. Corporal punishment for perceived misdeeds was not specifically a cross-sex pattern among Camp Trad families. It was considered socially acceptable for parents to discipline children and older siblings to discipline younger ones in this manner, regardless of gender.

7. Civil war erupted in Lebanon in 1975, two years after I completed the initial fieldwork, and continues to this writing.

8. See Bronislaw Malinowski, *The Family among the Australian Aborigines: A Sociological Study* (London: Univ. of London Press, 1913); A. R. Radcliffe-Brown, "The Mother's Brother in South Africa," *South African Journal of Science* 21 (1924): 542–55; Raymond Firth, *We, the Tikopia: A Sociological Study of Kinship in Primitive Polynesia* (London: Allen and Unwin, 1936); Kenelm O. L. Burridge, "Siblings in Tangu," *Oceania* 30 (1959): 128–54; David M. Schneider and Kathleen Gough, ed. *Matrilineal Kinship* (Berkeley and Los Angeles: Univ. of California Press, 1961); Annette B. Weiner, *Women of Value, Men of Renown; New Perspectives in Trobriand Exchange* (Austin: Univ. of Texas Press, 1976); Raymond C. Kelly, *Etoro Social Structure: A Study in Structural Contradiction* (Ann Arbor:

Univ. of Michigan Press, 1977); and Mac Marshall, ed., *Siblingship in Oceania. Studies in the Meaning of Kin Relations* (Boston: Univ. Press of America, 1983).

9. See Halim Barakat, "Arab Family"; Elizabeth Warnock Fernea, ed., *Women and the Family in the Middle East: New Voices of Change* (Austin: Univ. of Texas Press, 1985); Sharabi, *Neopatriarchy,* for pan-Arab discussions and comparisons. For specific national studies see Al-Haj, *Social Change;* Altorki, *Women in Saudi Arabia;* Davis and Davis, *Adolescence;* Christine Eickelman, *Women and Community in Oman* (New York: New York Univ. Press, 1984); Hatem, "Psychodynamics," 287–306; Henry Munson, Jr., *The House of Si Abd Allah: The Oral History of a Moroccan Family* (New Haven, Conn.: Yale Univ. Press, 1984); and Andrea B. Rugh, *Family.*

10. Much of the research on Arab patriarchy, patrilineality, patrilocality, and patrileal endogamy focuses on the preferred norms of FaBrDa/So marriage. The interest of most scholars has been on the *male* relationships in that marriage system. The debates concerning the FaBrDa/So marriage have spanned several decades. Scholars have evoked functionalist, structuralist, ecological, political-economic, and psychodynamic theories. See Robert F. Murphy and Leonard Kasdan, "The Structure of Parallel Cousin Marriage," *American Anthropologist* 61 (1959): 17–29; Raphael Patai, *Family, Love and the Bible* (London: McGibbon and Kee, 1960); M. M. Ripinsky, "Middle Eastern Kinship as an Expression of a Culture-Environment System," *Muslim World* 58 (1968): 225–41; Frederick Barth, "Father's Brother's Daughter Marriage in Kurdistan," *Southwest Journal of Anthropology* 10 (1954): 164–71; Fuad Khuri, "Parallel Cousin Marriage Reconsidered: A Middle Eastern Practice that Nullifies the Effects of Marriage on the Intensity of Family Relationships," *Man* 5 (1970): 597–618; and Justine McCabe, "FBD Marriage: Further Support for the Westermarck Hypothesis of the Incest Taboo?" *American Anthropologist* 85 (1983): 50–69.

11. See Prothro, *Child Rearing in Lebanon;* Ann Fuller, *Buarij: Portrait of a Lebanese Muslim Village* (Cambridge, Mass.: Center for Middle East Studies, Harvard Univ. Press, 1961); Williams, *Youth of Haouch El Harimi;* Samir Khalaf, "Family Associations in Lebanon," *Journal of Comparative Family Studies* 2 (1971): 235–50; and idem, "Primordial Ties"; Samih Farsoun, "Family Structure and Society in Modern Lebanon," in *Peoples and Cultures of the Middle East,* ed. Louise Sweet (Garden City, N.Y.: Natural History Press, 1978) 257–307; Prothro and Diab, *Changing Family Patterns;* Alamuddin and Starr, *Crucial Bonds;* and Joseph, "Family as Security and Bondage."

12. Hasan el-Shamy, *Brother and Sister Type 872: A Cognitive Behavioristic Analysis of a Middle Eastern Oikotype,* Folklore Monographs Series, 8 (Bloomington, Ind.: Folklore Publication Group, 1979).

13. Hasan el-Shamy, "The Brother-Sister Syndrome in Arab Family Life, Socio-Cultural Factors in Arab Psychiatry: A Critical Review," *International Journal of Sociology of the Family* 2 (1981): 319.

14. The folk tale has many renditions recorded in different Arab countries. Briefly, the main themes are as follows: a woman gives birth to a boy and a girl. The mother dies when the children are little, but before dying, entrusts the care of the brother to the sister. The sister lovingly raises the brother and gives him all the inheritance when he reaches manhood. He chooses a wife with the guidance of the sister, and they all live together. The sister-in-law attempts to drive a wedge between the brother and sister. Finally, she induces the sister to eat a "pregnancy egg" to make her appear pregnant and tells the brother to see what his sister has done. The brother, assuming the sister has had an illicit affair, takes her to a deserted place, intending to kill her. Unable to kill her, he abandons her there. The local people,

upon hearing the sister's story, build her a palace. One day, the sister sneezes two pigeons out her nostrils. The pigeons fly to the brother's house, proclaiming to the wife, who tries to shoo them away, that this is the home of their *khal* (mother's brother). The brother, upon hearing the pigeons, follows them to the spot where he had left his sister. Arriving at the palace, he is greeted by his sister dressed as a man. He asks about the story told by the pigeons and is told the whole story by the "man." The brother asserts that no one would know that story except his sister and asks to be taken to her to ask her forgiveness. At this, the sister reveals herself, and she and the brother embrace and cry. The brother renounces his wife and lives with the sister, begetting boys and girls.

15. Hasan el-Shamy, "The Traditional Structure of Sentiments in Mahfouz's Trilogy: A Behavioristic Text Analysis," *Al-'Arabiyya* 9 (1976): 53–74.

16. El-Shamy, "Brother-Sister Syndrome."

17. El-Shamy, *Brother and Sister Type 872,* 1.

18. Some of the literature on the Arab world reports more ambivalence in brother/sister relationships. Davis and Davis, *Adolescence,* 81 found considerable variation among brother/sister relationships in the Moroccan town of Zawiya. Sisters were both affectionate toward their brothers and resentful of the control they exercised. In the Moroccan village of Sidi Embarek, Susan Schaefer Davis, *Patience and Power: Women's Lives in a Moroccan Village* (Cambridge, Mass.: Schenkman, 1983), 132, found that sibling rivalry was greater among brothers and sisters than among sisters.

19. Hilma Granqvist, *Marriage Conditions in a Palestinian Village* Commentationes Humanarum Litterarum (Helsingfors: Societas Scientiarum Fennica, 1935), 2:254.

20. The brother said: "She has her father's house. Nobody can tread on the hem of her garment [insult her]. May it be as thou wishest. Our beard is on thy sack. We are thy camels [we bear all thy burdens and sorrows]" (*"ilha dar abuha ma hada byidar yuhbut 'a tarafha marhababic ilhana 'ala cisic ihna jmalic"*), ibid., 2:252.

21. Ibid., 2:253.

22. Ibid.

23. *"Hadi sagigti bukra bithasibni fi-l-ahre walakin uladi u marathi la,"* ibid., 2:254.

24. Michael E. Meeker, "Meaning and Society in the Near East: Examples from the Black Sea Turks and the Levantine Arabs," *International Journal of Middle Eastern Studies* 7 (1976): 388.

25. Parallels to this romantic view of brother/sister relationships have been reported for other cultures of the Mediterranean. Literature on the ancient Mediterranean, particularly ancient Egypt and Rome, seems to indicate that intimate relationships between brothers and sisters ranged from love to incest to marriage: J. S. Slotkin, "On the Possible Lack of Incest Regulations in Old Iran," *American Anthropologist* 49 (1947): 612–17; Patai, *Family;* Russell Middleton, "Brother/Sister and Father/Daughter Marriage in Ancient Egypt," *American Sociological Review* 27 (1962): 603–11; Keith Hopkins, "Brother-Sister Marriage in Roman Egypt," *Comparative Studies in Society and History* 22, no. 3 (1980): 303–59. Although fascinating, interpreting this literature in relation to the contemporary period must be done carefully to avoid assumptions of cultural continuities. Research on the contemporary Mediterranean also reveals some parallels. Lloyd A. Fallers and Margaret C. Fallers, "Sex Roles in Edremit," in *Mediterranean Family Structures,* edited by J. G. Peristiany (London: Cambridge Univ. Press, 1976), 250–58, contend that the brother/sister relationship in Edremit, Turkey, has "an almost romantic quality" and is, for many brothers and sisters, the "most intense cross-sex relationship they will ever experience." Ian Whitaker,

"Familial Roles in the Extended Patrilineal Kin-Group in Northern Albania," in *Mediterranean Family Structures,* ed. J. G. Peristiany (London: Cambridge Univ. Press, 1976), 198, claims that among the Ghegs, sheep-herding Albanians, a woman's dearest relation is with her brother.

26. Rugh, *Family in Contemporary Egypt,* maintains that, in Egypt, sisters are socialized to love their brothers and to focus on the affective aspects of the relationship. Brothers, although affectionate to sisters, are taught to focus on the jural duties of the brother to the sister. Hatem, "Psychodynamics," seems to indicate more ambivalence in Egyptian brother/sister relationships but does not discuss the relationship in detail.

27. Ahmed, "Between Two Worlds," 161.

28. Ibid., 172.

29. David G. Gilmore, ed., *Honor and Shame and the Unity of the Mediterranean* (Washington, D.C.: American Anthropological Association, 1987).

30. Perhaps no subject related to gender and family in the Mediterranean and the Middle East has received more anthropological attention than the relationship between honor and shame. Explanations have ranged from culture, David Campbell, *Honour, Family and Patronage: A Study of Institutions and Moral Values in a Greek Mountain Community* (Oxford: Clarendon Press, 1964); J. G. Peristiany, *Honor and Shame: The Values of Mediterranean Society* (Chicago: Univ. of Chicago Press, 1966); Julian Pitt-Rivers, *The Fate of Shechem or the Politics of Sex: Essays in the Anthropology of the Mediterranean* (London: Cambridge Univ. Press, 1977); to ecology and political economy, Jane Schneider, "Of Vigilance and Virgins: Honour, Shame and Access to Resources in the Mediterranean Societies," *Ethnology* 10 (1971): 1–24; Jane Schneider and Peter Schneider, *Culture and Political Economy in Western Sicily* (New York: Academic Press, 1976); to psychodynamics, Gilmore, *Honor and Shame.* For a feminist critical review of the honor/shame literature, see Forouz Jowkar, "Honor and Shame: A Feminist View from Within," *Feminist Issues* 6, no. 1 (1986): 45–63.

31. Richard T. Antoun, "On the Modesty of Women in Arab Muslim Villages: A Study in the Accommodation of Traditions," *American Anthropologist* 70 (1968): 692; Granqvist, *Marriage Conditions,* 2:255, quotes El-Barghuthi's study of judicial courts among Bedouins of Palestine in 1922 as reporting, " 'The good of a woman belongs to her husband and her evil to her family.' " Williams, *Youth of Haouch El Harimi,* 83, reports a similar attitude in the Lebanese Sunni village of Haouch El-Harimi.

32. Alois Musil, *The Manners and Customs of the Rwala Bedouins* (New York: American Geographical Society, 1928), 494.

33. Fuller, *Buarij;* Abner Cohen, *Arab Border-Villages in Israel: A Study of Continuity and Change in Social Organization* (Manchester: Manchester Univ. Press, 1965); Ahmed Abou-Zeid, "Honour and Shame among the Bedouins of Egypt," in *Honour and Shame,* ed. J. G. Peristiany (Chicago: Univ. of Chicago Press, 1966) 243–60; Emanuel Marx, *Bedouin of the Negev* (New York: Frederick A. Praeger, 1967); Antoun, "Modesty"; Pitt-Rivers, *Fate of Shechem;* and Altorki, *Women in Saudi Arabia.*

34. The hierarchy in brother/sister relationships was also affected by family demographics such as the number of children in the family and currently living in the household, residential proximity of adult siblings, gender and age orders, the presence or absence of one or both parents, the presence of extended family members in the household or in the neighborhood, and previous marriages of either parent or concurrent marriages of the father. Such demographic variables impact the expression of cultural norms in daily living and condition the practices associated with the brother/sister relationship. In general, though, older

brothers almost always had culturally sanctioned power over younger sisters (and brothers). Older sisters usually had control over younger brothers (and sisters) until the boys came into puberty, at which point brothers increasingly gained power over sisters. Although it is not within the scope of this chapter to account for all the variations in brother/sister love/power dynamics related to family size, birth order, life cycle, and other aspects of family demographics, it is important to note that despite the resultant variable practices, the cultural prescriptions of brothers' dominance over sisters and mutual love between them was generally accepted and upheld among the families I observed.

35. Most of the dynamics I describe here were found in families across religious sects. Arab Christians and Muslims shared basic patrilineal and patriarchal values about family life. Christians did not articulate a cultural norm of patrilineal parallel cousin marriage. They, like Muslims, practiced close bilateral kin marriage, however. Christians and Muslims shared beliefs concerning the primacy of family loyalty, duty, and honor. They alike supported the creation of connective social personas. And they shared similar beliefs about brother/sister relationships. Many of these dynamics appeared in Camp Trad Armenian families as well. Because of their special history in Lebanon, however, I will not discuss them except when it seems particularly useful to do so.

36. The scholarly research I cite, which indicates similar patterns in other Arab countries, needs to be contextualized historically, socially, and culturally. To do so would require a fuller treatment of the subject than I can undertake here.

37. Catherine Keller opposes the concept of connective selfhood to separative selfhood (Keller, Broken Web, 9). For her the concept of connective selfhood is a liberatory concept indicating a self that is relational and autonomous. I use the concept more broadly to indicate a self that is relational, but whose experience and expressions vary with different political economies.

38. Minuchin, Rosman, and Baker, *Psychosomatic Families.*

39. Luepnitz, *Family Interpreted,* 57.

40. See Joseph, *Connectivity and Patriarchy,* for a further discussion of the notion of connectivity and its relationship to Arab patriarchy and the limitations of family systems theory. Few scholars of the Arab world have researched the process of connectivity. Many have discussed the immersion of the individual in the family, however. See Rugh, *Family;* Barakat, "Arab Family"; Sharabi, *Neopatriarchy.* See Karen Ericksen Paige, "Gender, Family Systems and Theories of State Formation" (paper presented at Middle East Studies Association Meeting, San Francisco, 1984), for an application of the concept of enmeshment to Egyptian families.

41. Although it is not the subject of this chapter, I argue these Arab families supported connective relationships among their members in general.

42. Abu-Lughod, *Veiled Sentiments;* Catherine Lutz, *Unnatural Emotions;* Rosaldo, "Anthropology."

43. Abu-Lughod, *Veiled Sentiments,* 34.

44. El-Shamy, *Brother and Sister Type 872,* 79 argues that because of the possibility of polygyny, Arab children identified with their mothers more strongly than with their fathers and with their mothers' families more than with their fathers'.

45. Patai, *Family,* argues this marriage rule preserves property in the patrilineal line. Murphy and Kasdan, "Parallel Cousin Marriage," argue parallel cousin marriage allows for agnatic segmentation and structural opposition at the nuclear family level. Khuri, "Parallel Cousin Marriage Reconsidered," argues that the rule mitigates the effect of marriage on pa-

trilineality, that is, ensures that marriage will not undermine patrilineal solidarity. El-Shamy, *Brother and Sister Type 872,* 60, points out that despite the formal anticipation of political and marital alliance between patrilineal cousins, the relations between cousins and the siblings of their spouses in FaBr/So/Da marriages remains hostile as compared to the brother/sister relationship.

46. McCabe, "FBD Marriage," 58, found in the Southern Lebanese village of Bayt al-ʾAsir that unmarried opposite-sex first cousins displayed an intimacy very similar to that of cross-siblings. Her findings conflicted with those of Khuri, "Parallel Cousin Marriage Reconsidered," for two suburbs of Beirut.

47. El-Shamy, *Brother and Sister Type 872,* 43.

48. Ibid., 59.

49. Ibid., 79.

50. Donald Cole observes that the most affectionate relationship across generations among the Al Murrah Bedouin of Saudi Arabia is between young people and their mothers' brothers and sisters. Although he does not discuss the brother/sister relationship per se, he notes that the coldness and indifference with which a man greets his wife after a period of absence contrasts sharply with the lavish warmth he offers to his mother, father's and mother's sisters, and his own sisters; see Donald Powell Cole, *Nomads of the Nomads. The Al Murrah Bedouin of the Empty Quarter* (Arlington Heights, Ill.: Harlan Davidson, 1975), 73–75.

51. This structural limitation reinforced a woman's ultimate dependence on her own sons, if she had any. Structurally, in some ways, a woman was encouraged to look to her sons to fulfill what her father, brothers, and husbands did not. This partly explains the great intensity of the mother/son relationship, perhaps the only cross-sex family relationship that overshadowed the brother/sister in the cultural stress on love.

52. Granqvist, *Marriage Conditions,* 2:255, reports cases of Palestinian *fellahin* women risking their relationships with their husbands rather than risking being cut off from their natal families. Altorki, *Women in Saudi Arabia,* 78, reports similar cases among contemporary elite Saudi women.

53. Granqvist, *Marriage Conditions,* 2: 254, reports that Palestinian village men in the 1930s felt more responsible for their sisters than for their wives and children. I would not make a similar claim for the Camp Trad men. It was clear, however, that they did feel a strong responsibility for their sisters.

54. Fuller, *Buarji,* 52, observes that Sunni village women in Buarij realized that to gain the protection of fathers and brothers they had to conduct themselves with propriety.

55. I am indebted to Judith Walkowitz for pointing out the need to emphasize this point.

56. There has been no formal census in Lebanon since 1932. These percentages were estimated from interviews with local officials and residents.

57. Halim Barakat, *Lebanon in Strife: Student Preludes to the Civil War* (Austin: Univ. of Texas Press, 1977); Kamal Salibi, *Cross Roads to Civil War: Lebanon 1958–1976* (Delmar, N.Y.: Caravan, 1976).

58. Joseph, "Family as Security and Bondage"; and idem, "Working Class Women's Networks in a Sectarian State: A Political Paradox," *American Ethnologist* 10 (1983): 1–22.

59. Many families had lived in Lebanon and or Camp Trad less than one year; few had lived there more than two generations.

60. Suad Joseph, "Working the Law: A Lebanese Working Class Case," in *The Politics of Law in the Middle East,* ed. Daisy Dwyer (Hadley, Mass.: J. F. Bergin, 1990), 143–59.

61. Barakat, Lebanon in Strife,; P. Edward Haley and Lewis W. Snider, eds., *Lebanon in Crisis: Participants and Issues* (Syracuse, N.Y.: Syracuse Univ. Press, 1979); Suad Joseph, "Muslim-Christian Conflict in Lebanon: A Perspective in the Evolution of Sectarianism," in *Muslim-Christian Conflicts: Economic, Political and Social Origins,* ed. Suad Joseph and Barbara L. K. Pillsbury (Boulder, Colo.: Westview Press, 1978); B. J. Odeh, *Lebanon: Dynamics of Conflict* (London: Zed Books, 1985).

62. Joseph, "Family as Security and Bondage."

63. Khalaf, "Primordial Ties."

64. Prothro and Diab, *Changing Family Patterns,* 71, report that the approximately five hundred formally organized family associations in Lebanon outnumbered all other non-governmental welfare agencies recorded in the Ministry of Interior and Ministry of Social Affairs combined. See, also, Khalaf, "Family Associations."

65. Prothro's study, *Child Rearing in the Lebanon,* of rural and urban child rearing among Lebanese of different religious sects reveals that about one-half of the mothers reported that their children got along well with each other, whereas one-fourth reported open hostility among siblings (94). Prothro does not specify gender in his report.

66. Fallers and Fallers, "Sex Roles," similarly observe that marriage in Edremit, Turkey, breaks the highly charged brother/sister bond. The affection between brothers and sisters is so charged that the Fallers comment, "It is little wonder that marriage partners must be chosen by others and that they take so long 'to get to know each other' " (258).

67. This, like many of the patterns described here, was also characteristic of non-Arabs in the neighborhood. In one Armenian Catholic family an unmarried adult thirty-five-year-old woman lived with her married forty-three-year-old brother and his family. She stayed at home, helping with their seventy-eight-year-old mother and his four children.

68. El-Shamy, *Arab Family,* 319, claims that there are incestuous tendencies underlying the Arab brother/sister relationship. I cannot confirm such a tendency from my research. The distinction between gender and sexuality and the cultural specificity of these constructs warrants mention. If sexuality signals notions of the erotic and gender signals notions of masculinity and femininity and both are culturally constructed, as I believe they are, then evaluations of what constitutes a sexually charged relationship would have to be culturally specific. I believe it is important to raise this issue. Treating the subject of incest in the detail that it requires, however, necessitates more research than is available and more space than I have here.

69. For analysis of brother/sister marriages in the ancient Middle East, see Hopkins, "Brother-Sister Marriage" "Brother/Sister"; Middleton, and Slotkin, "Incest Regulations."

70. An Armenian resident of this street also reported that her mother had been adopted and raised by her father's family. She did not consider her parents to be "real" siblings although she acknowledged that they had a special relationship.

71. I am indebted to Richard Antoun for this insight.

72. Gender socialization was affected by sibling birth order and changed through stages of the siblings' lives. Older boys and girls often took care of younger siblings and became second parents. It was more common for girls to take on mothering roles than for boys to take on fathering roles. As boys came into puberty, however, they usually took power over sisters, regardless of age ranking or experience of having been parented by sisters.

73. Judith Williams observes in the Sunni Lebanese village of Haouch El Harimi that households with sons were more disciplined than houses that were predominately female. In the absence of fathers, brothers became an effective authority (39).

74. For a discussion of Abu Mufid as an entrepreneur, see Joseph, "Working the Law."

75. I am indebted to Joseph Massoud for this insight.

76. Prothro and Diab *Changing Family Patterns,* 65 survey of Sunni family patterns in Lebanon, Syria, and Jordan revealed that although the trend away from endogamy was strongest in Beirut and Tripoli, the preference for marriage among relatives was still very much in evidence throughout the region. Williams, *Youth of Haouch El Harimi,* 100, found a surprising two-thirds of the youth interviewed in the Lebanese Sunni village of Haouch El Harimi preferred cousin marriage. It was the preferred marriage form in the Sunni village of Buarij (Fuller, *Buarij,* 65). Alamuddin and Starr, *Crucial Bonds,* 75, report about one-third of Druze marriages recorded in the Beirut courts from 1931 to 1974 were clan endogamous, whereas Khuri, "Parallel Cousin Marriage Reconsidered," 598, found 27 percent of the marriages among Muslims in two Beirut suburbs, Chiah and Ghobeiri, to be endogamous, and among these the FaBrSo/Da marriage accounted for 38 percent.

77. In Lebanon inheritance was governed by religious courts. A fuller discussion of the impact of inheritance on brother/sister relationships, which is beyond the scope of this chapter, would need to account for the constraints imposed by these courts.

78. Granqvist, *Marriage Conditions,* 2:256, reports that Palestinian fellahin women were explicitly asserted that they kept their inheritances with their fathers and brothers so that they would have rights to return to their natal households should they need to do so.

79. Although this issue needs to be the subject of a separate discussion, it is worth noting here that women often felt that their security lay with their brothers until they, themselves, had sons and their sons became mature adults. Some women then refocused their energies and demands for support on their sons.

80. Altorki, *Women in Saudi Arabia,* 158, indicates that elite women of Jiddah are increasingly claiming their inheritances over the objection of male relatives.

81. Similar arguments are made by Antoun, "Modesty" 691; Henry Rosenfeld, "On Determinants of the Status of Arab Village Women," *Man* 60 (1960): 67; John Gulick, *Social Structure and Cultural Change in a Lebanese Village* (New York: Viking Fund Publications in Anthropology, 1955), 119.

82. Incidents of brothers or fathers killing their sisters or daughters in crimes of honor are reported in much of the literature: Rugh, *Family in Contemporary Egypt,* 85; Antoun, "Modesty," 694; and El-Shamy, *Brother and Sister Type 872,* 81.

83. *Batal* (*abtal,* pl.) means "brave man, hero, champion." It is used to refer to folk heroes and assertively domineering men. Locally, it was one of the strongest compliments one could pay to a man.

84. Granqvist, *Marriage Conditions,* 2:252, contends that Palestinian men who used their sisters to exchange for wives had even more responsibility for those sisters than they might otherwise have had. Rugh *Family in Contemporary Egypt,* 116, contends that some of the advantages of close kin marriage, in the absence of appropriate close kin, can be achieved by sibling marriages between unrelated families, that is, unrelated men exchanging their sisters as wives.

85. See Suad Joseph, "Zaynab. An Urban Working-class Lebanese Woman," in *Middle Eastern Muslim Women Speak,* ed. Elizabeth Warnock Fernea and Basima Qattan Bezirgan

(Austin: Univ. of Texas Press, 1977), 359–71, for a discussion of Zaynab and her friendship with Amira.

86. Although most of the Armenians later indicated to me that they supported the actions of the brothers, many remained indoors.

87. Granqvist, *Marriage Conditions*, 2:252–56.

88. An interesting parallel in the ancient Middle East is found in Herodotus, *The Histories*, trans. by Aubrey De Selincourt, rev. A. R. Burn (New York: Penguin Books, 1972), 250. He reports a story that is supposed to have occurred in about 520 B.C. during the rise to power of Darius, king of Persia. According to the story, Intaphrenes, one of six Persians who supported King Darius in an uprising against Magus, was disrespectful to Darius. Fearing a conspiracy, Darius had Intaphrenes and all his near relations arrested. Intaphrenes's wife pleaded with the king to save her family. Eventually moved by the woman's pleas, King Darius offered her the choice to save the life of only one member of her family. Her decision to save her brother surprised him, and he asked her for an explanation. She replied that she could find another husband and have another son, but she could never have another brother. Impressed with her reasoning, Darius gave her her brother and her eldest son.

I am indebted to Lyn Roller for pointing this story out to me and to Nicholas S. Hopkins for pointing out a parallel story in Sophocles's Theban Play, *Antigone*. Similar stories are also found in other Mediterranean cultures.

89. "*Ij-joz mawjud, il-walad mawlud il-ah il-'aziz min wen yi'ud?*" (Granqvist, *Marriage, Conditions*, 2:253).

90. Ibid., 254.

91. A similar reading can be taken from a story about the noted early Egyptian feminist Huda Sha'rawi's relationship with her brother. Ahmed, *Between Two Worlds*, 162, explains that Sha'rawi, although loving her brother, was dismayed that he was preferred to her. Her father's widow explained that she was a girl, and not the only girl, and her brother was a boy and the only boy. It would be his responsibility to perpetuate the name of the father. Ahmed reports that Sha'rawi was temporarily assuaged by this and loved her brother the more for it.

6. Wives or Daughters

1. See Fatima Mernissi, *Beyond the Veil: Male-Female Dynamics in Modern Muslim Society* (Bloomington: Indiana Univ. Press, 1985). pt. 1, chap. 3. See also, Lamya' al-Faruqi, *Women, Muslim Society and Islam*. (Indianapolis: American Trust Publishing, 1988), 2–3.

2. Aziza Hussein, "Recent Amendments to Egypt's Personal Status Law," in *Women and the Family in the Middle East: New Voices of Change*, ed. Elizabeth Warnock Fernea (Austin: Univ. of Texas Press, 1985), 231–32, argues that the fact that polygyny is permitted is an outrage and degradation to women, even when they are not actually subjected to it.

3. In recent (1992) survey J. Chamie found the percentage of polygynous marriages among Moslem Arab men to vary between a minimum of 1.9 percent in 1976 in Syria and a maximum of 12 percent among Kuwaiti nationals in 1965. Researchers in Lebanon in the sixties found 2 percent polygynous. Halim Barakat, Al-Mujtama'a al-Arabi al-mu'asir (Contemporary Arab society) (Beirut: Markaz Dirasat al-Wihda al-Arabiah, 1984), 210.

4. See, for example, Elizabeth Warnock Fernia, ed., *Women and the Family in the Middle East;* Abu Lughod, *Veiled Sentiments;* Barakat, *Al-Mujtama'a al-Arabi al-mu'asir;* and even ancient sources, for example, Shams al-Din Muhamad Abdul-Rahman al-Sakhawi, *Al*

Daw' al-lami' fi A'yan al-oarn al-tasi' (The bright light of the notables of the ninth century) (Cairo: Maktabat al-Qudsi, 1947), vol. 12, esp. case 388.

5. *Asha'ir* denotes collectively the descendants of known Arab tribes. The term carries a positive significance among the people of the Bekaa' and some other rural groups, where it imples observing certain moral standards such as generosity, helping the needy, and loyalty. In most cities of Lebanon, asha'ir has a negative significance, refering to those who usually take the law into their own hands. For example, they are known to avenge the killing of one of their kin by killing someone of the killer's kin. Ther are usually considered "backward" by urban, "modernized" groups.

Ashirah is a group of people who share a common lineage that is supposed to be traceable to a known Arab tribe, and ashirahs is the term I use to refer to more than one ashirah.

Ashirah and ashirahs are comparatively more neutral terms than asha'vir where emotive significance is concerned. The former terms do not necessarily imply a way of life that preserves tribal traditions. This is why a "modern" person may take pride in being a son or daughter of an ashirah, but may not appreciate being considered a member of the asha'ir.

6. "The Bedouins are among the proudest of races, believing the pure Arab strain is superior to any other." Nevins and Wright, *World without Time: The Bedouin* (New York: John Day, 1969), 218.

7. This anti-Marxist statement is based on my observation that the Asha'ir's values and aspirations remain drawn to the nomadic past with which they identify, even after being separated from it by the passage of centuries and by different economic conditions. The amazing observation in this context is that people who are affluent, or even rich, tend to copy the lifestyle of their poorer ancestors. Asha'ir who own mansions often have tents outdoors that they prefer to use as sitting rooms or for entertaining guests during weddings and other social occasions. Until the 1920s or 1930s, even the most prestigious families of the Asha'ir gave their children to the nomadic Bedouins for the first four or five years of life, thinking that this would give the youngsters better health and a greater proficiency and eloquence in the Arabic language.

8. Samar al-Zahr, a doctoral candidate in sociology at the Lebanese University, helped interview subjects of this study during one long weekend.

9. The Kora'nic verses that deal with polygyny are the following (my translation from Arabic): "Marry as many women as you wish, two or three or four. If you fear not to be fair in your treatment of them, marry only one" (Kora'n 4:2). Further, "Indeed you will not be fair in the treatment of your wives, even if you try" (Kora'n 4:128).

10. Eighty-one percent of first wives who are friendly to their co-wives believe the reason their respective husbands took more wives was other than love. Only 18 percent of first wives who are friendly to their co-wives believe that the subsequent marriage is the result of love.

11. *Muqayada* is an exchange of brides between two families. Two men give each other their respective sisters in marriage. Sometimes, as in the case of Amira, the father gives his daughter to a young man in exchange for the young man's sister. According to the traditions of muqayada, if one husband involved in the exchange repudiates his wife, the other husband will repudiate his. If one takes another wife or takes his wife for a vacation or buys her a dress, the other is expected to do likewise!

12. A current practice in Lebanese and other Arab cities, *bayt -al-ta'ah* (the house of obedience), enables a husband to bring home, by means of the legal authorities, an unwilling wife. Neither Bedouins nor early Moslems practiced, or practice, this custom. See Hasan

al-Turabi, *Al-Mar'a baina ta'aleem al-deen wa takaleed al-mujtama'* (Woman: Between religious teachings and social traditions), (Jeddah, Saudi Arabia: Al-Dar al-Saoudiah, 1984), 43; See, also, Shams al-Din Muhamad Abdul-Rahman al-Sakhawi, *Al-Daw' al-lami' fi a'yan al-qarn al-tasi'*.

13. Later, they were negotiating to give the young man some sheep in order to be released of their promise to give him the girl in marriage. He refused. The marriage was celebrated, but after several weeks was still not consummated (one of God's blessings according to Um Hussein), and the girl was returned to her family, which compelled the husband of Amira, her counterpart in muqayada, to do the same.

14. Nancy Chodorow, "Family Structure and Feminine Personality," in *Women, Culture, and Society,* ed. Michelle Zimbalist Rosaldo and Louise Lamphere. (Stanford, Calif.: Stanford Univ. Press, 1974), 64.

15. Abu-Lughod, *Veiled Sentiments.*

16. Ibid., 119, 148.

17. Ibid., 216–24.

18. In Lebanon there are currently only three women who have been elected members of parliament: one, whose husband was the assassinated late president of the Republic; another, who gained this office after the assassination of a politician brother; and the third, the sister of the previous prime minister, who is clearly his obedient ally. There is only one female director (general secretary) in the cabinet, in public affairs; she attained this position two decades after deserving it. During all that time she had to tolerate the frustration of continually being bypassed in favor of men of inferior seniority and experience.

19. In this connection I recall my late professor of physics, Salwa Nassar, who achieved international recognition as a nuclear physicist. Probably because of social conditioning, she always told us that her success was nothing compared to a baby in her arms, advising us, her female students, not to miss our chances to marry at an early age!

20. Abu-Lughod, *Veiled Sentiments,* 152–66.

21. Urban Muslim women in earlier times acted differently. In vol. 12 of *Al-Daw' al-lami' fi a'yan al-oarn al-tasi',* Abdul-Rahman al-Sakhawi tells of the lives of some thousand notable urban women of the fifteenth century. The story of the lives of these women, most of whom married several times, includes less than fifty who were in polygynous marriages. In these few cases, whenever the husband took a second wife, the first one either insisted on divorce or became so angry that the husband had to repudiate the second wife. The very few wives who accepted living in the polygynous situation were said to have gone crazy shortly afterward. This is an indication that the reactions observed in modern urban Lebanese co-wives in this study are similar to those of urban Arab women in the fifteenth century.

22. See Abu-Lughod, *Veiled Sentiments.*

23. See Gergen, "Social Understanding," 572.

24. See Barakat, *Al-Mujtama' al-Arabi al-Mu'asir.* 73.

25. See Simone de Beauvoir, *Le Deuxieme Sexe,* (France: Gallimard, 1949), 2:530–32.

26. The difference in attunement to and creative involvement with art and beauty between urban and Bedouin co-wives is similar to the difference that Roland, *In Search of Self,* observed between Americans, on the one hand, and the people of India and Japan, on the other. The values and modes of nurturing in Lebanese cities are, to a certain extent, more like those of the West, and Bedouin ways, which emphasize family and tradition and long, security-giving nurturing of children by an extended family, are more akin to the ways of the traditional Far East.

27. For a detailed account of poetry permeating the lives of Bedouins, see Abu-Lughod, *Veiled Sentiments.*

28. Sharabi, *Neopatriarchy,* 30–32.

29. Prothro and Diab, *Changing Family Patterns,* 6–7.

30. See Gergen, "Social Understanding," 285–87.

31. Ahmed, "Between Two Worlds," 168.

32. See, for example, Aziza al-Hibri, *Critique of Personal Status Codes in Selected Arab Countries,* Studies on Arab Women and Development, no. 25 (New York: United Nations, 1997, [E/ESCWA/SD-WOM/1997/2]); and Najla Hamadeh, "Islamic Family Legislation: The Authoritarian Discourse of Silence," in *Feminism and Islam,* ed. May Yamani (Lebanon: Ithaca Press, 1996).

33. In a conference, "Women's Court," in the Beirut Carlton Hotel, Mar. 15–17, 1998, Khadijah al-Haysami, from Yemen, said that women in her country realize that the sheikhs of the tribes protect them and give them rights beyond what is acknowledged by religious and civil laws.

34. One example indicative of the inefficiency and 'immobility' of the Lebanese situation is the controversy over the president of the Republic's 1998 proposal to institute an optional civil family law. After being approved by the cabinet, the proposal became the subject of a nationwide debate, which was prevented from being open and "democratic" by all the religious leaders, who joined forces to vehemently condemn it. They threatened to "excommunicate" people who marry under this proposed law and claimed that it is they, the religious leaders, and not the political leadership who have sovereignty over the country!

35. Louise E. Sweet depicts a more unified and more powerful process of social evolution between Bedouin and urban than my findings indicate. Indeed, she notices that things change in Syria: "Political unification of the area, under local or foreign control, has alternated with periods of areal disunity and local autonomy" (3). She adds that during the latter periods shepherd tribes lived independently. In Lebanon each sect has a measure of control over its members, which discourages social cohesion and preempts any kind of integrated or controlled social evolution. Louise E. Sweet, "Tell Toqaan: A Syrian Village" (Ph.D. diss., Univ. of Michigan, 1957).

36. This type of "capitalistic" self-construct is encouraged because it is considered to be conducive to enhancing economic productivity (as in Adam Smith's theory of the invisible hand in *The Wealth of Nations*). But this advantage comes with disadvantages for the community and for the individual, as is shown in the present work.

7. My Son/Myself, My Mother/Myself.

1. It is the custom in most Arab cultures to address a man or woman as the mother (um) or father (abu) of their eldest son. For example, Um George's oldest son was George. Although educated urban classes often no longer use this term of address, it is widely practiced in villages and in urban working classes.

2. My research in this village began in 1994 under an American Council of Learned Societies/Social Science Research Council grant. The five months in 1994 and two months each in 1995, 1996, and 1997 were part of a long-term project on children, selfhood, gender, and citizenship in postwar Lebanon. Yusfiyyi is my natal village, and some of the villagers are my relatives. Most villagers I came to know well, however, only after I began research in 1994.

3. Sitt Salma, like a number of women (and men), for various reasons was not addressed as the mother (father) of her eldest son. Sitt Salma married at a late age; possibly, the terms by which others addressed her had already become habituated. Some women and men were addressed in terms of roles or titles. For example, the wife of a long-term president of the municipality was called *sheikha* and he *sheikh,* honorific terms that some families claim genealogically and pass on to their children. The priest was simply addressed as *abuna* (father) or *el-khuri* (the priest) and his wife, *khuriyyi* or *el-khuriyyi'* (the priestess).

4. Most of the events and routines discussed here pertain to the research carried out in 1994, 1995, and 1996.

5. Barakat, *Arab World,* 199.

6. Sharabi and Ali, "Class and Culture," 240–256.

7. Rugh, *Family.*

8. Ibid., 82.

9. Joseph, "Connectivity and Patriarchy," 452–84.

10. Suad Joseph, "Women Between Nation and State in Lebanon," in *Between Women and Nation: Feminism and Global Issues,* ed. Norma Alarcon, Caren Caplan, and Minoo Moallem (Durham, N.C.: Duke Univ. Press, in press).

11. Murphy and Kasdan, "Parallel Cousin Marriage," 17–29.

12. Khuri, "Parallel Cousin Marriage Reconsidered," 597–618.

13. Joseph, "Connectivity and Patriarchy."

8. Microdynamics of Patriarchal Change in Egypt and the Development of an Alternative Discourse on Mother-Daughter Relations

1. Heidi Hartmann, "The Unhappy Marriage of Marxism and Feminism: Towards a More Progressive Union," *Women and Revolution,* ed. Lydia Sargent (Boston: South End Press, 1981), 1–42.

2. Gayle Rubin suggests that the original male traffic in women (their exchange among families through marriage) recognized the importance of women as contributors to the development of kinship relations among unrelated male groupings. See Gayle Rubin, "The Traffic in Women: Notes on the 'Political Economy of Sex,' " *Towards an Anthropology of Women,* ed. Rayna Reiter (New York: Monthly Review Press, 1975), 157–210.

3. Dorothy Dinnerstein, *The Mermaid and the Minotaur* (New York: Harper and Row, 1976); Chodorow, *Reproduction of Mothering;* Rubin, "Traffic in Women."

4. Abdel Rahman al-Rafi'i Bek, *'Asr Mohammed Ali* (Cairo: Maktabat al-Nahda al-Misriya, 1951), 523; Mohammed Kamal Yahyia, *Al-Juzur al-tarikhiya litahrir al-mara'at al-misriya* (Cairo: Al-Haya'at al-Misriya al-'Amma lil Kitab, 1983), 68; Margot Badran and Miriam Cooke, "Introduction," in *Opening the Gates: A Century of Arab Feminist Writing,* ed. Margot Badran and Miriam Cooke (Bloomington: Indiana Univ. Press, 1990), xxx.

5. Mayy Ziada, "Katiba tuqadim sha'irah," in *Hilyat al-tiraz: Diwan 'A'isha al-Tayymuriya* (Cairo: dar al-katib al-'Arabi, 1952), 56; Durriya Shafiq, *Al-mar'at al-misriya* (Cairo: Matba'at Misr, 1955), 89; Ahmed, *Women and Gender,* 135.

6. Ibid.

7. Barakat, "Arab Family," 32–33; Sharabi, *Neopatriarchy.*

8. Cynthia Nelson, "Public and Private Politics: Women in the Middle Eastern

World," in *Arab Society in Transition,* ed. Saad Eddin Ibrahim and Nicolas Hopkins (Cairo: American Univ. in Cairo, 1977), 131–47.

9. Judith Tucker, *Women in Nineteenth Century Egypt* (Cambridge, Eng.: Cambridge Univ. Press, 1985), chap. 1.

10. Afaf Lutfi al-Sayyid Marsot, *Egypt in the Reign of Muhammad ʿAli* (Cambridge, Eng.: Cambridge Univ. Press, 1984), 24.

11. Jonathan P. Berkey, "Women and Islamic Education in the Mamluk Period," in *Women in Middle Eastern History,* ed. Nikki Keddie and Beth Baron (New Haven, Conn.: Yale Univ. Press, 1991), 145–46.

12. Ahmad Kamal Zadah, "Jidati: ʿArd wa tahlil" in *Hilyat al-tiraz: Diwan ʿAʾisha al-Tayymuriya* (Cairo: Matbaʿat dar al-Kitab al-ʿArabi, 1952), 16.

13. Ziada, "Katiba tukadim shaʿirah," 56.

14. ʿAʾisha Taymur, *Nataʾj al-ʾahwal fi al-ʾaqwal wa al-ʾafʿal* (Cairo: Matbaʿat Muhamad Effendi Mustafa, 1887), 2–3. The translations of this passage and others from Arabic are mine.

15. For an interesting discussion of how Scheherazade represented a particular definition of narration and desire, see Fadwa Malti-Douglas, *Woman's Body. Woman's Word: Gender and Discourse Arabo-Islamic Writing* (Princeton, N.J.: Princeton Univ. Press, 1991), chap. 1.

16. Ibid.

17. ʿAʾisha Taymur, "Muqadimat al-diwan al-Farisi wa al-Turki," in *Hilyat al-tiraz: Diwan ʿAʾisha al-Taymuriya,* (Cairo: Matbaʿat dar al-Katib al-ʿArabi, 1952), 61.

18. Mayy Al-ʾAnisa, *Shaʿirat al-taliʿa: ʿAʾisha Taymur* (Cairo: Dar al-Hilal, 1956), 87.

19. Afaf Lutfi al-Sayyid Marsot, "The Revolutionary Gentlewomen in Egypt," in *Women in the Muslim World,* ed. Lois Beck and Nikki Keddie (Cambridge, Mass.: Harvard Univ. Press, 1978), 265–67.

20. Taymur, "Muqadimat," 68.

21. Ibid., 69.

22. Ziada, "Katiba tukadim shaʾirah," 71.

23. Ibid., 78.

24. Hatem, "Psychodynamics," 300.

25. Ibid.

26. Malak Zaalouk, *Draft of Community Schools. Alternative Approaches for Basic Education* (Cairo: UNICEF, 1995); idem, *Field Mission Report to Oena and Sohag with CIDA Canada* (Cairo: UNICEF, 1995).

27. UNICEF, *The Children of the Nile* (Paris: UNESCO, n.d), 13, 18.

9. Patriarchy and Imperialism

1. Barakat, *Arab World,* chap. 6 and 10.

2. The three volumes of Najib Mahfuz's Cairo trilogy are *Palace Walk,* trans. William M. Hutchins and Olive E. Kenny (New York: Anchor Doubleday, 1990); *Palace of Desire,* trans. William M. Hutchins, Lorne M. Kenny, and Olive E. Kenny (New York: Anchor Doubleday, 1991); and *Sugar Street,* trans. William M. Hutchins and Angele Botros Samaan (New York: Anchor Doubleday 1992).

3. For an analysis of Arab society as a whole as "neopatriarchal," that is, a patriarchal

system that, despite certain elements of modernization retains its essential qualities, see Sharabi, *Neopatriarchy.*

4. Kandiyoti, "Islam and Patriarchy," 23–42.

5. Joseph, "Connectivity and Patriarchy," 452–84.

6. Sharabi, *Neopatriarchy,* 18.

7. Deniz Kandiyoti, "The Paradoxes of Masculinity: Some Thoughts on Segregated Societies," in *Dislocating Masculinity: Comparative Ethnographies,* ed. A. Cornwall and N. Lindisfarne (London: Routledge, 1994), 197–213.

8. Abdelwahab Bouhdiba, *Sexuality in Islam* (London: Routledge and Kegan Paul, 1985).

9. Joseph, "Connectivity and Patriarchy."

10. Kandiyoti, *Paradoxes,* 2–3.

11. Joseph, "Connectivity and Patriarchy," 10–11. By contrast, "hot connectivity" refers to a relationship between a patriarch and household members in which he communicates with them. His character, accordingly, is significantly influenced by his interactions with them.

12. Ibid., 30 n. 7.

13. Jamal Ghaytani, *Najib Mahfuz yatadhakkar* (Najib Mahfuz remembers) (Cairo: Mu'asassat Akhbar al-Yawm, 1987).

14. Fatima al-Zahra' Muhammad Sa'id, *Al-Ramziya fi adab Najib Mahfuz* (Symbolism in the work of Najib Mahfuz) (Beirut: Al-Mu'asassa al-'Arabiyya li al-Dirasat wa al-Nashr, 1981), 110.

15. Afaf Lutfi al-Sayyid Marsot, *A Short History of Egypt* (New York: Cambridge Univ. Press, 1985), 75–77.

16. Although this date refers to the original meeting by the Wafdist leaders with Wingate in 1918, it did not become a holiday until after Zaghlul's death in 1927.

10. Constructions of Masculinity in Two Egyptian Novels

1. Edward W. Said, *The World, the Text, and the Critic* (Cambridge, Mass.: Harvard Univ. Press, 1983), 5, for example, affirms "the connection between texts and the existential actualities of human life, politics, societies, and events."

2. Hayden White, *The Content of the Form* (Baltimore, Md.: Johns Hopkins Univ. Press, 1987); Samia Mehrez, *Egyptian Writers Between History and Fiction: Essays on Naguib Mahfouz, Sonallah Ibrahim, and Gamal al-Ghitani* (Cairo: American Univ. in Cairo Press, 1994), 1–16, gives a nice synopsis of the intersections between fiction and history in Egyptian writing.

3. John Paul Eakin, *Fictions in Autobiography: Studies in the Art of Self-Invention* (Princeton, N.J.: Princeton Univ. Press, 1985); and idem, *Touching the World: Reference in Autobiography* (Princeton, N.J.: Princeton Univ. Press, 1992); James Olney, ed., *Autobiography: Essays Theoretical and Critical* (Princeton, N.J.: Princeton Univ. Press, 1980); and idem, ed., *Studies in Autobiography* (New York: Oxford Univ. Press, 1988).

4. Terry Eagleton, *Literary Theory: An Introduction* (Minneapolis: Univ. of Minnesota Press, 1983).

5. Teresa De Lauretis, *Technologies of Gender* (Bloomington: Indiana Univ. Press, 1987), 3.

6. Nina Auerbach, "Engorging the Patriarchy," in *Feminist Issues in Literary Scholarship*, ed. Shari Benstock (Bloomington: Indiana Univ. Press, 1987), 150.

7. Eakin, *Touching the World*, 135.

8. In spite of the above assertions, I caution readers against a tendency to generalize when confronting a "foreign" fictional text, a tendency that transforms characters into collective entities and replaces an Arab male with "the Arab male." Sidonie Smith and Julia Watson, ed., *De/Colonizing the Subject: The Politics of Gender in Women's Autobiography* (Minneapolis: Univ. of Minnesota Press, 1992) xvii, talk about the tendency to see the colonized as "an amorphous, generalized collectivity . . . an anonymous, opaque collectivity of undifferentiated bodies."

9. Ahmed, "Between Two Worlds," 159.

10. In Taha Husayn's, *Al-Ayyam* (The days) (Cairo: n.p., 1929), for example, which is perhaps the most well-known Arabic autobiography of this century, Husayn's mother and sisters might just as well have been nonexistent. More recently, however, there have been notable exceptions. The Moroccan Muhammad Shukri's autobiography, and he does not hesitate to call it one, *Al-Khubz al-hafi* (London: Dar al-Saqi, 1982), which has been translated by Paul Bowles under the title *For Bread Alone* (San Francisco, Calif.: City Lights Books, 1987), is uncompromising in its depiction of the horrors of growing up in a truly dysfunctional family. The Palestinian Fadwa Tuqan harshly criticizes her family in her autobiography *Rihla jabaliyya: Rihly sa'ba* (Mountainous journey: Difficult journey) (Beirut: Dar al-Shuruq, 1985), which has been translated into English by Olive Kenney under the title *A Mountainous Journey* (London: Women's Press, 1990), besides, of course, the memoirs of Huda Sha'rawi, which Leila Ahmed discusses in "Between Two Worlds."

11. Nancy K. Miller, *Getting Personal: Feminist Occasions and Other Autobiographical Acts* (New York: Routledge, 1991), 147.

12. Maxine Hong Kingston, *The Woman Warrior: Memoirs of a Girlhood among Ghosts* (New York: Random House, 1976), begins her memoirs: " 'You must not tell anyone,' my mother said, 'what I am about to tell you.' " In her memoirs Mary McCarthy expresses a reluctance to write about certain family experiences while her grandmother is alive, for she is afraid of "touching a sensitive nerve.

13. Eakin, *Touching the World*, 132.

14. For a criticism of the public/private demarcations even for the West, see Nancy F. Cott, "On Men's History and Women's History," in *Meanings for Manhood: Constructions of Masculinity in Victorian America,* ed. Mark C. Carnes and Clyde Griffin (Chicago: Univ. of Chicago Press, 1990), 205–11.

15. Chodorow, *Reproduction of Mothering*.

16. These theories also need modification when applied to other non-Western societies. See, for example, Sarane Spence Boocock, "The Social Construction of Childhood in Contemporary Japan," in *Constructions of the Self,* ed. George Levine (New Brunswick, N.J.: Rutgers Univ. Press, 1992), 165–88. Chodorow also has her critics in the West, for she "seems largely relevant to the white, Western, middle-class experience." Josephine Donovan, "Toward a Women's Poetics," in *Feminist Issues in Literary Scholarship,* ed. Shari Benstock (Bloomington: Indiana Univ. Press, 1987), 104. See, also, Jonathan Rutherford, *Men's Silences: Predicaments in Masculinity* (London: Routledge, 1992), 32–40; and Joseph H. Pleck, *The Myth of Masculinity* (Cambridge, Mass.: MIT Press, 1982), 108–10.

17. Leila Ahmed discusses the large household and "consequently relationally rich environment in which Sha'rawi was nurtured" although one that is more typical of the "wealthy

upper classes" (Ahmed, "Between Two Worlds," 160). Hisham Sharabi (*Neopatriarchy*, 31–32), in commenting on the proliferation of extended families in the Arab world, compares the two types of families and concludes that the nuclear family is democratic, promotes equality, and is a necessary, although not sufficient, condition for the liberation of women. Although I do not hasten to assert the opposite, Sharabi's view underrates the many advantageous aspects of life in an extended family and ignores the many disadvantages, for women, of living in a nuclear family, a fact of which some Western women are keenly aware.

18. The same remarks have been made about the sense of self that is presented in autobiographies of male minorities in the United States, such as African- and Native Americans. See, for example, Arnold Krupat, "Native American Autobiography and the Synecdochic Self," in *American Autobiography: Retrospect and Prospect*, ed. John Paul Eakin (Madison: Univ. of Wisconsin Press, 1991), 171–193; and William L. Andrews, "African-American Autobiography Criticism: Retrospect and Prospect," in *American Autobiography: Retrospect and Prospect*, ed. John Paul Eakin (Madison: Univ. of Wisconsin Press, 1991), 195–215. Mervat Hatem applied Chodorow's theories to the Egyptian context and concluded that "despite the existence of some important differences between the Egyptian and American/Western cultures . . . the Egyptian male personality, like its American counterpart, is based on the repudiation of the female aspects of personality, for example, nurturance and the importance of being connected to others. It also enjoys relatively more autonomy as well as firmer boundaries" (Hatem, "Toward the Study of the Psychodynamics," 301). Hatem observes, however, that whereas autonomy and fixed boundaries are by and large positive attributes and acquisitions in the West, in the Egyptian context individuality and strict spatial boundaries are still regarded as suspect. Suad Joseph, "Gender and Relationality," 15, 465–486, critiques the feminization of relationality in Western theory and talks about the importance of "developing the notion of patriarchal connectivity to account for masculine and feminine relationality that is not feminized but is gender and age-marked."

19. One could presumably argue that the first wife's condition, and that of her children, is still better than that of abandoned single mothers in the West, but that does not really make her pain any more acceptable. In both scenarios there are no large numbers of men who have to endure the same fate.

20. On the subject of homosocial, as distinct from homosexual, desire see Eve Kosofsky Sedgwick, *Between Men: English Literature and Male Homosocial Desire* (New York: Columbia Univ. Press, 1985); and Malti-Douglas, "Woman's Body."

21. These women come from the urban lower classes where codes for proper behavior are less rigid than they are for the middle class described in *Ahzan madina* (A city's sorrows).

22. Mothers in many cultures and eras have "provided a mediating role within the family, their conflict management often protecting their son from his father" (Rutherford, *Men's Silences*, 20).

23. Gilligan, *Different Voice*.

24. For a comparable indoctrination into femininity in the American South, see Harper Lee, *To Kill a Mockingbird* (New York: Warner Books, 1960), in which at a similar stage of growth the aunt wants the narrator, Scout, to dress and behave in "feminine" ways and to stop playing outside with her brother Jem and his male friends.

25. Muir and Ruggiero, eds., *Sex and Gender in Historical Perspective*, trans. Margaret A. Gallucci with Mary M. Gallucci and Carole C. Gallucci (Baltimore: Johns Hopkins Univ. Press, 1990).

26. Rutherford, *Men's Silences*, 40–48.

27. Much has been written about women's madness as a result of the misogynist struc-tures of patriarchy. See, for example, Shoshana Felman, "Women and Madness: The Critical Phallacy," in *Feminisms: An Anthology of Literary Theory and Criticism*, ed. Robyn R. Warhol and Diane Price Herndl (New Brunswick, N.J.: Rutgers Univ. Press, 1991), 6–19: and Linda Kauffman, "Devious Channels of Decorous Ordering: Rosa Coldfield in 'Absa-lom, Absalom,' " in *Feminisms: An Anthology of Literary Theory and Criticism*, ed. Robyn R. Warhol and Diane Price Herndl (New Brunswick, N.J.: Rutgers Univ. Press, 1991), 644–70.

28. His sorrow is intensified because his individuation parallels the replacement of com-munal values with the values of individualism in his neighborhood, a development that fills him with dismay. I have not discussed this important aspect of *Ahzan madina* (A city's Sor-rows) here owing to limitations of space and scope.

References

Abel, Elizabeth. "Race, Class, and Psychoanalysis? Opening Questions." In *Conflicts in Feminism,* edited by Marianne Hirsch and Evelyn Fox Keller, 184–204. New York: Routledge, 1990.

Abou-Zeid, Ahmed. "Honour and Shame among the Bedouins of Egypt." In *Honour and Shame,* edited by J. G. Peristiany, 243–60. Chicago: Univ. of Chicago Press, 1966.

Abu-Lughod, Lila. *Veiled Sentiments: Honor and Poetry in a Bedouin Society.* Berkeley and Los Angeles: Univ. of California Press, 1986.

Ahmed, Leila. "Between Two Worlds: The Formation of a Turn-of-the-Century Egyptian Feminist." In *Life/Lines: Theorizing Women's Autobiography,* edited by Bella Brodzki and Celeste Schenck, 154–74. Ithaca, N.Y.: Cornell Univ. Press, 1989.

———. *Women and Gender in Islam.* New Haven, Conn.: Yale Univ. Press, 1992.

Alamuddin, Nura S., and Paul D. Starr. *Crucial Bonds: Marriage among the Lebanese Druze.* Delmar, N.Y.: Caravan Books, 1980.

Al-'Anisa, Mayy. *Sha'irat al-tali'a: 'A'isha Taymur.* Cairo: Dar al-Hilal, 1956.

Alford, Fred. *The Self in Social Theory: A Psychoanalytic Account of its Construction in Plato, Hobbes, Locke, Rawls, and Rousseau.* New Haven, Conn.: Yale Univ. Press, 1991.

Altorki, Soraya. *Women in Saudi Arabia: Ideology and Behavior among the Elite.* New York: Columbia Univ. Press, 1986.

Ammar, Hammid. *Growing up in an Egyptian Village.* London: Routledge and Kegan Paul, 1954.

Andrews, William L. "African-American Autobiography Criticism: Retrospect and Prospect." In *American Autobiography: Retrospect and Prospect,* edited by John Paul Eakin, 195–215. Madison: Univ. of Wisconsin Press, 1991.

Antoun, Richard T. "On the Modesty of Women in Arab Muslim Villages: A Study in the Accommodation of Traditions." *American Anthropologist* 70 (1968): 671–97.

Anzaldua, Gloria. *Borderlands/La Frontera.* San Francisco, Calif.: Spinsters/Aunt Lute Press, 1987.

Auerbach, Nina. "Engorging the Patriarchy." In *Feminist Issues in Literary Scholarship,* edited by Shari Benstock, 150–60. Bloomington: Indiana Univ. Press, 1987.

Badran, Margot, and Miriam Cooke. "Introduction." In *Opening the Gates: A Century of Arab Feminist Writing,* edited by Margot Badran and Miriam Cooke. Bloomington: Indiana Univ. Press, 1990.

Barakat, Halim. *Al-Mujtama'a al-Arabi al-mu'asir* (Contemporary Arab society). Beirut: Markaz Dirasat al-Wihda al-Arabiah, 1984.

———. "The Arab Family and the Challenge of Social Transformation." In *Women and the Family in the Middle East,* edited by Elizabeth Warnock Fernea, 27–48. Austin: Univ. of Texas Press, 1985.

———. *The Arab World: Society, Culture and State.* Berkeley and Los Angeles: Univ. of California Press, 1993.

———. *Lebanon in Strife: Student Preludes to the Civil War.* Austin: Univ. of Texas Press, 1977.

Baron, Beth. "The Making and Breaking of Marital Bonds in Modern Egypt." In *Women in Middle Eastern History,* edited by Nikki Keddie and Beth Baron, 292–309. New Haven: Yale University Press, 1991.

Bart, Pauline. "Review of Chodorow's 'The Reproduction of Mothering.'" In *Mothering: Essays in Feminist Theory,* edited by Joyce Trebilcot, 147–52. Totowa, N.J.: Rowman and Allanheld, 1983.

Barth, Frederik. "Father's Brother's Daughter Marriage in Kurdistan." *Southwest Journal of Anthropology* 10 (1954): 164–71.

Beauvoir, Simone de. *Le Deuxieme Sexe.* Paris: Gallimard, 1949.

Bek, Abdel Rahman al Rafi'i. *Asr Mohammed Ali.* Cairo: Maktabat al-Nahda al-Misriya, 1951.

Benhabib, Seyla. "The Generalized and the Concrete Other. The Kohlberg-Gilligan Controversy and Feminist Theory." In *Feminism as Critique,* edited by Syla Benhabib and Drucilla Cornell, 77–95. Minneapolis: Univ. of Minnesota Press, 1987.

Berkey, Jonathan P. "Women and Islamic Education in the Mamluk Period." In *Women in Middle Eastern History,* edited by Nikki Keddie and Beth Baron, 143–60. New Haven, Conn.: Yale Univ. Press, 1991.

Boocock, Sarane Spence. "The Social Construction of Childhood in Contemporary Japan." In *Constructions of the Self,* edited by George Levine, 165–88. New Brunswick, N.J.: Rutgers Univ. Press, 1992.

Bouhdiba, Abdelwahab. *Sexuality in Islam.* London: Routledge and Kegan Paul, 1985.

Broughton, John. "Women's Rationality and Men's Virtues." *Social Research* 50, no. 3 (summer 1983): 597–642.

Brown, L. Carl, and Norman Itzkowitz. *Psychological Dimensions of Near Eastern Studies*. Princeton, N.J.: Darwin Press, 1977.

Burridge, Kenelm O. L. "Siblings in Tangu." *Oceania* 30 (1959): 128–54.

Butler, Judith. *Gender Trouble: Feminism and the Subversion of Identity*. London: Routledge, 1990.

Campbell, David. *Honour, Family and Patronage: A Study of Institutions and Moral Values in a Greek Mountain Community*. Oxford, Eng.: Clarendon Press, 1964.

Chami, J. "Polygyny among Arabs." *Population Studies* 40 (1986): 55–66.

Chodorow, Nancy. "Family Structure and Feminine Personality." In *Women, Culture, and Society*, edited by Michelle Zimbalist Rosaldo and Louise Lamphere, 43–66. Stanford, Calif.: Stanford Univ. Press, 1974.

———. *The Reproduction of Mothering*. Berkeley and Los Angeles: Univ. of California Press, 1978.

———. "What is the Relation Between Psychoanalytic Feminism and the Psychoanalytic Psychology of Women?" In *Theoretical Perspectives on Sexual Difference*, edited by Deborah L. Rhode, 114–30. New Haven, Conn.: Yale Univ. Press, 1990.

Chodorow, Nancy, and Susan Contratto. "The Fantasy of the Perfect Mother." In *Rethinking the Family: Some Feminist Question*, edited by Barrie Thorne and Maryland Lalom, 55–75. New York: Longmans, 1982.

Cohen, Abner. *Arab Border-Villages in Israel: A Study of Continuity and Change in Social Organization*. Manchester, Eng.: Manchester Univ. Press, 1965.

Cole, Donald Powell. *Nomads of the Nomads. The Al Murrah Bedouin of the Empty Quarter*. Arlington Heights, Ill.: Harlan Davidson, 1975.

Collins, Patricia Hill. "The Social Construction of Black Feminist Thought." *Signs* 14, no. 4 (1989): 745–73.

Cott, Nancy F. "On Men's History and Women's History." In *Meanings for Manhood: Constructions of Masculinity in Victorian America*, edited by Mark C. Carnes and Clyde Griffin, 205–11. Chicago: Univ. of Chicago Press, 1990.

Crapanzano, Vincent. *The Hamadsha: A Study in Moroccan Ethnopsychiatry*. Berkeley and Los Angeles: Univ. of California Press, 1973.

———. *Tuhami: Portrait of a Moroccan*. Chicago: Univ. of Chicago Press, 1980.

Davis, Susan Schaefer. *Patience and Power: Women's Lives in a Moroccan Village*. Cambridge, Mass.: Schenkman, 1983.

Davis, Susan Schaefer, and Douglas A. Davis. *Adolescence in a Moroccan Town: Making Social Sense*. New Brunswick, N.J.: Rutgers Univ. Press, 1989.

De Lauretis, Teresa. *Technologies of Gender*. Bloomington: Indiana Univ. Press, 1987.

Dinnerstein, Dorothy. *The Mermaid and the Minotaur*. New York: Harper and Row, 1976.

Diyab, Mahmud. *Ahzan madina: Tifl fi al-hayy al-'Arabi* (A city's sorrows: A child in the Arab quarter). Cairo: Al-Hay'a al-Misriyya al-'Amma lil-Kitab, 1971.

Donovan, Josephine. "Toward a Women's Poetics." In *Feminist Issues in Literary Scholarship,* edited by Shari Benstock, 98–109. Bloomington: Indiana Univ. Press, 1987.

Eagleton, Terry. *Literary Theory: An Introduction.* Minneapolis: Univ. of Minnesota Press, 1983.

Eakin, John Paul. *Fictions in Autobiography: Studies in the Art of Self-Invention.* Princeton, N.J.: Princeton Univ. Press, 1985.

———. *Touching the World: Reference in Autobiography.* Princeton, N.J.: Princeton Univ. Press, 1992.

Eickelman, Christine. *Women and Community in Oman.* New York: New York Univ. Press, 1984.

Eisenstein, Hester. *Contemporary Feminist Thought.* Boston: G. K. Hall, 1983.

Fallers, Lloyd A., and Margaret C. Fallers. "Sex Roles in Edremit." In *Mediterranean Family Structures,* edited by J. G. Peristiany, 243–71. London: Cambridge Univ. Press, 1976.

Farsoun, Samih. "Family Structure and Society in Modern Lebanon." In *Peoples and Cultures of the Middle East,* edited by Louise Sweet, 257–307. Garden City, N.Y.: Natural History Press, 1978.

Al-Faruqi, Lamya'. *Women, Muslim Society and Islam.* Indianapolis, Ind.: American Trust Publishing, 1988.

Felman, Shoshana. "Women and Madness: The Critical Phallacy." In *Feminisms: An Anthology of Literary Theory and Criticism,* edited by Robyn R. Warhol and Diane Price Herndl, 6–19. New Brunswick, N.J.: Rutgers Univ. Press, 1991.

Ferguson, Ann. "On Conceiving Motherhood and Sexuality: A Feminist Materialist Approach." In *Mothering. Essays in Feminist Theory,* edited by Joyce Trebilcot, 153–82. Totowa, N.J.: Rowman and Allanheld, 1983.

Fernea, Elizabeth Warnock, ed. *Women and the Family in the Middle East: New Voices of Change.* Austin: Univ. of Texas Press, 1985.

Firth, Raymond. *We, the Tikopia: A Sociological Study of Kinship in Primitive Polynesia.* London: Allen and Unwin, 1936.

Flax, Jane. *Thinking Fragments: Psychoanalysis, Feminism and Postmodernism in the Contemporary West.* Berkeley and Los Angeles: Univ. of California Press, 1990.

Foucault, Michel. "Two Lectures." In *Power/Knowledge,* edited by Colin Gordon, 98–99. New York: Pantheon Books, 1980.

Fox Keller, Evelyn. "Science and Gender." *Signs: Journal of Women in Culture and Society* 7 (1982): 589–602.

Frye, Marilyn. "The Possibility of Feminist Theory." In *Theoretical Perspectives on Sexual Difference,* edited by Deborah L. Rhode, 174–84. New Haven, Conn.: Yale Univ. Press, 1990.

Fuller, Ann. *Buarij: Portrait of a Lebanese Muslim Village*. Cambridge, Mass.: Center for Middle East Studies, Harvard Univ. Press, 1961.

Geertz, Clifford, Hildred Geertz, and Lawrence Rosen. *Order in Moroccan Society*. New York: Cambridge Univ. Press, 1979.

Gergen, Kenneth. *The Saturated Self: Dilemmas of Identity in Contemporary Life*. New York: Basic Books, 1991.

———. "Social Understanding and the Inscription of the Self." In *Cultural Psychology: Essays on Comparative Human Development*, edited by James Stigler, Richard Shweder, and Gilbert Herdt, 569–606. Cambridge, Eng.: Cambridge Univ. Press, 1990.

Gewertz, Deborah. "The Tchambuli View of Persons: A Critique of Individualism in the Works of Mead and Chodorow." *American Anthropologist* 86 (1984): 615–29.

Ghaytani, Jamal. *Najib Mahfuz yatadhakkar* (Najib Mahfuz remembers). Cairo: Mu'asassat Akhbar al-Yawm, 1987.

Gilligan, Carol. *In a Different Voice. Psychological Theory and Women's Development*. Cambridge, Mass.: Harvard Univ. Press, 1982.

Gilmore, David G., ed. *Honor and Shame and the Unity of the Mediterranean*. Washington, D.C.: American Anthropological Association, 1987.

Gilsenan, Michael. "Against Patron-Client Relations." *Patrons and Clients in Mediterranean Societies*, edited by Ernest Gellner and John Waterbury, 167–84. London: Duckworth, 1977.

Granqvist, Hilma. *Marriage Conditions in a Palestinian Village*. Commentationes Humanarum Litterarum, vol. 2. Helsingfors: Societas Scientiarum Fennica, 1935.

Gulick, John. *The Middle East: An Anthropological Perspective*. Pacific Palisades, Calif.: Goodyear Publishing, 1976.

———. *Social Structure and Cultural Change in a Lebanese Village*. New York: Viking Fund Publications in Anthropology, 1955.

Al-Haj, Majid. *Social Change and Family Processes: Arab Communities in Shefar-A'm*. Boulder, Colo.: Westview Press, 1987.

Hakim, George. "The Economic Basis of Lebanese Polity." In *Politics in Lebanon*, edited by Leonard Binder, 57–68. New York: John Wiley and Sons, 1966.

Haley, P. Edward, and Lewis W. Snider, eds. *Lebanon in Crisis: Participants and Issues*. Syracuse, N.Y.: Syracuse Univ. Press, 1979.

Hamadeh, Najla. "Islamic Family Legislation: The Authoritarian Discourse of Silence." In *Feminism and Islam*, edited by May Yamani. London, Eng.: Ithaca Press, 1996.

Hamady, Sania. *Temperament and Character of the Arabs*. New York: Twayne Publishers, 1960.

Harding, Sandra. "What is the Real Material Base of Patriarchy and Capital?" In *Women and Revolution*, edited by Lydia Sargent, 135–64. Boston: South End Press, 1981.

Hartmann, Heidi. "The Unhappy Marriage of Marxism and Feminism: Towards a More Progressive Union." In *Women and Revolution,* edited by Lydia Sargent, 1–42. Boston: South End Press, 1981.

Hartsock, Nancy. *Money, Sex and Power, Toward a Feminist Historical Materialism.* New York: Longman, 1983.

Hatem, Mervat. "Toward the Study of the Psychodynamics of Mothering and Gender in Egyptian Families." *International Journal of Middle East Studies* 19 (1987): 287–306.

———. "Underdevelopment, Mothering and Gender Within the Egyptian Family." *Arab Studies Quarterly* 8, no. 1 (1986): 45–61.

Herodotus. *The Histories.* Translated by Aubrey De Selincourt. Revised by A. R. Burn. New York: Penguin Books, 1972.

Al-Hibri, Aziza. *Critique of Personal Status Codes in Selected Arab Countries.* Studies on Arab Women and Development, no. 25. New York: United Nations, 1997. (E/ESCWA/SD-WOM/1997/2).

Hopkins, Keith. "Brother-Sister Marriage in Roman Egypt." *Comparative Studies in Society and History* 22, no. 3 (1980): 303–59.

Hourani, Albert. *A History of the Arab Peoples.* London: Faber and Faber, 1991.

Husayn, Taha. *Al-Ayyam.* Cairo: N.p., 1929.

Hussein, Aziza. "Recent Amendments to Egypt's Personal Status Law." In *Women and the Family in the Middle East: New Voices of Change,* edited by Elizabeth Warnack Ferned, 224–32. Austin: Univ. of Texas Press, 1985.

Jacobs, Jane Liebman. "Reassessing Mother Blame in Incest." *Signs* 15, no. 3 (1990): 500–514.

Jessup, Henry Harris. *Fifty-Three Years in Syria.* 2 vols. New York: Fleming H. Revell, 1910.

Johnson, Michael. "Political Bosses and Their Gangs: Zu'ama and Qabadayat in the Sunni Muslim Quarters of Beirut." In *Patrons and Clients,* edited by Ernest Gellner and John Waterbury, 207–24. London: Duckworth, 1977.

Joseph, Suad. "Brother/Sister Relationships: Connectivity, Love, and Power in the Reproduction of Arab Patriarchy." *American Ethnologist* 21, no. 1 (Feb. 1994): 50–73.

———. "Connectivity and Patriarchy among Urban Working Class Arab Families in Lebanon." *Ethos* 21, no. 4 (Dec. 1993): 452–84.

———. "The Family as Security and Bondage: A Political Strategy of the Lebanese Urban Working Class." In *Towards a Political Economy of Urbanization in Third World Countries,* edited by Helen Safa, 151–71. New Delhi: Oxford Univ. Press, 1982.

———. "Gender and Relationality among Arab families in Lebanon." *Feminist Studies* 19, no. 3 (fall 1993): 465–86.

———. "Muslim-Christian Conflict in Lebanon: A Perspective in the Evolution of Sectarianism." In *Muslim-Christian Conflicts: Economic, Political and Social*

Origins, edited by Suad Joseph and Barbara L. K. Pillsbury, 62–97. Boulder, Colo.: Westview Press, 1978.

———. "Women Between Nation and State in Lebanon." In *Between Women and Nation: Feminism and Global Issues,* edited by Norma Alarcon, Caren Caplan, and Minoo Moallem. Durham, N.C.: Duke Univ. Press, in press.

———. "Working Class Women's Networks in a Sectarian State: A Political Paradox." *American Ethnologist* 10 (1983): 1–22.

———. "Working the Law: A Lebanese Working Class Case." In *The Politics of Law in the Middle East,* edited by Daisy Dwyer, 143–59. Hadley, Mass.: J. F. Bergin, 1990.

———. "Zaynab. An Urban Working-class Lebanese Woman." In *Middle Eastern Muslim Women Speak,* edited by Elizabeth Warnock Fernea and Basima Qattan Bezirgan, 359–71. Austin: Univ. of Texas Press, 1977.

Jowkar, Forouz. "Honor and Shame: A Feminist View from Within." *Feminist Issues* 6, no. 1 (1986): 45–63.

Kandiyoti, Deniz. "Islam and Patriarchy: A Comparative Perspective." In *Women in Middle Eastern History,* edited by Nikki R. Keddie and Beth Baron, 23–42. New Haven, Conn.: Yale Univ. Press, 1991.

———. "The Paradoxes of Masculinity: Some Thoughts on Segregated Societies." In *Dislocating Masculinity: Comparative Ethnographies,* edited by A. Cornwall and N. Lindisfarne, 197–213. London: Routledge, 1994.

———, ed. *Women, Islam and the State.* Philadelphia: Temple Univ. Press, 1991.

Kauffman, Linda. "Devious Channels of Decorous Ordering: Rosa Coldfield in 'Absalom, Absalom.' " In *Feminisms: An Anthology of Literary Theory and Criticism,* edited by Robyn R. Warhol and Diane Price Herndl, 644–670. New Brunswick, N.J.: Rutgers Univ. Press, 1991.

Kay, Shirley. *This Changing World, the Bedouin.* New York: Crane and Russak, 1978.

Keddie, Nikki R., and Beth Baron. *Women in Middle Eastern History: Shifting Boundries in Sex and Gender.* New Haven, Conn.: Yale Univ. Press, 1991.

Keller, Catherine. *From a Broken Web: Separation, Sexism, and Self.* Boston: Beacon Press, 1986.

Kelly, Raymond C. *Etoro Social Structure: A Study in Structural Contradiction.* Ann Arbor: Univ. of Michigan Press, 1977.

Khalaf, Samir. "Changing Forms of Political Patronage." In *Lebanon, Patrons and Clients in Mediterranean Societies,* edited by Ernest Gellner and John Waterbury, 185–206. London: Duckworth, 1977.

———. "Family Associations in Lebanon." *Journal of Comparative Family Studies* 2 (1971): 235–50.

———. "Primordial Ties and Politics in Lebanon." *Middle Eastern Studies* 4, no. 3 (1968): 243–69.

Khuri, Fuad. "Parallel Cousin Marriage Reconsidered: A Middle Eastern Practice that Nullifies the Effects of Marriage on the Intensity of Family Relationships." *Man* 5 (1970): 597–618.

Kingston, Maxine Hong. *The Woman Warrior: Memoirs of a Girlhood among Ghosts.* New York: Random House, 1976.

Kondo, Dorinne. *Crafting Selves, Power, Gender and Discourses of Identity in a Japanese Workplace.* Chicago: Univ. of Chicago Press, 1990.

Krupat, Arnold. "Native American Autobiography and the Synecdochic Self." In *American Autobiography: Retrospect and Prospect,* edited by John Paul Eakin, 171–93. Madison, Wisc.: Univ. of Wisconsin Press, 1991.

Lee, Harper. *To Kill a Mockingbird.* New York: Warner Books, 1960.

Lerner, Daniel. *The Passing of Traditional Society: Modernizing the Middle East.* Glencoe, Ill.: Free Press, 1958.

Luepnitz, Deborah Anna. *The Family Interpreted. Feminist Theory in Clinical Practice.* New York: Basic Books, 1988.

Lutz, Catherine. *Unnatural Emotions. Everyday Sentiments on a Micronesian Atoll and Their Challenge to Western Theory.* Chicago: Univ. of Chicago Press, 1988.

Lutz, Catherine, and Lila Abu-Lughod, eds. *Language and the Politics of Emotion.* Cambridge, Eng.: Cambridge Univ. Press, 1990.

Mahfuz, Najib. *Palace of Desire.* Translated by William M. Hutchins, Lorne M. Kenny, and Olive E. Kenny. New York: Anchor Doubleday, 1991.

———. *Palace Walk.* Translated by William M. Hutchins and Olive E. Kenny. New York: Anchor Doubleday, 1990.

———. *Sugar Street.* Translated by William M. Hutchins and Angele Botros Samaan. New York: Anchor Doubleday, 1992.

Makdisi, Jean Said. *Beirut Fragments: A War Memoir.* New York: Persea Books, 1990.

Malinowski, Bronislaw. *The Family among the Australian Aborigines. A Sociological Study.* London: Univ. of London Press, 1913.

Malti-Douglas, Fadwa. *Woman's Body, Woman's Word: Gender and Discourse Arabo-Islamic Writing.* Princeton, N.J.: Princeton Univ. Press, 1991.

Marshall, Mac, ed. *Siblingship in Oceania. Studies in the Meaning of Kin Relations.* Boston: Univ. Press of America, 1983.

Marsot, Afaf Lutfi al-Sayyid. *Egypt in the Reign of Muhammad 'Ali.* Cambridge, Eng.: Cambridge Univ. Press, 1984.

———. "The Revolutionary Gentlewomen in Egypt." In *Women in the Muslim World,* edited by Lois Beck and Nikki Keddie, 265–67. Cambridge, Mass.: Harvard Univ. Press, 1978.

———. *A Short History of Egypt.* New York: Cambridge Univ. Press, 1985.

Marx, Emanuel. *Bedouin of the Negev.* New York: Frederick A. Praeger, 1967.

McCabe, Justine. "FBD Marriage: Further Support for the Westermarck Hypothesis of the Incest Taboo?" *American Anthropologist* 85 (1983): 50–69.

McCarthy, Mary. *Memories of a Catholic Girlhood.* New York: Harcourt, 1957.

Meeker, Michael E. "Meaning and Society in the Near East: Examples from the Black Sea Turks and the Levantine Arabs." *International Journal of Middle Eastern Studies* 7 (1976): 383–422.

Mehrez, Samia. *Egyptian Writers Between History and Fiction: Essays on Naguib Mahfouz, Sonallah Ibrahim, and Gamal al-Ghitani.* Cairo: American Univ. in Cairo Press, 1994.

Meneley, Anne. *Tournaments of Value: Sociability and Hierarchy in a Yemeni Town.* Toronto: Univ. of Toronto Press, 1966.

Mernissi, Fatima. *Beyond the Veil: Male-Female Dynamics in Modern Muslim Society.* Bloomington: Indiana Univ. Press, 1985.

Middleton, Russell. "Brother/Sister and Father/Daughter Marriage in Ancient Egypt." *American Sociological Review* 27 (1962): 603–11.

Miller, Nancy K. *Getting Personal: Feminist Occasions and Other Autobiographical Acts.* New York: Routledge, 1991.

Minces, Juliette. *The House of Obedience. Women in Arab Society.* London: Zed Press, 1982.

Minuchin, Salvador, Bernice L. Rosman, and Lester Baker. *Psychosomatic Families. Anorexia Nervosa in Context.* Cambridge, Mass.: Harvard Univ. Press, 1978.

Moore, Henrietta. *A Passion for Difference.* Bloomington: Indiana Univ. Press, 1994.

Moughrabi, Fouad. "The Arab Basic Personality: A Critical Survey of the Literature." *International Journal of Middle Eastern Studies* 9 (1978): 99–112.

———. "A Political Technology of the Soul." *Arab Studies Quarterly* 3, no. 1 (1981): 68–89.

Muir, Edward and Guido Ruggerio, eds. *Sex and Gender in Historical Perspective.* Translated by Margaret A. Gallucci with Mary M. Gallucci and Carole Gallucci. Baltimore: Johns Hopkins Univ. Press, 1990.

Munson, Henry, Jr. *The House of Si Abd Allah: The Oral History of a Moroccan Family.* New Haven, Conn.: Yale Univ. Press, 1984.

Murphy, Robert F., and Leonard Kasdan. "The Structure of Parallel Cousin Marriage." *American Anthropologist* 61 (1959): 17–29.

Musil, Alois. *The Manners and Customs of the Rwala Bedouins.* New York: American Geographical Society, 1928.

Nails, Debra. "Social-Scientific Sexism: Gilligan's Mismeasure of Man." *Social Research* 50, no. 3 (1983): 643–65.

Nelson, Cynthia. "Public and Private Politics: Women in the Middle Eastern World." In *Arab Society in Transition,* edited by Saad Eddin Ibrahim and Nicolas Hopkins, 131–47. Cairo: American Univ. in Cairo, 1977.

Nelson, Cynthia, and Virginia Olesen. "Veil of Illusion: A Critique of the Concept of Equality in Western Thought." *Catalyst* 10, no. 11 (1977): 8–36.

Nevins, Edward and Theon Wright. *World without Time: The Bedouin.* New York: John Day, 1969.

Odeh, B. J. *Lebanon: Dynamics of Conflict*. London: Zed Books, 1985.

Olney, James, ed. *Autobiography: Essays Theoretical and Critical*. Princeton, N.J.: Princeton Univ. Press, 1980.

——, ed. *Studies in Autobiography*. New York: Oxford Univ. Press, 1988.

Paige, Karen Ericksen. "Gender, Family Systems and Theories of State Formation." Paper presented at Middle East Studies Association Meeting, San Francisco, Calif. 1984.

Patai, Raphael. *Family, Love and the Bible*. London: McGibbon and Kee, 1960.

Peristiany, J. G. *Honor and Shame: The Values of Mediterranean Society*. Chicago: Univ. of Chicago Press, 1966.

Pitt-Rivers, Julian. *The Fate of Shechem or the Politics of Sex: Essays in the Anthropology of the Mediterranean*. London: Cambridge Univ. Press, 1977.

Pleck, Joseph H. *The Myth of Masculinity*. Cambridge, Mass.: MIT Press, 1982.

Prothro, Edwin Terry. *Child Rearing in Lebanon*. Harvard Middle Eastern Monographs, no. 8. Cambridge, Mass.: Harvard Univ. Press, 1961.

Prothro, Edwin Terry, and Lutfy Najib Diab. *Changing Family Patterns in the Arab East*. Beirut: American Univ. of Beirut Press, 1974.

Qasim, ʿAbd al-Hakim. *Ayyam al-insan al-sabʿa* (The seven ages of man). Cairo: Dar al-Katib al-ʿArabi, 1969.

Radcliffe-Brown, A. R. "The Mother's Brother in South Africa." *South African Journal of Science* 21 (1924): 542–55.

Rhode, Deborah L. "Theoretical Perspectives on Sexual Difference." In *Theoretical Perspectives on Sexual Difference*, edited by Deborah L. Rhode, 1–9. New Haven, Conn.: Yale Univ. Press, 1990.

Ripinsky, M. M. "Middle Eastern Kinship as an Expression of a Culture-Environment System." *Muslim World* 58 (1968): 225–41.

Roland, Alan. *In Search of Self in India and Japan*. Princeton, N.J.: Princeton Univ. Press, 1988.

Rosaldo, Michelle. *Knowledge and Passion: Ilongot Notions of Self and Social Life*. Cambridge, Eng.: Cambridge Univ. Press, 1980.

——. "Toward an Anthropology of Self and Feeling." In *Culture Theory, Essays on Mind, Self and Emotion*, edited by Richard Shweder and Robert LeVine, 137–57. Cambridge, Eng.: Cambridge Univ. Press, 1984.

Rosenfeld, Henry. "On Determinants of the Status of Arab Village Women." *Man* 60 (1960): 66–70.

Rubin, Gayle. "The Traffic in Women: Notes on the 'Political Economy of Sex.' " *Towards an Anthropology of Women*, edited by Rayna Reiter, 157–210. New York: Monthly Review Press, 1975.

Rubin, Lillian B. *Intimate Strangers: Men and Women Together*. New York: Harper, 1983.

Rugh, Andrea B. *Family in Contemporary Egypt*. Syracuse, N.Y.: Syracuse Univ. Press, 1984.

————. *Within the Circle: Parents and Children in an Arab Village*. New York: Columbia Univ. Press, 1997.

Rutherford, Jonathan. *Men's Silences: Predicaments in Masculinity*. London: Routledge, 1992.

Said, Edward W. *The World, the Text, and the Critic*. Cambridge, Mass.: Harvard Univ. Press, 1983.

Sa'id, Fatima al-Zahra' Muhammad. *Al-Ramziya fi adab Najib Mahfuz* (*Symbolism in the work of Najib Mahfuz*). Beirut: Al-Mu'asassa al-'Arabiyya li al-Dirasat wa al-Nashr, 1981.

Salibi, Kamal. *The Modern History of Lebanon*. London: Weidenfeld and Nicolson, 1965.

Al-Sakhawi, Shams al-Din Muhamad Abdul-Rahman. *Al-Daw' al-lami' fi a'yan al-qarn al-tasi'* (The bright light of the notables of the ninth century). Vol 12. Cairo: Maktabat al-Qudsi, 1497.

Salibi, Kamal. *Cross Roads to Civil War: Lebanon 1958–1976*. Delmar, N.Y.: Caravan, 1976.

————. *The Modern History of Lebanon*. London: Weidenfeld and Nicolson, 1965.

Schneider, David M., and Kathleen Gough, eds. *Matrilineal Kinship*. Berkeley and Los Angeles,: Univ. of California Press, 1961.

Schneider, Jane, and Peter Schneider. *Culture and Political Economy in Western Sicily*. New York: Academic Press, 1976.

Schneider, Jane. "Of Vigilance and Virgins: Honour, Shame and Access to Resources in the Mediterranean Societies." *Ethnology* 10 (1971): 1–24.

Scott, Frances E. *Dare and Persevere*. London: Lebanon Evangelical Mission, 1960.

Sedgwick, Eve Kosofsky. *Between Men: English Literature and Male Homosocial Desire*. New York: Columbia Univ. Press, 1985.

Shafiq, Durriya. *Al-Mar'at al-misriya*. Cairo: Matba 'at Misr, 1955.

El-Shamy, Hasan. *Brother and Sister Type 872: A Cognitive Behavioristic Analysis of a Middle Eastern Oikotype*. Folklore Monographs Series, 8. Bloomington, Ind.: Folklore Publication Group, 1979.

————. "The Brother-Sister Syndrome in Arab Family Life, Socio-Cultural Factors in Arab Psychiatry: A Critical Review." *International Journal of Sociology of the Family* 2 (1981): 313–23.

————. "The Traditional Structure of Sentiments in Mahfouz's Trilogy: A Behavioristic Text Analysis." *Al-'Arabiyya* 9 (1976): 53–74.

Sharabi, Hisham. *Neopatriarchy: A Theory of Distorted Change in Arab Society*. New York: Oxford Univ. Press, 1988.

Sharabi, Hisham and Mukhtar Ali. "The Impact of Class and Culture on Social Behavior: The Feudal-Bourgeois Family in Arab Society." In *Psychological Dimensions of Near Eastern Studies*, edited by L. Carl Brown and Norman Itzkowitz, 240–56. Princeton, N.J.: Darwin Press, 1977.

Shukri, Muhammad. *Al-Khubz al-hafi (For bread alone)*. London: Dar al-Saqi, 1982.

———. *For bread alone (Al-Khubz al- hafi)*. Translated by Paul Bowles. San Francisco, Calif.: City Lights Books, 1987.

Slotkin, J. S. "On the Possible Lack of Incest Regulations in Old Iran." *American Anthropologist* 49 (1947): 612–17.

Smith, Sidonie, and Julia Watson, eds. *De/Colonizing the Subject: The Politics of Gender in Women's Autobiography*. Minneapolis: Univ. of Minnesota Press, 1992.

Spelman, Elizabeth. *Inessential Woman. Problems of Exclusion in Feminist Thought*. Boston: Beacon Press, 1988.

Stack, Carol. "Different Voices. Different Visions: Gender, Culture and Moral Reasoning." In *Uncertain Terms. Negotiating Gender in American Culture,* edited by Faye Ginsburg and Anna Lowenhaupt Tsing, 19–27. Boston: Beacon Press, 1990.

Sweet, Louise E. "Tell Toqaan: A Syrian Village." Ph.D. diss. Univ. of Michigan, 1957.

Taussig, Michael. *Shamanism, Colonialism and the Wild Man: A Study in Terror and Healing* (Chicago: Univ. of Chicago Press, 1986).

Taymur, 'A'isha. "Muqadimat al-diwan al-Farisi wa al-Turki" (Introduction to the Persian and Turkish anthology). In *Hilyat al-tiraz: Diwan 'A'isha al-Taymuriya*, 61. Cairo: Matba'at dar al-Katib al-'Arabi, 1952.

———. *Nata'l al-'ahwal fi al-'aqwal wa al-'af'al*. Cairo: Matba'at Muhamad Effendi Mustafa, 1887.

Thorne, Barrie. "Children and Gender: Constructions of Difference." In *Theoretical Perspectives on Sexual Difference,* edited by Deborah L. Rhode, 100–113. New Haven, Conn.: Yale Univ. Press, 1990.

Tibawi, A. L. *American Interests in Syria, 1800–1901*. Oxford, Eng.: Clarendon Press, 1966.

———. *British Interests in Palestine, 1800–1901*. London: Oxford Univ. Press, 1961.

Trinh, T. Minh-ha. *Woman, Native, Other: Writing Postcoloniality and Feminism*. Bloomington: Indiana Univ. Press, 1989.

Tristram, Rev. H. B., ed. *Daughters of Syria*. London: Seeley, Jackson, and Halliday, 1872.

Tucker, Judith. *Women in Nineteenth Century Egypt*. Cambridge, Eng.: Cambridge Univ. Press, 1985.

Tuqan, Fadwa. *A Mountainous Journey*. Translated by Olive Kenny. London: Women's Press, 1990.

———. *Rihla Jabaliyya, Rihla Sa'ba*. Beirut: Dar al-Shuruq, 1985.

Al-Turabi, Hasan. *Al-Mar'a baina ta'aleem al-deen wa takaleed al-mujtama'* (Woman: Between religious teachings and social traditions). Jeddah, Saudi Arabia: Al-Dar al-Saoudiah, 1984.

UNICEF. *The Children of the Nile*. Paris: UNESCO, n.d.

Weiner, Annette B. *Women of Value, Men of Renown: New Perspectives in Tro-briand Exchange*. Austin: Univ. of Texas Press, 1976.

Whitaker, Ian. "Familial Roles in the Extended Patrilineal Kin-Group in Northern Albania." In *Mediterranean Family Structures*, edited by J. G. Peristiany, 195–203. London: Cambridge Univ. Press, 1976.

White, Hayden. *The Content of the Form*. Baltimore, Md.: Johns Hopkins Univ. Press, 1987.

Williams, Judith. *The Youth of Haouch El Harimi: A Lebanese Village*. Cambridge, Mass.: Center for Middle East Studies Harvard Univ. Press, 1968.

Yahyia, Muhammid Kamel. *Al-Juzur al-tarikhiya litahrir al-mara'at al-misriya*. Cairo: Al-Hay'a al-Misriyya al-'Amma li'l-Kitab, 1983.

Yanagisako, Sylvia J., and Jane F. Collier. "The Mode of Reproduction in Anthropology." In *Theoretical Perspectives on Sexual Difference*, edited by Deborah L. Rhode, 131–41. New Haven, Conn.: Yale Univ. Press, 1990.

Young, Iris Marion. "Is Male Gender Identity the Cause of Male Domination?" In *Mothering, Essays in Feminist Theory*, edited by Joyce Trebilcot, 129–46. Totowa, N.J.: Rowman and Allanheld, 1983.

Zaalouk, Malak. *Draft of Community Schools, Alternative Approaches for Basic Education*. Cairo: UNICEF, 1995.

———. *Field Mission Report to Oena and Sohag with CIDA Canada*. Cairo: UNICEF, 1995.

Zadeh, Ahmed Kamal. "Jidati. 'Ard wa Tahlil." In *Hilyat al-Tiraz: Diwan 'A'isha al-Taymuriya*, 16. Cairo: Matba 'at dar al-Kitab al-'Arabi, 1952.

Ziada, Mayy. "Katiba tukadim sha'irah." In *Hilyat al-tiraz: Diwan 'A'isha al-Taymuriya*. Cairo: Matba 'at dar al-Kitab al-'Arabi, 1952.

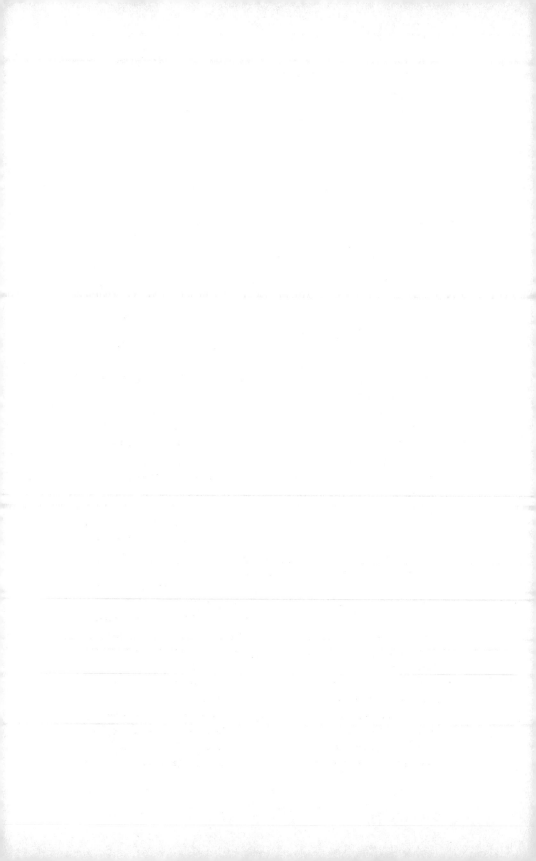

Index

Abdullah, Rafik, 136, 137

Abu-Lughod, Lila, 122, 159, 161

age: patriarchy as aged dominion, 13, 188; in sexual segregation, 251–52. *See also* elders; juniors

agency: individuation as condition for, 4; of the knowing subject, 8; relationality and, 2–3, 4, 15, 70

agl (wisdom), 161–62

Ahmed, Leila, 118–19, 170, 236, 288nn. 10, 17

Alamuddin, Nura S., 280n. 76

Ali, Mukhtar, 187

Altorki, Soraya, 17, 211–12, 280n. 80

'am (paternal uncle), 134

American Junior College (Beirut), 33, 35

American School for Girls (ASG) in Beirut, 33

American University of Beirut (AUB), 29, 35

'amta (paternal aunt), 134

Antun, Amira, 135, 136, 137–38, 139

Antun, Edward, 135, 136–37, 139

Antun, Francis, 135, 137–38, 139

Arab children: as following their fathers, 174–76; as identifying with their mothers, 277n. 44; love between mother and, 176; parents sleeping in rooms with adult, 179; socialized to

feel responsible for parents and siblings, 11. *See also* brothers; daughters; sisters; sons

Arab family: aunts, 134; as central to Lebanese social life, 128, 279n. 64; cousin relationships, 77–91; ethnographic and historical excavations of the self in, 107–208; hypervalorization of, 9; intimate selving as practice of biography and autobiography in, 19–105; in literature, 236; microdynamics of power in Egyptian, 192–94; relationality in, 14; theories and dynamics of gender, self, and identity in, 1–17. *See also* Arab children; Arab parents; uncles

Arab fathers: as authoritarian, 10; change as supported by, 192; children as following, 174–76; competing with their wives over sons, 187; Muslims, 124; in power dynamics in Egyptian families, 192–94. *See also* father-daughter relationships; father-son relationships

Arab men: aging parents as responsibility of, 125, 183–84; change as supported by, 192; as head of the family that the woman turns, 44; names used by,

305

232; Western impact on, 170. *See also*
patriarchal connectivity
patrilineage, 117, 188, 216
polyarchy, 219
polygyny. *See* co-wife relationships
power: complex character of patriarchal,
192–93; connectivity as, 132–33;
Diyab's *Azhan madina* on power
dynamics between parents, 252–53;
domestic power of women, 28, 44,
192; in Egyptian families, 192–94;
gender in organization of, 132; and
love in brother-sister relationships,
126, 127, 132–33, 139–40
private-public distinction. *See* public-
private distinction
prostitutes, 257–58, 259–62
Prothro, Edwin Terry, 170, 279nn. 64,
65, 280n. 76
psychoanalytic theory, 8, 269n. 29
psychological theory: on the family
drama, 172; family systems theory, 4,
122; the individuated self in Western,
1, 17; on the nuclear family as
normative, 238; object relations
theory, 6–8, 14, 260; relationality in,
3–6
public-private distinction, 238–39. *See
also* separate spheres
public sphere, 7
Puritanism, 47

Qasim, ʿAbd al-Hakim. *See Ayyam al-
insan al-sabʿa* (Qasim)

Rafik, Abu Mufid, 133, 135, 138
Rafik, Adnan, 135, 136–37, 138
Rafik, Mufid, 137
relationality, 9; agency and, 2–3, 4, 15,
70; in Arab families, 14; in the Arab
world, 9, 11; versus autonomy, 3–4;

connectivity contrasted with, 122; in
feminist theory, 6–9; as gendered, 2,
14; versus hegemonic individualized
selfhood, 1–2; and individualism, 9,
17, 237, 238, 250, 263; masculinity as
set of relationalities engaged with
femininity, 212; as motorizing force,
14; paradoxical relationalities of
patriarchal connectivity, 174–90; and
patriarchy, 2, 8, 14–15; political claims
based on relationships in Lebanon,
67, 73; in psychological theory, 3–6;
romanticizing, 70; self as understood
in terms of relationships in Lebanon,
54, 73; as situational, 68; in women
and men, 6–7, 239, 242. *See also*
connectivity
religion, politicizing in Lebanon, 64
Rihla jabaliyya: Rihly saʿba (Tuqan),
288n. 10
Roland, Alan, 5–6, 283n. 26
Roller, Lyn, 281n. 88
Rubin, Gayle, 285n. 2
Rugh, Andrea B., 10, 187, 276n. 26
Rwala Bedouins, 119–20

Said, Edward W., 236, 287n. 1
Al-Sakhawi, Abdul-Rahman, 283n. 21
Scheherazade, 21, 23–24
Scheherazade (*Thousand and One
Nights*), 198
segregation, sexual, 195, 197, 200,
251–52, 257
self, the. *See also* connectivity;
individuation; intimate selving;
relationality: Cartesian dualism in
Western notions of, 8; closely-bound
self-constructs, 172–73, 284n. 36;
connective self, 54–55, 61, 189, 277n.
37; as constantly contested, 112;
constructedness of, 3; embeddedness
of other and, 2; enmeshment of, 4;